THE TROPICAL SILK ROAD

THE TROPICAL SILK ROAD

The Future of China in South America

Edited by
Paul Amar, Lisa Rofel,
María Amelia Viteri,
Consuelo Fernández-Salvador,
and Fernando Brancoli

Stanford University Press
Stanford, California

STANFORD UNIVERSITY PRESS
Stanford, California

Printed in the United States of America on acid-free, archival-quality paper

Library of Congress Cataloging-in-Publication Data

Names: Amar, Paul (Paul Edouard), 1968- editor. | Rofel, Lisa, 1953-
    editor. | Viteri, María Amelia, editor. | Fernández Salvador, Consuelo, editor. |
    Brancoli, Fernando, editor.
Title: The tropical silk road : the future of China in South America /
    edited by Paul Amar, Lisa Rofel, María Amelia Viteri, Consuelo Fernández-
    Salvador, and Fernando Brancoli.
Description: Stanford, California : Stanford University Press, 2022. |
    Includes bibliographical references and index.
Identifiers: LCCN 2022008366 (print) | LCCN 2022008367 (ebook) |
    ISBN 9781503633193 (cloth) | ISBN 9781503633803 (paperback) |
    ISBN 9781503633810 (ebook)
Subjects: LCSH: Investments, Chinese—South America. | South America—Foreign
    economic relations—China. | China—Foreign economic relations—South America.
    | South America—Economic conditions—21st century. | South America—Social
    conditions—21st century. | South America—Environmental conditions.
Classification: LCC HF1508.Z4 T86 2022 (print) | LCC HF1508.Z4 (ebook) |
    DDC 337.5108—dc23/eng/20220803
LC record available at https://lccn.loc.gov/2022008366
LC ebook record available at https://lccn.loc.gov/2022008367

Cover design: Rob Ehle

Cover images: Mural in Amazon region of Ecuador, Paul Amar;
aerial photo of forest, PxHere

Typeset by Newgen in 10.2/14.4 Minion Pro

Contents

Part 2: Indigenous Epistemologies and Maroon Modernities

**Part 3: Grassroots Perspectives on the Fragmentation
of BRICS**

Part 7: Hybridity of Transnational Labor

Acknowledgments

This collectively produced volume reflects the hard work, creativity, and vision of a group of scholars on four continents, all responding generously, fiercely, and brilliantly to the challenges of a set of intersecting crises. We would like to thank here our colleagues and team members who made this collective exercise in global knowledge production and public engagement possible.

First, we would like to acknowledge each other's efforts, those accomplishments from among our team who made special efforts and faced certain risks and terrific challenges to launch and guide our project research and team formation. We thank Professor Lisa Rofel for her bold and visionary leadership that initiated this project and the community around it. Her brilliance, inclusiveness, innovative methodologies, and collective-oriented research ethic have served as models for all of us, and this book and the projects that generated it would not exist without her. Paul Amar is the sine qua non of this book project. This book simply would not exist without his leadership, creativity, and capacity to manage a research team across four continents and four languages. We also offer deepest thanks to Professor Maria Amelia Viteri and Professor Consuelo Fernández-Salvador, who elaborated a profound and inclusive network of case-study sites, research partners, activist contacts, and trusted students and collaborators in Ecuador and in the Amazon region. We are grateful for all the support from

Universidad San Francisco de Quito (USFQ) starting with the provost at the time, Carlos Montúfar, and the dean of the School of Social Sciences, Carmen Fernández-Salvador, who brought us together with professors working in similar areas of interest such as José Salazar to foster further collaborative work. This preparation enabled our research and collective knowledge-formation project to bring on board Indigenous student activists from across the country, Indigenous leaders, feminist activists, LGBTQI+ movements, lawyers, journalists, Chinese business and project specialists, ecologists, economists, and community leaders. This group also set up a conference that brought together stakeholders and researchers in Quito as well as working meetings in Cuenca and in the Amazonian area of Tundayme, Ecuador. Our heartfelt thanks to Kaleidos Center for Interdisciplinary Ethnography and LGBQTI+ activist Pedro Gutierrez for his support in convening key actors on a very tight schedule while travelling from Cuenca to the Amazon. Also, many thanks to Dr. William Sacher from Universidad Andina Simón Bolívar in Quito for his compelling insights and vast experience regarding large-scale mining in the Amazon Region, and to INSUCO (Observatorio de Transformaciones Territoriales–Los Encuentros) for sharing valuable information from their work that addresses social dynamics in a mining project in the province of Zamora. In El Chaco, province of Napo, Ecuador, the information and support provided by the mayor, Ing. Javier Chávez, was key for the team to be able to understand the socioeconomic dynamics around the Coca Codo Sinclair project. We are also very appreciative of the opportunity provided by Ing. Marcelo Reinoso, manager of CELEC's Business Unit, to visit Project Coca Codo Sinclair and provide a guide to explain the water intake facility, and other technical details of the project.

For Brazil, Fernando Brancoli and Paul Amar spearheaded the selection of case-study sites, research networks, and partners among Indigenous leaders, youth activists, investigative journalists, social movement leaders, Black *quilombolas*, feminist movements, engineers, businessmen, political-economy specialists, political ecologists, anthropologists, and geographers. And this group produced a major interdisciplinary conference on "China's Futures in South America" hosted in March 2020 at the ABIA NGO in Rio de Janeiro, which included experts from China and across South America, and whose participants were identified with the expert assistance and generosity of Professor Lena Lavinas and Professor Monica Herz. We would also like to thank Sonia Correa and the staff at ABIA for hosting this conference and for their generous advice and guidance in how to manage the COVID-19 risks and context that was materializing around us ominously right at that time. We would also like to express our profound gratitude to our Chinese colleague Cai Yiping, specialist in international gender policy, development, and Chinese diplomacy in the Global South, who very much shaped this project but was trapped by the first wave of COVID lockdowns in Beijing and so was unable to join us for the research missions. Beijing-based documentary filmmaker He Xiaopei, a member of our research team, captured our work on film in all its complexity. Her Mandarin Chinese translation as we met with Chinese workers and businessmen in South America was a crucial added bonus. She is producing a set of wonderful short documentary films that track our research and this volume's themes.

Second, we would like to thank the funders, grant managers, and coordinators of this project for their essential and enthusiastic support. Most of all we thank Ford Foundation China for their stalwart support of this kind of research on Chinese overseas development finance, social impact, and environmental contexts. We have been very lucky to benefit from the guidance, expertise, and wisdom of Ford Foundation project officer Enjiang Cheng and grants manager Yingjie Zhang. Their intelligence, guidance, and vision have been so inspiring! We also would like to thank former Ford Foundation project officers Susie Jolly and Cai Yiping for their invaluable suggestions and wisdom throughout the years. We would also like to thank University of California, Santa Barbara, and the Orfalea Center for Global and International Studies, supported in turn by our benefactor and friend Paul Orfalea and Christine Brozowski of the Audacious Foundation, for providing a degree of matching funding and for supporting graduate student activities and some translation and editing services that were crucial to the production of this book. Huge thanks to Dr. Melissa Bator for her academic coordination, vision, leadership, and Lacy Olivera at ISBER (University of California, Santa Barbara) for her implementation and financial management genius. And we would like to thank the Center for Emerging Worlds at University of California, Santa Cruz, for hosting this project officially from the start, and for hosting the extraordinary major conferences in 2017 and 2018 that catalyzed this community of ideas and researchers.

Third, we would like to thank the team of genius collaborators and consultants who are appreciated as a core part of our team and whose contributions, efforts, and leadership have been definitive. Zahirah Suhaimi was Herculean in her project management work, organizing the travel, accommodations, and per diem funding for the research team as we journeyed across South America. And then she airlifted us all out on March 15, 2020, when, quite suddenly, COVID-19 had us cornered. Alix Johnson and Kali Rubai offered their amazing skills and hard work in organizing the international conferences at University of California, Santa Cruz, and in Beijing that generated this project and the intellectual framework for this book. Fernando Brancoli continued to serve not just as a superb researcher, contributor, and coeditor but also as our brilliant project manager and dexterous academic diplomat in Brazil and with our contributors there. We would also like to thank our talented and hard-working team of translators from Spanish to English, starting with John M. Hughson. Jesse Crane-Seeber was immensely dedicated to the initial formatting of this English translation. These translators brought the Ecuadorian and Indigenous contributions to an English-speaking public. And we would like to thank Rodrigo Bezerra, our translator from Brazilian Portuguese to English, for doing such a fantastic job. We would also like to thank CY Xu at University of California, Santa Barbara, for his brilliant translation of articles in Mandarin Chinese into English. What a brilliant group of translators!

We would also like to extend a very special thanks to Dr. Hatem Hassan, editor extraordinaire, who worked for months and months with every member of this team to polish each chapter, improve the lucidity of each argument, and bring each contribution to the highest level of readability and accessibility, and then beautifully formatted text, notes, and references. Extraordinary work, Hatem! And we also extend profound gratitude to Professor Thaddeus Blanchette who beautifully revised and enriched all Portuguese-English translations, edited and reedited each chapter, helping in particular to identify and encourage cross-talk among the contributors, slimming down the texts, and rendering this book perfect for the general public, teaching in the classroom, and for scholarly and business reference.

Finally, we would like to thank the incredible team at Stanford University Press for their guidance, fantastic ideas, vision, and support. We convey our gratitude to Marcela Cristina Maxfield, acquisitions editor for the first year of our project, who graciously accepted our proposal and guided the shaping of our book. And we thank the more recently arrived acquisitions editor Dylan Kyung-lim White, who guided us through the exciting period of responding to peer reviews and finalizing the volume for transmission. We also thank Sunna Juhn, assistant editor, for shepherding our volume through production, as well as copy editor Kristine Hunt and cover designer Rob Ehle. And we express deep gratitude and appreciation to Kate Wahl, editor-in-chief and publishing director of Stanford University Press.

Contributors

Diana Aguiar serves as an advisor to the National Campaign in Defense of the Cerrado, and has a PhD in urban and regional planning from the Institute of Urban and Regional Research and Planning (IPPUR) of the Federal University of Rio de Janeiro (UFRJ).

Paul Amar serves as department chair and professor, Global Studies Department, and director of the Orfalea Center for Global & International Studies, University of California, Santa Barbara. Professor Amar is a political scientist and anthropologist with affiliate appointments in Political Science, Feminist Studies, Sociology, Comparative Literature, Middle East Studies, and Latin American and Iberian Studies. A three-time Fulbright Fellowship winner who speaks six languages, Prof. Amar is an accomplished scholar and campus leader, having served as founding director of the PhD Program in Global Studies and the cofounder of the Area-Global Institute at UCSB. Before he began his academic career, he worked as a journalist in Cairo, a police reformer and sexuality rights activist in Rio de Janeiro, and as a conflict-resolution and economic development specialist at the United Nations. His books include *Cairo Cosmopolitan* (2006); *New Racial Missions of Policing* (2010); *Global South to the Rescue* (2011); *The Middle East and Brazil* (2014); *Dispatches from the Arab Spring* (2013); and *The Security Archipelago*, which was awarded the Charles Taylor Award for "Best Book of the Year" in 2014 by the Interpretive Methods Section of the

American Political Science Association. This was published in Brazil as *O Arquipélago de Segurança* (Editora UFRJ, 2018). In 2019 he was awarded Mentor of the Year by the Latin American Studies Program at UCSB.

Yasmin Bitencourt is a researcher and popular educator of the Alternative Policies for the Southern Cone Institute (Instituto Políticas Alternativas para o Cone Sul-PACS).

Emilia Bonilla is an undergraduate student at the Espiritu Santo University in Ecuador.

Cleiton Ferreira Maciel Brito holds a doctorate in sociology from the Federal University of São Carlos.

Fernando Brancoli is an associate professor of international security and geopolitics at the Institute of International Relations and Defense at the Federal University of Rio de Janeiro (IRID–UFRJ), with a PhD granted by the Graduate Program in International Relations San Tiago Dantas–Unesp, Unicamp and PUC-SP. Previously, he served as a visiting scholar at the University of California, Santa Barbara. Brancoli's research is centered on South-South relations, with emphasis on narratives of security and development, with field work on three continents. His articles have appeared in the *New York Times*, *Al Jazeera*, and *Folha de São Paulo*. His books include *Arab Spring: Squares, Streets and Revolts* (Desatino, 2016) and *Private Security Companies in the Global South* (UFRJ, 2020, forthcoming).

Alana Camoça holds a doctorate in International Political Economy at UFRJ.

Sofía Carpio is a member of Kaleidos Center for Interdisciplinary Ethnography.

Israel Chumapi received a BA in international relations from Universidad San Francisco de Quito. He continues to collaborate in the development of the Shuar nationality and for the benefit of his own community, by strengthening and improving local institutions.

Julia Correa was born and raised in Quito, Ecuador, holds a BA in anthropology, and is conducting graduate work in visual anthropology.

Lucilene Raimunda Costa is a human rights activist and a community leader of traditional populations in Brazil.

Sabrina Felipe is an independent investigative reporter, covering human rights and the right to land and territory in urban and rural areas.

Consuelo Fernández-Salvador is an associate professor at the Department of Anthropology, Universidad San Francisco de Quito. Professor Fernandez has a PhD in development studies from the International Institute of Social Studies-Erasmus University Rotterdam. Her research has focused on Indigenous politics and extractivism, particularly around large-scale mining in the southern Amazon Region in Ecuador. She is the coeditor of the book *La Amazonía Minada. Minería a Gran Escala y Conflictos en el Sur del Ecuador* with K. van Teijlingen, E. Leifsen, and L. Sanchez Vázquez (USFQ Press-Abya Yala, 2017). This book offers an analysis of a variety of socioenvironmental, sociocultural, and territorial conflicts surrounding Project Mirador, the first and most emblematic large-scale mining in Ecuador, now owned by the Chinese consortium CCRC-Tonguan.

Mayra Flores is a member of Kaleidos Center for Interdisciplinary Ethnography.

Ana Saggioro Garcia is an associate professor of international relations at the Federal Rural University of Rio de Janeiro (UFRRJ) and the Graduate Program in Social Sciences (PPGCS/ UFRRJ). Garcia is also a coordinator of the Interdisciplinary Laboratory for International Relations Studies (LIERI /UFRRJ).

Wander Guerra is an environmental engineer who holds a PhD from the Urban and Regional Research and Planning Institute. Guerra holds a master's degree in population, territory and public statistics from the National School of Statistical Sciences (ENCE/IBGE).

Pedro Gutiérrez Guevara is a member of Kaleidos Center for Interdisciplinary Ethnography.

Bruno Hendler is an adjunct professor of international relations at UFSM.

Milton Reyes Herrera is a professor and researcher at the Security and Defense Center, and coordinator of the Chinese Studies Center, at the Ecuadorean National Institute of Advanced Studies (IAEN).

Juan Pablo Hidalgo Bastidas is a senior lecturer and researcher in water governance at the Universidad Central del Ecuador. He is a postdoctoral fellow at the Water Resources Management Group at Wageningen University and Research. Since 2009, he has been an active member of the Water Justice Alliance and the Ecuadorian National Water Forum.

David F. Delgado del Hierro is a lawyer from the Universidad San Francisco de Quito, a member of ProPrivacidad and USFQ Law Working Papers, and works in the State Attorney General's Office in the Directorate of Legal Control and Evaluation of Fiscal Activity.

Andrea Piazzaroli Longobardi is part of the editorial commission of *Revista Leste Vermelho*, and received their PhD in history from the University of São Paulo and University of Bologna.

Diego Trindade d'Ávila Magalhães is a professor of international relations and a collaborating professor of the Graduate Program in Political Science at the Federal University of Goiás.

Paúl Ghaitai Males was born in the Indigenous community of Compañía-Otavalo and is currently an anthropology student at the Universidad San Francisco de Quito. His work revolves around Indigenous cultural rights and heritage, including preserving the Kichwa language among the new generations. He wants to direct his efforts to support local institutions in Otavalo communities in the areas of education, law, and environmental protection.

Rina Pakari Marcillo is a Kichwa-Otavalo student of cultural anthropology at the Universidad San Francisco de Quito. She is an active member of the YACHANA project, which is devoted to working with Indigenous young people from different communities, and is also part of the Federation of Indigenous Peasants of Imbabura (FICI). She is a young activist interested in promoting and strengthening the Kichwa language.

Aline Regina Alves Martins is a professor in international relations and the Graduate Program in Political Science at the Federal University of Goiás.

Jennifer Yajaira Masaquiza is Kichwa Salasaka, and a student of cultural anthropology at the Universidad San Francisco de Quito. She was elected as secretary general of the Governing Council of the Kichwa Salasaka People.

David Menacho grew up with his grandparents in the Kichwa community of Colimbuela, land of ex-Wasipungueros that are former Indigenous people who worked and lived in a peonage system known as haciendas. He was an anthropology student at the Universidad San Francisco de Quito.

Luísa Pontes Molina is a doctoral candidate of anthropology at the Universidade de Brasília (UnB).

Alessandra Korap Silva Munduruku is one of the most respected Indigenous leaders in Brazil and a law student at the Universidade Federal do Oeste do Pará (Ufopa).

David Mosquera Narváez is an economist from the Central University of Ecuador, and holds a MA in international relations and diplomacy from Instituto de Altos Estudios Nacionales.

Gustavo Oliveira is an assistant professor in the Graduate School of Geography at Clark University. Oliveira is also member of the international secretariat of the BRICS Initiative for Critical Agrarian Studies, editor of the book *Soy, Globalization, and Environmental Politics in South America* (Routledge 2018, with Susanna Hecht), and guest editor of special issues in the *Journal of Peasant Studies* (v. 43, n. 2), *Political Geography*, the *Canadian Journal of Development Studies*, and *Globalizations*.

Marcos A. Pedlowski is a professor at Universidade Estadual do Norte Fluminense Darcy Ribeiro.

Rodrigo Curty Pereira is an undergraduate student in the international relations major at the Federal Rural University of Rio de Janeiro.

Rui Jie Peng is a PhD candidate in the Department of Sociology at the University of Texas at Austin.

Marina Praça is a researcher and popular educator of the Alternative Policies for the Southern Cone Institute (Instituto Políticas Alternativas para o Cone Sul-PACS).

Jefferson Pullaguari is vice president of the Indigenous Shuar Federation of Zamora Chinchipe.

Ana Luisa Queiroz is a researcher and popular educator of the Alternative Policies for the Southern Cone Institute (Instituto Políticas Alternativas para o Cone Sul-PACS).

Maria Elena Rodríguez is a professor at the Institute of International Relations at PUC-Rio and a researcher at the Brics Policy Center. Rodríguez received a PhD in sociology from IESP-UERJ, and holds law and master's degrees from the Université de Génève.

Lisa Rofel is an emerita professor at University of California, Santa Cruz. Professor Rofel has consistently brought feminist, postcolonial, and Marxist poststructuralist approaches to bear on questions of modernity, postsocialism, capitalism, desire, queer identities, and transnational encounters. She has written extensively about China. Rofel was trained in East Asian history at Brown University in the 1970s and cultural anthropology at Stanford

University in the 1980s. Her publications include *Desiring China* (Duke University Press), which addresses how public culture events in China produce desiring subjects, including soap operas, gay public life, cosmopolitan practices, and financial news; and *Other Modernities: Gendered Yearnings in Post-Mao China*, an ethnography of women workers that addresses how modernity is not a universal logic or an evolutionary tale of progress but a disparate and shifting set of discourses and practices about otherness. Rofel recently published the *Twenty-First Century Silk Road between Italy and China* (with Sylvia Yanagisako), a coedited volume *Beyond the Strai(gh)ts: Transnationalism and Queer Chinese Politics* (with Petrus Liu), and a co-edited volume on contemporary documentary filmmaking in China (with Chris Berry).

Karolien van Teijlingen is a postdoctoral research fellow at Radboud University Nijmegen (the Netherlands), and a human geographer with a PhD in social sciences from the University of Amsterdam.

Laís Forti Thomaz is an associate professor of international relations at the Federal University of Goiás, coordinator of the Global Studies Center (NEG) and the Politizar Project, and collaborating professor of the Graduate Program in Political Science (PPGCP) at UFG.

Pedro Henrique Vasques is a postdoctoral fellow at INCT-INEU/ Unicamp. He holds a law degree from the Pontifical Catholic University of Rio de Janeiro, a master's degree in law from the State University of Rio de Janeiro, a doctorate in political science from the State University of Campinas, and a doctorate in law from the University of Rio de Janeiro. He is currently a researcher at the National Institute of Science and Technology for Studies on the United States (INCT-INEU) and at the Center for the Study of Contemporary Culture (CEDEC).

Sigrid Vásconez D. is a researcher and consultant at the Ñeque Foundation.

María Amelia Viteri is a professor of anthropology at Universidad San Francisco de Quito (USFQ), the director of UNIDiversidad Program, and an associate researcher at the Department of Anthropology at University of

Maryland, College Park. Professor Viteri is a linguist and anthropologist working as an applied social scientist and professor of gender, queer theory and LGBT studies, globalization, and Migration. As such, she has examined the central role "race," ethnicity, class, gender, sexuality, and migrant status play in structural inequality, including displacement, environmental degradation, access to health, housing, and education, across the Americas. Some of her publications include *Desbordes: Translating Racial, Ethnic, Sexual and Gender Identities across the Americas* (SUNY Press, 2014), "IntenSiones: Tensions and Queer Agency and Activism in LatinoAmérica" (*Feminist Studies Journal*, 2018), and "Cultural Imaginaries in the Residential Migration to Cotacachi" (*Journal of Latin American Geography*, 2016).

Laura Trajber Waisbich is a researcher at the Brazilian Center for Analysis and Planning (Cebrap), associate at the Center for Studies and Articulation of South-South Cooperation (Articulação SUL), and is currently pursuing her PhD in geography at the University of Cambridge.

Yasunidos Guapondélig Collective consists of the following activists: David Fajardo Torres (law, University of Cuenca), María Paola Granizo Riquetti (biologist from the Universidad del Azuay, MA in interdisciplinary studies from the Universidad Autónoma de Barcelona), Carolina Vallejo (civil engineer, University of Cuenca), and Carlos Quizhpe Parra (environmental engineer, University of Cuenca).

Li Zhang (PhD in development studies from the China Agricultural University) serves as Assistant Professor in the Department of Anthropology and Sociology and Department of Environmental Studies at Amherst College. She served as visiting fellow at Cornell University and in positions at Henan Agricultural University and in the Global and International Studies Department at the University of California, Irvine. She is author of *The Origins of COVID-19: China and Global Capitalism* (Stanford University Press, 2021).

Zhou Zhiwei is a research fellow and deputy director of the Department of International Relations at the Institute of Latin American Studies (ILAS), Chinese Academy of Social Sciences (CASS). Zhiwei is the executive director of the Center for Brazilian Studies of ILAS/CASS, and was a visiting scholar at São Paulo University.

THE TROPICAL SILK ROAD

INTRODUCTION

China Stepping Out, the Amazon
Biome, and South American Populism

Paul Amar, Lisa Rofel, María Amelia Viteri,
Consuelo Fernández-Salvador,
and Fernando Brancoli

OUR BOOK *The Tropical Silk Road: The Future of China in South America* captures the epochal juncture of two of the world's most transformative processes: China's "Stepping Out"[1] into the Global South and the disintegration of the Amazonian, Cerrado, and Andean biomes. These two mega processes play out against the backdrop of new deployments of authoritarian populist repression and the emergence of voices and forms of resistance. And we illuminate fractious debates within the Left around the costs and benefits of alliances with the People's Republic (PRC) and its politics of promoting "extractivism"—mining, fossil fuel extraction, and infrastructure (Gómez-Barris 2017). These projects and partnerships may promise revenue for South American states and state-allied groups and a veneer of high-modernist developmentalism. But how does this "extractivist futurism" and statist development agenda impact the environment and groups that desire autonomy from the state or who advocate alternative notions of futurity, participation, and South-South solidarity with Asia? Our volume provides answers to this question through a set of engaging case studies and activist perspectives. In addition, our book interrogates "tropicalist" figures of race, gender, sexuality, and indigeneity that animate these projects and debates.

The intersection of rising Chinese influence and new patterns of social-environmental struggle has been studied in Africa, but almost no studies of this scale exist for South America—certainly none with an inclusive methodology that creates space for intersectional critique and voices of resistance. Our project zeroes in on a critical political juncture, as cracks in the legacy of the left-leaning "Pink Tide" and failures of racist, ecocidal populisms shape new grassroots struggles, global political economies, and geopolitical possibilities. This spectrum of issues requires the mobilization of voices never before published in English: Black community leaders across South America, critical Chinese media and Latin America specialists, Indigenous organizers, feminist activists, environmental movements, and progressive economists. Here, we provide the first grounded, grassroots-based, and comprehensive analysis of a post-US-centered world order, and an accompanying map of the stakes for local communities. And this book aims to serve as a catalyst for reading groups, teaching seminars, and policy-making conversations.

QUESTIONS AND CONTEXT

What does a world look like in which China is the primary, if not exclusive, partner in trade, defense, investment and debt, contracting, and social policy? Which social landscapes and ecological geographies are shaped by the structures built and economies fostered by China in South America? Which cultural imaginaries and media representations are articulated? Which communication gaps or expectation lags occur? What forms of negotiation, resistance, and accommodation emerge?

US wealth, military power, cultural impact, and diplomatic influence are far from disappearing in a South America shaped by the Monroe Doctrine. China's influence in the region has risen enormously, however. In the 1990s, countries across South America resisted US-centered neoliberal hegemony, shifting away from the Washington Consensus and toward the Beijing Consensus. The latter model gave pride of place to state planning and public coordination of developmentalism. During the 2000–2010s—an era dominated by the left-leaning Pink Tide in South America—China moved into position as a primary partner, funder, and contractor of infrastructure projects, mining and extraction industries, agrobusiness expansion, and military-defense relations. China is reshaping the dynamics of the region. In Ecuador, conflicts surrounding Chinese corporations have given rise to large-scale violence, such as the takeover of the Andes Petroleum oilfield in Tarapoa in

November 2006. In July 2007, protests against the Chinese firm Petroriental in Orellana led to more than twenty-four deaths and the declaration of a national state of emergency (Ellis 2013). After the 2016–2019 wave of right-wing populism swept the continent, it momentarily seemed that China's leverage in South America might be lost, as new authoritarian-leaning regimes fanned anti-Chinese sentiment and anti-Asian racism.

However, in 2020, another revolution happened. With the US retreating into radical isolationism and atavistic nationalism, the COVID-19 pandemic triggered the collapse of financial markets and exposed the catastrophic incapacity of the antidevelopmentalist political coalition. China moved into this gap, propping up state and local government infrastructure and healthcare budgets across the region, and reviving partnerships that had been frozen since the end of the Pink Tide era (Zhang 2021; Amar 2020). Municipal and provincial governments in São Paulo, Rio de Janeiro, Maranhão, Quito, Guayaquil, and elsewhere basked in Chinese attention. The press began describing an "inevitable marriage" between China and South America in an era of declining US hegemony. In April 2020, Chinese president Xi Jiping launched a "New Health Silk Road" agenda of aid and investment that would target South America, extending the Eurasian-African Belt and Road Initiative to the southern half of the Americas, creating a medical-humanitarian agenda for an age of pandemics. And this New Health Silk Road complemented and extended the PRC's previously announced "digital silk road" project that would include "innovation action plans for e-commerce, digital economy, smart cities and science and technology parks" (Brown 2017).

In recent years, a flurry of editorials, debates, and blog posts have grappled with the implications of this tectonic shift in global hegemony toward China. However, no publication has yet explored in-depth the local realities and socio-ecological implications of these recent shifts. What does this new Tropical Silk Road and this "inevitable" courtship or marriage between China and South America look like for communities and ecologies on the ground? This book aims to answer that question.

In the pages that follow, we provide in-depth case-study analysis. We go beyond armchair theorizing and the satellite-eye view. Our specialists speak from grassroots contexts, offering unique, lucid perspectives and insights. Our contributing authors include economists, anthropologists, political scientists, think-tank directors, and ecologists—but also community organizers, journalists, diplomats, and activists. We bring together a wide range of voices rarely privileged in these conversations: Indigenous leaders, members of Black women's groups, feminist theorists, and environmental analysts, as well as specialists uniquely qualified in local political economy and in the analysis of transnational mobilization.

FOCUS AND PERSPECTIVE

To better provide this fine-grained analysis, we have chosen to focus on two countries in South America: Brazil and Ecuador. These represent two ends of a spectrum of relations with China. Brazil is an empire in itself: a huge country with a strong state, massive contracting and agribusiness sectors, and a highly militarized society. Brazil has a long history of aggressive economic, commercial, and religious extension into Africa and, of course, into its own internal indigenous territories. Ecuador is a smaller nation, but strategically positioned at the gateway between the vast Amazonian region, the Andean nations, and the increasingly metropolitan Pacific world. Ecuador's Port of Manta is one of the closest on the South American mainland to China. It is a strategic point for expediting Chinese–Latin American trans-Pacific trade, through which Brazil and Ecuador will develop a transcontinental corridor connecting the Pacific with Coastal Brazil (Narins 2012). Although the presidencies of Pink Tide leaders Lula da Silva in Brazil and Rafael Correa in Ecuador were distinct, they both launched megaproject partnerships with China celebrated as marking an epochal shift away from US and neoliberal domination.

In Ecuador, the focus of these partnerships has been overwhelmingly extractivist: copper mining, gold mining, oil drilling, hydroelectric dams (producing the energy needed for these extraction projects), and roads and ports to carry these products to China and its global markets. In Brazil, the focus has been on agribusiness, and particularly on soybean harvesting and cattle ranching that has encroached on the Amazon rainforest. Here too has also been investment in oil and gas extraction, dam building, and the construction of ports and free-trade zones to service new commodity exports. Chinese public companies have also invested in Brazil in energy grids, dams, Olympic megaprojects, railroads, and port complexes.

Ecuador and Brazil also share social concerns that arise in response to Chinese investment. Both countries have significant Indigenous populations in the Amazon regions as well as in the big cities. These populations have mobilized in response to the impacts of Chinese-backed projects. Both nations have active Black and racialized populations, particularly in coastal urban and port zones. These have confronted, accommodated to, or resisted the new realities.

In the following pages, we have been insistent on tracing the gender, sexuality, and class dimensions of the new geopolitical and social profile of China in South America. Community responses to China's mega infrastructure and extraction projects (and accompanying transportation infrastructure expansion) have included concerns about changing gender and sexual relations, unequal access to livelihoods, and the varying racialized and gendered impact of environmental hazards.

The wording of our title, *The Tropical Silk Road*, is a self-conscious and carefully made choice. In the Middle East and East Asia, distinct forms of power referred to as "Orientalism" have served as matrices of racial/sexual representation that enable forms of colonial and postcolonial governance, population control, economic development, and military incursion. In analogous ways, in South America and the Caribbean, "tropicalism" thrives as a persistent legacy of colonial and imperial representations of race, sex, and desire. Tropicalism in South America was not just a colonial-imperial doctrine. It was embraced by postcolonial nationalists and modernists. "Luso-tropicalism" became a founding doctrine of Brazilian twentieth-century state-driven modernization, and the Andean nationalist focus on *mestizaje* is narrated through profoundly tropicalist tropes. *Mestizaje* is a doctrine of race/gender mixing that values the "whitening" of the population as the seed of post-Spanish identity (Moreno Figueroa 2010). Articulated in the case of Ecuador by Benjamín Carrión, the founder of the Casa de la Cultura Ecuatoriana in the 1940s (Rosado 2021; Olson 2012). Carrión wrote passionately about *mestizaje* as "the national human climate [in Ecuador]" promoted by "political tropicalism, and its highest expression, the passion for freedom." His book, *Letters to Ecuador* (1944) "constitutes an interpretation of the themes of tropicalism, Ecuadoriany, and the periods of configuration of the national personality" (Tite Mallitasig 2017). Similarly and even more (in-)famously, the influential founding father of Luso-tropicalism in Brazil, Gilberto Freyre, presented a lecture "Why Tropical China" in 1944 in the United States, which eventually was published in a book entitled *New World in the Tropics* in 1959, and then reissued more recently in Portuguese in São Paulo in 2011 as *China Tropical* to coincide with a moment in which the PRC launched a vast array of extractive and infrastructure partnerships with the administration of President Lula in Brazil and when the PRC had surpassed the US to became Brazil's number one trading partner and investor.

Freyre's term "Tropical China" suggested explicitly that Brazil, and maybe South America in general, had many "Oriental" sociocultural characteristics: mass rural agricultural populations socially reproduced through supposedly "positive" models of plantation-based race/sex intimacies, and so-called traditional values that could serve as a solid basis for an enriched project of modernization and expansive development and as a "tropical" alternative to Mao's revolutionary model. Cultural expressions in Brazil were also affected by reflections on different interpretations of "tropical." The best example was the Movimento Tropicalista, a cultural movement that flourished in the second half of the 1960s. Also identified as Tropicália, it embraced a wide range of cultural genres, including film, theater, and poetry, in addition to music transposing proposals made in the 1920s and 1930s by artists associated with the Anthropophagic Movement (among them, Mario de Andrade and Tarsila do Amaral) that proposed that Brazil should "cannibalize," digest and regurgitate, cultural expressions exported by dominant Western cultural powers and combine them with local ideas.

Our book turns this tropicalist analytic inside out, offering critical insights into the legacies of "tropical" doctrines and uniquely exploring how China has figured in these imaginaries. Our studies also exist in a world of "tropically" identified struggles around tropical ecosystems and populations, tropical medicine in a time of pandemic, and social movements such as the Tropical Forest Alliance. In the twenty-first century, a "modern Silk Road"[2] slicing through "tropical forests" has become an evocative image of futurity for enraged activists and developmentalist champions alike. In the context of these emergent and imagined futures, we launch our debates, analyses, and engagements.

BOOKS IN THIS FIELD

Numerous books have tracked China's increased presence in the Global South, beginning around the turn of the twenty-first century in the era of "new developmentalism." These have focused on the Beijing Consensus of the 1990s, the BRIC (Brazil, Russia, India, and China) alliance of the 2000s, and the Belt and Road Initiative of the 2010s. The majority of these books take a bird's-eye view of geopolitical trends, mapping large-scale shifts or recounting the diplomatic maneuvers of statesmen and negotiators. Much less work has been done on grounded analyses based on fieldwork, ethnography, and social scientific methodologies. The books that have so far been published have largely focused on environmental impacts or social conflicts around Chinese investments in the African continent. Latin America—and South America, in particular—has received far less scholarly attention. That lacuna has begun to be filled by a series of recent publications.

Among these publications are David Dollar, *China's Investment in Latin America* (2017); Margaret Myers and Carol Wise, eds., *The Political Economy of China–Latin American Relations In the New Millennium: Brave New World* (2017); Julia Strauss and Ariel C. Armony, eds., *From the Great Wall to the New World: China and Latin America in the 21st Century* (2013); Gastón Fornez and Alvaro Mendez, *The China–Latin America Axis: Emerging Markets and Their Role in an Increasingly Globalised World* (2018); R. Evan Ellis, *China-Latin America Military Engagement: Good Will, Good Business, and Strategic Position* (2011); Kevin Gallagher, *The China Triangle: Latin America's China Boom and the Fate of the Washington Consensus* (2016); Alex Fernández Jilberto and Barbara Hogenboom, eds., *Latin America Facing China: South-South Relations beyond the Washington Consensus* (2010); R. Evan Ellis, *China on the Ground in Latin America: Challenges for the Chinese and Impacts on the Region* (2014); Rebecca Ray et al., eds., *China and Sustainable Development in Latin America: The Social and Environmental Dimension* (2017); and Karolien van Teijlingen et al., eds., *La Amazonía Minada. Minería a Gran Escala y Conflictos en el Sur del Ecuador.* (2017). With the exception of the last two titles, however, this body of work largely adopts the lens of US-based business investors, looking from afar and strategizing about long-term prospects.

New models of public-facing scholarship weave together themes of antiextractivism, indigeneity, feminist and queer mobilizations, and environmental justice. These intersectional models have inspired this collective. Macarena Gómez-Barris's (2017) pioneering book *The Extractive Zone: Social Ecologies and Decolonial Perspectives* "works across spaces that might not

otherwise be organized together in one study, delinking from the natural-
ization of national histories and from the heteronormativity of the nation
state" (2), and "attends to the regions of extractive capitalism by foreground-
ing submerged perspectives" (1). Thea Riofrancos (2020) has also inspired
our collaboration with *Resource Radicals: From Petro-Nationalism to Post-
Extractivism in Ecuador*. In this timely book, she "explores the conditions
and consequences of the radical politicization of resource extraction. . . .
[her approach] expands the study of resource politics well beyond the halls
of the petro-state. In Ecuador, grassroots activists were key protagonists in
the contentious politics of oil and mining. In dynamic conflict with state
and corporate elites, popular mobilization shaped the political and economic consequences of resource extraction" (3). Finally, Manuela Lavinas
Picq (2018) has taken a lead role with her book *Vernacular Sovereignties:
Indigenous Women Challenging World Politics*, highlighting case studies and
new analyses that prove that "from their positions of marginality, Indigenous women actively challenge state sovereignty and are more enmeshed in
international relation than many would imagine" (4). We also draw upon
the rich conversations and field-shaping interventions in the special issue
of *Feminist Studies* edited by Lisa Rofel and Megan Sweeney (2021), entitled
"Global Intimacies: China and/in the Global South."

We believe that public actors, classrooms, and reading audiences may
eagerly appreciate perspectives that conceptualize change in new ways and
convey stories that capture new relations of power, desire, wealth, and violence in this time of change. In this context, the three principal contributions that our community of "Global Asia" scholars and their intersectional
perspectives offer are (1) mapping the lived experience of geopolitical change
and launching a new set of global and transregional conversations, (2) cen-
tering a new generation of young activists and publicly engaged scholars in
dialogue with leaders in academic fields, and (3) highlighting methodological and epistemological innovations from perspectives situated in the Global
South and in sites of radical-alternative grassroots knowledge production.

SETTING THE SCENE

In April 2020, Brazil's vice-president Hamilton Mourão (an army general) proclaimed that Brazil and China will be united in an "inevitable
marriage." Brazil seduces with its large-scale supplies of food and fuel.

And China is a superpower longing for both. For Mourão, this relationship needed to be guided by "pragmatism, not dogma," as Asia becomes the strategic and economic hub of the world. Anticipating new kinds of geo-economic "marriages" in this changing global order, Latin American newspapers and diplomats described China as "courting" (*cortejo*) or "flirting" (*flerte, coqueteo*) with countries across the region.

These courtship metaphors are not coincidental but reflect a historic shift in sexualized subjects and metaphors of intimacy. This shift marks a set of transformations in relations between China and South America, as the two regions move away from revolutionary Third Worldism and toward bilateralism and possibly new relations of dependency. "Brotherhood" among Global South countries was the favored term used to describe a twentieth-century age that stretched from the Bandung Conference of 1955 through the 2010s Pink Tide era. At the Bandung Conference, Chinese foreign minister Zhou Enlai spoke charismatically of global cooperation through brotherhood and peaceful coexistence. The term *brotherhood* resonated with the masculinism of the alliance between male nationalist heads of state, leaders who had led coups or revolutions that ejected colonial rulers. The gender and class exclusivity of the "brotherhood" brand of mid-twentieth-century Bandung-era Third World Solidarity has been noted by feminist and queer scholars of the Global South. Postcolonialists, including Kwame Nkrumah of Ghana, have argued that ideologies of "brotherhood" evoke a false sense of fraternal equality among Global South countries that, in fact, are characterized by extreme inequality in terms of size, wealth, and influence (Allman 2013). Within Global South countries, "brotherhood" legitimizes masculinist gender/sexual normativity and nationalist tendencies, leaving domestic patriarchy, class systems, and gender binaries unchallenged. This language of brotherhood (*fraternidad* in Spanish and *fraternidade* in Portuguese) continued through the Pink Tide era and the founding of the BRICs forums (Wanming 2019).

By 2020, however, China–South American relations had crossed a threshold. A notable shift had occurred in the gendered and social imagining of the relationship between China and its Global South partners. The previously mentioned metaphors of intimacy "courtship," "flirting," and "inevitable marriage" emerged in Latin America (López 2020) while the Chinese term *zou xiang shijie*, meaning "stepping out toward the world," erased the era of socialist internationalism and previous eras of transregional engagement (Rofel 2019). As a synonym for "going global," the phrase has been criticized because it implies that China was closed in on itself before. Since at least the sixteenth century, China has had economic, political, and ideological entanglements with other countries in Asia, then with European colonial powers, and, finally, with the nonaligned and socialist worlds. Nevertheless, "stepping out," in English, does resonate in certain registers that interest us. It is defined as engaging in a more active social life, wearing new clothes and meeting new people, increasing one's pace and scale of socializing. The term also means to begin to sexually experiment in an open marriage (Urban Dictionary 2020).

We think it is revealing that in an era of high-stakes bilateralism and renewed dependency, metaphors of courtship and marriage are supplanting those of brotherhood. "Brotherhood," of course is also a sexualized metaphor, infused with homosocial desire and a yearning for manliness and aspirations for heteronormative validation. Perhaps the fact that "handshake politics" between strongmen leaders is described in social media and even sometimes in the conventional media as "bromances" or "courtship" or "marriage" indicates that the homosocial subtexts or the critiques of Third World brotherhood articulated by feminists and queer analysts are shaping public consciousness. This could be true. But this shift in metaphors from brotherhood to marriage implies a recognition of the binary, coupling, and unequal division of labor and affect in these emerging relationships. "Brotherhood," for all its limitations as a concept, signifies mutuality and group solidarity. Marriage, as it is conventionally understood, signifies privacy and exclusivity. It is a bond sealed between two and only two contracting individuals. Conventionally (even in homosexual marriages), it implies a hierarchical division of productive and reproductive labor, which becomes extractive and ritualized in the context of normativity. Marriage signals a "sexual contract" of possession over desire and property. The imaginary of courtship and marriage is quite distinct, with its interpellation of a newly desiring China (as Lisa Rofel has described) and fresh logics of attraction (Rofel 2007). With gendered and sexualized metaphors that treat communities as singular actors, it is no wonder that the actual relations between China and Latin America are complex and require careful analysis.

This book addresses what the new imaginary of courtship and marriage between China and South America reveals in terms of romanticized gender, race, and sexual relationships; new structures of desire and mastery; as well as progressive yearnings for mutuality and conviviality. China's presence in Ecuador is strategic because of Chinese regional ambitions. As Ecuadorian economics professor Milton Reyes Herrera discusses in this book, however, China's relationship with each country in Latin America has unique features, depending on the internal political discourse of each state-society. It should be noted that Ecuador and the surrounding nations do not represent priority areas in terms of China's strategic national defense profile (Shi 2010). Neither Ecuador nor Brazil is located within the first of China's concentric "rings" of diplomatic and security interests (Yuan 2013; Clarke 2016; Nathan and Scobell 2012; Nathan 2015; Brown 2017). South America falls within the third and/or fourth rings, concerned with international trade, economic relations and the strengthening of state sovereignty through participation in post–World War II international institutions, for which China has developed mechanisms for regional and bilateral dialogues.

The specificity of the gendered and sexualized imaginaries that animate geopolitical dynamics between China and Ecuador is addressed by our research activists from Cuenca, Ecuador: Pedro Gutiérrez Guevara, Sofía Carpio, and Mayra Flores. In their examination of new kinds of development and its attendant masculinities, they shed light on the political rationality materializing in the form of phallic infrastructure projects that exacerbate gendered and racialized inequities faced by local populations. These authors discuss how the provision of infrastructure is intimately related to a masculinist rationality that idealizes and concretizes geopolitical "marriages" and modernist visions. In Latin America, this understanding is embedded in the colonial (Quijano 2000) dimension of development. While political imaginaries that romanticize mega infrastructure projects abound in the world, the projects themselves are linked to historic heteronormative state formations (Viteri and Picq 2016), where epistemological framings of South-South cooperation are embedded in gendered imaginings (Fernández-Salvador and Viteri this volume).

Zhou Zhiwei describes in this volume how the metaphor of marriage, discussed above, perfectly captures the moment: "This kind of metaphor is very appropriate. It very vividly summarizes the basis, motivation, and expectations of cooperation between China and Brazil. Without a solid 'affec-tion' as basis, how can there be a natural marriage? Without passionate moti-vation toward each other, how can there be a long-lasting marriage? Without a good expectation of future life, how can there be a stronger marriage? The words 'inevitable' emphasized by Vice President Mourão precisely reflect the reality that China and Brazil are 'indivisible'" 75). Chinese social media and development scholar Li Zhang analyzes the rise of a heroic and desiring "wolf warrior" culture in the wake of the blockbuster success of the Chinese film *Wolf Warrior II*. As analyzed elsewhere by Petrus Liu and Lisa Rofel (2018), the film depicts a handsome Chinese ex-soldier speeding through Africa to rescue local and Chinese victims of mercenaries and pandemics, developing passionate pairings along the way. Here, Zhang traces how "China's new 'wolf warrior' culture among diplomats and 'netizens' transformed [the COVID pandemic] crisis into an engine of nationalist fervor domestically, and an instrument of diplomacy" abroad (52). Zhang continues, revealing that "the Chinese diaspora in Brazil juggles a transnational identity that places them in the crossfire of cultural struggles·... narratives about Brazil ultimately reveal how official and unofficial, formal and informal, domestic and dias-poric voices reinforce Chinese nationalism" (53). Cinematic investigation reveals the global and individual effects of such a marriage.

Duality, division of labor, and desiring subjects interpellated by the language of "marriage" and "courtship" smooth over significant tensions and contradictions in the new ideologies of China–South American part-nership. Does marriage imply that Brazil must loyally stand by China as a spouse, losing flexibility to deal with the US or to challenge the economic dependency that might result from a rigid two-partner system? Will Latin America be forced into a dispute between China and the US, rearticulating perspectives in which Beijing emerges as an ally of the global south or just another imperialist agent. In this context, Ana Saggioro Garcia and Rodrigo Curty Pereira, in this volume, explore if China is installing relations of dom-ination that foster geo-economic dependency practices like those of the last century—while legitimizing them with attitudes and performances of Global South bonding? "The ideas and narratives regarding China-Latin America relations... tend to either emphasize South-South cooperation and inclusive and sustainable growth or push for the exploitation of natural and primary resources" (227). Is this romanticized "marriage" just a deal cut between

China and the *comprador* classes in South America, through which China establishes alliances with local elites to guarantee extractive industries?

BEYOND DEVELOPMENTALISM AND THE STATE

The benefits of such extractions do not remain static. David Delgado del Hierro illustrates why Ecuador has less leverage and thus fewer options for negotiation, facing a debt with China that has become onerous due to declining petroleum prices (Ecuador's main source of export income). Rafael Correa agreed to pre-sell petroleum to China "committing . . . 90% of [Ecuador's] exportable crude . . . until 2024" (Kraul 2018). In December 2018, then president Lenín Moreno visited China to link Ecuador to its "New Silk Road" initiative (*La República* 2018), with the objective of securing more flexible terms for the repayment of its Chinese debt (Delgado del Hierro, this volume, 390). Meanwhile, other communities, private actors, and municipalities that have been marginalized from the privileged negotiating status of the *comprador* elites have seized upon the new opportunities offered by "marriage" with China, imagining this as the beginning of a new age of respect and diversification in South-South flows. As Fernando Brancoli and Wander Guerra argue in their chapter that these new discourses specifically disidentify with the forms of domination deployed by the Global North, fostering a belief that "Chinese investment tools would be linked to a reality of respect for sovereignty and local development. . . . [A new] grammar is one of investments focused on the communities . . . a discourse of horizontality and reconstruction" (370–71). This disidentification transforms the PRC in South America into a distinct presence that diverges from paradigms set by US and European superpowers.

South American Indigenous community leaders and youth activists have been articulating their own concepts and agendas for analyzing the PRC's Stepping Out and the paradigm shifts this entails. Part 2 provides a vital alternative to nation-scale accounts that methodologically privilege national capital, statist actors, or commercial elites. Here, we center the voices of Indigenous communities, Black organizers, laborers and the working class. Alessandra Korap Munduruku, leader of the Mundukuru Indigenous nation, describes here the degree to which China represents a new ontological paradigm for indigenous communities affected by megaprojects: in addition to the risks of material displacement or biological extinction, new investments have set in motion dynamics that desecrate that which is eternal and of the ancestors. In this sense, Munduruku and Luísa Pontes Molina highlight that "the damage caused by megaprojects has reached spaces animated by nonhuman subjectivities" (125). Indigenous community organizers convey their epistemological perspectives and their existential resistance. As they insist, the phenomena we are analyzing here amount to the "putting Indigenous people and their communities at risk not only in terms of their physical integrity but also endangering the world of spirits and the organization of the cosmos" (121). We also include authors who are leaders of Black and mixed "maroon" communities in South America. Maroons constitute autonomous urban-peripheral or rural societies, self-liberated zones where enslaved Black peoples and insurgent Indigenous groups merged to create self-governed polities and economies, free from the state. In Spanish, these communities are called *cimarrones* or *palenques*. In Portuguese, maroon societies are called *quilombos*, drawing the word from the Kimbundo African language. These societies have survived across the continent from the sixteenth century into the modern period. Those that persisted until the 2010s achieved some degree of recognition and protected status from the government of President Lula in Brazil (Moraes 2017) and President Correa in Ecuador (specifically, in that country, for *palenques* near Esmeraldas, Limones, and Guayaquil) (Defensoria del Pueblo Ecuador 2016).

Indigenous territories and maroon communities have generated historic and increasing levels of mobilization, effecting dramatic large-scale changes. In Ecuador, the first large-scale copper mining project located in the Amazon Region, the Mirador mining project, has motivated both resistance and negotiation among the Shuar leadership and local communities. For many Shuar, a megaproject such as Mirador could offer material improvement and access to a better life and education. These possibilities compelled the Shuar leaders to negotiate. As Jefferson Pullaguari (136), then leader of the Shuar federation in the province of Zamora Chinchipe, writes, "because the state had a history of not treating Indigenous populations fairly, the feeling among the Shuar was that this was an opportune time to demand reasonable compensation for the exploitation of resources in their territories." However, there was much disenchantment within the Indigenous organization after both the Chinese company and the Ecuadorean government disavowed its role in the negotiation process:

"Relations between the Chinese company and the FESZCH-Shuar Federation (which had a new president) became tense, mainly because it no longer recognized the federation as an important player or as representing Shuar communities" (139). Opportunity had, once again, led to further marginalization.

The nationalist developmentalist agenda in which extractive and mega projects financed by China are key has not only worked to delegitimize and neutralize indigenous organizations at all levels, but also criminalized resistance and opposition (Arsel and Avila Angel 2011; Méndez 2012). Indigenous activists Julia Correa, Israel Chumapi, Paúl Ghaitai Males, Jennifer Yajaira Masaquiza, Rina Pakari Marcillo, and David Menacho—all students at the Universidad San Francisco de Quito—have generated an illuminating ethnographic and analytical narrative of the national Indigenous protests that occurred in Ecuador in October 2019. They trace the reasons for this mobilization to the impacts of extractivism: "China's interest in Ecuador is based primarily on its natural resources, which are located in protected wilderness areas close to rural mestizo and Indigenous populations" (152). The government did not accept opposition from local populations directly affected by these projects. Instead, as Cholango—an Indigenous leader—asserts, the president accused "them of opposing development, technology and progress," criminalizing, persecuting, and neutralizing organizations and resistance efforts (Cholango 2012). The authors argue that the October 2019 uprisings were a response to Indigenous organizations' need to regroup after years of conflict, fragmentation, and suffering resulting from persecution for opposing extractivism in Indigenous territories.

The statist, "neodevelopmentalist Left" (in both Brazil and China) tends to describe Chinese-Brazilian joint megaprojects as "anti-imperialist." They promise to "manage risk" and "mitigate impact" on ecosystems and society. In Ecuador, large-scale extractive projects are directly linked to notions of well-being. This concept, translated from the Kichwa *Sumak Kawsay*[3] and incorporated in the Constitution of 2008, served as a guideline for state policy, justifying the need to generate wealth through oil and mineral extraction (Arsel, Hogenboom, and Pellegrini 2011).

In this volume, Munduruku and Molina make a claim that they link to a counterdevelopmentalist manifesto: "What would the white man say if we built our villages on top of their properties, their sanctuaries and cemeteries? We had this sacred place and when we died, we went there. But as the government is now exploding everything, even things of the spirit, we will end. We will die as spirits too" (122).

Similarly, Shuar leader Jefferson Pullaguari shares his concerns and goals regarding the extractivism of the Mirador Project: "[We must] protect and keep alive ancient customs, defend *Li Nunke*, our Mother Earth, protect the water, protect life and defend the legacy of the future generations that will want to know these majestic green mountains" (141).

Megaprojects constructing ports, mines, or dams in the Amazon region, or fossil fuel platforms, pipelines, or spaceports in the coastal areas, have been displacing long-standing autonomous communities. As this volume underlines, these processes often threaten to transform *quilombos* into depopulated industrial enclaves or shipping hubs. Under certain circumstances, however, the same processes can bring "modern maroon" activists from the periphery of the periphery into the nodular centers of global economies, suddenly giving them leverage and influence. Will this corrupt and coopt their historical, epistemological, and eco-social alterity? As analyzed here by *quilombo* activists Sabrina Felipe and Lucilene Raimunda Costa, "The [infrastructure projects] threaten to remove quilombolas from that municipality . . . Maranhão has been designate as a territory for the extraction and export of commodities, a designation that comes at a high price for the communities that have lived on these lands for centuries" (274).

In this context, the recent investments sponsored by China and Brazil are interpreted by *quilombola* leaders as deliberately ignoring what these intellectuals call their "nonspacialized societies"—that is, they acknowledge forms of presence or ontologies that are not immediately perceptible as currently living social beings or proximate structures. Felipe and Raimunda Costa insist that megaprojects alter the landscape and the lives of residents at multiple levels and scales. They point out that it is impossible to separate and protect "'culture' or mitigate social impact, since in their conception of the world, it is impossible to disassociate the material 'resources' from the symbolic marks inscribed in the territories" (272–75).

These massive projects have also increased the presence of foreign workers. In the case of Rio de Janeiro, Chinese men occupying management positions have begun to work in the region. In this context of intensifying "interactions between 'outsider' workers and the local community, the vulnerability of women and foreign workers is simultaneously aggravated: the former related to patriarchy and the latter to xenophobia" (Ana Luisa Queiroz, Marina Praça, and Yasmin Bitencourt, 358). The social imaginaries and moral panics (often racialized sex panics) that orbit around the presence of male laborers and businessmen shape conceptions of the gendered violence that accompanies megaprojects. This intersects with increasing mobilization of awareness of anti-Asian violence and Sinophobia, stoked by right-wing populism. Our intervention offers community feminist perspectives on the undeniable gender skewing of the social violence of these investments. Our authors resist victim subjectivities and convey narratives and strategies of women's organizing in the context of the rise in levels of rape, lack of access to reproductive health, sexual rights, and family planning, and the denial of paternity and public and private support for children born in and around project sites. Their activism highlights the intensified patriarchal nature of these sites and their unequal engendered division of labor, as well as the "sexual social contract" underpinning their social organization. Although China presents itself as different from the Global North, *quilombola* activists do not see much difference on the ground. "Women and other residents mobilized through the legal system by filing lawsuits claiming financial damages as compensatory measures for the impacts caused by [the steel plant]," say Felipe and Raimunda Costa (358). To avoid perspectives that unilaterally critique Asian businessmen and elites, our chapters also give space for Asian workers, managers, and social media influencers to articulate nuance and forms of agency.

Quilombolas in the state of Maranhão provide an in-depth analysis of how northeastern Brazil has become a "stopover territory," treated as a shipping corridor between commodity producing regions and China. Local organizers want to interrupt this dynamic, insisting upon sovereignty, participation, and redistribution. From investors' perspective, the presence of Black communities is an obstacle to regional development. Community researchers offer an alternative notion of participatory development that centers upon racial justice, history, and environmental protection. They work to reimagine development through a nonstatist lens, creating a nontransitory feminist geography and bringing to life new alliances as China and Brazil "flirt" with each other across the region.

New projects have been enabled by the bilateralism being forged between China and individual countries in Latin America. This has fragmented the fragile unity of BRICS as a forum for rising powers from the Global South. As Gustavo Oliveira argues, "that Chinese capital and corporate control becomes refracted through Brazilian public and private actors. This enables Chinese firms to circumvent socioenvironmental resistance, promoting continuities in Chinese investment strategies despite Brazilian politics" (179). Brazilian scholars Alana Camoça and Bruno Hendler continues, "Logisitical corridors for the export of agricultural production through the Tapajós River Basin . . . contribute to irreversible socioenvironmental impacts in the region" (257). These "logistics corridors" are not made without resistance, however, and social struggles have gained important victories.

In 2016 in Brazil, the federal Public Prosecutor's Office transferred responsibility for environmental licensing of ports on the Tapajós from the state to the federal government, halting further construction because previous projects were licensed individually, without considering the compounded interaction of their impacts as a block. "That triumph for local environmentalists was soon followed by a victory for the Munduruku, whose campaign reversed the environmental license of the Chinese-backed São Luis do Tapajós hydroelectric dam" (Oliveira, this volume, 187).

Local communities and governments in Brazil's Amazon and northeast have seized upon the opportunities and aid offered by China in a time when the national government has abandoned the region to fire and pandemic, describing it with racist invective and contempt. In this context, China's courtship gestures, expressed in humanitarian assistance, have been welcomed at the grassroots level. Zhou Zhiwei, director of the Center for Brazilian Studies in the Chinese Academy of the Sciences, describes in this volume that "The PR government has expressed a commitment to global cooperation and sharing Chinese experience in combating pandemics. . . . The government actively deployed medical resources to support Brazil and coordinated online exchanges between experts from the two countries. . . . The sincere and voluntary character of this assistance marks a historic shift in the two countries' relationships" (77).

In Ecuador, the Yasunidos Guapondélig Collective tells the story of a partnership between these environmental activists and the Río Blanco indigenous community in the highlands of Ecuador, which fought for their right to be consulted before any company could extract minerals in their territory. While there has been resistance to mining activity in this area for almost twenty-four years, the authors argue that two factors prepared the ground for the development of a successful coalition: the shift from a Canadian to a Chinese company, which negatively affected the dynamics with the community, and the ties developed between the collective and the Río Blanco community. After a period of organization, protests, and uprisings that halted the mining project's activities, "a civil court issued a preliminary injunction finding a violation of the communities' right to free, prior, and informed consultation, and ordering the suspension of mining activities in the Río Blanco area . . . a ruling which 'marked the first time an Ecuadorian community has been able to legally suspend the operations of a foreign-operated metal mining project'" (213).

LOCAL INITIATIVES AND NATIONALIST FRAGMENTATION

The fragmentation of governance in Brazil is perhaps one of the clearest consequences of the COVID-19 pandemic that swept through South America, beginning in February 2020. With the Brazilian federal government's refusal to adopt practices to curb the spread of the virus, state governors and even mayors tried to fill the vacuum. This has been particularly relevant when considering Brazil as a country in which the budget and the decision-making process are centralized at the federal level. Even though governors received support from the population at the beginning of the health crisis, recent polls indicate that this support is falling, reflecting a certain exhaustion with isolation measures and concern with increased unemployment.

The fragmentation of political leadership has also changed the way in which Brazil deals with international partners like China, opening possibilities for leveraging among different international actors and lobbies. Traditionally, Brazilian foreign policy has been administered by the Ministry of Foreign Affairs, with few windows of opportunity for other Brazilian political groups. Although in recent years there have been some attempts by organized groups and social movements to be included in decision-making processes, most of the relevant activities have been concentrated in the hands of the federal government. The inauguration of Jair Bolsonaro as president in January 2018 resulted in dramatic changes in Brazilian foreign policy, creating space for subnational actors (right-wing lobbies more often than not) to produce different narratives. This had shocking effects in the environmental arena. Brazil was subsequently criticized for not battling the fires that ravaged the Amazon in 2019. Bolsonaro, backed by the newly mobilized agrobusiness, military, and nationalist lobbies, proclaimed that the Amazon "belongs to Brazil" (*BBC News* 2019) and that he would not tolerate external interference in the region, implying that local indigenous and environmental activists were agents of global enemies betraying Brazil's national interests. The governors of the states of the northeast and Amazon regions rejected this nationalistic framework, however, moving to push for closer ties with the European Union, fearing that the bloc would create barriers to local products to retaliate for Brazil's lack of care for the Amazon.

In the context of Bolsonaro's presidency, the demagogue harshly criticized Beijing, in spite of the fact that China is Brazil's largest trading partner. Bolsonaro complained that the Chinese want to "buy the whole country" (Senra 2019). A dispute erupted over the implementation of 5G Internet in Brazil. The United States already made public statements that if Brazil accepts Huawei's offer, it could suffer reprisals from Washington. Anti-Chinese rhetoric, often containing strong anti-Asian overtones, spilled into the debates surrounding COVID-19, with Brazilian federal ministers and the president's son, Eduardo Bolsonaro, calling it the "Chinese virus" (*Jornal Nacional* 2020) and repeating conspiracy theories (Chade 2020) regarding Beijing's supposed hidden agenda during the crisis.

Li Zhang's chapter details the nationalist uproar that Eduardo Bolsonaro caused in China. The day after his tweet blaming China for COVID, the Chinese Embassy in Brazil tweeted back, in true "wolf warrior" fashion, suggesting the president's son had become infected with a "mental virus" in the United States, which was now "poisoning" Brazil-China relations (48). These tweets quoted Li Yang, the Chinese Consul for Rio de Janeiro, who also stated that Eduardo Bolsonaro had been "brainwashed" into becoming a US "vassal," as his "remarks are not unfamiliar, just clearly parroting his [US] friends" (48). Despite some differences in tone, members of the Chinese diaspora and domestic social media narratives in Brazil came together to argue that right-wing, pro-US politicians in Brazil were harmful to positive China-Brazil relations.

Government fragmentation, however, also opened space for state governors and mayors to negotiate directly with China, taking advantage of the fact that the "diplomacy of masks" (donation by the PRC of personal protective equipment and vaccine supplies) was being ignored by the Brazilian government (Amar 2020).[4] Beijing was quick to establish agreements with states such as São Paulo and Maranhão, providing hospital supplies and respirators. With the advance of vaccine research, China passed over the formal structures of the Brazilian federal government and established partnerships with state laboratories, promising to distribute vaccines as soon as possible.

This aspect of the prospects for China in Brazil must be taken into account when analyzing Beijing's influence in Latin America. In the United States, there seems to be a bipartisan consensus regarding the possible threats that China entails for US hegemony. In Brazil, however, political elites are polarized into two camps with regard to the future of alliances with China. The creation of the "Consortium of the Northeast" is interesting in this context, as it brought together state governments from the Brazilian Northeast and Amazon to establish a lobby favoring massive joint projects with China. This consortium has declared it would set up a "Parallel Ministry of Foreign Affairs" (Madeiro 2020), rivaling that of the federal government in Brasília. By mid-2020, then, the age of the BRIC consensus had been irrevocably split in two in Brazil, with wildly different—even opposed—projects being proposed (Benites 2020).

Academically, Brazil's reflections on China are not well institutionalized. Asian studies and Chinese studies research centers across South America are still scattered and poorly integrated, with the important exception of the Confucius Institutes. As Andrea Piazzaroli Longobardi (91) points out in this volume, China has been analyzed by academics in Brazil largely through epistemologies and methodologies imported from the Global North. Brazilian higher education is still widely based on European scholarly traditions and Eurocentric agendas. For a long time, "China and other Asian countries . . . [were] not even mentioned in History and Social Sciences courses, with Asians being portrayed as a 'picturesque appendix' of the world, and not presented as world historical subjects" (91). Piazzaroli's founding of the unique interdisciplinary journal *Leste Vermelho* (Red East) and her contributions to this volume assert a more critical, Global South approach to China Studies (and to Asian Studies in general) in Latin America. *Leste Vermelho*'s critique has highlighted the historical tradition in Brazilian scholarship that sees Asian countries through an Iberian worldview: i.e., through lenses formed by imperial Portugal or Spain. Although there were significant waves of immigration from many Asian countries (principally Japan, Korea, and China) to Brazil, notably in the nineteenth and twentieth centuries, Brazilian higher education does not engage with Asian perspectives and life-worlds, much less with Asian diasporic or ethnic studies, global Asia studies, or critical East Asian studies.

In Ecuador, the IAEN, a governmental institute, funded a Chinese studies program during the Correa regime. This program is coordinated by Professor Milton Reyes Herrera, who is also a contributor to this volume. The emergence of Chinese studies in Ecuador reflects what international relations scholar David Mosquera Narváez describes as the emergence of a wave of progressive politics throughout the region during the first decade of the 2000s. This coincided with China's win-win approach. Beginning with a strengthening of politico-diplomatic ties in 2007, Chinese financing and development financial institutions in Ecuador increased. Narváez discusses how the two countries combined China's Stepping Out policy of international deployment with the interventionist policy of former president Rafael Correa at a time when China was already in the process of increasing its presence in the Latin America and Caribbean region. The Stepping Out geo-economic strategy primarily serves the interests of the Chinese state. The institutions channeling Chinese capital flows are state-owned (Narváez 102). During the administration of former president Rafael Correa (2007–2017), contracts were awarded to various Chinese companies—notably CAMC, Gezhouba, and Sinohydro Corporation—for the construction of large infrastructure projects. Sinohydro was the contractor in charge of building the Coca Codo Sinclair (CCS) hydroelectric project, the "largest construction in national history" (Pallares 2020). It was later found that the construction "used substandard materials . . . [and] did not carry out adequate quality control or technical procedures" (Contraloría General del Estado 2018). The Correa administration also tended to use no-bid contracts and "insider deals" when negotiating investment contracts with Chinese companies, again reflecting how bilateralism has upended the BRICs initiatives. These practices paved the way for nepotism and corruption (Delgado del Hierro, this volume, 388–91). In fact, Correa has been convicted on corruption charges and sentenced to eight years in prison. Correa was among twenty people, including his vice president, Jorge Glas, accused of accepting $8 million in bribes in exchange for public contracts from 2012 and 2016 (León Cabrera 2020).

Anthropologists Maria Amelia Viteri and Consuelo Fernández-Salvador illustrate the multiple ways in which strategic projects such as CCS alter the socioeconomic well-being of local populations. These Ecuadorian scholars analyze the promises of development, beginning with the construction of the CCS dam during the Correa government in 2009, and including the erosion of the Coca River that in turn collapsed the San Rafael waterfall, causing an oil spill in 2020. This polluted the Coca and Napo Rivers (tributaries of the Amazon), creating massive erosion due to the hydroelectric dam's sediment management strategies (Orozco 2020). According to activists Pedro Gutiérrez Guevara, Sofía Carpio, and Mayra Flores (Part 1, this volume), the dam increased the Coca River's erosion rate by 42 percent and caused creeping erosion along its margins—an effect known as the "white waters" effect (56).

AGENCY OF SCIENTISTS, ENVIRONMENTALISTS, AND CHINESE STAKEHOLDERS

The research presented in this volume provides a detailed and useful mapping of the disintegration of the Amazon biome, emerging logistics and extraction regimes, and the battles around infrastructure projects that have flared up across South America. Chinese business leaders and diplomats have certainly not been passive in these struggles. As analyzed by Laís Forti Thomaz, Aline Regina Alves Martins, and Diego Trindade d'Ávila Magalhães in this volume, China has shown itself to be a sophisticated actor in dealing with environmental procedures in Brazil. In the case of the largest hydroelectric plant in the country, Belo Monte, where it operates, Beijing mobilized an expressive number of experts, journalists to build its presence normatively and in the media (299). Diana Aguiar builds on this analysis, insisting that China in Brazil must also be understood as an actor in the agricultural sector with regard to the relations the country establishes with local actors through "a complex chain that includes corporate technological packages, computerized machinery, and transnational financial and logistical schemes." (323)

In Ecuador, Chinese projects such as the CCS and the Mirador open-pit copper have faced strong criticism. Environmental organizations and scientists, economists, political analysts, and journalists have gone beyond local resistance and conflicts, digging deep into the technical problems that might cause or contribute to environmental damage (Casey and Krauss 2018). Critics have also focused on the debt negotiations between China and Ecuador, much of which were designed to facilitate extractive infrastructure projects, since a portion of the debt is to be paid in oil shipments at a fixed, preset price. For the construction of the CCS, Ecuador agreed to a loan of US$1.682 billion, which was increased to US$2.3 billion. An oil debt set at high interest rates was also revealed after Correa left office (see Delgado del Hierro, this volume, 389, and Vásconez, this volume, 292).

Megaprojects such as Mirador and CCS are rarely understandable simply in terms of their infrastructure and technical aspects. They also have huge political and economic implications. As van Teijlingen and Hidalgo Bastidas argue in this volume, the Ecuadorian government's technocratic dream and the Chinese ambition to become the new strategic ally of Latin America resulted in disaster. The authors refer to a series of disastrous events that took place between February and April 2020 around the CCS project (events that began with the destruction of one of the largest waterfalls in Ecuador and the progressive erosion of the river that fed it). "Both Mirador and the CCS were marked by controversies about the studies and data that undergirded their design. In both cases, alternative claims by communities, civil society, critical engineers, or researchers related to environmental impacts were denied or brushed off as politically motivated nonsense. . We have seen the first indications of where such problematic politics of knowledge lead." (242)

In this context, environmental consultant and activist Sigrid Vásconez examines the role of scientists who caught the public's attention during the first months of the COVID-19 lockdown period, drawing news media and social media attention to catastrophic technical flaws in the CCS project. Vásconez writes that "confinement has actually favored the dissemination of news and allowed certain scientific questions about waterfall destruction to enter into the public discourse. Digital media, postings and links in social media, and some mainstream media coverage brought forth into the national arena (Basantes 2020; Pallares 2020) scientific questions that challenge the technical characteristics of the CCS on the national stage, a so far unseen form of criticism" (291). Both Vásconez and contributors van Teijlingen and Hidalgo Bastidas confirm that the government and the company were warned of technical problems that could lead to fatal consequences in both the CCS and Mirador projects. For the latter authors, not only did local communities and environmental organizations raise concerns about possible dangers, but even mining engineers' "latest critique concerns the mine's designs, saying are fraught with errors and are incorrectly executed. The question is not if, but when a major catastrophe will take place, they assure us" (234). These authors analyze the ways that environmental knowledge is appropriated by Chinese operators to advance projects despite possible dangers, and how the government made decisions to approve the projects. Questioning notions of "responsible mining" they show that both ECSA, the Chinese company that owns Project Mirador, and the government openly ignored crucial information on environmental impacts of copper extraction: "In the case of Mirador, the risks for water contamination with heavy metals and acid drainage was mentioned in the studies but were eventually assessed as 'insignificant.' . . . In a similar vein, the impacts of a possible collapse of the tailings facilities were deemed to be local, only affecting 10 km of the river downstream. In its public relations, ECSA meanwhile simply reiterated its environmental responsibility and minimal water use" (237).

Attention has also been directed to the rights of Indigenous people to defend their territories and to participate in appropriate processes of consultation in relation to extractive projects. In this regard, Emilia Bonilla, an Ecuadorian law student at Universidad San Francisco de Quito, provides an analysis of the contradictions in the 2008 Ecuadorian Constitution, a document that claims to recognize "the right of the population to live in a healthy and ecologically stable environment, which guarantees sustainability and well-being." In 2007, President Correa convened a Constitutional Assembly to draft a new constitution in conformity with the Citizens' Revolution platform. This was in line with the principle of *Sumak Kawsay* (mentioned above), which envisions a country where all people "effectively enjoy their rights and exercise responsibilities within the framework of interculturality, respect for diversity, and harmonious coexistence with nature."[5] The new constitution recognized the environment as having judicially protected rights.[6] Likewise, the Constitutional Assembly expanded the rights of Indigenous peoples. The new Article 57 recognizes and guarantees the collective rights of Ecuador's Indigenous peoples in accordance with international human rights instruments. While the 2008 Ecuadorian Constitution boasts of guaranteeing respect for nature and the autonomy of Indigenous peoples, corruption and opportunism were effectively prioritized over Indigenous rights (Restrepo Echavarría 2017) under the guise of so-called Socialism for the 21st Century (Bonilla, this volume, 246).

As analyzed by Thomaz et al. in this volume, as they examine "the participation of social actors in the decision making process," (299) China has shown itself to be a sophisticated actor in dealing with environmental procedures in Brazil such as in the case of Chinese involvement in the largest hydroelectric plant in the country, Belo Monte.

It is interesting to note that traditional resistance groups, such as those linked to the democratization of land use or the rights of indigenous peoples, are also acting as deal-makers and breakers around Chinese investment projects in South America. As Saggioro Garcia and Curty Pereira reveal, "One example is the Landless Rural Workers Movement (MST), which worked in partnership with local peasant and Indigenous communities to prevent iron mining and the construction of a pipeline by Sul-Americana Metais (controlled by the Chinese company Honbridge Holding) in Grão Mogol in Brazil" (226). These struggles around Chinese foreign investment transnationalize regional nonstate political mobilizations. In their study of these processes, Thomaz et al. show that Brazilian institutions have been the scene of disputes between local groups and megaproject entrepreneurs. The Brazilian state, in this analysis, becomes the subject of conflicts.

Diana Aguiar's activist work and research reveal the interconnections of "statism," or the state coordination of Chinese investment strategies, that channels public goods to the private sector for corporate profit making in Brazil. Statism creates a landscape of territorial control and hyperconnectivity designed by the state and materializing as a geography of hydroelectric power. "The spatial reorganization of capitalism's metabolism around China implies the redesign or reconfiguration of practices that commodify goods to generate value. It is a phenomenon of global proportions" (Aguiar, 234).

It is also a global phenomenon with high costs that are overlooked in the face of the gleaming promises of megaprojects.

Building dams and hydroelectric plants reflects the core dilemmas of Chinese investment in Latin America, obfuscating processes of South-South finance and investment, particularly as these impact the Amazon region. On the one hand, these megaprojects are presented as "clean construction," since they produce energy without consuming fossil fuels. They also provide hundreds of thousands of jobs (at least temporarily). On the other hand, this narrative of "clean construction" hides the necessary social engineering that must be deployed for these constructions to be realized. This includes the removal of Indigenous and traditional communities and the devastation of landscapes and biomes. The resulting dichotomy highlights the relevance of the environmental and development issues discussed by regional political groups in this volume, which spill over into the grand imaginaries of China's "stepping out" into a "South-South marriage" that incubates national development.

Anthropologists Fernández-Salvador and Viteri focus on the substantial expectations that great hydroelectric projects create in local populations, framing their analysis in terms of the political imaginaries that romanticize mega-infrastructure projects and the discourses that favor extractive-based development models. "The construction period between 2009 and 2016 saw the impact area thrive, both in terms of people's affluence and in terms of construction-spurred economic activity. As trucks and heavy equipment became part of the everyday landscape, the construction sites and the magnificent and powerful infrastructure work started to take shape, greatly altering the landscape. Similarly, expectations of economic development, land speculation, and a variety of commercial investments also increased among the local population, who truly believed the project to be a source of hope and opportunity" (309). While the government symbolically asserted its presence in the regulation of such projects and promised development and well-being for the local population, social and economic dynamics were greatly altered during the construction years. The authors document the rise and fall of expectations, as well as of economic activity and human mobility. In this context, they also pose essential questions about the future of marginal Amazonian societies in the wake of the oil spill in the CCS area and the coronavirus pandemic.

Ultimately, the central imperative of appropriating territories feeds the wheel of capital accumulation, devouring space by converting it into future-deferred progress, as Aguiar argues (this volume, 329–30). This process takes the form of subordinating regions marked by other logics. The Tapajós Basin is thus transformed into a "New Soy Road," an Amazonian mirror of the "New Silk Road." Along the soy corridor "new agribusiness sees the potential to fulfill its self-proclaimed 'logistical imperative': namely, to transport soy more efficiently from central Brazil to its new priority destination, China." This works by creating "corridors" as a new formation of "global territory." Aguiar generates the novel concept of "corridor-territory" in order to better describe the unique set of management techniques and logistical flows that compose each link in the supply chain (324–25).

"Global corridor-territories" such as the New Soy Road have been shaped over years of multiscale political disputes and negotiations, generating new cargo-only railways, highways, and container port facilities. These are the infrastructural fruit of agreements and megaprojects launched by previous governments, both Left and Right, which give continuity to the "logistical logics" that confer legitimacy in public debates. Many of these projects have not been completed after several years (or even a decade) of breaking ground. In some cases, they have not even broken ground. This delay in implementation is characteristic of the nature of investments in infrastructure megaprojects due to their size and the long term of return on investment. These aspects have been aggravated, however, by the political crises of recent years. In this context, our researchers demonstrate the subtlety of "speculative projection" that underlies investment announcements. This must be understood with caution, as part of the speculative "imagination-projection" character intrinsic to what is called "the War of the Routes."

An example of this process is the CCS, the largest project in the new Ecuadoran energy grid. This became an intensely politicized domain in which the Ecuadorian state asserts power to boost its legitimacy. The authors underline the heteronormative and homophobic discourses in Correa's authoritarian and populist administration, which instrumentalized Ecuador's strategic sectors and nonrenewable resources as bait to attract the PRC. The sexist analogy offered by President Rafael Correa in a 2014 interview is one among many examples: "Banks, the holders of financial power, are like a slightly vain girl, in the sense that if someone shows too much interest, they start playing 'hard to get.' But if he pretends like he's not interested, maybe the girl is the one that will call the boy. That's what financial markets are like" (Correa 2014). In interviews with Ecuadorian workers, author Rui Jie Peng shares how she heard many call the CCS "the president's project." They remarked upon presidential visits to project sites and some recalled moments when they personally shook hands with President Correa and Vice President Glas (418). As Pedro Gutiérrez Guevara, Sofía Carpio, and Mayra Flores discuss in Part 1, asymmetries of power reside in the symbolically male figures of the president and vice president, as exemplified on a plaque at the entrance of the CCS hydroelectric plant that reads, "To Rafael Correa Delgado,[7] Jorge Glas Espinel,[8] for being the true forgers and visionaries of this monumental work."

The analytical narratives and conceptual innovations presented in this volume flow from one text to the next. As our dialogue builds, we highlight the everyday neoextractivism and developmental imaginaries that reshape (and are shaped by) local Black, Indigenous, and worker communities. Our volume's collaborative, grassroots methodology has demonstrated its relevance even as Amazonian populations' precarity was exacerbated by the COVID-19 pandemic and Asian communities have been targeted.

By giving space for these voices, analyses, empirical findings, and conceptual innovations, we hope to illuminate the processes by which disparate and asymmetrical agendas collide in the transnational spaces of Brazil and Ecuador. We demonstrate how local and global flows of desire, people, and capital reconfigure inequalities along with gendered and racialized imaginaries and social relations. (Fernández-Salvador and Viteri, this volume, 310). Marginalized communities have been interacting with extractivism, rethinking their position and relationships with regard to it. During this struggle, they are engaging in forms of resistance and/or negotiation. In this book, we present examples of this—such as the Shuar in the Amazon Region and the Río Blanco in the highlands—and the coalitions that local peoples and groups have formed with external allies.[9]

International relations scholar, feminist, and journalist Manuela Picq (2018) illustrates how Chimborazo Kichwa women's advocacy led to the adoption of gender clauses in Indigenous rights protections in Ecuador's 2008 Constitution. These explicitly require "women's participation in decision-making processes" in the development of all collective rights and the administration of justice and territory. "Deserted by lawyers, dismissed by the national women's movement, and opposed by Pachakutik legislators, the women of Chimborazo themselves assembled legal strategies and improvised alliances along the way" (128).

As these many authors describe at length, in implementing its international development strategy of Stepping Out, the PRC imposes its geostrategic-economic interests under the cover of the principle that "everyone wins" without considering the unequal power relations that are unfolding. PRC projects and coordinated investment strategies have allowed governments like those of Correa, Moreno, and Bolsonaro to impinge on the human and constitutional rights of Indigenous and peasant communities. Just as nineteenth-century "free trade" advocates saw a "harmony of interests" between the British Empire and global colonial economies (Carr 1964), our studies reveal that PRC leaders and corporate managers cannot imagine themselves as doing anything *but* good.

As Rui Jie Peng argues in her chapter, in order to encourage Chinese government agencies to act "responsibly," it is not enough to pressure the China Development Bank and their sponsored projects. More synergistic measures are needed to identify political allies in destination countries and leverage domestic legal and regulatory change that can aid in efforts to achieve equity and protection for workers, communities, and the environment (423).

QUESTIONS OF CLASS STRUCTURE AND RACIALIZATION

Race and class nuance are absent in the majority of scholarly accounts of investment in South America, which typically view the region's political actors as pawns in a geoeconomic chess game. At best, local actors are seen as involved in a struggle between the environment and big business, in which "environmental racism" plays a constitutive role. But even in that frame, such local activists are portrayed as victims rather than as theorists, researchers, and agents on their own terms.

In the lead-up to the Olympic Games in 2016, community leaders of Black women's groups in the working-class neighborhoods of Rio de Janeiro organized against displacement and pollution caused by the megaprojects implemented by Global South partnerships with Chinese contractors, along with Chinese, Brazilian, European, and other investors. Of particular interest here were the projects of the Ternium Company. Black community leader Ana Luisa Queiroz and participatory community researcher Marina Praça, along with movement organizer Yasmin Bitencourt, argue in this volume that "Chinese performance in Brazil and Latin America is structurally inserted in a capitalist, racist, and patriarchal model. The relationship between Ternium Brasil and China is structural. It involves production in the sector that receives the greatest Chinese investments in Brazil, with the company directing part of its export to Asia" (350). Chinese megaprojects are understood by women—especially Black women—in the Global South as a result of practices based on patriarchal societies, with the distinction of added symbolic elements of Global South solidarity, which mask oppression (Quieroz, et al, this volume, 350). In the impoverished state of Maranhão in Brazil, Governor Flávio Dino of the Communist Party of Brazil actively partners with China to bring social aid to his state's residents. Paradoxically, he also makes grand capitalist deals with Beijing. From the view of grassroots community activists Sabrina Felipe and Lucilene Raimunda Costa, "Between these two opposing worldviews that have the same horizon of capitalist development stand the original and traditional peoples of the lands of Maranhão" (278).

As seen in previous sections, resource extraction goes hand in hand with race and class. In Ecuador, the impoverished mestizo and Indigenous populations have been the most affected by extractive projects. Interestingly enough, the Shuar organization in the area where the Mirador Project is located has employed discourses of class and race, arguing that they have been neglected by a racist state and society, This, in turn, has served to justify Shuar attempts to negotiate with mining companies (Fernández-Salvador 2017). This volume's Indigenous authors make it clear that government policies favoring extractivism are part of an unjust socioeconomic structure. In this structure, inequality is revealed and has been exacerbated by the COVID-19 pandemic. As a group of Indigenous student authors write, inequality calls for resistance and protest: "The October protests, the COVID-19 pandemic, and even the Coca Codo Sinclair Hydroelectric Project's disasters brought to light our society's inequalities and shown us once again that it is the most vulnerable groups who most suffer the impacts from these events while continuing to be made invisible: Indigenous peoples, rural mestizos, and Afro-Ecuadorians. For this reason, we recognize that it is imperative to legitimize the protest spaces where Indigenous peoples and others have succeeded in calling the non-Indigenous public's attention to ask them to 'acknowledge our reality'" (Correa and Chumapi, et al, 153–54).

This volume appreciates the agency of Chinese workers in South America, intersecting in spaces of labor, sociability, and struggle with Indigenous and other local workers. As described here by Cleiton Ferreira Maciel Brito, Chinese workers share spaces and sociability with Brazilians, however Brazilians often see their colleagues as agents of oppression and loss of rights (401–3). The interaction between Chinese and Brazilian workers in the Brazilian Amazon provides a space for generating new analytical and interpretive lenses regarding Chinese development in Latin America, shedding new light on debates regarding Sinophobia and racial violence against Asians in non-US contexts.

In his chapter, Brito draws upon ethnography among Brazilian workers at a factory in Manaus who reinforces the view that Beijing factories are not seen as private enterprises, but as a geopolitical strategic tools. Factory workers complain of the lack of accountability that this long-distance reporting fosters. They describe systematic physical aggressions, nonpayment of wages, and noncompliance with Brazilian laws. In the contributions assembled below, we can see the fine grain of the relationship between Chinese investments in the Global South and workers' perspectives and imaginations. The arrival of investments coordinated by Beijing delivers a plethora of new jobs but profoundly alters the grievance and alliance mechanisms that structure labor relations. In this context, certain workers have created a grammar of complaint that has nationalistic and racist tones, including the metaphor of an "invasion by the Chinese state."

The production of camaraderie among employees is lost insofar as Asian workers are represented by companies and communities, as if they were an organic part of the Chinese corporate ensemble rather than as autonomous subjects with their own economic interests. "The Chinese company does not have many benefits and the workers themselves do not complain. They say they don't have these things because they are not going to buy the worker. They say that the person has to be motivated for the good of the company and do things willingly," one Brazilian worker claims (Brito, 403).

This is how global capital, national hierarchies, and development priorities shape the structure of labor control and workplace inequalities, according to Latin Americanist scholar Rui Jie Peng, who conducted ethnographic field research on the Ecuadorian hydroelectric project (CCS). Peng addresses two different sets of labor rights and laws applied to Chinese and Ecuadorian workers. She studied how workers from different racial and national backgrounds interpreted and managed workplace inequalities, with the goal of understanding how transnational workplace inequality and national-racial boundaries interrelate. Her research suggests that workers' race, gender, nationality, citizenship, and legal status stratify their labor tasks and statuses (414). Since most Chinese state-owned enterprises were "concerned about the political stability and safety in their host countries," they developed a "tough hydro-worker" persona who "would work overtime without pay and remain compliant," all in the hope of "securing permanent employment and future higher-paying opportunities abroad with the company." In turn, when Ecuadorian workers observed Chinese workers' long work hours and lack of negotiation with management, "they stereotyped their Chinese counterparts as 'workaholics' and 'model workers,' portraying them as submissive and unconcerned about better labor conditions. Such stereotyped interpretations, however, ignored the underlying constraints Chinese workers experienced" (417). As a result, Ecuadorian workers (but not their Chinese colleagues) could leverage governmental oversight and appeal to labor laws to make demands on management. This is how they were able to maintain eight-hour work days and uphold higher safety standards compared to their Chinese counterparts (416).

The rich empirical, ecological, and social data provided by the chapters assembled here can inform and guide this process of legal, regulatory, and political transformation. The metaphors of "courtship" and "marriage" have pushed aside older "brotherhood" frameworks and have made more visceral the destructive paternalism of megaprojects that attempt to render Chinese, Ecuadorian, and Brazilian workers into mass publics of authoritarian populism. The words of the organizers and analysts presented here negate this massification without minimizing the scale of environmental degradation and social conflict. Our contributions—the words of economists, environmentalist, scholars, and activists, and Indigenous, Black, and queer leaders—have drawn a series of new maps that multiply the nuances of race, class, and gender/sexuality, so commonly rendered invisible by authors unfamiliar with the on-the-ground experiences of the region. Maroon and Indigenous communities challenge the PRC-Brazilian assertion that their joint projects are "anti-imperialist" because they embody South-South "solidarity," ignoring how this representation ignores and erases internal populations and sovereignties. Counterdevelopmentalist manifestos emerge in this volume, not only in the face of megaprojects—railroads, highways, and so on—but also in the context of state neglect and failure to respond adequately to a paralyzing pandemic. Fragmented political leadership threatens unity from above while grassroots organizing does what is familiar to it: locating coordinates in a shared effort to claim autonomy and prevent catastrophe. The neoextractivists logic of states cannot hide their patriarchal features when these are analyzed, here by Black women's groups in Rio during the months before the 2016 Olympics.

The movement leaders and organizers in this volume are not organized according to a typology. They are ordered and sequenced to reflect an evolving conversation among authors, activists, and theorists. Case studies and perspectives build and intersect as the volume's chapters unfold. The contributions engage each and reinforce each other's interventions. Readers are thus advised to peruse the chapters sequentially.

Reading groups outside the classroom will find that the discussions in the present volume can be understood as the preservation of oral histories recounted during an exceptional rise in militarism and authoritarianism during a pandemic. This moment also provoked unprecedented collaborations against these dehumanizing projects. These accounts of urban and local confrontations between state actors and workers, organizers, and indigenous populations demystify our stereotypes of how states and the global political economy work. The novel concepts introduced by this volume may be used to reorient policies, sensibilities, and solidarities. At their best, these contributions will inspire readers to locate the matrices of emerging and collapsing desires, currencies, regimes, and actors in their own worlds, and to imagine a more just and sustainable future.

ORGANIZATION OF CHAPTERS

In order to highlight the unique perspectives our book brings together, we have grouped our contributions into parts:

Global Asia, New Imaginaries, and Media Visibilities
Indigenous Epistemologies and Maroon Modernities
Grassroots Perspectives on the Fragmentation of BRICS
Logistics Regimes and Mining
Hydroelectrics and Railroads
Race, Class, and Urban Geographies
Hybridity of Transnational Labor

Each chapter focuses on the future, examining in particular the patterns and struggles opened up in the first two decades of the twenty-first century. Each contribution analyzes dimensions of China-Brazil or China-Andes/ Amazon relations, taking into account grassroots perspectives, neglected diplomatic or media aspects, or transnational civil-society relations. Our chapters answer questions including the following:

- Which new perspectives are emerging after the crisis of state-driven projects of extractivist developmentalism in the era of the "Beijing Consensus" in South America, and forged in the struggles with new articulations of authoritarian populisms?
- How do the controversies over the handling of the COVID-19 pandemic and China's assertive humanitarian, diplomatic, and financial response impact these issues on the ground?
- What is new or changing about the social profile and media-cultural impact of Chinese investors, laborers and migrants, humanitarian interventions, and diplomatic initiatives?

Our contributors highlight dimensions of social, cultural, and community communication, impact, and representation, as these interact with class and regional differences, gender, sexuality, indigeneity, and rurality. Specifically, these chapters provide case studies concentrating on one or two actors, including "bottom-up" perspectives, decolonial and deimperial lenses (Amar 2021), and identifying new lines of controversy, solidarity, or intervention. They point to trends that are otherwise ignored, tracking changing regimes or modes of articulation between and among discourses, policies, strategies, and actors.

NOTES

1. The expression "stepping out" may be better translated from Mandarin Chinese (走向世界) to English as "marching into the world." And we are very attentive

to debates around translation. However, we have found that Stepping Out (a phrase without the military implications of marching or the Long March) is how the term is utilized by business leaders and in social media, for example in Eisenman and Heginbotham 2018.

2. "Modern Silk Road" referenced on page 14 and "tropical forests" referenced on page 8 of Rosenthal, Moskovits, and Reid 2019.

3. *Buen Vivir* or *Sumak Kawsay*, a Kichwa concept that can be translated as "life in fullness."

4. https://globalejournal.org/global-e/september-2020/diplomacy-masks-china -and-crisis-populism-south-america.

5. *Constitución de la República del Ecuador*, Article 257.

6. *Constitución de la República del Ecuador*, Article 71.

7. Correa is currently living under political asylum in Belgium in the wake of an eight-year prison sentence issued by an Ecuadorian court for the crime of bribery in the *Sobornos 2012–2016* case.

8. Jorge Glas is currently serving a six-year sentence, having been convicted as an accessory to bribes received by the Brazilian construction conglomerate Odebrecht, as well as an eight-year sentence for a separate bribery conviction in the *Sobornos 2012–2016* case.

9. Indigenous activism did not begin with China's increased investments. This is also the case of the Kichwa Sarayaku who, in 2003, took their demands for the protection of their territory from the Argentinian oil company CGC to the Interamerican Commission of Human Rights.

REFERENCES

Allman, Jean. 2013. "Kwame Nkrumah, African Studies, and the Politics of Knowledge Production in the Black Star of Africa." *International Journal of African Historical Studies* 46 (2): 181–203.

Amar, Paul. 2020. "Diplomacy of Masks: China and the Crisis of Populism in South America." *global-e* 13, no. 60 (September 4). https://globalejournal.org/global-e/ september-2020/diplomacy-masks-china-and-crisis-populism-south-america.

Amar, Paul. 2021. "Insurgent African Intimacies in Pandemic Times: Deimperial Queer Logics of China's New Global Family in 'Wolf Warrior 2.'" *Feminist Studies* 47 (2): 419–48.

Arsel, Murat, and Natalia Avila Angel. 2011. "State, Society and Nature in Ecuador: The Case of the Yasuní-ITT Initiative." NEBE Working Paper 2, ISS/Hivos/ USFQ/LIDEMA.

Arsel, Murat, Barbara Hogenboom, and Lorenzo Pellegrini, eds. 2016. "The Extractive Imperative and the Boom in Environmental Conflicts at the End of the Progressive Cycle in Latin America." *Extractive Industries and Society* (4): 877–79.

Basantes, A. C. 2020. "Ecuador: la rotura del oleoducto OCP revela el impacto de construir en zonas de alto riesgo." *Mongabay Latam*, May 4, 2020.

BBC News. 2019. "Amazon Rainforest Belongs to Brazil, Says Jair Bolsonaro." September 24, 2019.

Benites, Afonso. 2020. "Desconfiados de Bolsonaro, governadores recorrem à China por ajuda contra coronavírus." *El Pais Brasil*, March 25, 2020.

Brown, Rachel. 2017. "Beijing's Silk Road Goes Digital." Council on Foreign Relations, June 6, 2017. https://www.cfr.org/blog/beijings-silk-road-goes-digital.

Carr, Edward Hallett. 1964. *The Twenty Years' Crisis, 1919–1939: An Introduction to the Study of International Relations*. London: Macmillan, 1939. Second edition, New York: Harper and Row.

Casey, Nicholas, and Clifford Krauss. 2018. "El gobierno ecuatoriano apostó por China para una represa que ahora se resquebraja." *New York Times*, December 24, 2018.

Chade, Jamil. 2020. "Pandemia: ministro denuncia 'plano comunista,' cita China e questiona OMS." *UOL*, April 22, 2020.

Cholango, Humberto. 2012. "Los pueblos y nacionalidades de Ecuador frente al extractivismo." Foro de Estudiantes Latinoamericanos de Antropología y Arqueología conference, Universidad Politécnica Salesiana, Quito, July 17–23, 2011.

Clarke, Michael. 2016. "Beijing's March West: 'One Belt, One Road' and China's Continental Frontiers into the 21st Century." Paper presented at the Political Studies Association conference, Brighton.

Congreso Em Foco. 2020. "Mourão, 'O Brasil e a china têm um casamento inevitável.'" April 29, 2020.

Contraloría General del Estado. 2018. "Contraloría identifica 7648 fisuras en Coca Codo Sinclair." November 15, 2018.

Correa, Rafael. 2014. "Rafael Correa: 'Para muchos, quedar mal frente a la banca internacional es terrible'—Salvados." *LaSexta* (canal de YouTube), December 14, 2014. https://www.dailymotion.com/video/x2cwh5d.

Defensoria del Pueblo Ecuador. 2016. "Defensoria del Pueblo participó en el evento 'Retorno al Palenque de Libertad' en Esmeraldas." November 14, 2016.

Dollar, David. 2017. *China's Investment in Latin America*. Foreign Policy at Brookings, paper 4, January 2017.

Eisenman, Joshua, and Eric Heginbotham, eds. 2018. China Steps Out: Beijing's Major Power Engagement with the Developing World. New York: Routledge.

Ellis, R. Evan. 2011. *China–Latin America Military Engagement: Good Will, Good Business, and Strategic Position*. Carlisle, PA: Strategic Studies Institute, US Army War College.

Ellis, R. Evan. 2013. *Beyond Win-Win and the Menacing Dragon: How China Is Transforming Latin America*. Coral Gables, FL: University of Miami, Center for Hemispheric Policy.

Ellis, R. Evan. 2014. *China on the Ground in Latin America: Challenges for the Chinese and Impacts on the Region*. New York: Springer.

Eo, Kyunghee. 2019. "Queering the Dreams of a Third World Brotherhood: Black Women in Early 1890s South Korean Literature and Film." In *Revisiting Minjung: New Perspectives on the Cultural History of 1980s South Korea*, edited by Sunyoung Park. Ann Arbor: University of Michigan Press.

Escárcega, Oscar González. 2015. "¿Qué intereses tiene Latinoamérica en China?" *Forbes* México, January 21, 2015.

Fernández-Salvador, Consuelo. 2017. "Los shuar frente al proyecto estratégico de El Mirador: el manejo de identidades y prácticas políticas fragmentadas." In *La Amazonía Minada. Minería a Gran Escala y Conflictos en el Sur del Ecuador*, edited by Karolien van Teijlingen, Esben Leifsen, Consuelo Fernández-Salvador, and Luis Sánchez-Vázquez. Quito: Universidad San Francisco de Quito, Ediciones Abya Yala.

Fornez, Gastón, and Alvaro Mendez. 2018. *The China–Latin America Axis: Emerging Markets and Their Role in an Increasingly Globalised World*. New York: Springer.

Freyre, Gilberto. 2011 (reissue of 1944 lecture and subsequent publications). *China Tropical*. São Paulo: Global Editora.

Gallagher, Kevin. 2016. *The China Triangle: Latin America's China Boom and the Fate of the Washington Consensus*. Oxford: Oxford University Press.

Gómez-Barris, Macarena. 2017. *The Extractive Zone: Social Ecologies and Decolonial Perspectives*. Durham, NC: Duke University Press.

Gurovitz, Helio. 2019. "O flerte entre Bolsonaro e Xi." *Mundo*, November 14, 2019.

Hornby, Lucy, and Andrés Schipani. 2015. "Cortejo de China a América Latina." *El Espectador*, January 10, 2015.

Ikeuchi, Suma. 2019. *Jesus Loves Japan: Return Migration and Global Pentecostalism in a Brazilian Diaspora*. Stanford, CA: Stanford University Press.

Jilberto, Alex Fernández, and Barbara Hogenboom, eds. 2010. *Latin America Facing China: South-South Relations beyond the Washington Consensus*. New York: Berghahn Books.

Jornal Nacional. 2020. "Weintraub insiste em responsabilizar China pelo coronavírus em declaração à PF." June 5, 2020.

Koch, Gabriele. 2020. *Healing Labor: Japanese Sex Work in the Gendered Economy*. Stanford, CA: Stanford University Press.

Kraul, Chris. 2018. "Por los créditos negociados con China, Ecuador se enfrenta a un enorme déficit presuprestario." *Los Angeles Times* en Español, December 10, 2018.

La República. 2018. "Ecuador se suma a la iniciativa china de la Nueva Ruta de la Seda." December 12, 2018.

Lee, Christopher J., ed. 2010. *Making a World after Empire: The Bandung Moment and Its Political Afterlives*. Athens: Ohio University Press.

León Cabrera, José Maria. 2020. "Ecuador's Former President Convicted on Corruption Charges." *New York Times*, April 7, 2020.

Liu, Petrus, and Lisa Rofel. 2018. "Introduction." In *Wolf Warrior II: The Rise of China and Gender/Sexual Politics*, edited by Petrus Liu and Lisa Rofel. MCLC Resource Center, Ohio State University. https://u.osu.edu/mclc/online-series/liu-rofel/.

López, Julio. 2020. "Cortejo latinoamericano." *Connectas*. https://www.connectas.org/cortejo.

Madeiro, Carlos. 2020. "Governadores do NE consultam China e pedem material para tratar covid-19." *UOL*, March 20, 2020.

Méndez, Johan. 2012. "Eurocentrismo y modernidad: Una mirada desde la Filosofía Latinoamericana y el Pensamiento Descolonial." *Revista OMNIA* (3): 49–65.

Moraes, Ricodo. 2017. "In Rio, the Descendants of Slaves Try to Hang on to Their Historic Communities." *Agence France-Presse*, December 29, 2017.

Moreno Figueroa, Monica. 2010. "Distributed Intensities: Whiteness, Mestizaje and the Logics of Mexican Racism." *Ethnicities* 10 (3): 387–401.

Myers, Margaret, and Carol Wise, eds. 2017. *The Political Economy of China–Latin American Relations in the New Millennium: Brave New World.* New York: Routledge.

Narins, Tom. 2012. "China's Eye on Ecuador: What Chinese Trade with Ecuador Reveals about China's Economic Expansion into South America" *Global Studies Journal* 4 (2): 295–308.

Nash, Andrew. 2003. "Third Worldism." *African Sociological Review* 7 (1): 94–116.

Nathan, Andrew J. 2015. "China's Challenges." *Journal of Democracy* 26 (1): 156–70.

Nathan, Andrew J., and Andrew Scobell. 2012. *China's Search for Security.* New York: Columbia University Press.

Olson, Crista J. 2012. "'Raíces Americanas': Indigenist Art, América, and Arguments for Ecuadorian Nationalism." *Rhetoric Society Quarterly* 42 (3): 233–50.

Orozco, M. 2020. "El Coca-Codo puede esfumarse en el río." *El Comercio*, April 13, 2020.

Pallares, Martín. 2020. "Coca Codo Sinclair: ¿pagará la China por el inminente desastre?" *4Pelagatos*, April 20, 2020.

Paz Cardona, Antonio. 2020. "Ecuador: gobierno reconoce que la erosión de la cascada San Rafael podría afectar la hidroeléctrica Coca Codo Sinclair." *Mongabay Latam*, July 14, 2020.

Perez Lopez, Yvonne. 2017. "Mestizaje Ideology as Color-Blind Racism: Students' Discourses of Colorism and Racism in Mexico." PhD dissertation, Syracuse University.

Picq, Manuela Lavinas. 2018. *Vernacular Sovereignties: Indigenous Women Challenging World Politics.* Tucson: University of Arizona Press.

Quijano, Anibal. 2000. "Coloniality of Power, Eurocentrism, and Latin America." *Nepantla: Views from the South* 1 (3): 533–80.

Ray, Rebecca, Kevin Gallagher, Andres López, and Cynthia Sanborn, eds. 2017. *China and Sustainable Development in Latin America: The Social and Environmental Dimension.* London: Anthem.

Restrepo Echavarría, Ricardo. 2017. "Sovereign Democratic Transformation in Ecuador (2007–2016)," *Review of European Studies* 9, no. 4: 20–33.

Reyes, Victoria. 2019. *Global Borderlands.* Stanford, CA: Stanford University Press.

Riofrancos, Thea. 2020. *Resource Radicals: From Petro-Nationalism to Post-Extractivism in Ecuador.* Durham, NC: Duke University Press.

Rofel, Lisa. 2007. *Desiring China: Experiments in Neoliberalism, Sexuality, and Public Culture.* Durham, NC: Duke University Press.

Rofel, Lisa. 2017. "China's Tianxia Worldings: Socialist and Post-socialist Cosmopolitanisms." In *Chinese Visions of World Order: Tianxia, Culture and World Politics*, edited by Ban Wang. Durham, NC: Duke University Press.

Rofel, Lisa. 2019. "Between Tianxia and Postsocialism: Contemporary Chinese Cosmopolitanism." In *Routledge International Handbook of Cosmopolitanism Studies*, edited by Gerard Delanty. London: Routledge.

Rofel, Lisa, and Megan Sweeney. 2021. "Global Intimacies: China and/in the Global South." Special issue, *Feminist Studies* 47, no. 2.

Rosado, Erika. 2021. "Concebir la 'Patria Nueva' a través del arte: el discurso cultural de Benjamín Carrión y su representación en la pintura ecuatoriana (1944–1957)." *Memoirs of the First and Second Congress of Inter-American Students*.

Rosenthal, Amy, Debra Moskovits, John Reid, eds. 2019. China and the Amazon. Washington, DC: Inter-American Dialogue.

Senra, Ricardo. 2019. "Um ano após reclamar que China 'compraria o Brasil,' Bolsonaro quer vender estatais e commodities em visita a Xi Jinping." *BBC News*, December 23, 2019.

Shams, Tahseen. 2020. *Here, There and Elsewhere: The Making of Immigrant Identities in a Globalized World*. Stanford, CA, Stanford University Press.

Shi, Yinhong. 2010. "Fe común con los países en Desarrollo." Milton Reyes-Herrera and Diego Pérez Enriquez, interviewers. Revista China Hoy.

Soutar, Robert. 2020. "How China Is Courting New Latin American Partners." *Americas Quarterly*, January 13, 2020.

Spira, Tamara Lea. 2014. "Intimate Internationalisms: 1970s 'Third World' Queer Feminist Solidarity with Chile." *Sage Journals* 15, no. 2: 119–40.

Strauss, Julia, and Ariel C. Armony, eds. 2013. *From the Great Wall to the New World: China and Latin America in the 21st Century*. Cambridge: Cambridge University Press.

Tite Mallitasig, Bryan Enrique. 2017. "Cartas al Ecuador: interpretaciones históricas." Bachelor thesis, Pontifica Universidad Católica de Ecuador (Quito). http://repositorio.puce.edu.ec/handle/22000/13778?show=full.

Urban Dictionary. 2020. "stepping out," 4. Accessed September 6, 2020. https://www.urbandictionary.com/define.php?term=stepping%20out.

Van Teijlingen, Karolien, and Consuelo Fernández-Salvador. Forthcoming. ¿"La Minería para el 'Buen Vivir?' Large-Scale Mining, Citizenship and Development Practice in Ecuador's Correa." *Latin American Perspectives*.

Van Teijlingen, Karolien, Esben Leifsen, Consuelo Fernández-Salvador, and Luis Sánchez- Vázquez, eds. 2017. *La Amazonía Minada. Minería a Gran Escala y Conflictos en el Sur del Ecuador*. Quito: Universidad San Francisco de Quito, Ediciones Abya Yala.

Viteri, María Amelia, and Manuela Lavinas Picq, eds. 2016. *Queering Paradigms V: Queering Narratives of Modernity*. Bern, Switzerland: Peter Lang.

Wanming, Yang. 2019. "China e Brasil: aspirações e fraternidade compartilhadas." *Diário do Povo Online*, August 14, 2019.

Yuan, P. 2013. "China's Grand Periphery Strategy." *Contemporary International Relations* 23 (6): 59–62.

Zhang, Li. 2021. *The Origins of COVID-19: China and Global Capitalism*. Stanford, CA: Stanford University Press.

PART 1
GLOBAL ASIA, NEW IMAGINARIES,
AND MEDIA VISIBILITIES

China's State and Social Media Narratives about Brazil during the COVID-19 Pandemic

Li Zhang

INTRODUCTION

The recent wave of Chinese investment in Latin America (with Brazil and Ecuador receiving 86 percent of this, according to Maria Elena Rodríguez, this volume) brought Brazil and China into rapid approximation. While this development was supported by many, it also faced opposition and grew more fraught during the COVID-19 pandemic. Chinese and Brazilians are dealing with each other in unprecedented numbers, but as economic relations move ahead of cultural connections, old interpretations of the Other are refashioned, overflowing "official" and state-controlled avenues of approximation, communication, and cooperation.

Most of the chapters contained within the present volume speak of how China is viewed by Brazilians and Ecuadorians. In the chapter by Queiroz, Praça, and Bitencourt, Chinese workers are seen as mysterious and somewhat threatening interlopers by young female residents of the peripheries of Rio de Janeiro. Meanwhile, Brito remarks on how workers in the Manaus Free Trade Zone see Chinese managers and capitalists as "the worst Asian businessmen," overturning processes of worker comanagement of production put in place by the Japanese and Koreans. Finally, as Longobardi points out, few Brazilians know much about China—even among Brazil's academic elites. Popular understandings of China are often refracted through early twentieth-century Orientalist tropes.

The following chapter takes a different tack: it speaks to how China and Chinese are learning to see Brazil and Brazilians. In Chinese eyes, Brazil is a distant place, full of resources but risky and underdeveloped. The US-China trade war and Jair Bolsonaro's successful election provoked anti-Chinese sentiments and resulted in geopolitical shifts during a global pandemic. The emergence of COVID-19 in China and the explosion of the epidemic in the US and Brazil thus also became a crisis of international relations for China and a lightning rod for nationalist sentiment among Chinese people (Zhang 2021).

I draw upon a digital "living archive" (Carlin and Vaughan 2015) to analyze Chinese narratives about Brazil during the pandemic, revealing how China's new "wolf warrior" culture among diplomats and social media users (Liu 2018) has transformed this crisis into an engine of nationalist fervor and an instrument of diplomacy. I focus on Chinese narratives about Brazil and narratives created by the Chinese diaspora in the Brazil, examining how these narratives seek to produce a "common sense" about how the Chinese government and people ought to respond to the crisis (Han 2018).

I argue that although these Chinese narratives are nominally "about Brazil," they are in fact about China itself. Their purpose is to counter Sinophobic discourses and practices, strengthening nationalism and China's position in the world. The new wolf warrior culture underlying these narratives has elements that echo "white savior" colonial ideologies (Liu 2018), portraying China as a leader in efforts to "rescue" the world from the pandemic and lead the global economic recovery, thereby strengthening China's power. We must add more nuance to this view, however. Chinese narratives about Brazil during the pandemic do not emanate from a point of view of "Chinese supremacy," but rather from injured pride. They seek to reverse the negative identification of COVID-19 with China and the Chinese people, while grappling with the challenges China still faces in its quest for development and modernization.

Below, I examine three moments when Chinese state and social media narratives about Brazil shifted during the course of the pandemic. I aim to contribute to debates about China's new wolf warrior culture and the COVID-19 pandemic, demonstrating how research in the living archives of social media may be useful for critical scholarship.

THEORY, METHODS, AND POLITICS

I draw upon critical media studies' and global studies' critiques of national-ism, which focus upon transnational identities. Particularly useful here are studies of the technological and political forces through which national iden-tities come into being, as well as analyses of how top-down and bottom-up social forces combine to produce nationalist fervor and identity in Chinese cyberspace (Han 2018). I reject contrasts between government media and unofficial social media, showing instead how the Chinese state has adopted social media as a platform for communication. Microblogs like Sina Weibo and social media platforms (WeChat in particular) have assumed a central place in public discourse (DeLisle, Goldstein, and Yang 2016; Chen, Chao Su, and Chen 2019). More useful than a state/society dichotomy is an analysis of the convergences and divergences between "domestic" and "transnational" commentators in the Chinese diaspora. Although there is an extensive liter-ature on the Chinese diaspora's negotiations of transnational identities (Ong 1999), few examine the recent transformations that occurred due to the rise of social media. Reilly is an exception, showing how "China's new media en-vironment has stimulated lively policy debates and focused public attention on citizen safety overseas," mobilizing social media to "influence the prac-tice and priorities of China's foreign policy" (2016, 186 and 199).

I trace Chinese state and social media narratives domestically and among the diaspora in Brazil from January to June 2020, mapping how shifts in the pandemic dovetailed with shifts in China-Brazil relations and, in turn, shaped and were shaped by China's digital nationalism. My method is the creation and analysis of a digital living archive from the microblog and social media platforms Sina Weibo and WeChat. A digital living archive is an ongoing collection that transcends the fixed standards of description, control, and taxonomy of traditional archives, including material sampled from the open, porous, and informal universe of user-generated content in participatory platforms (Carlin and Vaughan 2015).

I begin with an examination of Sina Weibo entries tagging the topic "South America epidemic." These listed 760 million views and 11,000 dis-cussion threads by June 30, 2020, with the "Brazil epidemic" topic having over 200 million views, 9,173 discussion threads, and 22 related pages. I analyzed WeChat entries to confirm whether a particular topic was trending broadly in China's social media sphere, as WeChat provides mechanisms to gauge the most-read articles. I also analyzed Chinese diaspora social media platforms, focusing on the websites and official Sina Weibo accounts of the South American Overseas Chinese News Network, the Brazilian Overseas Chinese Network, the Brazilian Chinese Diaspora Network, and their associated user accounts on WeChat.

RESCUE FLIGHTS? RESCUE THE MOTHERLAND

In early 2020, Chinese public discourse focused on the Spring Festival (January 24–25), although there was already some debate on social media about government cover-ups and information control regarding the new disease. Once Wuhan was shut down, however, government statements, official media, and social media platforms all focused attention, advocacy, and news coverage on COVID-19 in China. Narratives about foreign countries centered on how the US and other countries began to evacuate their citizens from Wuhan.

On February 7, the Brazilian government evacuated forty Brazilian citizens and six foreigners. There was some online discussion following this news in China, but no mention that Brazilians had to pressure their own government through social media to be evacuated.[1] The silence was notable among the Chinese diaspora in Brazil, who certainly would have heard through mainstream Brazilian news about the Brazilian diaspora's campaign. Instead, Chinese narratives simply argued that Brazil was "following" the US, emphasizing that the Brazilian plane was "very small" and could "only carry 58 persons," so the evacuation was mostly to "show their alliance with the US," and "discredit" China. But these narratives were marginal in Chinese public debate. Only in March, when the epidemic was being controlled within China but growing in Europe and the US, did Chinese narratives began to pay more attention to COVID-19 abroad.

During this first stage, the Chinese response was mass mobilization to contain the epidemic and address the shortage of personal protective equipment (PPE). Most donations went to Wuhan, even though supplies dwindled throughout China. The need for donations was communicated mostly through WeChat, rather than through official government statements posted on Weibo. Evidently, the emergence of COVID-19 in China (overwhelming the healthcare system in Hubei) and the resulting fear created a crisis of trust and legitimacy for the Chinese government.

When transferred to friends and family members abroad, however, calls for help took on a nationalist dimension that blunted this crisis of trust and legitimacy. The Chinese diaspora was called upon to "rescue the motherland" in partnership with Chinese companies and government authorities, collecting money for Chinese charities and purchasing PPE abroad for shipment to China. Most donations were organized by formal associations of Chinese abroad and transferred through the All-China Federation of Returned Overseas Chinese, the United Front Work Department of the CCP Central Committee, the Red Cross, and local-level associations in the Chinese diaspora. In return, these institutions urged the Chinese diaspora to stay alert for COVID-19 outbreaks in the countries where they lived, particularly as they returned from the Spring Festival in China. A case that received much attention involved the Chinese Consulate in São Paulo, which secured an emergency appointment with the Customs Director of the São Paulo International Airport to clear the export of PPE donations from the diaspora in Brazil to China.

The pandemic stoked anti-Chinese sentiments throughout South America. Leaders of Chinese associations abroad began to take an increasingly public stance in combating anti-China rhetoric, rallying around the news report on February 25 that the first confirmed case of COVID-19 in Brazil was "not Chinese," but a "Brazilian who traveled to Italy for tourism." These narratives were defensive, circulating in parallel with narratives about teams of Chinese military who deployed to the newly built hospitals alongside the "heroic" healthcare workers in Wuhan.

Up until then, China-Brazil relations were warming (as Bolsonaro's anti-China campaign rhetoric softened once he came into office) and Chinese diplomats coordinated with the diaspora to "recover China's image." This changed, however, when Bolsonaro visited Trump on March 8. If up until then South America was hardly mentioned in the Chinese media, Bolsonaro's visit placed Brazil firmly in the Chinese public debate.

THE MINISTER OF INSULTS KNEELS IN APOLOGY TO CHINA

Bolsonaro's visit to Trump occurred when new cases of COVID-19 in China fell below one hundred per day and temporary hospitals in Wuhan were being deactivated. Chinese narratives were pivoting from "emergency" toward "victory over the epidemic." Social media reveals that the masses were regaining trust and confidence in the government, reinforcing nationalism at home and in the diaspora. By contrast, outbreaks began to spike in South Korea, Iran, and especially Italy, which became the epicenter of the pandemic and the source of Brazil's first confirmed case.

Once Bolsonaro returned from the US, a member of his delegation was diagnosed with COVID-19 and Bolsonaro himself was tested for the disease. Chinese media first reported that the Brazilian president had tested positive, then negative, triggering discussion on social media. Although social media accounts of the Chinese diaspora in Brazil largely abstained from speculation, consensus emerged among Chinese social media users that Bolsonaro—the "Brazilian Trump"—was infected with COVID-19 but was covering this up. Moreover, this was evidence that Trump and other top US government officials were also likely infected.

This conversation also noted that Bolsonaro and his third son, Eduardo, like Trump, were referring to SARS-CoV-2 as the "Chinese virus," infuriating Chinese officials and social media users alike. Eduardo Bolsonaro's tweets from March 18 and April 1 claiming that the pandemic was "China's fault" and calling it the "Chinese virus" caused an uproar in China. Although Chinese narratives had compared Bolsonaro to Trump before, lamenting Brazil's geopolitical realignment with the US against China, Bolsonaro's visit and his son's tweets triggered an explosion of nationalist anger. The day after Eduardo Bolsonaro's tweet, the Chinese Embassy in Brazil tweeted back (in true wolf warrior fashion), suggesting the president's son had become infected with a "mental virus" in the US that was now "poisoning" China-Brazil relations. They quoted the Chinese consul in Rio de Janeiro, Li Yang, who stated that Eduardo Bolsonaro was "brainwashed" and a US "vassal," as his "remarks are not unfamiliar, just clearly parroting [his] friends" in the US.

Even Chinese diaspora social media accounts in Brazil, which were mostly silent regarding Bolsonaro's visit, joined the debate. They republished Consul Li's remarks and quoted Brazilian op-eds to show that "people from all sectors in Brazil praised Consulate General Li's article, which clearly and unequivocally sent a strong message to Eduardo [Bolsonaro], not only expressing China's dissatisfaction, but also reaffirming China's willingness to cooperate with Brazil in the fight against the epidemic, showing the style of an outstanding diplomat." Despite differences in tone, Chinese diaspora and domestic social media narratives came together in the argument that right-wing, pro-US politicians in Brazil were harmful for good China-Brazil relations.

Then, in early April, Chinese diaspora and domestic narratives began to diverge in their focus. While China's mainstream social media turned fully to the victory over the epidemic at home, celebration in diaspora accounts was tempered with concern about the epidemic's surge in South America, as increasingly negative and terrifying narratives emerged about the onset of COVID on that continent. The intersection between these two narratives was the shared belief that China was the "good model" other countries should follow, rebuilding nationalist pride. However, this was cold comfort for the diaspora abroad.

For example, news circulated widely in the domestic Chinese media that, in the absence of an efficient government, gangs were stepping in to impose quarantines in the favelas of Rio de Janeiro. A public debate ensued. Several notable "netizens" with a high social-media profile in China reveled in the fact that Brazilian gangsters were more organized and responsible than the federal government. Other Internet commentators, however, cautioned against this celebration and called for "civility" (cf. Yang 2018). These calls were as much addressed to the Chinese people's domestic behavior as to their analysis of Brazil. The diaspora largely abstained from this public debate.

This period was the turning point for Chinese state and social media narratives. The defensive posture and informal networking of shipments of PPE back to China began to give way to wolf warrior counterattacks against Bolsonaro and his team, as well as celebrations of China and its allies. South American demand for PPE, ventilators, and other medical supplies became the central focus of these narratives. Chinese state and social media accounts emphasized that while Bolsonaro dismissed COVID-19 as a "little flu," state governors in Brazil were left scrambling to import ventilators and medical supplies on their own. When a major deal was finally announced with a Chinese exporter, mainstream news in China reported that the Brazilian minister of health had to turn to China after being rejected by four other countries who were unable to provide the huge amount of medical equipment Brazil needed. Social media users were quick to point out that Cuba,

Venezuela, Uruguay, and even Paraguay (which recognizes the Republic of China government in Taiwan, rather than the People's Republic in mainland China) had aligned themselves more closely with China than with the US and were able to secure medical supplies far more easily than the Brazilian federal or state governments.

This narrative peaked when the Brazilian minister of education (who blamed China for the pandemic and became identified in Chinese social media as the "minister of insults") said during a radio interview that "If they [China] sell us one thousand ventilators at cost, I'll get down on my knees, apologize, and say I was an idiot." The context of the interview, as explained in Chinese mainstream media outlets, was that the minister remained skeptical China would ever help Brazil by supplying ventilators without a profit and was speaking sarcastically. Nonetheless, the headline that circulated throughout Chinese social media was that "The Brazilian minister of insults would like to kneel and apologize to China!"

Meanwhile, the Chinese diaspora found itself caught in the crossfire. Overseas Chinese had to respond to increasing accusations that they were taking advantage of the epidemic to import PPE and medical supplies from China at exorbitant prices and playing part of a political strategy to leverage the "Chinese virus" to defeat other countries. This began to create a growing divergence between the discursive needs of Chinese nationalist narratives at home and abroad.

RIDICULING BOLSONARO'S "FANTASIES" AT HOME AND "HELPING" BRAZILIANS OVERSEAS

Between early May and the end of June, new cases of COVID-19 in Brazil jumped from about 5,000 to over 40,000 per day, reaching 1.5 million cases and 60,000 deaths in total. This surge made the WHO declare South America as the pandemic's newest hotspot, with Brazil jumping to second place in the global roster behind the US. At that moment, these two countries accounted for about 40 percent of all COVID-19 cases in the world. Meanwhile, China had effectively curtailed the resurgence of the disease.

This consolidated Chinese narratives that Brazil, like the US, had fallen into a catastrophic situation because of its lack of scientific, principled, and strong government action. Chinese social media users remarked that "Brazil does not have a strong economic foundation or the good fortunes of the US, but it gets sick like the US." Thus, Brazilian politicians like Bolsonaro who "follow the US" are even more "irresponsible" and "absurd" than Trump and his followers. This narrative framework shifted from defending China to ridiculing Bolsonaro, linking the Brazilian president's anti-Chinese rhetoric to a "chaotic" and "populist" attitude that rejects science in favor of a "magical" approach to the pandemic. This rhetoric also simultaneously celebrated China, its "victory" over the epidemic at home, and its capacity to "lead by example" on the global stage.

Headlines about Bolsonaro riding on a Jet Ski while the pandemic ravaged Brazil circulated widely in Chinese social media, drawing ridicule and disdain from nationalist social media users. News in June that the Brazilian government was suppressing information about the number of COVID-19 cases, and reports that Bolsonaro had admitted to being infected, reignited earlier claims about a cover-up. A social media user commented that "they falsely blame China for covering up the outbreak, but they are the ones who are actually censoring scientific facts." This comment received much positive feedback. Major Chinese social media personalities and wolf warrior diplomats alike circulated reports that a Brazilian judge ordered Bolsonaro to wear a mask, something he had resisted for months. Chinese social media users reveled in these stories, as Brazil's tragedy became explicitly contrasted with the triumph of Chinese nationalism.

Public social media accounts of the Chinese diaspora in Brazil reveal a slightly different narrative, however. The shift of the COVID-19 hotspot from China to Brazil was interpreted as a shift from their "motherland to their second homeland." Those who had previously offered to "rescue the motherland" back in January and February were now needing aid in return. Moreover, the diaspora began to feel the need to organize themselves for "self-protection"—economically, politically, socially, and culturally. After all, the right wing in Brazil did not stop blaming China just because some wolf warrior diplomats and Chinese social media personalities had responded with sharp words. In fact, the nationalist pushback only placed the diaspora in a more precarious position. While China-based nationalists stoked nationalism by ridiculing Bolsonaro and reveling in the growing case and death counts in Brazil, the Chinese diaspora began to respond more strategically and delicately to the catastrophe. Some diaspora members became popular vloggers, sharing information with compatriots at home about the front lines of the COVID-19 disaster abroad. Despite their own needs, diaspora members also began to organize publicized donations of medical supplies and food to local governments and communities.

Some of the most celebrated examples came, once again, from the leaders of Chinese associations, joined by the directors of Chinese companies operating abroad. Political elites, particularly the ambassador and consuls, facilitated Chinese exports of medical equipment to Brazil and helped to organize meetings between healthcare experts from China and Brazil. These elites also appeared on Brazilian mainstream media to respond to anti-Chinese statements from Brazilian politicians, relating China's successful experience in containing COVID-19 domestically. In the diaspora's social media, there were far fewer negative reports about Brazil. It is rare to find discussions gloating about the pandemic abroad, ridiculing Brazilian officials, or speaking about the situation with the sarcastic tone that predominates in state and social media narratives emanating from China itself. Business elites, leaders of Chinese associations abroad, and high-level diplomats adopted a more constructive tone than the hypernationalist social media users in China (Schneider 2018). These efforts culminated in the highly publicized fact that Sinovac, one of China's leading pharmaceutical companies, had partnered with the Butantan Institute in Brazil for the final stage of the clinical trials of its COVID-19 vaccine and began distributing it in Brazil in early 2021. Since there are no longer enough COVID-19 cases in China for such large-scale clinical trials, Chinese companies needed international partners. Chinese narratives now emphasize that even though US and European companies refuse to collaborate, China has been able to find partners in countries like Brazil, improving its standing in the eyes of many Brazilians through vaccine diplomacy.

CONCLUSION

By drawing upon the living archive of China's state and social media narratives about Brazil during the COVID-19 pandemic, I have revealed how China's new wolf warrior culture among diplomats and social media users domestically transformed this crisis into an engine of nationalist fervor, while employing it as an instrument of diplomacy abroad. I also showed how the Chinese diaspora in Brazil juggles a transnational identity that places them in the crossfire of the cultural struggles triggered by the pandemic. This allows us to examine China's "mask and vaccine diplomacy" in a more nuanced way. Such efforts are not simply top-down directives from China's central government, but also a product of bottom-up initiatives from the Chinese diaspora and diplomatic corps (Reilly 2016; Chen et al. 2019), who leverage China's digital nationalism for multiple purposes of their own. These objectives sometimes—but not always—align with narratives emanating from China itself. And, of course, there is also a minority of critical and open-minded voices that do not reproduce shallow nationalist narratives about China and its relations with other countries.

The findings underline how members of the Chinese diaspora are political subjects in their own right (Reilly 2016). China's digital nationalism cannot be reduced to mere propaganda, or to tension between social media users and the imposition of "civility" by an authoritarian state (Creemers 2016). Chinese narratives about Brazil ultimately reveal how official and unofficial, formal and informal, domestic and diasporic voices reinforce Chinese nationalism. This occurs partly through the new wolf warrior culture that not only counters anti-China rhetoric abroad but also portrays China as a leader in efforts to "rescue" the world from the pandemic, echoing "white savior" and colonial discourses entrenched in Euro-American imperialism and white supremacy (Liu 2018). These discourses do not arise from a standpoint of presumed Chinese supremacy; rather, they emanate from a position of damaged self-esteem during a moment when government legitimacy was challenged by the outbreak of a pandemic in China. Instead of seeking to impose Chinese hegemony abroad, this narrative emerges with the far humbler goals of reversing the negative identification of China with COVID-19 and self-protection among diasporic communities, in the context of an often fumbling quest for development and modernization.

NOTES

1. As evidenced by discussions organized through several WeChat groups for Brazilians living in China, which Gustavo Oliveira brought to my attention.

REFERENCES

Carlin, David, and Laurene Vaughan. 2015. *Performing Digital: Multiple Perspectives on a Living Archive.* London: Routledge.

Chen, Zhuo, Chris Chao Su, and Anfan Chen. 2019. "Top-Down or Bottom-Up? A Network Agenda-Setting Study of Chinese Nationalism on Social Media." *Journal of Broadcasting & Electronic Media* 63, no. 3: 512–33.

Creemers, Rogier. 2016. "Cyber China: Upgrading Propaganda, Public Opinion Work and Social Management for the Twenty-First Century." *Journal of Contemporary China* 26, no. 103: 85–100.

DeLisle, Jacques, Avery Goldstein, and Guobin Yang. 2016. *The Internet, Social Media, and a Changing China.* Philadelphia: University of Pennsylvania Press.

Han, Rongbin. 2018. *Contesting Cyberspace in China: Online Expression and Authoritarian Resilience.* New York: Columbia University Press.

Liu, Petrus. 2018. *Wolf Warrior II: The Rise of China and Gender/Sexual Politics.* Modern Chinese Literature and Culture Resource Center, University of Ohio. https://u.osu.edu/mclc/online-series/liu-rofel/.

Ong, Aihwa. 1999. *Flexible Citizenship: The Cultural Logics of Transnationality.* Durham, NC: Duke University Press.

Reilly, James. 2016. "Going Out and Texting Home: New Media and China's Citizens Abroad" In *The Internet, Social Media, and a Changing China,* edited by Jacques DeLisle, Avery Goldstein, and Guobin Yang, 180–99. Philadelphia: University of Pennsylvania Press.

Schneider, Florian. 2018. *China's Digital Nationalism.* Oxford: Oxford University Press.

Yang, Guobin. 2018. "Demobilizing the Emotions of Online Activism in China: A Civilizing Process." *International Journal of Communication* 12: 1945–65.

Zhang, Li. 2021. *The Origins of COVID-19: China and Global Capitalism.* Stanford, CA: Stanford University Press.

Cracks in the Coca Codo Sinclair Hydroelectric Project: Infrastructures and Disasters from a Masculine Vision of Development

Pedro Gutiérrez Guevara, Sofía Carpio, and Mayra Flores

INTRODUCTION

The San Rafael cascade on the border between the provinces of Napo and Sucumbíos had been one Ecuador's tallest waterfalls. It disappeared on February 2, 2020, when erosion in the Coca river caused the riverbed upstream to collapse into a large sinkhole.[1] Just five days later, another sinkhole formed about one mile upstream, fracturing three pipelines belonging to the Trans-Ecuadorian Pipeline System (TEPS) and the Heavy Crude Pipeline (HCP), spilling some 15,000 barrels of crude petroleum. This socio-environmental disaster has affected approximately 120,000 members of 105 different Kichwa and Shuar communities located near the Coca and Napo rivers.

As Vásconez discusses in this volume, drawing upon Pallares (2020) the two implosions are the result of a phenomenon that caused the river to become more erosive, provoking loss of sediment. According to Pallares:

> This hydrostatic imbalance hypothesis is based on a phenomenon called "hungry waters," which is caused by the loss of sediments. . . . With reduced sediments, the river's downstream erosive capacity increases, which in turn accelerates the erosive hollowing of the riverbed. In poorly consolidated volcanic soils, such as those in the Coca River basin, erosive forces act like a blade, cutting and dislodging everything they encounter.

This process is thought to have been caused by the Coca Codo Sinclair (CCS) dam, located approximately eleven miles upstream of the TEPS and HCP pipeline ruptures. According to an investigation conducted by Ecuador's National Polytechnic School, the dam increased the Coca river's erosion rate by 42 percent and has also caused regressive erosion along its margins—an effect known as "white waters" (Escuela Politécnica Nacional 2020). Meanwhile, Ecuador's comptroller general confirmed the existence of 7,648 fissures in the CCS's pressure distribution system, a sensitive part of the plant exposed to high levels of water pressure (Controlaría General del Estado 2019).

Like the chapters in this volume by Fernández-Salvador and Viteri, and van Teijlingen and Bastidas, the present chapter situates this disaster within a wider social and theoretical framework. It relies on a critical and interdisciplinary interpretation of documents related to the construction of the CCS hydroelectric dam (a project that required substantial government investments), the testimony of experts who raised questions about the CCS project prior to its construction, communications from environmental and human rights organizations in the wake of the TEPS and HCP pipeline ruptures, and related pieces of investigative journalism. Ultimately, this chapter seeks to complicate the conception of hydroelectric infrastructure within the theoretical framework of masculinity, development, and the ethnography of science and technology to better understand the structural conditions that give rise to disasters.

NATIONAL DEVELOPMENT AND LARGE-SCALE INFRASTRUCTURE PROJECTS

The role of the rationalities and political meanings that converge in the conceptualization and materialization of infrastructures has been extensively studied elsewhere (Barker and Scheele 2016, 91). The legitimation of hydroelectric and other large-scale infrastructure projects, occurring within a framework of national development, has also been documented in Latin American (Catullo 1991) and global literature (Larkin 2013).

The first development programs designed for the Global South by multilateral organizations of the Global North were drafted under the presumption that substantial sums of capital would be invested in large-scale infrastructure projects. The idea was that this would close the development gap between these two worlds (Easterly 2002). This nexus is reflected in how development is conceived, measured, and presented (Acosta and Gudynas. 2011). Moreover, the emphasis on GDP growth and other domestic macroeconomic indexes has overshadowed and relegated logics of redistribution and concern for how development projects impact people on a local level.

As Larkin comments, the provision of infrastructures is intimately related to a rationality that idealizes modernity (2013). In Latin America, this appears in the colonial[2] dimensions of the region's visions of development. For example, in their analysis of other Amazon basin projects of the Citizens' Revolution,[3] Wilson and Bayón describe these infrastructure achievements as decontextualized "utopian fantasies," conceived through imported notions of modernity (2017, 31).

The construction of large-scale infrastructure projects does not bring about prosperity for local populations, who often find themselves absorbing social and environmental costs, as Camoça and Hendler, and Felipe and Costa have described in their chapters on the Brazilian Amazon. According to these authors, while the exportation of soy is touted as an answer to Brazil's economic woes, the construction of the transportation corridors that make it possible have disrupted lives and polluted the environments of the communities they displace. The notion of *development*, along with its programs and projects, is laden with ideological presuppositions. Not only does it not fulfill the promise of closing the gap between the developed and the undeveloped, but it creates new abysses between fantasies of promised well-being and the reality of dealing with the negative effects caused by an imposed infrastructure. As Marcos Pedlowski's interlocutors report regarding the population removals occasioned by the Porto do Açu Project in Brazil, described by that author in this volume, "outsiders arrived to take without asking or paying for that which already had owners" (431).

In his critique of the concept of development, Quijano starts with the question "What is it that is being developed?" He concludes that the answer is capitalism and the institutions that keep it functioning (2001). Critical theories of development, such as the world systems theory, maldevelopment, and postdevelopment (to mention the most important ones) highlight the exploitative character of this concept (Tortosa 2011; Wallerstein 1997).

Through decades of development programs that have failed in their objective of bringing prosperity to the Global South, the concept of development has come to take on different meanings, as other dimensions of human well-being beyond the purely chrematistic are identified and incorporated (Acosta and Gudynas 2011)

The principal discourse of the Rafael Correa administration initially centered on the creation of alternatives to development: specifically, the promotion of *Buen Vivir* or *Sumak Kawsay*.[4] Its theoretical formulation, based on the Ecuadorian Andean worldview, sought to move away from development-related prejudices. It presumed a different conception of time (nonlinear), a harmonious relationship with nature and the construction of a plurinational society (Acosta and Gudynas 2011). The promise of this political project, incorporated into the 2008 Constitution, was internationally recognized by academics (Martínez Novo 2018) and enthusiastically received by the people of Ecuador, as evidenced by the success of Correa's platform in national elections (de la Torre 2013).

Within a few years, however, the administration began taking on a more neodevelopmentalist, extractivist, and—ultimately—authoritarian character (Gudynas 2010; Martínez Novo 2018). Correa's development program attempted to fuse progressive social policies with transformations of Ecuador's productive sectors. Included in the latter was a plan to improve Ecuador's energy matrix. The CCS hydroelectric project was an important component of this plan.

COCA CODO SINCLAIR AND CHANGES IN THE ENERGY MATRIX

The CCS project had been the subject of a 1992 prefeasibility study for an 859-megawatt plant. The proposed site, however, had a high seismic risk, as it was located near the epicenter of a 1987 earthquake that had destroyed a major segment of the TEPS pipeline.[5] Moreover, erosion from the nearby Antisana, Cayambe, and Reventador[6] volcanoes carries a large amount of sediment into the area.

In 2007, after winning Ecuador's presidential election, Correa promised his administration would construct a 1,500-megawatt hydroelectric project at the site. Included in his Master Electrification Plan for 2007–2016 (Agencia de Regulación y Control de Electricidad 2016), this would be the largest such project in Ecuador. The inauguration of the completed CCS project, which was paid for through the largest public infrastructure investment

Ecuador has made to date (US$2.3 billion) was attended by China's president Xi Jinping (CELEC 2015).

Among the objectives of the CCS project was guaranteeing a national energy supply that would be consistent with a post-oil economy and sufficient to support the Correa administration's national development strategy (Castro 2011, 67). One of the principal motives of the project was to increase the electrical supply for basic industries,[7] consistent with an extractivist development model (Morán 2019). Between 2006 and 2017 Ecuador's energy supply was increased by 111 percent (ARCONEL 2018).

This logic excluded any national conversation about energy alternatives from Ecuador's energy agenda (for example, a possible decentralized system of micro-hydroelectric projects that could provide energy to specific localities) (Moreno Ronquillo 2019, 72). Instead, the government negligently and ineffectively implemented a large-scale energy development model.

CHINESE INVESTMENT IN ECUADOR AND THE COCA CODO PROJECT

In 1988, Deng Xiaoping announced that "the twenty-first will be the era of Latin America" (Diálogo Chino 2016). This prophecy was fulfilled two decades later in the context of the global economic crisis of 2008 and the fact that several South American governments were allied under the "Socialism for the 21st Century" movement. As Waisbich, Reyes Herrera, and Narváez all detail in their chapters in this volume, the dynamic relationships between China and the region saw both sides of the partnership turn to each other as a way of bypassing multilateral institutions controlled by the US and Europe.

Chinese loans operate under the logic of the "iron triangle," a term coined by the China Development Bank. This means that "the Chinese bank loans money to a foreign government under the condition that the government will contract Chinese companies and hire a percentage of Chinese workers" (Garzón 2014, 260). Chinese capital has landed in Latin America without social or environmental considerations. With the support of the Ecuadorian government, Chinese companies consolidated themselves in the petroleum, mining, and hydroelectric sectors and have been awarded more than 70 percent of Ecuador's public contracts. The China Petrochemical

Corporation has come to own 45 percent of the HCP pipeline's operations (Garzón 2014, 261).

The Correa administration used Ecuador's strategic sectors and non-renewable resources as bait to hook China's intervention, as betrayed by a sexist metaphor offered up by Correa in a 2014 interview:

> Banks, the holders of financial power, are like a slightly vain girl, in the sense that if someone shows too much interest, they start playing "hard to get." But if [the boy] pretends like he's not interested, maybe the girl calls the boy. That's what financial markets are like. (Correa 2014)

This discourse is one of several examples of the heteronormative and homophobic views of the Correa administration (Viteri 2020, 43), which were also evident in its moral agenda and in public speeches (Larraz 2017; Granda Vega 2016).

MASCULINE LOGIC IN CAPITALIST AND PATRIARCHAL DEVELOPMENT

Ecuadorian politics has maintained an archetypal masculinity in Correa and former leaders (Moore and Gillette 1993) through characteristics like control, wisdom, and the use of different modes of violence. This performativity is related to the discursive power to impact the world materially through mere pronouncements. It imposes a heterocentric,[8] hegemonic power as the creator of sociocultural realities removed from constituents' desires and needs (Duque 2010).

Correa's personality and exercise of power were marked by images of hegemonic masculinity (Connell 1987). His administration adopted a strategy of power concentration that operated in three arenas: the consolidation of forces, institutional design, and the propaganda state (Meléndez and Moncagatta 2017). It was also hyperpresidentialist in the way it married his personal charisma to strong technocratic support (de la Torre 2013), maintaining a pattern of investment and debt. In the words of former energy minister Fernando Santos, Ecuadorians "are addicted to loans" (Casey and Krauss 2018).

Masculinity in Latin America oscillates between two ideal types of manhood (Andrade 2001; Gutmann 1998; Herrera 2002; Viveros 2007; Figueroa

2010): underdevelopment (rural customs) and development (urban mentality) (Hernández 2008). This polarity manifests through dominators (decision makers, government officials, Chinese companies) ruling over the lives of the dominated (women, children, communities, villages, nationalities), resulting in a binary hierarchical structure (Fuss 1991, 10) and, at the same time, forms of resistance (Picq 2018).

The directorship of Compañía Hidroeléctrica Coca Codo Sinclair S.A. was composed entirely of upper middle-class, heteronormative men socialized as white in Ecuadorian society. The hegemonic definition of virile masculinity is a man in/with/of power (Kimmel 1997) and is associated with characteristics of strength, success, confidence, and ostentation of the kind of effective power that was used by the Ecuadorian government and the Chinese entity Sinohydro Corporation in the CCS megaproject.

Discourses, decision making, the intervention of those who signed construction and financing contracts, the inauguration, and the labor involved in the CCS project were all sustained by virile masculine bodies and virile masculine gambles. This is consistent with the kind of heteropatriarchal structure that impacts on otherness, seating all relations and interpellations under an androcentric, developmentalist, and capitalist worldview. For this reason, we understand *political dominators* as those who impose both horizon and meaning under such banners as *progress*, *development*, or *modernization* while ignoring the opinions of subordinates who experience this domination as exploitation, oppression, dispossession, and humiliation (Sierra 2014, 32).

This is exemplified by the symbolic character of the power constituted in the male figures of the president and vice president on an altar of contemplation and redemption: a plaque at the entrance of the CCS hydroelectric plant that reads, "Rafael Correa Delgado,[9] Jorge Glas Espinel,[10] for being the true forgers and visionaries of this monumental work."

While the *Correista* project purported to adhere to the humanist principle of Socialism for the 21st Century, it ignored the internal dynamics of the subjects and intersections in which inequalities are maintained (Vera 2013, 173). The CCS project became an infrastructure of disaster for the people, communities, and environment impacted by the sinkholes, oil spills, and COVID-19 pandemic that loom over the lives of those who should have been the beneficiaries of *Sumak Kawsay* (Acosta 2011, 88).

IMPACT ON COMMUNITIES IN AFFECTED AREAS

In the wake of the April 7, 2020, oil spills, affected persons and human rights defenders filed a lawsuit[11] on April 29, seeking a precautionary injunction based on violations of the rights to food, health, life in a healthy environment, information, and Indigenous territories, as well as environmental rights. The defendants included the Ministry of Energy and Nonrenewable Natural Resources, the Ministry of the Environment, the Ministry of Public Health, Empresa Pública Petroecuador,[12] and privately owned OCP Ecuador S.A.[13]

Specifically, the lawsuit alleges that the oil spill was foreseeable by the state and OCP Ecuador, in light of alerts offered by experts who had warned of the zone's instability due to its proximity to the Reventador volcano, frequent seismic activity, heavy rainfall in the month prior to the accident, the San Rafael waterfall implosion, and soil erosion caused by the CCS hydroelectric project that was threatening the TEPS and HCP pipelines. In other words, the allegations suggest a series of omissions and negligence that point in the most literal sense to the construction of a socioecological disaster.

While the state did announce that it was taking measures to contain and remediate the situation, affected communities (in a public complaint dated June 23, 2020) alleged that "the existence of traces of petroleum remnants and oils in the river 75 days after the oil spill . . . confirms the lethal risk to the communities from the consumption of contaminated water and fish" (Alianza por los Derechos Humanos 2020a).

The hearing on the injunction has been suspended and postponed on multiple occasions, contrary to Ecuador's principle of procedural celerity, which should apply with special force as the country now faces simultaneous problems of floods, the dengue virus, and the COVID-19 health emergency.

Bernal (2020, 17) warns that rising erosion will continue to damage infrastructure near the Coca river, including the CCS hydroelectric project and segments of highways that connect Ecuador's petroleum region to the capital. The danger of a collapse of the CCS dam and the accelerated erosion such a calamity would cause demonstrate the gravity of embarking on large-scale engineering projects without environmental and social impact studies that fully consider the geography of affected rivers, as Vásconez, Molina and Munduruku, and others have illustrated in this volume (see also Sacher 2020).

Among the consequences are the loss of biodiversity, deterioration of the landscape, and health consequences for communities that have intimate connections to the river. Devastation of aquatic life, skin diseases, digestive problems, and food scarcity are already presenting themselves. In the words of Andrés Tapia, leader of the Confederation of Indigenous Nationalities of the Ecuadorian Amazon Region (CONFENIAE):

> The spilling of crude oil spells death for biodiversity and life itself. The Ecuadorian state must remedy this problem, suspend all extractiv-ist activities and choose a new course of economic development that is post-extractivist. The exploitation of petroleum and other minerals isn't really profitable, since it only contaminates the environment . . . [and] this pandemic has shown the world that people don't survive by eating petroleum, but rather by working the land, which is the production of indigenous and rural communities. (Amazon Frontlines 2020)

Far from fulfilling the vision of well-being that it promised, CCS's energy infrastructure has become a disaster for nearby communities. As affirmed by Leopoldo Gómez, who worked in the construction of water treatment facilities during the Correa administration, "Now we realize there are things that we never really needed . . . like the dam" (Casey and Krauss 2018).

CONCLUSIONS

The CCS hydroelectric project threatens natural resources (rivers, forests, petroleum), infrastructures (TEPS and HCP pipelines, highways, the CCS project itself), and the continued viability of river communities, which demonstrates an economic impact. But this is incomparable to the impact on the lives of those who live near the river.

Our analysis, based on a critical examination of development and mas-culinity, has shed light on the rationalities that materialize in the form of infrastructure projects that aggravate the inequities suffered by local populations. Like van Teijlingen and Hidalgo Bastidas, Vásconez, Molina and Munduruku, and Fernández-Salvador and Viteri in this volume, our analysis finds that the CCS dam project reveals problematic structural and epistemological issues, whose consequences will be faced by vulnerable populations for decades to come.

The CCS project, a product of developmentalist logics that are alien to the territorial and geographic realities of Amazonian people, has laid the foundation for its own failure, despite the enormous investment that was made in it and the fact that it is still being paid for with presold oil to China. This is an infrastructure project conceived from a developmentalist model, under the power and virile decisions of political actors who not only failed to measure its risks, but also failed to consider the medium- and long-term socioenvironmental costs of their gambling.

NOTES

1. The vacuum of this riverbed implosion caused the waters to plunge through a new gorge formed immediately upstream from the original falls.

2. According to Quijano (2001), *coloniality* refers to the Ibero-American societies and white minorities in control of the state, whose perspective tended to focus more on the interests of the European bourgeois than on their own interests, while ignoring the interests of their own Indigenous and Black populations.

3. The administration of former president Rafael Correa was conceived as the first stage of what Correa dubbed the *Revolución Ciudadana* (Citizens' Revolution), and Ecuadorians often refer to his administration with this phrase.

4. *Sumak kawsay*, a Kichwa phrase that can be translated as "life in fullness," was adopted as a theme by Indigenous movements in Bolivia and Ecuador in the 1990s and eventually entered Ecuador's mainstream political discourse as novel framework for cultural and social progress (Vera Rojas 2013).

5. The epicenter was located next to the Reventador volcano in an area of steep slopes. The most important infrastructure damage was the destruction and local severing of approximately forty-three miles of pipeline (belonging to TEPS, since this was the only pipeline in the country at the time). While the actual repairs to the pipeline were not especially costly, the macroeconomic impact was substantial—as petroleum exports were halted for more than five months (Albornoz 2013).

6. Reventador is Ecuador's most active volcano.

7. Basic industries include metallurgy, shipyards, flat steel, paper pulp, aluminum, copper, and iron and petrochemical operations and would require 1,500 megawatts and US$9.213 billion in investments by 2025 (Ministerio Coordinador de Producción, Empleo y Competitividad y Ministerio de Industrias y Productividad 2015).

8. Heterocentric thought, which is oppressive in nature, is consequently unable to conceive of a culture or society in which heterosexuality does not rule over all human relations as well as the very production of concepts—and thereby all processes that emanate from human consciousness—in its tendency to formulate and universalize generalized laws that are intended to apply to all societies, all periods, and all individuals.

9. Correa is currently living in political asylum in Belgium, in the wake of an eight-year prison sentence issued by an Ecuadorian court for the crime of bribery in the *Sobornos 2012–2016* case.

10. Jorge Glas is currently serving a six-year sentence, having been convicted as an accessory to bribes received by the Brazilian construction conglomerate Odebrecht, as well as an eight-year sentence for a separate bribery conviction in the *Sobornos 2012–2016* case.

11. Case No. 22281-2020-00201.

12. Translator's Note: EP Petroecuador is an Ecuadorian state-owned petroleum company.

13. Translator's Note: OCP Ecuador S.A. is the company that operates the HCP pipeline.

REFERENCES

Acosta, Alberto, and Eduardo Gudynas. 2011. "El buen vivir o la disolución de la idea del progreso." In *La Medición Del Progreso y Del Bienestar. Propuestas Desde América Latina*, edited by Mariano Rojas. México D.F.: Foro Consultivo Ciéntifico y Tecnológico AC.

Acosta, Alberto. 2012. *Buen Vivir. Sumak Kawsay*. Quito: Ediciones Abya-Yala.

Agencia de Regulación y Control de Electricidad. 2016. "Plan Maestro de Electrificación 2007–2016." https://www.regulacionelectrica.gob.ec/plan-maestro-de-electrificacion-2007-2016/.

Albornoz, Vicente. 2013. "El terremoto de 1987." *El Comercio*, October 27, 2013. https://www.elcomercio.com/opinion/terremoto-1987.html.

Alianza por los Derechos Humanos. 2020a. "Denuncia Pública 4. Comunidades indígenas alertan sobre la presencia de crudo y otros derivados en el río Coca; su situación de riesgo y vulnerabilidad se agudiza." June 23. https://ddhhecuador .org/2020/06/23/documento/denuncia-publica-4-comunidades-indigenas-alertan-sobre-la-presencia-de-crudo-y-.

Alianza por los Derechos Humanos. 2020b. "Press Release "Organizaciones indígenas, religiosas y de derechos humanos presentan acción de protección y medidas cautelares contra el Estado y empresas petroleras por derrame de petróleo."

Alianza por los Derechos Humanos. 2020c. "Boletín De Prensa." No. 4. https://ddhhecuador.org/sites/default/files/documentos/2020-06/Denuncia Pública _04.pdf.

Andrade, Xavier. 2001. "Introducción. Masculinidades en El Ecuador: Contexto y particularidades." In *Masculinidades en Ecuador*, edited by Xavier Andrade, Gioconda Herrera, and (Comps.), 13–26. Quito: FLACSO; UNFPA.

Amazon Frontlines. 2020. "Organizaciones indígenas, religiosas y de derechos humanos presentan acción de protección y medidas cautelares contra el Estado y empresas petroleras por derrame de petróleo" https://www.amazonfrontlines .org/es/chronicles/derrame-ecuador-demanda-2/.

Appel HC. 2012. "Walls and White Elephants: Oil Extraction, Responsibility, and Infrastructural Violence in Equatorial Guinea." *Ethnography* 13:439–65.

ARCONEL. 2018. "Estadística Anual y Multianual Del Sector Eléctrico Ecuatoriano." Quito. https://www.regulacionelectrica.gob.ec/boletines-estadisticos/.

Barker J. 2005. "Engineers and Political Dreams: Indonesia in the Satellite Age." *Current Anthropology* 46 (5): 703–27.

Barker, Meg-Jhon, and Julia Scheele. 2016. "Queer una historia gráfica" *Mesulina* (Spain).

Bernal, Isabel. 2020. "Revista EcoAméricas realiza un artículo sobre las situaciones que ocasionaron el derrame de petróleo en la Amazonía ecuatoriana." *EcoAméricas*, May, 14–17. https://www.ecoamericas.com/issues/article/2020/5/4A758326-B1B1-4B78-AA70-E420A7513166.

Carse Ashley. 2012. "Nature as Infrastructure: Making and Managing the Panama Canal Watershed." *Social Studies of Science* 42 (4): 539–63.

Casey, Nicholas, and Clifford Krauss. 2018. "El gobierno ecuatoriano apostó por China para una represa que ahora se resquebraja." *New York Times*, December 24. https://www.nytimes.com/es/2018/12/24/espanol/ecuador-china-prestamos-represa.html.

Castro, Miguel. 2011. *Hacia una matriz energética diversificada en Ecuador*. Edited by Joerg Elbers. Quito: Ecuadorian Environmental Law Center.

Catullo, María Rosa. 1991. "Antropología y proyectos de Gran Escala: Los estudios sobre represas hidroeléctricas en Brasil." *Anuario Antropológico* 15 (1): 205–29. https://dialnet.unirioja.es/servlet/articulo?codigo=7401530.

CELEC. 2015. (Corporación Eléctrica del Ecuador), "Resumen de estudios—Central Hidroeléctrica Coca Codo Sinclair." September 7. https://www.celec.gob.ec/cocacodosinclair/index.php/2015-09-07-17-45-09/footers/coca-codo-sinclair2/resumen-de-estudios.

Connell, R. W. 1987. *Gender and Power*. Stanford, CA: Stanford University Press.

Controlaría General del Estado. 2019. "Press Release Controlaría confirma 7,648 fisuras en Coca Codo Sinclair." March 28, 2019. https://www.contraloria.gob.ec/CentralMedios/PrensaDia/21525.

Correa, Rafael. 2014. "Rafael Correa: 'Para muchos, quedar mal frente a la banca internacional es terrible'—salvados." *LaSexta* (channel on YouTube). https://www.youtube.com/watch?v=pS6mWv1IKlk.

Correa, Rafael. 2016. "El Enlace Ciudadano, la mejor opción para la rendición de cuentas." June 4. https://www.presidencia.gob.ec/el-enlace-ciudadano-la-mejor-opcion-para-la-rendicion-de-cuentas/.

De la Torre, Carlos. 2013. "Latin America's Authoritarian Drift: Technocratic Populism in Ecuador." *Journal of Democracy* 24 (3): 33–46.

De la Torre, Carlos. 2016. "Rafael Correa y la muerte lenta de la democracia en Ecuador." In *Elecciones y legitimidad democrática en América Latina*, edited by Fernando Mayorga, 139–64. La Paz: Consejo Latinoamericano de Ciencias Sociales.

Diálogo Chino. 2016. "Inversiones responsables requieren participación de la sociedad civil." April 25, 2016. https://dialogochino.net/es/actividades-extractivas-es/5984-inversiones-responsables-requieren-participacion-de-la-sociedad-civil/.

Duque, Carlos. 2010. "Judith Butler y la teoría de la performatividad de género." *Revista de Educación y Pensamiento* 17: 85–95.

Easterly, William. 2002. *The Elusive Quest for Growth: Economists' Adventures and Misadventures in the Tropics*. Cambridge, MA: MIT Press.

Escuela Politécnica Nacional. 2020. "Investigación muestra erosión en Cauce del Río Coca en el Sector de San Rafael." https://www.epn.edu.ec/investigacion-muestra-erosion-en-cauce-del-rio-coca-en-el-sector-de-san-rafael/.

Figueroa, Juan. 2010. "El sentido del ser hombre como categoría política." In *Relaciones de Género. Tomo VIII de Los Grandes Problemas de México*, edited by Ana María Tepichín, Karine Tinat, and Luzelena Gutiérrez de Velasco, 109–33. México D.F.: El Colegio de México.

Frank, Andre Gunder. 1988. "The Development of Underdevelopment." In *The Political Economy of Development and Underdevelopment*, edited by Charles K. Wilber, 109–20. New York: McGraw-Hill.

Fuss, Diana. 1991. *Inside/Out: Lesbian Theories, Gay Theories*. New York: Routledge.

Garzón, Paulina. 2014. "Una cuestionable alianza sur sur: las inversiones chinas en Ecuador y en la región." In *La restauración conservadora del correísmo*, edited by Alberto Acosta et al., 259–267. Quito: Montecristi Vive.

Granda Vega, M. P. 2016. "El macho sabio: Racismo y sexismo en el discurso sabatino del presidente ecuatoriano Rafael Correa." *Ecuador Debate* 100: 197–211. https://repositorio.flacsoandes.edu.ec/handle/10469/13576.

Gudynas, Eduardo. 2010. "Si eres tan progresista ¿Por qué destruyes la naturaleza? Neoextractivismo, izquierda y alternativas." *Ecuador Debate* 79: 61–81. https://repositorio.flacsoandes.edu.ec/handle/10469/3531. 2010.

Gutmann, Matthew C. 1998. "Traficando con hombres: La antropología de la masculinidad." *Revista de Estudios de Género. La Ventana.*, No. 8: 47–99. https://www.redalyc.org/articulo.oa?id=88411133004.

Hernández, Oscar. 2008. "Estudios Sobre Masculinidades. Aportes desde América Latina." *Revista de Antropología Experimental* 8: 67–73. http://revista.ujaen.es/huesped/rae/articulos2008/05hernandez08.pdf.

Herrera, Gioconda, María Troya, and Jacques Ramírez. 2002. "Masculinidades en América Latina, más allá de los estereotipos. Diálogo Con Mathew C. Guttman." *Iconos—Revista de Ciencias Sociales*, no. 14: 118–24. https://revistas.flacsoandes.edu.ec/iconos/article/view/600.

Kimmel, M. 1997. "Homofobia, temor, vergüenza y silencio en la identidad masculina." In *Masculinidad/es. Poder y crisis*, edited by T. Valdés and J. Olavarría. Santiago, Chile: Ediciones de las Mujeres 24.

Larkin, Brian. 2013. "The Politics and Poetics of Infrastructure." *Annual Review of Anthropology* 42: 327–43.

Larraz, Irene. 2017. "El lenguaje machista de Rafael Correa" *Diario El País*, https://elpais.com/elpais/2017/05/23/planeta_futuro/1495560980_079621.html.

Martínez Novo, Carmen. 2018. "Discriminación y colonialidad en el Ecuador de Rafael Correa (2007–2017)." *Alteridades* 28, no. 55: 49–60.

Meléndez, Carlos, and Paolo Moncagatta. 2017. "Ecuador: Una década de correísmo." *Revista de ciencia política* (Santiago) 37, no. 2: 413–48. https://www.redalyc.org/pdf/324/32453264009.pdf.

Moore, Robert L., and Douglas Gillette. 1993. *La nueva masculinidad: Rey, Guerrero, Mago, Amante*. Barcelona: Paidós Ibérica.

Morán, Susana. 2019. "Una hidroeléctrica preocupa a los habitantes del Río Piatúa." *Plan V*. https://www.planv.com.ec/historias/sociedad/una-hidroelectrica-preocupa-habitantes-del-rio-piatua.

Moreno Ronquillo, Martha Cecilia. 2019. "Caudales ambientales como herramienta para la gobernanza hídrica: Limitaciones discursivas y debates para su aplicación en la actividad hidroeléctrica del país." Facultad Latinoamericana de Ciencias Sociales (FLACSO) Sede Ecuador. https://repositorio.flacsoandes.edu.ec/handle/10469/15887.

Pallares, Martin. 2020. "Coca Codo Sinclair: ¿Pagará la China por el inminente desastre?" *4 Pelagatos*, April 20, 2020. https://4pelagatos.com/2020/04/20/coca-codo-sinclair-pagara-la-china-por-el-inminente-desastre/.2020.

Patel, Kasha. 2020. "La desaparición de la cascada más alta de Ecuador." *Observatorio de La Tierra de La NASA*. https://ciencia.nasa.gov/la-desaparición-de-la-cascada-más-alta-de-ecuador.

Ministerio Coordinador de Producción, Empleo y Competitividad, y Ministerio de Industrias y Productividad. 2015. *Politica industrial del Ecuador 2016–2025*. http://servicios.produccion.gob.ec/siipro/downloads/estudios.html.

Ministerio de Industrias y Productividad (MIPRO) y Ministerio Coordinador de Producción, Empleo y Competitividad (MCPEC). 2015. "Presentación de la política industrial Del Ecuador (Ppt)." http://servicios.produccion.gob.ec/siipro/estudios.html.

Ministerio de Industrias y Productividad (MIPRO) y Ministerio Coordinador de Producción, Empleo y Competitividad (MCPEC). 2015. "Política industrial del Ecuador 2016–2025." Quito. http://servicios.produccion.gob.ec/siipro/estudios.html.

Picq, Manuela. 2018. *Vernacular Sovereignties: Indigenous Women Challenging World Politics*. Tucson: University of Arizona Press.

Quijano, Aníbal. 2001. "Colonialidad del poder, globalización y democracia." *Utopías, Nuestra Bandera: Revista de Debate Político* 188: 97–123. https://www.rrojasdatabank.info/pfpc/quijano2.pdf.

Sacher, William. 2020. "La erosión regresiva, el derrame y la represa: Detalles sobre el derrumbe de La Cascada de San Rafael en La Provincia de Napo, Ecuador." *Mutantia*. https://mutantia.ch/es/cascada-de-san-rafael-la-primera-tragedia-de-una-larga-lista/.

Sierra, Natalia. 2014. *La restauración conservadora del correísmo: Breves reflexiones sobre el poder como instrumento de dominación. Radiografía de la dominación correista.* Quito: Blanda.

Tortosa, J. M. 2011. *Maldesarrollo y mal vivir—Pobreza y violencia a escala mundial.* Edited by Esperanza Martínez and Alberto Acosta. Quito: Abya-Ayala. https://web.ua.es/es/iudesp/documentos/publicaciones/maldesarrollo-libro.pdf.

Vera Rojas, María Teresa. 2013. "Humanismo, heteronormatividad y homofobia en el socialismo del siglo XXI: El amor como consigna." In *Resentir lo queer en América Latina: Diálogos desde/con el Sur,* edited by Diego Falconí Trávez, Santiago Castellanos, and María Amelia Viteri. Madrid: Editorial Egales.

Viteri, María Amelia. 2020. "Anti-Gender Policies in Latin America: The Case of Ecuador." *LASA Forum Dossier: Las ofensivas antigénero en América Latina* 51, no. 2: 42–46.

Viveros, Mara. 2007. "Teorías feministas y estudios sobre varones y masculinidades. Dilemas y desafíos recientes." *La Manzana de La Discordia* 2, no. 4: 25–36. https://doi.org/10.25100/lmd.v2i2.1399.

Wallerstein, Immanuel. 1997. "La reestructuración capitalista y el sistemamundo." In *Conferencia magistral en el XX° Congreso de la Asociación Latinoamericana de Sociología, México, 2 al 6 de Octubre de 1995.*

Wilson, Japhy, and Manuel Bayón. 2017. *La selva de Los elefantes blancos: Megaproyectos y extractivismos en la Amazonía ecuatoriana.* Quito: Mundo, Instituto de Estudios Ecologistas del Tercer.

Wolff, Jonas. 2016. "Business Power and the Politics of Postneoliberalism: Relations between Governments and Economic Elites in Bolivia and Ecuador." *Latin American Politics and Society* 58, no. 2: 124–47.

Brazil and China's "Inevitable Marriage"? Post-Bolsonaro Futures and Beijing's Shift from North America to South America

Zhou Zhiwei

CHINA'S INCREASED PRESENCE in Latin America, particularly in Brazil and Ecuador, occurred at a moment when the region is undergoing great political change. As the chapter by Correa et al. demonstrates, Ecuador faced widespread popular revolts after ten years of authoritarian, neodevelopmentalist rule that had as one of its cornerstones Chinese investment in mega development projects. As the authors put it, "the development of strong ties between Ecuador and China in the context of a populist and authoritarian government contributed not only to environmental destruction in the Amazon Region, but also to reinforce inequalities and the disempowerment of minorities in a racist society" (144). This, in turn, fueled nationwide revolts against a regime that had been entrenched for over a decade. Meanwhile in Brazil, the political collapse of the Workers' Party governments and their local allies, which were guiding lights for Chinese investors (Vasques, 375, and Pedlowski, 429, this volume), resulted in a wave of Sinophobia emanating from the highest levels of Brazil's fascist-leaning federal government. As Li Zhang reports in their chapter, the aggressiveness of the Bolsonaro government's insulting anti-Chinese rhetoric was seen as an affront to China's new generation of "wolf warrior" diplomats—even as the two countries become more aware of their growing economic interdependence.

After nearly twenty years of the "Pink Tide" in Latin America, the region is now undergoing political, ecological, and economic transformations, as well as diplomatic adjustments. Uncertain factors in the geopolitical environment have also significantly increased. The most intuitive presentation of the changes taking place in Latin America would be to call it an adjustment of political ecology. The rotation of left and right political power, the emergence of new political forces, and the resurgence of populism are the main characteristics of this current round of political environmental adjustment. In contrast to the "Pink Wave" created by left-collectivist governments in the early twenty-first century, most Latin American countries have taken a "right turn" following the 2017–2019 "super election cycle," and left-wing governments are facing increasing challenges. This also reflects the current governance dilemma faced by Latin America. Both the left and right models have difficulty in resolving the region's development dilemma, and the rotational frequency of regional political forces may thus accelerate. Additionally, traditional Latin American political groupings have been greatly impacted by the groupings emerging in the current round of adjustment. The rise of Bolsonaro in Brazil was the result of emerging political forces, right-wing populism, media-based politics, and many other factors. This will inevitably aggravate the degree of fragmentation of Brazil's political party system, increasing the cost and difficulty of governance and increasing political risks.

This problem of asynchronized political cycles has caused great disruption to the integration process in Latin America. Latin American countries must take sides on the Venezuelan issue, which seriously endangers the unity of the region, directly affecting regional integration, which has basically come to a standstill. Some regional organizations are facing difficulties in terms of their survival. The Union of South American Nations exists in name only, due to the fact that its member countries are part of two disagreeing sides. At the same time, the Community of Latin American and Caribbean States has lost the vitality it had in the past, particularly impacting the greater connections to the world it had forged.

The Latin American economy has turned from prosperity to decline or even failure. Unsuccessful economic governance is the key reason for the adjustment of Latin American political ecology. With the outbreak of the global financial crisis and the sharp decline in commodity prices, the Latin

American economy has decelerated significantly since 2010. The growth rate of the region has fallen from 6.1 percent in 2010 to 0.5 percent between 2014 and 2018. The Latin American economy has decreased from US$6.4 trillion in 2014 to US$5.8 trillion in 2018. From 2011 to 2016, the size of the Brazilian economy dropped from US$2.6 trillion to US$1.8 trillion, shrinking by as much as 31 percent in five years. Latin America's oscillating economy of the past two decades reflects the fragile characteristics of the region's economy, including economic structures based on one or a few products, the deterioration of industrial structure, and the lack of autonomous development. From the perspective of the internal and external environment, the Latin American economy may show large fluctuations in the short to medium term. In the context of the continued economic downturn, social conflicts in Latin America have become prominent. Considering the pessimistic economic growth expectations for Latin America, the ideological polarization at national and regional levels, and the acceleration of the rotation of political forces, the Latin American social situation demonstrates a greater risk of volatility. Chinese investments in Latin America—and particularly in Brazil—have reflected this volatility, as Rodríguez's chapter in this volume has shown.

At the diplomatic level, with the ideological polarization in Latin America, the normalization of competitive Sino-US relations, and the rapid advancement of Sino-Latin American relations, current US–Latin American relations show a strong "exclusivity." In the past two years, the United States has strengthened its diplomacy with Latin America. The policy focus is to exert pressure on the left-wing regimes of Venezuela, Cuba, and Nicaragua, squeezing their diplomatic space in the region, and to increase the exclusion of foreign powers by positioning China and Russia as "new imperialist powers," specifically demanding that Latin American countries reject China's Belt and Road Initiative. In general, there is a huge difference between the current US attitude toward China and the view that, at the beginning of the new century, "China–Latin America cooperation is conducive to Latin America's prosperity." With the complication of Sino-US relations, the US is likely to further strengthen the restrictions on China–Latin America cooperation (Zhiwei 2019).

Brazil is one of China's most important partners in Latin America. Over the past two decades, China-Brazil relations achieved many breakthroughs.

As emerging powers, China and Brazil greatly improved their regional and international influence over the past decade, and with this process, the status of China and Brazil in the international system is improving. Gradually transitioning from "peripheral players" to "central players," the relationship between the two countries has increasingly become a major bilateral relationship that has an important influence in international affairs. From the perspective of national identity and cooperation, China-Brazil relations are progressing along three axes: bilateral, multilateral, and transregional/ regional (China and Latin America). The latter two axes have growing and vital aspects supporting China-Brazil bilateral relations.

When Jair Bolsonaro took over the presidency in Brazil in 2019, Brazilian diplomacy gave off signs that it is readjusting. For example, it alienated Latin American left-wing neighbors (especially Venezuela and Cuba), and its attitude toward multilateral cooperation tended to be cold. Bolsonaro's Brazil followed the US position on regional and international issues, contrasting sharply with Brazilian diplomacy at the beginning of the new century. In fact, President Bolsonaro and Foreign Minister Araújo repeatedly criticized the foreign policy of the left-wing Workers' Party during its control of the presidency (2003–2016) as having a strong "ideological" color. From the current perspective, however, Brazil's diplomatic preferences are possibly driving the country to the other extreme, a phenomenon that is in fact an "ideological" operation. Bolsonaro heavily criticized left-wing government, socialism, and Marxism during his election program, further strengthening external expectations of a "big adjustment" in Brazilian diplomacy.

Bolsonaro's foreign policy closely followed that of the US. This is reflected in his diplomatic decision-making team's position on issues such as the relocation of embassies in Israel, antiglobalism, and withdrawal from relevant multilateral mechanisms of the United Nations. But the US and Brazil have also had a high frequency of interactions during the Trump and Bolsonaro presidencies. Multiple bilateral forms of cooperation between Brazil and the United States have accelerated. In September 2019, the US and Brazil launched the Strategic Partnership Dialogue; in October, the US-Brazil Political and Military Dialogue was convened; and in November, the US-Brazil Joint Committee on Science and Technology Cooperation was restarted.

Since the global outbreak of the COVID-19 epidemic, members of Brazil's far-right government have repeatedly stigmatized China. As Zhang's chapter in this volume demonstrates, China-Brazil relations have witnessed diplomatic storms that have been rare since the establishment of diplomatic relations between the two countries. On March 18, 2020, Eduardo Bolsonaro, the son of Brazilian president Bolsonaro (and a federal representative and the chairman of the House Committee on External Relations and National Defense), used social media to slander China's efforts to fight the new pandemic. On April 5, Brazilian education minister Abraham Weintraub (who, as Zhang points out in this volume, is known to China as "Brazil's minister of insults") publicly slandered China for trying to "rule the world" via the pandemic. On April 22, Brazilian Foreign Minister Ernesto Araújo posted on his personal social media account that "the spread of the new coronavirus is part of a plan for globalists to spread a new road to communism." The Chinese Embassy in Brazil condemned these allegations and asked the Bolsonaro government to correct their mistakes and stop making unjustified accusations against China. Afterward, many people from Brazil's political, business, academic, and media communities expressed their solidarity with China, criticizing extreme right-wing forces for their opinions and for the violation of diplomatic principles. This played a role in avoiding the complete derailment of bilateral relations between the two nations.

Because of the COVID-19 epidemic, in fact, Brazil's attitude toward China has changed significantly, especially with regard to synchronized diplomatic policy in collaboration with the US. After the outbreak of the epidemic, Bolsonaro expressed solidarity with and support for China's fight against the virus while meeting with Ambassador Yang Wanming on February 6, 2020. Coincidentally, on February 7, Trump also praised China's excellent organization and coping ability during a phone call with President Xi Jinping. Obviously, at the beginning of February, the channels of dialogue running between the United States, Brazil, and China were relatively smooth with regard to responding to the pandemic. From March 7 to 10, 2020, Bolsonaro visited Miami, Florida. After this visit, the US and Brazilian stock markets suffered multiple meltdowns, which put the two presidents who "most questioned the new coronavirus" under public pressure.

It was also at this point that both the United States' and Brazil's attitudes toward China took a turn once again. On March 17, Trump called the new virus "the China Virus" on Twitter; a day later, Congressman Eduardo Bolsonaro attacked China on the same platform. Brazil's former foreign minister Magalhães claimed that this "double act" amounted to a specific calculation: "What is good for Trump is good for Bolsonaro; what is good for Bolsonaro is good for Brazil." In addition to maintaining a consistently aligned attitude toward China, Bolsonaro's approach to the pandemic showed the same populist tones as Trump's. Following Trump's promotion of hydroxychloroquine as a miracle cure, Bolsonaro began to promote the drug as well. Brazil's attacks on the World Health Organization also followed the lead of the United States. When public opinion and ideology are highly polarized, extreme right-wing populism can emerge, even in a Brazil that is inclusive. For the Bolsonaro government, rational policy making was not important; what was key is a political "survival" strategy that influences (and is influenced by) public opinion. However, there is no doubt that Bolsonaro's populist diplomacy profoundly changed Brazil's diplomatic tradition and caused irreparable damage to its international image.

In the last week of April 2020, two auspicious signs appeared in China-Brazil relations, demonstrating Brazilian pragmatic forces' determination to cooperate with China. The first good sign was Vice President Hamilton Mourão likening China-Brazil relations to "an inevitable marriage." Mourão made this statement when talking about the future development of Embraer. This kind of metaphor is very appropriate. It vividly summarizes the basis, motivation, and expectations of cooperation between China and Brazil. Without solid "affection," how can there be a natural marriage? Without passionate motivation toward each other, how can there be a long-lasting marriage? Without a good expectation of a future life together, how can there be a strong marriage? The word "inevitable," emphasized by Vice President Mourão, precisely reflects the reality that China and Brazil are "indivisible."

In fact, since entering the new century, China-Brazil cooperation has achieved a series of breakthroughs that have attracted the attention of the international community. In 1993, Brazil established its first strategic partnership with China, which was upgraded in 2012 to a comprehensive partnership. In 2009, China became Brazil's largest trading partner. And more recently, in 2018, China-Brazil bilateral trade exceeded US$100 billion, with Brazil becoming the first country in Latin America to cross that monetary threshold with China. Over the past decade, Brazil's trade surplus with China accounted for about 40 percent of Brazil's total foreign trade surplus.

China simultaneously became a significant source of investment for Brazil. Efficient economic and trade cooperation between the two countries has provided the impetus for Brazil's economic and social development. Cooperation between the two countries in the high-tech field has also made great breakthroughs. Since the 1980s, more than thirty years of space cooperation have resulted in the development and launching of six earth resource satellites, providing means to monitor environmental changes in the Amazon basin. This process broke the monopoly in remote-sensing technology of the developed countries and was hailed as a model of South-South cooperation by leaders of both China and Brazil. In fact, Embraer—the company Vice President Mourão had referred to—maintained close cooperative ties with China. At the end of May 2000, Embraer's Beijing Representative Office was established to formally enter the Chinese market. At the same time, Embraer and Sichuan Airlines signed a letter of intent to purchase five ERJ145 jets. In September of the same year, the first aircraft was successfully delivered to Sichuan Airlines and started commercial operations. Sichuan Airlines has thus become the first customer of the ERJ145 in the Asian market. In January 2003, Embraer, together with China Aviation Industry Corporation and its subsidiary Harbin Aircraft Industry, jointly invested in the establishment of Harbin AnBoWei Aircraft Industry to produce fifty-seat ERJ145 jet aircraft in China. To date, Harbin AnBoWei has delivered a total of forty-one ERJ145 jets and five Legacy 650 business jets to the Chinese market, while Tianjin Airlines, China Southern Airlines, Colorful Guizhou Airlines, Guangxi Beibu Gulf Airlines, Hebei Airlines, and Urumqi Airlines together operated more than one hundred E-Series jets. Much can be learned from China-Brazil aerospace cooperation.

The BRICS Special Foreign Ministers' Meeting regarding the COVID-19 outbreak, held on April 28, was the first coordinated BRICS meeting regarding the pandemic. The key words for this meeting were *multilateralism* and *collaboration*. In particular, the meeting emphasized that BRICS countries must adhere to multilateralism, strengthen solidarity and cooperation, closely share information on outbreaks, exchange experience, carry out drug and vaccine research and cooperation, respond more effectively to viruses, maintain world public health security, and strive to mitigate the effects of the outbreak. This foreign ministers' video meeting sent a signal from the five countries to strengthen cooperation and fight the epidemic together. At the same time, the meeting's communiqué mentioned that there was a difference in understanding among the BRICS members regarding the epidemic. This referenced the recent politicization and stigmatization of the 2020 pandemic by members of the Brazilian cabinet.

The PRC government has expressed a commitment to global cooperation and sharing Chinese experience in combating pandemics. It portrays itself as being inspired by a humanitarian ethic without ideological considerations or geopolitical private interests. The era we are in is quite different from the Cold War period, even in the PRC, and it has been that way for some time. By abandoning the zero-sum-game thinking of the Cold War and carrying out mutually beneficial cooperation with countries around the world, China believes that its reforms and pragmatic thinking have achieved results. The government actively deployed medical resources to support Brazil and coordinated online exchanges between experts from the two countries. Chinese companies and overseas Chinese diaspora in Brazil have participated in the fight against the COVID-19 pandemic in solidarity with the Brazilian people. The sincere and voluntary character of this assistance marks a historic shift in the two countries' relationship.

Brazil has expressed a desire to maintain a harmonious atmosphere with its neighbors in South America—this may even be called the country's "soft power." Brazil has been much recognized by the international community for this. There is a well-known saying in China: travel with a good companion and live with a good neighbor. The COVID-19 pandemic has demonstrated regional and global interconnection. The core of neighborly relationships is mutual respect, consideration of interests, and mutual solidarity. Perhaps this pandemic is an important test of Sino-Brazil relations. My choice of an optimistic expectation resonates in the words of Vice President Mourão: it is an inevitable marriage, a better way to cherish one another and maintain solidarity.

The Bolsonaro government brought changes in ideologies and values, regional strategy adjustments, and changes in Brazil's multilateralism, established as its diplomatic tradition since the early twentieth century. In fact, Brazilian national identity is also undergoing redefinition. How these changes will affect Brazil's national development and international agenda is a question that will require time to answer. In the early days of World War II, the Getúlio Vargas administration adopted a strategy of balancing US and German interests. This not only ensured trade with Germany but also laid the foundation for the country's heavy industry through US assistance. The diplomatic arrangements during the Vargas period may be something that future Brazilian governments may try to emulate. This, in fact, may be seen by some Brazilian leaders as the most rational choice.

REFERENCE

Zhiwei, Zhou. 2019. "The 'Three-Dimensional' Structure of China-Brazil Relations: Connotation and Policy Ideas" in *The Yellow Book of Portuguese-Speaking Countries Social Sciences Archives: Report on the Development of Cooperation between China and Portuguese-Speaking Countries*. Guangdong University of Foreign Studies.

The China-Ecuador Relationship: From Correa's Neodevelopmentalist "Reformism" to Moreno's "Postreformism" during China's Credit Crunch (2006–2021)

Milton Reyes Herrera

Using a historical-structural approach, this chapter examines the China-Ecuador relationship from a decision-making perspective. This dynamic is also analyzed through a review of two periods: reformism (the Rafael Correa administration, 2006–2017) and postreformism (the Lenín Moreno administration, May 2017–2021), as well as certain aspects of the impact of the COVID-19 pandemic. Along with some of the other authors in this book, I'm interested in how the transition between the two governments was complex and contested, as well as the lasting impacts of what Mosquera Narváez calls Ecuador's "stepping out [into the world]" after 2017.

I propose an approach through the lens of critical international political economy, which, in a complementary manner, recognizes the dynamic of increasing the wealth-power of nations, but which also takes into account the reality that countries are not cohesive units, but rather state-social complexes with competitive dynamics between hegemonic and subordinate social forces (Cox 1993). As numerous authors in this volume have attested (Gutiérrez, Carpio, and Flores; Molina and Munduruku; and Brito, among others), social movements, Indigenous rebellions, and other "nonstate" political forces have played roles in shaping the political economies of Ecuador and Brazil, particularly in terms of containing the deepening of neoliberalism. As Sigrid Vásconez shows in her article in this volume, happenstance

(COVID-19 coinciding with the implosion of a waterfall caused by the Coca Codo Sinclair [CCS] hydroelectric project in Ecuador) can act as an accelerant on these forces, pushing them into new alliances and critiques of power. The confinement of the Ecuadoran population due the pandemic "actually favored the dissemination of news and allowed certain scientific questions about waterfall implosion to enter into the public discourse. Digital media, postings, and links in social media and some mainstream media coverage brought to the fore scientific questions that challenged the technical suitability of the CCS project in national forums" (Vásconez, this volume, 290).

This is especially visible in Latin America, whereas China—a state-civilization with a very long history—has a certain contrasting continuity, as Braudel argued (1978). In Latin America, we find structural weaknesses in the state, present since the independence struggles of the early nineteenth century. These resulted in a course of development driven by the interests of a white, land-owning, conservative oligarchy that fashioned its approach to the world market through the exportation of primary products (Centeno 2002; Sevilla 1992; Sánchez 1981; Biarritz Forum 2009). They had no interest, whether economically or territorially, in channeling resources derived from their accumulated wealth toward domestic development—as, for example, happened in the twentieth century in the case of Japan, the Asian Tigers, China, and other Asian economies (Medeiros 1997).

Ecuador and other countries in the region thus settled into a material posture and political orientation (which materialized institutionally) whose perspective was oriented toward foreign markets. In the aftermath of the wars of independence (which involved substantial losses of goods and means of production) existing prerevolutionary plans for domestic development were abandoned, just as similar plans would be destined for a similar defeat in the future.

A dichotomy thus emerged in the form of a hegemonic competition between two kinds of state projects: those of a more outward-looking nature, oriented toward a situation of minimal governmental intermediation; and what began as protodevelopmentalist projects, which presumed a state that was increasingly involved in the direct administration of social (and productive) forces and the nation's place in the world order (the state's role from the Coxian perspective). From there, the dichotomy continues to reproduce itself at the level of ideas (Cox 1993): perceptions that tend to reinforce

colonial exclusion, coinciding with civilizational, political, and even es-
thetic ideals driven by Eurocentric representational parameters (Quijano
2000). In historical terms, Ecuador developed along a path of "spasmodic
modernization," prioritizing projects of a more outward-looking nature,
with brief periods in which the state implements developmentalist policies
(Páez-Cordero 1994). It was this kind of developmentalist period that characterized the reformism that emerged in 2006 and marked the beginnings
of Ecuador's stronger relationship with China.

CHINA-ECUADOR RELATIONS DURING THE REFORMIST PERIOD

By way of background, it is worth mentioning that China's presence in
Ecuador is not a purely bilateral situation, but rather part of a regional
presence (although China's relationship with each individual country has
unique features, depending on the internal political discourse of each
state-society complex).

The administration of Ecuador's former president Rafael Correa began
with what could be described as a neo-national-populist project, with the
goal of articulating a national powerbase of Ecuadorians who identified with
the middle and upper-middle classes; lower socioeconomic classes (not just
working classes, given the deterioration of the workers' movement during
the two previous decades); social movements, rural and Indigenous sectors,
environmentalists, etc., many of whom object to globalization and US efforts
to form a Free Trade Area of the Americas (FTAA) (Pullaguari as well as
Correa et al., this volume); and a proposed state project based on a new
modernized and technocratic institutionalism. This coalition gained legitimacy through robust voter support and an enthusiastic popular reception.

Insofar as this proposed project opened the possibility of an expanded
state role as the mediator of social forces and Ecuador's place in the world
order (oriented toward the redistribution of material resources)—and insofar as China's traditional international policy elevates and prioritizes
bilateral dialog at the state-state level—the two countries began to conceive
of mutuality of interests in the following areas:

- Ecuador needed to overcome foreign restrictions and the global
  financial crisis of 2007–2008 (through credit or loans-for-oil mech-

anisms), which would put it in a position to freely acquire resources without finding itself pressured to implement economic policies that could disrupt its proposed state project (as often tended to happen with loans from international banks and multilateral loans based on the "exchange rate regime").

- The proposed model depended on the generation of a level of investment that would strengthen Ecuador's economic dynamics, for example, in infrastructure, thereby creating demand as well as supply, and stimulating national businesses and production.
- China needed to acquire strategic resources, like petroleum, minerals, and other materials, which are crucial not only to China's economy but also to its defense (Klare 2008); and to satisfy other kinds of security demands—the acquisition of food commodities, for example—to maintain a supply of products for an ever-more-sophisticated middle class.
- China needed to diversify its surpluses in a manner that was both financially sound and productive and to utilize its workforce abroad ("going global"), which would allow it to expand domestic accumulation.
- Both countries shared the policy of developing and strengthening a discourse in international organizations that was oriented toward the maintenance of a strong national sovereignty (through voting in the United Nations, for example); and generating space for a relative increase in their political autonomy in the international sphere.
- Both countries expressed a need for a strong state, although in distinct dimensions. In the case of Ecuador, this was oriented toward a perspective of reformist planning, without the need (let alone capacity) for a complete centralization of the government's mediating role, as is the case with China.

It should be noted, however, that because they are not located within any adjacent area of national interest, Ecuador and the surrounding region do not represent any concern in terms of China's national defense (Shi 2010). Neither is Ecuador located within the first of China's concentric rings of diplomatic and security interests (Yuan and Wang 2013; Clarke 2016; Nathan and Scobell 2012; Nathan 2015; Brown 2017). South America falls within the third and/or fourth rings, which are specifically concerned with international trade, economic relations, and the strengthening of states' sovereignty through participation in post–World War II international institutions, for which China developed mechanisms for bilateral dialogs.

The strategic attitude behind China's foreign policy is informed by a long history of military thought with numerous influences (chief among them Confucianism) in the deployment of its "soft power" policy and Mao Zedong's Three Worlds Theory in maintaining support for nonaligned countries; the nationalist notion of "the century of humiliation," which informed China's sovereignty policy; and ancient traditions of realism with regard to authoritarian rule. This can be seen in China's conception of the state as a unit in dialog with equals ("one state, one unit"). It is also visible in China's policy of regarding different countries and regions as having different levels of importance according to their standing in the world order, focusing on roles as regional and global leaders, available resources, material capacities, and geopolitical positions.

China currently continues to reinforce its expanded international presence in two areas: acceleration of foreign trade and direct foreign investment, allowing other countries to overcome restrictions in their access to international capital markets through the offering of credit and financing; and avoiding entering into agreements or submitting to evaluation measures perceived as an inappropriate form of control (such as measures to adjust and reduce public spending or investment, as a precondition for obtaining resources from bilateral organizations).

With the entry of the Correa administration in 2006, an unprecedented acceleration of Chinese-Ecuadorian relations took place in direct foreign investment and financing. Between direct credits and resources generated from the "loans for oil" program, it is estimated that Ecuador has taken in around US$21 billion, approximately 22 percent of its GDP (Reyes and Chun-Lee 2017), which in 2016 totaled about US$100 billion. By 2015, Ecuador, along with Venezuela, Brazil, and Argentina, took in approximately 90 percent of the Chinese resources invested in the entire region (Reyes 2012).

The Correa administration's perspective on this activity could be characterized as "optimism portrayed as pragmatism," as it maintained that China had imposed enormous challenges during negotiations. But given the realities of the situation and the asymmetries between the two countries, the agreements were generally regarded as setting a standard for viability and optimality (Reyes 2012).

Returning to our analysis, it is worth noting that while the Correa administration's neodevelopmentalist orientation supported policies aimed at expanding domestic economic redistribution and sovereignty, this was accomplished by an administrative environment that favored technocracy and distanced itself from the social movements that had been key to Correa's election. This had the effect of slowly weakening his voting base and explains why his political movement only secured narrow victories in presidential elections. The effectiveness of Ecuador's economic policy was weakened during Correa's 2013–2017 term, which generated two overlapping macroconsequences: (a) a boom in consumer spending, with improvements in Ecuador's Gini Index (from 53.3 in 2007 to 45 in 2016);[1] and a simultaneous confluence of several factors that threatened the domestic economy and, along with it, the possibility of maintaining "the purity of [the administration's] model." Such factors include:

- the end of the commodities boom that had started in 2014, which demonstrated Ecuador's susceptibility to external economic shocks, a consequence of the historical structure of its productive sector's dependency on foreign markets;
- the strengthening of the US dollar, which weakened the competitivity of export products, thereby directly affecting national production (since Ecuador uses the dollar as its official currency); and
- the 2016 earthquake (in the Ecuadorian province of Manabí), which resulted in a 3 percent GDP decrease.

During this period, bilateral China-Ecuador relations remained strong at the economic level through credits and nonrefundable aid (that Ecuador did not fully make use of),[2] but also in terms of cooperation, which occurred through Chinese donations of medical assistance and supplies in the wake of the 2016 earthquake.

Simultaneously, the Correa administration attempted a controlled reformulation of its economic policy in view of decreasing oil prices (since petroleum sales are a key pillar of Ecuador's public revenue). Attempts were made to partially recalibrate the orientation of the administration's political project, through proposed public-private alliances and the Multiparty Agreement signed with the European Union in 2015, for example.[3] This reorientation was foreshadowed in 2014 when Ecuador renewed traditional multilateral banking operations, with the Interamerican Development Bank, global bonds, Development Bank of Latin America, Credit Suisse, and Goldman Sachs, and the issuance of US$15.513 billion in bonds. Prior to this, the administration's largest direct transaction was US$6.555 billion in financing from the Chinese government (Reyes, Pérez, and Barreiro-Santana 2020).

As decreasing commodity prices were impacting the regional economy, South America was experiencing a wave of political shifts, beginning with anti-Maduro protests in Venezuela in December 2015 (*La Salida*, "The Exit") and the impeachment of Brazilian president Dilma Rousseff in May 2016. At the same time, China was reorienting its political attitudes toward South America (a process that began in 2014), retreating from what was primarily a biregional approach[4] and returning to a more bilateral emphasis.

China's approach toward biregional relations continued in accordance with the initiatives of the First China-CELAC Forum and the 2016 White Paper. Meanwhile, China was also attempting to strengthen its bilateral relationships through a series of "Strategic Association" agreements (Oviedo 2014) with countries in South America.[5]

In November 2016, during Xi Jinping's visit to Ecuador (the first time that a Chinese president had visited Ecuador in an official capacity), China and Ecuador signed the Integral Strategic Association Document. However, several of the projects set forth in the document have failed to materialize, in part due to structural weaknesses in the state's ability to execute projects, and in part due to the election of President Lenín Moreno. Notably, Moreno campaigned as a member of Correa's political movement. Upon taking office, however, he moved toward a postreformist model (which slowly morphed into economic liberalism), as well as a reorientation of Ecuador's foreign policy.

POSTREFORMISM (2017–2020)

Starting in 2017, the Moreno administration began distancing itself from the former administration's reform project. At the political level, the process began with outreach to sectors that were structurally opposed to the Correa administration (hegemonic sectors of the Ecuadorian establishment), as well as to those that had been systematically excluded from the political decision-making process during Correa's transition from a neonationalist project to one that was more neodevelopmentalist and technocratic.

Beginning with the Popular Consultation of 2018, the transition began orienting itself toward a more outward-looking project, including a substantial reduction in public spending, which resulted in a pause in infrastructure development (an area where China and Ecuador had completed various major projects); a realignment toward US hemispheric leadership in terms of foreign policy and international security; and the renewal of a more unrestricted engagement with financial markets and multilateral organizations.

This postreformist economic attitude was a response to the interests and ideological perspectives of more traditional political sectors with links to the government, but also to certain problems inherited from the Correa administration: low commodity prices[6] as well as the need for large-scale financing to confront a projected 8 percent fiscal deficit for December 2018, for example. This latter was only partially paid with a US$900 million loan from China (*El Universo* 2018), less than 12 percent of the expected deficit. Importantly, the remaining deficit and related fiscal imbalances led the Moreno administration to seek financial and technical cooperation, as well as supervision, from international financial organizations like the International Monetary Fund, the World Bank, and the Interamerican Development Bank, resulting in agreements in early 2019 (Reyes and Diaz 2019).

As for the interests at play in the China-Ecuador relationship during this new period, bilateral trade continued at levels like those of the former administration, but, in this new environment, Chinese direct investment was more limited. In the area of finance, China—following its policy of adjusting its relations to the posture of its counterparts—continued disbursing resources but at a notably reduced rate (considering its enormous economic capacity), a decrease framed as prudence in deference to Ecuador's new orientation. In other words, the relationship entered into a waiting period as a result of a new Ecuadorian posture, which coincided with a bilateral and biregional scene that was quite different from what China had encountered in 2007.

Particularly since the intensification of the postreformist project in 2019, this new dynamic coincided with a series of images and interests that are repositioning themselves hegemonically within the Moreno administration as well as the media—interests that were already present in hegemonic social blocs and critiques of the bilateral China-Ecuador relationship during the Correa administration. This dynamic considers China to be a predatory world power existing beyond the boundaries of democratic and liberal reason that has possibly acted as an instrument of destabilizing political interests through its increased interest in Ecuador.

In May 2020, as the COVID-19 pandemic deepened to affect Ecuador, Economic Minister Richard Martínez announced that the government was expecting approximately US$2.4 billion in new Chinese credits. This, despite the fact that opinions favoring a renewal of financial relations with China had not been visible in the media. Of this amount, between US$300 and $400 million would be used as payment against a debt from an earlier operation with the Industrial Commercial Bank of China, thereby allowing Ecuador to restructure its obligations under better conditions. In the end, because of the political recalibration of the Ecuadorian government, the country received credit from multilaterals. Consequently, the Chinese credit operation had not materialized as of the first trimester of 2021 (*El Comercio* 2020).

In spite of the ongoing problems with the Chinese credit operation, the government's intentions allow us to infer that China is prepared to offer the kind of financial assistance that could generate an economic recovery in which Ecuador maintains access to resources, legitimacy, and prestige in the world order, as well as to markets (however small they might be) that are crucial to the sustainability of a global commercial arena in which China is becoming the principal player. If and when the Ecuadorian state reactivates this channel, it could make use of such a position. Nevertheless, the question is whether China will really have enough funds to lead a global recovery. Should they fall short, countries of our region could end up falling into a competitive logic that could weaken their positions in future negotiations with China, as well as with other global powers.

NOTES

1. World Bank data accessible at https://datos.bancomundial.org/indicador/SI. POV.GINI.

2. According to consulted sources, more than a year after China offered this financial aid, Ecuador had still not planned or proposed enough projects to fully utilize this resource—yet another illustration of the state's historical-structural weaknesses.

3. This was a decision that "empathized with proposals from Ecuador's business sectors, which viewed the country as having become less competitive in the European market when compared to its neighbors and having fallen into a kind of commercial isolation from other markets, for example in the Far East" (Larenas, Rubio, and Flores 2018, in Reyes and Díaz 2019).

4. For example, with UNASUR and CELAC.

5. Despite the term "strategic," the meaning here is not related to defense.

6. This situation persisted even after a relative recovery of oil prices, which, according to Ecuador's Central Bank, rose from an average of US$43.21 per barrel in 2016 to US$50.91 per barrel in 2017.

REFERENCES

American Enterprise Institute. 2017. China Global Investment Tracker. https://www.aei.org/china-global-investment-tracker/.

Barreiro-Santana, Katalina, Milton Reyes Herrera, and Diego Pérez-Enríquez. 2019. "The Role of the Ecuadorian Armed Forces: Historical Structure and Changing Security Environments," *REPATS*. special edition no. 2: 50–72.

Braudel, Fernando. 1978. *Escritos sobre Historia*. Sao Paulo: Perspectiva.

Biarritz Forum [Foro de Biarritz]. 2009."El estado-nación latinoamericano: Los atolladeros de dos siglos de reproducción de un modelo: Efectos socioeconómicos y manejo." FLACSO-Ecuador. http://www.corporacionescenarios.org/zav_admin/spaw/uploads/files/Biarritz09.Bicentenario-Long.pdf.

Brown, Kerry. 2017. "What Beijing's Ring Roads Say about China's Foreign Policy," *South China Morning Post*, August 6, 2017. http://www.scmp.com/week-asia/opinion/article/2105476/what-beijings-ring-roads-say-about-chinas-foreign-policy.

CEAP-EAFIT. 2016. "La presencia de China en América Latina comercio, inversión y cooperación económica." CEAP-EAFIT. Medellín: Centro de Estudios Asia Pacífico de la Universidad.

Centeno, Miguel A. 2002. *Blood and Debt: War and the Nation-State in Latin America*. University Park: Pennsylvania State University Press.

Clarke, Michael. 2016. "Beijing's March West: 'One Belt, One Road' and China's Continental Frontiers into the 21st Century." Political Studies Association conference paper. https://www.psa.ac.uk/sites/default/files/conference/papers/2016/Clarke-PSA-2016-paper.pdf.

Cox, Robert. W. 1993. "Fuerzas sociales, estado y ordenes mundiales: Más allá de las relaciones internacionales." In *El Poder y el Orden Mundial*, edited by Abelardo Morales, 119–97. San José, Costa Rica: FLACSO.

The Dialogue. 2017. China-Latin America Financial Database. https://www.thedialogue.org/map_list/.

Ellis, Robert E. 2014. *China on the Ground in Latin America: Challenges for the Chinese and Impacts on the Region*. New York: Palgrave-Macmillan.

El Comercio. 2020. "Ecuador recibirá créditos de China por US$ 2 400 millones entre junio y octubre del 2020; la próxima semana arranca renegociación de bonos." May 29, 2020. https://www.elcomercio.com/actualidad/ecuador-credi tos-china-economia-deuda.html.

El Universo. 2018. "Ecuador consigue crédito chino por $ 900 millones, sin comprometer más petróleo." December 12, 2018. https://www.eluniverso.com/no ticias/2018/12/12/nota/7095084/ecuador-consigue-credito-chino-900-millones -comprometer-mas.

IMF. 2017. World Economic Outlook Database. https://www.imf.org/external/pubs/ ft/weo/2015/02/weodata/index.aspx.

Gallagher, Kevin, Amos Irwin, and Katherine Koleski. 2013. "¿Un mejor trato? Análisis comparativo de los Préstamos Chinos en América Latina," Cuaderno de Trabajo 1. México: Centro de Estudios China México.

Klare, Michael. 2008. *Rising Powers, Shrinking Planet*. Glasgow: Bell & Bain.

Larenas, Galo, Jennifer Rubio, and Gabriela Flores. 2018. "La alianza del Pacífico: Consideraciones político-económicas para Ecuador." Quito: Documento Técnico de Integración Monetaria y Financiera Regional Banco Central del Ecuador. https://contenido.bce.fin.ec/documentos/PublicacionesNotas/doctec18 .pdf.

Medeiros, Carlos. 1997. "Globalização e a inserção internacional diferenciada da Ásia e América Latina." In *Poder e Dinheiro: uma Economia Política da Globalização*, edited by Maria da Conceição Tavares and Jose Luis Fiori. Petrópolis: Vozes.

Nathan, Andrew, and Andrew Scobell. 2012. "How China Sees America. The Sum of Beijing's Fears." *Foreign Affairs* 91, no. 5: 31–47.

Nathan, Andrew. 2015. "China's Search for Security." Roundtable Remarks, 1–8. Seoul: The Asian Institute for Policy Studies. http://en.asaninst.org/contents/ andrew-j-nathan-chinas-search-for-security/.

OVIEDO, Eduardo Daniel. 2014. "Las Relaciones entre China y América Latina: Una visión contextualizadora." *Observatorio Política China.* http://politica -china.org/wp-content/plugins/download-attachements/includes/download .php?id=908.

Páez-Cordero, Alexei. 1994. "Democracia y ajuste estructural en Ecuador: Del orden mundial a los actores sociales." Mimeo. Ponencia presentada al Instituto Francés de Estudios Andinos y Universidad Nacional de Bogotá.

Quijano, Anibal. 2000. "Colonialidad del poder, Eurocentrismo y América Latina." In *Colonialidad del saber, Eurocentrismo y ciencias sociales*, edited by Edgardo Lander, 201–46. Buenos Aires: CLACSO-UNESCO.

Reyes-Herrera, Milton. 2012. "Comprendiendo China: Elementos fundamentales para una agenda de beneficios mutuos." *Revista de Política Exterior Línea*

Sur 2, May, 126–43. Quito: Ministerio de Relaciones Exteriores, Comercio e Integración.

Reyes-Herrera, Milton. 2019. "Conferencia de apertura: La geopolítica y economía política internacional de la Iniciativa Franja y Ruta; y ¿Sudamérica?" In *Actas del III Encuentro de Economía Política Internacional*, 16–54. Rio de Janeiro. UFRJ. https://enepiufrj.wixsite.com/enepi/edicao-atual.

Reyes-Herrera, Milton, and Po Chun-Lee. 2017. "La relación China-Ecuador en el siglo XXI: elementos relevantes para la discusión." Working Paper. Quito: Instituto de Altos Estudios Nacionales. https://editorial.iaen.edu.ec/wp-content/uploads/2017/09/La-relacio%CC%81n-China-Ecuador-en-el-siglo-XXI-ilovepdf-compressed.pdf.

Reyes-Herrera, Milton, and Andrea Díaz. 2019. "Ecuador y su interés por ingresar a la Alianza del Pacífico." In *Segundo Informe CELAC-China: Avances hacia el 2021*: 43–51. Santiago de Chile: Consejo de Relaciones Internacionales de América Latina.

Reyes-Herrera, Milton, Diego Pérez-Enríquez, and Katalina Barreiro-Santana. 2020. "El reposicionamiento del Ecuador: Competencia Intra-estatal, y coyuntura en la Administración 2017–2019." *Revista Desafíos* 1, no. 33.

Sánchez, Walter. 1981. "Relaciones internacionales de América Latina: Marginalidad y autonomía." *Estudios Internacionales* 14, no. 55: 322–56.

Sevilla, Rosario. 1992. "Hacia el estado oligárquico. Iberoamérica: 1820–1850." *Rábida* 11: 88–102.

Shi, Yinhong. 2010. "Fe común con los países en desarrollo." *China Today*. http://www.chinatoday.com.cn/ctspanish/se/txt/2010-01/29/content_243399.htm.

World Bank. n.d. "Índice de Gini—Ecuador." https://datos.bancomundial.org/indicator/ SI.POV.GINI?locations=EC.

Yuan, Peng, and Hui Wang. 2013. "China's Grand Periphery Strategy," *Contemporary International Relations* 23, no. 6: 59–62.

China Studies in Brazil:
Leste Vermelho and Innovations
in South-South Academic Partnership

Andrea Piazzaroli Longobardi

UNTIL VERY RECENTLY, Brazilian academics did not consider China, other Asian countries, or even African countries as primary topics of history and social sciences courses, much less full-career specializations. As Antonio Candido remarks regarding Brazilian eighteenth- and nineteenth-century literature, Asia appeared as a "picturesque appendix" of the world (Candido 1989), not as a world historical subject. This may be the core of problem that we face in Brazil: the human sciences have historically cultivated a methodological flaw that disregards Asian countries as historical forces or subjects. For a long time, China and other countries appeared in national literature as *chinoiseries*, as sets of cultural and aesthetic curiosities. As a result, current university libraries contain only a handful of books on Asian history, most of them with sweeping and vague historical summaries encompassing thousands of years in two hundred pages or less.

Leste Vermelho was conceived as journal that would confront and change this pattern of neglect. After contacting researchers and students interested in Asian studies (in particular, Chinese studies) and encountering the same problems—a lack of academic instructors, sources, and references—we realized that there are many research initiatives in Asian studies in Brazil. Most of these were without institutional support or lack a community of collaboration, however. The primary aim of *Leste Vermelho* was thus to become an arena of debate, uniting students' research, professors' articles, and even translations. The journal takes Asia as a complex, multidimensional, and interdisciplinary subject of inquiry, comprehending contradictory inner forces and exterior dynamics within a world system.

This chapter is an eyewitness report on how Brazil's first academic journal promoting Chinese studies, *Leste Vermelho* ("Red East"), was organized and launched in 2015, as it struggled against the limitations that Asian studies faces in Brazil. Below, we shall outline a historical panorama and some possible outcomes for the journal in the context of the political situation during a time in which academic research and human sciences, in particular, are being demonized.

As we see in so many chapters of this volume, Chinese investments in Brazil are enormous, but direct contact between the two nations is relatively new. As Queiroz et al. point out, although the "relationship between China and Latin American countries has attracted the attention of scholars, investors, and politicians since the 2000s, due to the significant increases in trade flows and political exchanges between the Asian giant and the region," commercial relations has been the focus of this axis. "However," they go on, "many Chinese investments in energy, infrastructure, agriculture, manufacturing, technological innovation, information technology, and services have taken place over the past few decades" (350). In the case of port projects in the Amazon (Camoça and Hendler; Felipe and Costa, this volume), traditional riverine peoples have often literally woken up one day to find themselves at ground-zero of Chinese-backed mega-infrastructural projects. But as Zhang has pointed out in her chapter, members of the Chinese diaspora in Brazil have also organized donations of medical supplies and food baskets to local Brazilian governments and communities in the face of COVID-19 and the Bolsonaro's government's stoking of Sinophobic panics.

China's "Stepping Out" policy onto the Latin American stage has placed new segments Brazilian society in contact with the Asian giant's projects and peoples. However, academic fields in Brazil have been late to focus on China as an object of historical, social, cultural, political, or economic research.

OVERCOMING HISTORICAL PREJUDICES

The area studies formula combining geographical, sociocultural, and historical viewpoints is not often employed in Brazil, although some scholars have been pushing to develop this methodological approach. This helps to explain why Chinese and Asian studies are not taught in Brazilian universities. However, the limitations Asian-focused academics face in Brazil go beyond the lack of formal organization of Asian studies or Chinese studies courses.

International financial cooperation has grown exponentially over the last thirteen years. In Brazil, the commercial liberalization of national enterprises (ongoing since the 1990s but accelerating in the early 2000s under President Luiz Ignacio "Lula" da Silva) has created wider and deeper cooperation with Asian countries, most notably China and South Korea (Paulani 2003; Cosnenza 2016). What began as commercial partnerships have become complex relationships involving entrepreneurial cooperation, land leasing, joint investments in energy production, and even political innovations in labor policy, as both Brito and Oliveira show in this volume. Following the increasing importance of Brazil's international relations with Asian countries (particularly with China), Brazilian universities began to develop courses promoting Chinese studies in different disciplines.

Even though considerable efforts have been made to promote the study of Asia as a whole, Chinese studies is by far the most widespread of all Asian studies specializations in Brazil. Chinese studies centers are being set up in some universities, with or without direct cooperation from Chinese education institutions (the Confucius Institute, for example). They can also involve the Chinese Academy of Social Sciences or direct partnerships with individual Chinese universities. Partnerships between Brazil and China's education ministries have also grown considerably over the last twenty years. For example, if we observe Chinese Education Ministry scholarships to study Mandarin, there were only two full scholarships for Brazilian students in 2004. By 2018, however, this number had increased to twenty. Direct partnerships between universities have also been made over the last ten years.

These initiatives may appear remarkably tiny, especially to an English-speaking readership. However, considering Brazil's academic history, such tiny steps represent the development and opening of possibilities for students who wish to specialize in Asian or Chinese studies. Although still restricted in numbers, these opportunities are valuable.[1] Among the other seven editors at *Leste Vermelho*, three have studied abroad in China or in

Japan with the support of international scholarships during their undergraduate or graduate studies.

There are already some influential Asian or Studies Chinese centers
in universities in Brazil, offering students possibilities for study and research. The obstacles professors and students confront are mostly due to
the historical conditions of Brazilian cultural and scholastic contexts.
The first Brazilian university is only a century old, founded in 1920 in Rio
de Janeiro by uniting already-existing law, medicine, and engineering
colleges. According to the National Higher Education Census of 2017,
there are currently 296 public universities in Brazil (INEP 2018). Most
of the (few) Asian or Chinese studies centers that exist are within public universities, since very few private universities have graduate-level
research centers.

There are several reasons for this situation. An article published in 2003
(Pereira 2003) brought to light some historical obstacles the development of
Asian studies faces in Brazil. It highlighted an important factor: cultural mediation between Brazil and any Asian country has historically been through
the Iberian worldview. Although there was significant immigration from
many Asian countries to Brazil, notably in the nineteenth and twentieth
centuries, Brazilian higher education is still widely based on European academic traditions.

Asian languages suffer from the same prejudice, commonly being described as "impossible" to learn. Even among those dedicated to Asian studies, very few scholars know the language of the country they study. These are
in no way problems restricted to Brazil, as many other countries confront
the same prejudices fertilized by antiquated Eurocentrism. In Brazil, however, these ideas are still dominant and have barely even been challenged.
They still impact the present opportunities of students who want to overcome the cultural boundaries between Brazil and Asia.

THE ORIGIN OF *LESTE VERMELHO*

In 2013, I entered the University of São Paulo's Economic History doctoral
program with a research project to study a particular event that had happened during the Chinese Cultural Revolution. My topic of research was
a grassroots initiative called the Workers University, which had begun in
Shanghai in 1969. I had learned about this though the work of Alessandro

Russo, a professor at the University of Bologna who would become my co-mentor a year later.

Before starting my doctoral program, I spent a year preparing my research project. During this time, I was repeatedly shocked by the paucity of the bibliography on China in Brazil. There were only a handful of books in published Portuguese on Chinese modern and contemporary history, and all of them were introductory texts or the personal statement of an author's experiences (Secco 1998; Pomar 2003; Changsheng 2011; Spencer 1990). Most of the books did not employ social scientific methodology or consult specific archives or documents collections. Articles tended to be based on second-hand narratives and personal testimonies.

Trying to use English and other language sources proved marginally less frustrating. As it turns out, many of these publications employ the same sort of approach outlined above. The problem with these texts is not that they associate different types of historical sources with personal narratives collected after the fact; rather, they assemble these references without a specific methodological or analytical purpose. They consider divergent sources and personal impressions as equally relevant, often employing them without clear references as part of a linear narrative that is only vaguely linked to historical facts. This is specifically the case of many publications regarding Chinese contemporary history. There are, of course, numerous serious and relevant books and articles available worldwide on Chinese topics, but it's often hard to gain access to these, let alone separate the wheat from the chaff, particularly for researchers operating in a Brazilian academic context.

A few Chinese studies researchers in Brazil base their work on significant statistical surveys (Pires and Paulino 2009), but their main interests are not to relate these numbers to historical or social contexts. Instead, their aim seems to be employing statistics to demonstrate current or future business opportunities for Brazilian governments or private enterprises.

Nevertheless, over the years I found many professors and students who have engaged in consistent research and/or were interested in dedicating themselves to developing work on important Asian topics by employing appropriate scientific methodologies. Most of these colleagues complained about the lack of two things: the ability to discuss their work with other researchers, in Brazil or in other countries, and the fact that Brazilian university libraries do not contain adequate material for research.

Most books on Chinese studies are published in languages other than those typically collected by Portuguese and Brazilian universities. Importing a book can be very expensive. Even in today's postdigital age, many specialized and important texts in the field of Asian studies are not available digitally and cannot be shipped to South America. Many individual research initiatives begun in Brazil were frustrated by these conditions and abandoned after the researcher had published only one or two articles.

Given this context, I thought it would be interesting and useful to publish an academic journal that would create opportunities for Brazilian students of Asia to associate and exchange ideas. This would be a necessary first step toward building whatever else would be needed to launch Asian and Chinese studies as recognized and consolidated fields in our country. My two main references at the time were the journals *Critical Asian Studies* and *Positions—Asia Critique*.

The start-up process was relatively simple. I wrote emails to many professors and graduate students in Brazil, proposing to launch a journal on critical Asian studies, asking their support as editors or members of the scientific community. Almost all of them quickly wrote me back, inspired by the idea. I proposed that the first number focus on the Chinese Cultural Revolution, since this is a lesser-known topic in Brazil even though it is the source of many debates.

We chose the name *Leste Vermelho* (Red East) because of a poem written by Mao Zedong in 1964, which proposed a contradiction between his conceptions of the ideal of a politically active "red East" and the then-politically suppressed "white East."[2] The journal's proposition was to organize each edition with three sections: articles written by Brazilian researchers, translations of relevant documents and articles, and reviews of books or artistic productions. The aim of the translation section was to disseminate important international references on that issue's main topic, preferably articles that linked together different sources.

The first problem we faced was a lack of reviewers for our articles. We could not find professors who were specialized in the main topics. Selection and reviews were therefore made by the group of editors themselves. This problem has persisted and, so far, we have not been able to solve it. Whenever there is a Brazilian specialist on a certain topic related to Asian studies willing to collaborate with the journal, we normally prefer they write an article rather than review a submission. They can participate in both activities, of course, but considering the amount of work that universities are requiring from full-time professors, this dual role is generally not feasible.

Leste Vermelho's inaugural number contained articles presenting different viewpoints of the same historical event (the Cultural Revolution). This was, of course, one of the journal's main goals. This first number established contact between interested students and professors, resulting in at least one new master's degree research project analyzing the transformation of ballet during the Chinese Cultural Revolution—a project formalized two years later at the University of São Paulo. This was an interesting case, because the researcher in question speaks and reads Chinese fluently, is a ballet dancer, and had been trying to research their topic for years but had not found a mentor in Brazil. This first edition of *Leste Vermelho* brought this researcher and their future mentor together.

Putting together the translation section was also an interesting experience. Translations were made directly from Chinese to Portuguese—very rare in Brazil. Up to then, almost all translations of Chinese texts came from English or Spanish versions. Our translations were made by a group of Chinese language undergraduate students. This project was the first professional experience working as translators of historical documents for some of these students.

DISPARITIES BETWEEN HUMAN AND MATERIAL RESOURCES

After *Leste Vermelho*'s first two editions, we decided to organize a congress or seminar to allow professors and students to meet and discuss possibilities of association and development of Asian studies. The congress, like the journal, began as a bold initiative. It was a long shot because, at first, we did not have any financial support from the university.

We started by writing to known specialists from other countries and recognized Brazilian professors such as Christine Dabat, Isabela Nogueira, and Marcos del Roio. After these scholars showed interest in coming to an event in São Paulo, we applied for a grant offered by the Association for Asian Studies through the China and Inner Asia Small Grants Program. Fortunately, our proposal was approved. This allowed us to formalize our invitation for most of the professors and even offer opportunities for some undergraduate students to attend the congress without paying for lodging and transportation.

We wanted the congress to promote more than just lectures, organized discussion groups, and short-term courses. The organization of the event was exclusively undertaken by undergraduate and graduate students, with crucial aid from university administrative and operations workers. Even so, the congress was relatively large: approximately thirty professors attended from Brazil, India, Canada, the United States, Ecuador, and Argentina. Two hundred participants registered for it. It lasted four days and contained many different types of activities. Considering that we were only able to offer lodging and transportation to a handful of students, this was quite a happening. São Paulo is a very expensive city, and it was therefore not easy for many students to participate in the event.

The congress was nationally promoted through *Leste Vermelho*. In the third issue of the journal, we published articles that were based on the event's panels. The event made it clear that there was a discrepancy between human and material resources in Brazilian universities in general, and in human sciences and Asia studies in particular. There are, in fact, many students interested in developing research topics in the area, but, as I mentioned above, scholarships and study centers are rare in Brazil, especially in the human sciences. This problem was greatly aggravated under Bolsonaro's leadership.

Approximately 30 percent of the more than sixty articles were written by graduate students. Their topics are varied, ranging from international politics to cinema, environmental issues, history, and technological developments. Most of the remaining articles were written by professors. The readership includes undergraduate and graduate students, as well as established professors.

In December 2018, we attempted to organize a fifth volume. However, because we had only two submissions, we decided not to publish it. Another factor influencing the decision to stop publication for a period was that the group of editors had decided to re-create the journal to amplify its readership and organize it according to the national criteria for academic journals, such as blind peer review of submitted articles. To that end, we decided to change the name from *Leste Vermelho* to simply *Leste* (East) and restart, if necessary, with smaller editions—maybe containing fewer original articles but always with blind peer review.

Our next step will be a cycle of videoconferences and online interviews with researchers from different universities and countries. *Leste*'s editors committee will keep working to offer opportunities for scholars to interconnect and share their work, as well as promoting the circulation of important research that is being conducted in Brazil and other countries. Our hope is to disseminate Asian studies in Brazil as a rich, wide, and politically active field of research, connected with the present and our social contexts. We are keeping the flame alive while working to build new and better conditions for continued publication.

CONCLUSION

Leste Vermelho—now, *Leste*—is an example what can be done even under adverse conditions by focusing on existing resources. Amid rapid changes in international politics, economics, and technology, a new generation of Brazilian students is being formed. Some of these new academics are already finding their places as professors in Brazil or, unfortunately, in other countries. Study centers are being set up in many cities, even with extremely limited material resources. These initiatives should be interconnected to amplify their range of possibilities and promote joint projects.

Leste seeks to aid in promoting and facilitating this growth in Asian studies in Brazil. It is a space for debating and propagating these initiatives, promoting a network that can help beginning researchers and offer solid support to veteran scholars, while promoting collaboration with international professors and study centers.

NOTES

1. The author was one of the two students chosen to go to Beijing in 2004 to study Mandarin with a full scholarship from the Chinese Ministry of Education.

2. This poem was written in 1964, but only published in 1974, in the September edition of *Red Flag*, under the title "Spring of 1964" (一九六四年春).

REFERENCES

Candido, Antonio. 1989. *A educação pela noite e outros ensaios*. São Paulo: Editora Ática.

Changsheng, Shu. 2011. *A história da China popular do século XX*. Rio de Janeiro: Editora FGV.

Cosenza, Apoena Canuto. 2016. "Apontamentos sobre o comércio entre Brasil e China (2003–2014)." *Revista Leste Vermelho* 2, no. 1: 62–83.

INEP, Instituto Nacional de Estudos e Pesquisas. 2018. *Censo da Educação Superior* (Higher Education Census).

Lima, Marcos Costa (org). 2018. *Sobre a China*. Recife: UFPE.

Paulani, Leda. 2003. "Brasil *delivery*: a política econômica do governo Lula." *Revista de Economia Política* 23, no. 4 (92): 58–73.

Pereira, Ronan Alves. 2003. "Estudos Asiáticos no Brasil" In *Ásia, América Latina, Brasil: a construção de parcerias*, edited by Lytton L. Guimarães, 105–24. Brasília: NEASIA/ CEAM/ UnB.

Pires, Marcos Cordeiro, and Luis Antonio Paulino. 2009. *Nós e a China: o impacto da presença chinesa no Brasil e na América do Sul*. São Paulo: LCTE.

Pomar, Vladimir. 2003. *A Revolução Chinesa*. São Paulo: UNESP.

Secco, Lincoln. 1998. *A Revolução Chinesa: até onde vai a força do dragão*. São Paulo: Scipione.

Spencer, Jonathan. 1996. *In Search of Modern China*. Brazil: W. W. Norton.

Chinese Financing and Direct Foreign Investment in Ecuador: An Interests and Benefits Perspective on Relations between States through the Lens of the Win-Win Principle

David Mosquera Narváez

INTRODUCTION

The sustained economic growth of China, traceable to its 1978 Open Door Policy and other reforms, has allowed it to become a dominant player in the world economy and to accumulate large capital reserves. China has invested its reserves on a global level through direct foreign investment (DFI) and financing. As Maria Elena Rodríguez points out in her chapter for this volume,

> With regard to Latin America, official sources point out that Chinese FDI has grown significantly since 2010, a year in which it jumped to almost US$30 billion, a value equal to everything that China had invested in the region up to that moment. Nevertheless, these sources differ significantly in terms of the values they report. For example, ECLAC estimates a value of $6.9 billion in 2015 while Mofcom reports that $12.6 billion has been invested—almost double the amount reported by ECLAC. Reports regarding amounts invested per country also differ greatly. According to Mofcom, the Virgin and Cayman Islands captured 86.35 percent of Chinese FDI between 2010 and 2015. Meanwhile, ECLAC claims that Brazil and Peru received about 75 percent. (339)

China's international economic expansion focusses on the pursuit of its national interests under what is presented as a win-win discourse. Of course, as Bonilla and Vásconez, among other contributors to this volume, have noted, even a win-win at the macro level leaves certain communities and populations more vulnerable or further from security and autonomy.

Research on China's presence in the Latin America and the Caribbean region (LAC) and Ecuador presents different characterizations of the interests involved in this international projection, as well as its political and economic benefits. As Reyes Herrera notes in this volume, different types of state projects are at stake, and China's funding for infrastructure development when commodity prices were high contributed to the success of a certain vision of the state. While some of the extant literature relies excessively on economic-commercial analyses, other studies focus heavily on the nature of the cooperation. In the former case, studies tend to focus on increased economic flows attributed to the mutual satisfaction of needs. For example, the Economic Commission for Latin America and the Caribbean (ECLAC) maintains that China places exports and investments in LAC in exchange for raw materials from the region that are crucial to its industry, which in turn allows LAC countries to benefit from increased demand for its products and an increased supply of financing and DFI (OCDE/CEPAL/CAF 2015).

In the latter case, studies tend to analyze whether China's relations with LAC and Ecuador adhere to the precepts of South-South cooperation. According to Valencia (2008), for example, the Chinese government has been aware of the need for cooperation within the Global South, and most of its international collaboration involves commercial cooperation and technical assistance based on the principles of equality and mutual benefit. Detractors of this analysis frame China as a predatory power that exploits its advantages for its own benefit. For Castro (2014), China is not an ally of South-South cooperation, as this concept contemplates solidarity and horizontal alliances between partners with similar levels of development, complementary interests, and balanced mutual benefits.

Amid this debate, Chinese financial activity in Ecuador intensified. Beginning in 2007, along with a strengthening of politico-diplomatic ties, Chinese financing and DFI in Ecuador began increasing. The two countries married China's "Stepping Out" policy of international deployment with the interventionist policy of former president Rafael Correa at a time when China was in the process of increasing its presence in the LAC region.

During the first decade of the 2000s, China's win-win approach to international relations coincided with the emergence of a wave of progressive politics throughout the region. By 2008, eleven of the eighteen Latin American countries were operating under center-left or left-wing administrations. This regional phenomenon that came to be known as "the left turn" (Stoessel 2014).

By the mid-2010s, the movement was losing steam. Progressive administrations throughout the LAC region began to be replaced by more neoliberal governments. Left-oriented governments had struggled with widespread criticism throughout the region. Part of the discourse used to justify this turnaround focused on unsustainable public spending, worrisome levels of corruption, excessive foreign debt, unfavorable international negotiations, and other problems observed in these progressive regimes. In terms of international policy, the criticism fell both directly and indirectly on the advisability of closer relations with China, which was argued as contrary to the austerity policies recommended by the International Monetary Fund.

Despite this reversal, in late 2018 the Ecuadorian Moreno government returned to China to reduce its fiscal deficit through external financing. Moreover, China continues to maintain a keen interest in Ecuador's resources, which matches Ecuador's continued interest in exporting these resources. This renewed activity with China now coincides with the COVID-19 pandemic that has shocked the world economy, further aggravating Ecuador's fiscal problems and creating an even greater demand for external resources and a need to restructure debt to China.

Considering these observations, this chapter proposes that China, when implementing its international deployment strategy, presents its geo-economic interests under a win-win framework without fully appreciating the different perspectives or political realities of the Ecuadorian government. In support of this argument, the chapter will describe the general characteristics of China's Stepping Out policy. It will also discuss the main interests of China's international presence and win-win discourse from a geo-economic perspective. In this context, historical and current data on China's financing and DFI in Ecuador will be presented to examine changes made by the current Ecuadorian government with respect to the previous administration.

STEPPING OUT: BASIC ELEMENTS OF CHINA'S GEO-ECONOMIC STRATEGY

Following the implementation of China's 1978 Open Door Policy and related reforms, China began receiving significant amounts of DFI. For companies from the US and other Asian countries, this new policy of incentivizing foreign investment resulted in the relocation of many of their industrial operations (Harvey 2007). By the first few years of the 1990s, China was no longer interested in simply receiving DFI, but also in channeling capital abroad. Thus began the international deployment policy known as Stepping Out or Going Out.

The idea for the policy was born on October 12, 1992, when Secretary General Jiang Zemin stressed the importance of opening more to the outside world to take better advantage of the funds, resources, technologies, and administrative experience the country had acquired (Jiang 2014, 1). On December 24, 1997, at the National Conference on the Use of Foreign Capital, Jiang again indicated that in addition to attracting foreign companies to invest in China, it was also necessary to organize national companies to invest abroad in order to make use of foreign markets and resources (2).

Subsequently, on October 11, 2000, the Fifth Plenary Session of the Chinese Communist Party's approved the Stepping Out strategy (2001–2005). In this way, China adopted a policy of using resources abroad, encouraging outgoing investments, expanding methods of technical-economic cooperation with foreign countries, and providing credit. In view of pronouncements made by Jiang Zemin, it is apparent that one of the intentions of the Stepping Out policy is to make use of foreign markets and resources.

This argument is supported by the work of Ellis;[1] Gallagher, Irwin, and Kolesli (2013); and Reyes (2017), who have observed the following:

- China justifies its presence abroad in terms of a search to expand its interests in the service of its continued survival, as well as a strategic insertion in the world in service of increased growth, influence, and power (Ellis 2009).
- Chinese investments abroad, made by state-owned companies, will tend to be linked to political objectives. Several Chinese companies have mentioned that their ability to pursue investment projects abroad has been bolstered by the government facilitation of access

to permits and foreign currency. In addition, a complementary relationship has been observed between demand and supply both in China and in the countries of the world. For example, China can offer infrastructure development, and, in exchange, the world supplies resources for China's development (Gallagher, Irwin, and Kolesli 2013).

- The main motives for the consolidation and application of the Stepping Out policy, despite the profit incentive produced by market logic, is the assurance of the medium- and long-term acquisition of strategic resources (Reyes 2017).

In this context, particularly in view of the motivations for the implementation of the Stepping Out policy, it is argued that China's presence abroad, apart from being understood in terms of economic benefits, can be explained in terms of its interest in obtaining resources for its subsistence, growth, security, and defense. In view of its grounding in "the use of economic instruments to promote and defend national interests and produce geopolitical benefits," the Stepping Out policy can thus be analyzed from a geo-economic perspective (Blackwill and Harris 2016).

It should be emphasized that the Chinese state's geopolitical advantages are deployed as a means to obtain vital resources, a dynamic that resonates with Ratzel, Kjellén and Haushofer's definition of geopolitics[2] as political action with geographic factors (vital spaces), in view of the fact that "states depend on certain natural conditions" (Costa 1992, 33). Accordingly, states obtain the vital resources that geographical spaces provide.

When viewed within the framework of geopolitics, China's interaction with foreign resources and markets refers not only to its interest in the capital, consumer goods, and services demanded by its economic actors, but also to those goods considered strategic, such as oil and copper. These resources are crucial to the sustained growth of China's economic system as well as its security and defense (Reyes 2018).

However, it is important to distinguish that geo-economics uses the logic of geopolitics through the use of economic tools. From this perspective, as Blackwill and Harris (2016) have observed, China is able to obtain geopolitical benefits without using military force, relying instead on the economic tools of trade and investment.

Having outlined the general characteristics of the Chinese Stepping Out strategy and related geo-economic interests, we now turn to China's deployment of financing and DFI in the LAC region generally and specifically in Ecuador—as well as China's adaptation to the perspectives of different Ecuadorian social and political sectors.

CHINESE FINANCING AND DIRECT FOREIGN INVESTMENT IN LATIN AMERICA AND THE CARIBBEAN

With its implementation of the Stepping Out strategy, China became a key player in the global economy. In the area of international finance, it began distinguishing itself as a global lender. Countries in the LAC region were among the principal targets of this money supply. During the 2005–2014 period, China disbursed US$118.665 billion in the form of seventy-six loans to fifteen countries in the region. By 2017, China became Latin America's principal financial creditor, surpassing the World Bank, the Export-Import Bank of the United States (U.S. Eximbank) and the Inter-American Development Bank (Pautasso 2018).

In terms of DFI, in 2016 China channeled US$216.424 billion abroad, a historical record for the country that represented 10.75 percent of the year's global money flows (World Bank 2017). By the mid-2010s, the LAC region became the second most important destination for Chinese investments, receiving 13.3 percent of the total—followed by Europe (5.5 percent), North America (4.5 percent), Oceania (3.5 percent), and Africa (3.2 percent), and surpassed only by Asia (70.1 percent) (Roldán et al. 2016).

China's prioritization of investment in LAC countries was in full swing during the region's "left turn" period. However, from a geo-economic perspective this investment is not explained by political affinities, but rather by China's intent to procure natural resources required for its national interests. This is evident from the fact that China's DFI in the region is concentrated mainly in the exploration and extraction of natural resources (Lin 2013). In a recent breakdown of LAC countries' exports to China, a concentration of 73 percent is observed in products classifiable as strategic: refined copper, oil, copper and its concentrates, iron and its concentrates, soybeans, scrap metal, fish meal, wood, and sugar (CEPAL 2012).

In this context, China's geo-economic strategy can also be seen in the deployment of financing to the LAC region, where these monetary flows (beyond satisfying the market logic that seeks a return on capital) can be explained by China's needs: to generate the necessary infrastructure conditions for the exploration, exploitation, and commercialization of natural resources (Lin 2013); and to increase its capacity to impose negotiation conditions in ways that favor its geopolitical preferences (for example, credits tied to guaranteed shipments of strategic resources like oil).

This study concludes that China's geo-economic presence not only generates benefits in the service of its own national interests but also has generated win-win opportunities for the LAC region. Some countries have benefited from increased exports and access to financing. During the 2000–2010 period, Brazil, Chile, Peru, Cuba, and Costa Rica covered part of China's increased demand for raw materials. During the same period, China became the primary market for exports from Brazil and Chile, and the second-largest market for exports from Peru, Cuba, and Costa Rica (CEPAL 2015). Since 2005, Venezuela, Brazil, Argentina, and Ecuador have received large Chinese loans for infrastructure projects (Roldán et al. 2016), although the social and environmental impact of these projects has been strongly questioned (Teijlingen et al. 2017). Indeed, as contributors to this volume such as Fernández-Salvador and Viteri, Molina and Munduruku, Felipe and Costa, as well as van Teijlingen and Hidalgo Bastidas all explore, the lack of even minimal socioecological impact mitigation helped produce what Vásconez convincingly describes as preventable disaster.

CHINESE FINANCING AND DIRECT FOREIGN INVESTMENT IN ECUADOR: INTEREST-BASED PERSPECTIVES

Relations between China and Ecuador intensified when the countries mated the implementation of China's Stepping Out strategy (2001) with the policies of former president Rafael Correa (2007–2017) (Reyes and Chun Lee 2017). This period of intensified political-diplomatic relations saw a substantial increase in Chinese economic deployment in Ecuador in the areas of DFI and financing.

Almost all of China's DFI in Ecuador was concentrated in mines and quarries. During the 2000–2017 period, this sector received US$780 million (92 percent of the total)—followed by business support services (3.85 percent) and construction (2.11 percent).

Despite the arrival of a new president in 2017 and the strong disapproval from social sectors (primarily Indigenous groups and environmentalists) (Yasunidos Guapondélig Collective, this volume; Pullaguari, this volume; Flores, Carpio, and Gutiérrez Guevara, this volume), Chinese DFI in Ecuador continued to focus on mining. In July 2019, Ecuador's minister of energy announced a new large-scale mining project. Under this concession, the Chinese company EcuaCorriente S.A. (ECSA) is now mining the El Mirador copper deposit in Tundayme, thought to be among the twenty largest such deposits in the world. With a DFI of US$1.348 billion, ECSA expects to exploit the deposit for twenty-five years and export the copper to China. Between royalties and taxes, the Ecuadorian government expects to receive US$2.250 billion from the El Mirador concession (*El Universo* 2019).

In view of the foregoing data and geo-economic theoretical considerations, it is apparent that China's FDI in Ecuador has been used as a tool to fulfill its geopolitical objectives. Considering that its domestic copper production does not satisfy its demand, China's acquisition of Ecuadorian mining resources is clearly in the service of the country's commercial and military industrial requirements (Chicaiza 2014).

Beyond its consistency with China's geopolitical objectives for the LAC region, as analyzed by Lin (2013), this argument is also corroborated by the official policies set forth in China's tenth Five-Year Plan for the 2001–2005 period (Torres and Sanborn 2009).

It cannot be ignored that the Stepping Out geo-economic strategy thus primarily serves the interests of the Chinese state—a reality confirmed by the fact that the institutions channeling Chinese capital flows are state owned. The operator of the El Mirador copper deposit, ECSA, for example, is owned by CRCC-Tongguan Investment, which in turn is jointly owned by Chinese public companies (Chicaiza 2014).

Likewise, in financing, China has become Ecuador's largest creditor. In 2017, Ecuador received thirteen new Chinese loans, increasing its total Chinese debt to US$17.4 billion (Gallagher and Myers 2017) and reaching fourth place among LAC countries on the same measure. Ecuador began receiving Chinese loans in 2010, again tying former president Correa's development policy with China's strategy of international projection. The loans have mainly been directed toward energy projects such as hydroelectric plants and renewable energy; infrastructure, for example transportation, highways, roads, and urban streets; education and health projects such as the construction of schools, universities and hospitals; and discretionary credits used to finance Ecuador's fiscal deficit.

As has been the case with its reception of Chinese DFI, Ecuador has continued to avail itself of Chinese financing against strong societal objections and despite current president Lenín Moreno's neoliberal policy reversals. In 2018, for example, Ecuador borrowed US$900 million from the China Development Bank under the minister of economics and finance's justification—in response to widespread criticism of both China and the International Monetary Fund—that if the loan conditions are favorable, Ecuador should not "demonize" any source of financing.[3]

Within the geo-economic framework, it can be observed that the channeling of financial capital to Ecuador also serves China's geopolitical interests. In view of observations made by Lin (2013), it is thus notable that Chinese loans in Ecuador have been directed toward the development of the infrastructure that facilitates the exploitation, extraction, and commercialization of natural resources. The development of hydroelectric plants, for example, provides the energy required for the exploitation of natural resources; likewise, the development of highways, roads, and streets helps transport the same resources. While it is true that China's financing has not imposed conditions that directly interfere with Ecuador's national sovereignty or domestic politics, it is also true that China has conditioned its loans in a way that guarantees the country's ongoing receipt of strategic resources from Ecuador, particularly oil (Chicaiza 2014). China has also included conditions that have provoked questions as to the relationship's overall favorability.

In his analysis of the cooperation between the two countries, Castro (Castro 2014) concluded that hydroelectric projects developed with Chinese financing and technical support show unfavorable asymmetries in terms of benefits for Ecuador. China has enjoyed profits of 6–7 percent in financing, payment in the form of presold oil shipments, and lucrative contracts (which stipulate the use of Chinese labor and technology) to develop and build hydroelectric infrastructure.

Questions have not only been raised about the conditions attached to Chinese loans, but also about the socioenvironmental impact of Chinese construction in Ecuador. In 2019 structural problems were discovered at the Chinese-built Coca Codo Sinclair (CCS) hydroelectric project,[4] which carried the risk of plant failure (Miranda 2019). Moreover, the February 2020 sinkhole-related disappearance of the downstream San Rafael waterfall has been attributed to regressive erosion processes in the Coca River basin that have been accelerated by the CCS project's operations. A second, related landslide caused the rupture of three petroleum pipelines—which has seriously impacted the Ecuadorian economy and necessitated preventive measures that will require substantial investment (Gonzáles 2020; Fernández-Salvador and Viteri, this volume; Vásconez, this volume).

Despite these questions, from a win-win perspective Ecuador has benefited from China's deployment of DFI and financing. Through Chinese DFI, for example, Ecuador has managed to obtain a substantial supply of capital for mining investments. Because this frees Ecuador from having to tap its own scarce mining budget, and because the country now receives substantial income, royalties, and taxes from China's extraction of metallic minerals, Ecuador's economy has grown, allowing the government to focus its budget on other priority items. Chinese mining investments also generate employment for the Ecuadorian population.

Whereas China's financial supply allowed the Correa administration to obtain resources in service of its ambitious public investment policy, Chinese financing during the current Moreno administration is now allowing Ecuador to partially cover its budget deficit. Here, it is important to note that Ecuador is presently facing serious budgetary problems. Since taking office, President Moreno has had to adjust public spending to mitigate this predicament. To prevent further cuts and cover the remainder of the deficit, the administration has had no alternative but to seek external financing.

This problem is currently exacerbated by the COVID-19 pandemic, which has caused a partial paralysis of economic activities and therefore a decrease in tax revenues, a reduction in exports, and a drop in the price of oil. These and other issues contributed to the employment crisis described by Delgado del Hierro in this volume. The injection of external resources into a dollarized Ecuadorian economy has thus become a priority. It will be interesting to observe how China chooses to address the possibility of channeling its monetary reserves to countries most affected by this global crisis, perhaps through a Marshall Plan–type reconstruction program—which could conceivably be integrated with its existing Belt and Road Initiative.

CONCLUSIONS

Despite the shifting political affinities between China and Ecuador, there remains a basic set of compatible interests and potential benefits that can work to serve both states in their respective efforts to ensure continued subsistence and growth. This analysis therefore regards as tangential the shifting perspectives or political trends in Ecuador's attitude toward Chinese relations and finds that bilateral relations with the Asian country can be favorable for Ecuador, so long as they are based on pragmatic concepts and objective win-win opportunities.

Finally, it is important to recognize that, as the balance has tended to tip in favor of China, the benefits derived from the relationship have not been symmetrical. To balance it in the direction of a true win-win scenario, Ecuador must improve its capacities for effective administration and negotiation—with due regard for China's interests, as well as its own economic, social, and environmental realities.

NOTES

1. Ellis, *El impacto de China en Ecuador y America Latina*.

2. These were some of the principal developers of geopolitical theory see (Cuéllar 2012; Ratzel 1983).

3. It should also be noted that during his December 2018 visit to China, President Moreno signed a memorandum of understanding formally joining Ecuador to the Belt and Road Initiative (China's 2013 global infrastructure development strategy) (*El Comercio* 2018).

4. The project was designed and built by Sinohydro Corporation, a Chinese state-owned hydropower engineering and construction company.

REFERENCES

Blackwill, Robert, and Jennifer Harris. 2016. *War by Other Means: Geoeconomics and Statecraft*. London: Cambridge.

Castro, D. 2014. "'Cooperación energética' China-Ecuador: ¿Una relación de mutuos beneficios?" Master's thesis, Universidad Andina Simón Bolívar.

CEPAL. 2012. *China América Latina y el Caribe: hacia una relación económica y comercial estratégica*. Santiago: Naciones Unidas.

CEPAL. 2015. *Foreign Direct Investment in Latin America and the Caribbean*. Santiago: Naciones Unidas.

Chicaiza, G. 2014. *Mineras chinas en Ecuador: nueva dependencia*. Quito: Acción ecológica.

El Comercio. 2018 "Ecuador vuelve a financiarse con China luego de once meses." December 12, 2018. https://www.elcomercio.com/actualidad/negocios/ecuador-financiamiento-china-credito-finanzas.html.

Costa, W. M. 1992. *Geografia política e geopolítica. discurso sobre o territ ório e o poder.* São Paulo: Edusp/Hucitec.

Cuéllar, Rubén. 2012. "Geopolítica. Origen del concepto y su evolución." *Revista de Relaciones Internacionales de la UNAM.* México.

Ellis, Robert. 2009. *El impacto de China en Ecuador y America Latina.* Quito: FLACSO.

Gallagher, E. 2010. "La estrategia del "Go Out." Buenos Aires: Consejo Argentino para las Relaciones Internacionales.

Gallagher, K., and M. Myers. 2017. "China–Latin America Finance Database." Washington: Inter-American Dialogue.

Gallagher, K. P., A. Irwin and K. Kolesli, 2013. "¿Un mejor trato? Análisis comparativo de los préstamos chinos en América Latina." Cuadernos de Trabajo del Cechimex no. 19 (January–February 2013).

Gonzáles, Mario Alexis. 2020. "Coca Codo Sinclair, el principal sospechoso de la erosión en el río Coca."*Primicias,* April 27, 2020. https://www.primicias.ec/noticias/economia/erosion-rio-coca-coca-codo-sinclair/.

Harvey, David. 2007. *Breve historia del neoliberalismo.* Madrid: Akal.

Jiang, S. 2014. *Chinese Investment in the EU.* Beijing: Institute of European Studies, Chinese Academy of Social Sciences.

Lin, Yue. 2013. *Inversión extranjera directa de China en América Latina.* México: UNAM.

Miranda, Boris. 2019. "Coca Codo Sinclair: los problemas de la multimillonaria represa que China construyó en Ecuador." *BBC News Mundo,* February 25, 2019. https://www.bbc.com/mundo/noticias-america-latina-47144338.

OCDE/CEPAL/CAF. 2015. *Perspectivas económicas de América Latina 2016: Hacia una nueva asociación con China.* Paris: OECD Publishing.

Pautasso, D. 2018. "China y la nueva arquitectura financiera mundial." Recuperado el October 8. http://www.globaldev.blog/es/blog/ Globaldev.

Ratzel, F. J. 1983. "A Relação entre o Solo, a Sociedade e o Estado." *Revista do Departamento de Geografia* no. 2: 92–101.

Reyes, M., and P. Chun Lee. 2017. *La relación China-Ecuador en el siglo XXI: elementos relevantes para la discusión.* Quito: Instituto de Altos Estudios Nacionales.

Reyes, Milton. 2018. "La proyección política de la República Popular China: El caso Sudamérica, 2002–2015." PhD diss, Instituto de Economia da Universidade Federal—Rio de Janeiro.

Reyes, Milton. 2017. "La relación de la República Popular China y América del Sur: Una mirada desde la EPI Crítica." *Revista de estudos críticos asiáticos—Revista Leste Vermelho* 3, no. 1.

Roldán, Adriana, Alma Castro, Camilo Pérez, Pablo Echavarría, and Robert Ellis. 2016. *La presencia de China en América Latina.* Bogotá: Centro de Estudios Asia Pacífico de la Universidad EAFIT.

Stoessel, Soledad. 2014. "Giro a la izquierda en la América Latina del siglo XXI." *Polis* 39. http://journals.openedition.org/polis/10453.

Teijlingen, K, E Leifsen, C Fernández, and L Sánchez. 2017. *La Amazonía Minada: Minería a gran escala y conflictos en el Sur del Ecuador.* Quito: Abya-Yala / Universidad San Francisco de Quito USFQ.

Torres, Víctor, and Cynthia Sanborn. 2009. *La economía China y las industrias extractivas: desafíos para el Perú.* Lima: Universidad del Pacífico.

El Universo. 2019. "Ecuador comienza explotación minera a gran escala con el proyecto Mirador en Zamora Chinchipe." July 18, 2019. https://www.eluniverso .com/noticias/2019/07/18/nota/7430958/ecuador-comienza-explotacion-minera -gran-escala-proyecto-mirador/.

Valencia, M. 2008. *La cooperación Sur-Sur del gobierno de la República Popular China como mecanismo de Ayuda Oficial al Desarrollo en el Ecuador.* Cuenca: Universidad del Azuay.

World Bank. 2017. "Foreign Direct Investment, Net Outflows (BoP, Current US$)—China." https://data.worldbank.org/indicator/BM.KLT.DINV. CD.WD?locations=CN.

PART 2
INDIGENOUS EPISTEMOLOGIES AND MAROON MODERNITIES

An Indigenous Theory of Risk: The Cosmopolitan Munduruku Analyze Chinese Megaprojects at Tapajós–Teles Pires

Luísa Pontes Molina and Alessandra Korap
Silva Mudukuru

INTRODUCTION

Heads of state or corporate executives see the Amazon and its waterways as vague abstractions when, in fact, these forest lands represent the means and cosmos of the Native peoples of the region. The lives and lifeways of these peoples are thrown into risk whenever "enterprises" are planned for the lands they inhabit, as Hendler and Camoça, and Oliveira have shown in this volume in non-Native contexts in the Amazon. Over the last ten years, the Munduruku people have seen several threats advance against the region they have occupied for at least the past four centuries. These include dams, waterway expansions, ports, roads, and railways composing a mosaic of projects that put the Tapajós and Teles Pires watersheds (and all who depend on them) at risk. The following essay discusses these risks and the destruction that comes with them from the point of view of the Munduruku, particularly their cosmopolitical view of these "enterprises."

We begin by presenting this mosaic of threats, revealing its composition at different scales, and how it involves both local political arrangements and the characteristics of life in these places. As Fernando Brancoli and Wander Guerra (this volume) remind us, Chinese investments in Brazil amounted to US$8.8 billion. With the rise to power of the far-right Bolsonaro government, however, and the worsening Brazilian economic crisis, Chinese strategies toward Brazil changed: "With the arrival of diplomats who are younger and aligned with the 'wolf warrior' style of leadership, China's diplomatic performance has become more mediatized and assertive," as well as willing to directly deal with agents of power at the regional, state, and even municipal levels. "It is important to understand that this is not a question of replacing the strategic actors with whom Beijing is engaged, but in engaging with a wide range of agents who have the capacity to meet China's strategic objectives (Brancoli and Guerra, this volume, 370).

While Chinese capital has been concentrated along the Rio–São Paulo axis, Maria Elena Rodríguez's chapter demonstrates that the Chinese have also vigorously moved into Brazil's energy sector in the Amazon, constructing transmission lines and hydroelectric dams. No foreign presence in the Amazon has been as strong and broad as the Chinese presence today. The Amazon is strategic: the "vital space of the 21st Century" (Amin 2015, 17), due not only to its huge stock of natural resources but also to the wide-open opportunities the region offers. In the new international dynamic, the Amazon has become a center of attention in the search for the resources needed to keep the global economy growing. (Rodríguez, this volume).

Our second section will comment on the specific damage caused by two hydroelectric plants on the Teles Pires River (one of them the UHE São Manoel, which has China Three Gorges Corporation [CTG] among its principal shareholders) on the sacred places and objects of the Munduruku people. Finally, we will show how these damages are linked to a Munduruku theory of risk and destruction, which animates their cosmopolitical criticism of other logistics and hydroelectric projects currently advancing over their territories.

PROGRESS AND ITS DEATH PROJECTS

Along the road that leads to the Praia do Índio Indigenous Reserve, where Alessandra was born and grew up, one can see successive signs of the "progress" that is taking over the city of Itaituba: a new residential subdivision is announced with seductive imagery; hotels and mansions boast impressive facades and well-paved access roads (in frank contrast to the bumpy asphalt that is the norm throughout the municipality); transport companies occupy large portions of the Tapajós's river bank with their heavy machinery, ferries, boats, and other working vessels.

Less than two decades ago, the landscape was different. There were still large portions of forest on the outskirts of Praia do Índio, where the Munduruku, who reside there, could find raw materials for their traditional crafts, buildings, and home remedies. Alessandra's generation, today's adults, is at an impasse: without access to the forest, how can they teach younger Munduruku to manufacture handicrafts? How can they teach them to fish, if they risk being run over by the soybeans barges that scrape by the banks of Praia do Índio?

The city rapidly advances over and around the Indigenous reserve. And "progress" and "development" is not just about the city and reserve: it takes in the entire region. Currently, Tapajós is considered "one of the high-risk speculation frontiers of the most frantic expansion yet in the Brazilian Amazon" (Aguiar 2017, 12). The fronts of this expansion are many. Although Indigenous and riverside peoples' resistance managed to interrupt the licensing of the São Luiz do Tapajós dam due to lack of prior consultation, the project has already been included in the investment plans of CTG. This and other hydroelectric dams in the Tapajós Complex are a source of concern (Alarcon et al., 2016). Mining is also advancing across the region. In addition to gold and diamond mining—the main drivers of the economy of the middle and upper Tapajós, which already puts demands on the fragility of protected areas[1]—large mining companies have moved into southwest Pará, targeting Munduruku lands (Angelo 2020).

The Wuyjuyū (as they call themselves) have been Tupi-speaking (Munduruku family) inhabitants of the Tapajós basin since time immemorial. The coauthor of this chapter, Alessandra Korap Silva Mundukuru, is a member of the Wuyjuyū. Their documented presence stretches back to at least the second half of the eighteenth century (Rocha 2017). Today, the Munduruku number about fifteen thousand people living in the states of Amazonas, Mato Grosso, and Pará. It is in the last that most of the population is concentrated, distributed throughout the Indigenous reserves of Praia do Índio and Praia do Mangue (within the urban perimeter of Itaituba), in the Sawre Bapim and Sawre Muybu Indigenous Lands (TIs) (in the middle Tapajós), in the Munduruku and Sai Cinza TIs (upper Tapajós), and in the Kayabi TI (lower Teles Pires). Two of these areas—Sawre Muybu and Sawre Bapim—have not yet been formally recognized by the Brazilian government as Indigenous lands. Legal and administrative apparatuses allow such recognition, and several technical studies have been conducted that prove that the Munduruku have traditionally[2] occupied these lands. It not bureaucratic obstacles or the land's supposedly recent occupation by the Munduruku that has placed the legal recognition of these two TIs on indefinite hold. The apparent inability of the Brazilian state to recognize the Indigenous lands is the result of a complex game of political chess, susceptible to all sorts of arrangements between various powers of the executive branch, pressures from the private sector on the legislative and judiciary branches, and the persistent advances of foreign investors (Molina 2018).

Part of this chess game is the pressure from projects that aimed at exporting agricultural commodities in the Tapajós region. During the 2020 COVID-19 pandemic, the National Land Transport Agency (ANTT) granted a right of way for the Ferrogrão, a railway project aimed at facilitating the flow of soybeans and corn from the center-west of the country to the north (and from there to the Atlantic), connecting Sinop (MT) to the ports of Miritituba in the district of Itaituba (PA). Despite the persistent opposition from Indigenous and traditional communities directly affected by the project,[3] ANTT approved the grant, the technical studies, and public notice and contract drafts by Ferrogrão, forwarding these to the Ministry of Infrastructure (Agência Nacional de Transportes Terrestres 2020). The federal government expected the public notice to be launched in late 2019. In May of the same year, Minister of Agriculture Tereza Cristina met with potential Chinese investors in Shanghai who had shown "interest in railway projects such as Ferrogrão," according to the Brazilian government (Governo Federal 2020).

It is not surprising that potential financiers were anticipating this project, considering the history of Chinese insertion in the Amazon, China's relationships with Brazilian agribusiness (De Assis and da Silva 2020; Escher, Wilkinson, and Pereira 2018; Aguiar 2017; De Oliveira 2015), and remembering the previous involvement of Chinese companies in railroad projects in Brazil. We are referring here to the giant Bioceânica (or Transoceânica) route, which integrates with Ferrogrão and other railroads into the Logistics Investment Program. Subject to an agreement between the governments of Brazil, Peru, and China in 2014 and 2015, Bioceânica had its viability confirmed by the China Railway Eryuan Engineering Group in 2016 (Aguiar 2017, 43). Both railroad projects aim to fill a supposed gap in multimodal logistics corridors in Brazil. In the case of Tapajós, the railway joins a series of projects such as the construction of at least twenty port terminals (to add to the five already in operation (Cardoso Rodrigues 2018), industrial waterways (Tapajós–Teles Pires), and paved roads.

Private port terminals help to visualize the complexity of the capital relations involved, interweaving three of the largest trading companies in the agricultural sector (the North American Bunge and Cargill and the French Louis Dreyfus Commodities), joint ventures involving Chinese capital (Cianport), an Algerian steel and agribusiness giant (Cevital), Mato Grosso companies (Ammagi), and a publicly traded private company (Hidrovias do Brasil SA), which have channeled investments from the International Finance Corporation (the corporate arm of the World Bank), the National Bank for Economic and Social Development, and other financial organizations (Aguiar 2017, 13–14).

HYDROELECTRIC DAMS IN TELES PIRES AND THE "DEATH OF THE SPIRIT"

Given all this, it is no wonder that Indigenous leaders like Alessandra lie awake at night: it is the future of their communities that is at stake. It is the very possibility of persevering in their uniqueness, living according to their culture, that is being called into question. The Munduruku people see the arrival of the projects listed above as what they call *death projects*[4]: works that directly or indirectly affect their territories and lives, promoting effects in complex chains of events and among nonhuman beings, putting Indigenous people and their communities at risk not only in terms of their physical integrity but also endangering the world of spirits and the organization of the cosmos. This is what *development* and *enterprise* often mean when seen from the Munduruku point of view.

In April 2013, during the construction of the Teles Pires Hydroelectric Plant (HPP), which would transform a stretch of the left bank of Teles Pires river (on the border between the states of Pará and Mato Grosso) into a reservoir, the Seven Falls Rapids (Karobixexe, following Munduruku toponymy) were dynamited, submerging a Munduruku sacred site. Karobixexe was "a place where you shouldn't move," according to the "Kayabi, Apiaká and Munduruku Manifesto Against Hydroelectric Developments on the Teles Pires River" (Agência Nacional de Águas 2011). This 2011 document explains the seriousness of the threats to the sacred places along the Teles Pires, calling on the Federal Public Ministry (MPF) to insist upon the imperative need for large development projects to consult Indigenous peoples. This imperative was overwhelmed by pressure from agents interested in completing the dam's works at any cost. National and international legislation that insists upon free, prior, and informed consultation with affected communities was ignored in this rush. A judicial decision in favor of the Indigenous peoples' demands was delivered only after the dam had already been built—that is, too late.[5] "How can we give up our rights, our sacred places, like Seven Falls Rapids, Jabuti Hill and Macaco Hill?" ask the Indigenous peoples in the manifesto mentioned above. "What would the white man say if we built our villages on top of their properties, their sanctuaries, their cemeteries?"

This is not a mere allegory: in addition to housing funerary urns (*itiğ'a*, which were removed without any authorization by the Munduruku), Karobixexe was a central place in the cosmography of this people. Its rapids were a portal where the souls of the dead went. In addition, it was there that the fish reproduced and where the spirit of the *mother of fish* and *mother of game* lived: matrices of abundance and sources of life from which the main foods of Indigenous communities ultimately come. With the destruction of the rapids, the matrices were also destroyed and the posthumous destination of Munduruku spirits disintegrated. "We had this sacred place and when I died I would go there," said elder Krixi Biwün to Torres and Branford. "But as the government is now dynamiting everything, we will end even in spirit. We will die in spirit, too" (de Oliveira 2014; Torres and Branford 2017).

Only one of the sacred places mentioned in the manifesto has survived the onslaught of the dams along the Teles Pires. Like the Seven Falls, Macaco Hill (Dekoka'a) was dynamited despite the open and vocal opposition of the Indigenous people. The destruction of this place (where the spirits watched over Karobixexe) took place in 2014 during the construction of the Manoel dam, an "enterprise" conducted by EDP Brasil SA, Furnas Centrais Elétricas and CTG.[6] The target of seven MPF civil suits due to the various illegalities that took place in its environmental licensing process, the HPP was built less than 1 km away from the Kayabi Indigenous Land without properly consulting the Kayabi, Apyaká, and Munduruku who reside there. To guarantee the progress of the works, the consortium responsible for the dam legally suspended parts of the oversight process. Legal decisions such as these have been criticized for having made possible the unilateral implementation of megaprojects along Amazonian rivers (Oliveira and Vieira 2016).

On January 19, 2018, the São Manoel dam was authorized to begin commercial operations. This authorization took place less than a month after the MPF filed suit requesting an injunction to suspend the plant's operating license, claiming that the project was proceeding under its own legal regime, disconnected from its socioenvironmental implications. The reason for the suit was noncompliance with several stages of the environmental licensing process, including the so-called Indigenous component, by the dam's construction company. But it was not only in the legal and administrative spheres that São Manoel overran the opposition of Indigenous peoples. The beginning of the plant's operations crowned a succession of episodes in a conflict between the Munduruku (who had already suffered four years of violations) and Empresa Energia São Manoel (EESM) and the Companhia Hidrelétrica Teles Pires (CHTP). The MPF and Funai (Brazil's Indian Affairs bureaucracy) acted as mediators in this conflict, but in a political context that was becoming increasingly unfavorable to the Indigenous peoples (Molina 2020). In July 2007, a group of two hundred Munduruku men, women, and children occupied the São Manoel construction site for five days in intense cold, after crossing hundreds of kilometers over several days in crowded outboard boats. Installing themselves without interrupting the activities of workers, the Indigenous people demanded recovery of the funerary urns, which the CHTP maintained in a museum in Alta Floresta (MT). They also demanded remedial measures for the damages suffered from the destruction of Karobixexe and Dekoka'a, in addition to an apology from EESM and CHTP (Roach 2020).

The end of the occupation came about through an agreement for the transfer of the *itiğ'a* to Munduruku territory. An audience was also scheduled to discuss the impacts of the two hydroelectric dams and the demands of the Munduruku. This was to be held at Missão Cururu, a village located in the township of Jacareacanga, about 1,700 kilometers distant from Belém, the state capital. Only the MPF attended this meeting in September 2017. FUNAI did not send any representatives. The companies not only failed to send representatives but sent letters to the MPF, denying that they could be held responsible for the damage caused to the Indigenous people and refusing to apologize. Nor did they return the burial urns, as agreed. A month later, the Munduruku moved again on the São Manoel dam. They were received with crowd control bombs launched by the National Force for Public Security (FNSP). Responding to a request from the EESM, the

FNSP remained on guard at the construction site until the completion of the dam to prevent Indigenous peoples from approaching it again. As a result, the Munduruku were unable to perform the necessary rituals to calm the spirits—something of vital importance not only for the Munduruku but, as their shamans explained (Munduruku 2017), for the balance of the cosmos.

Two more years passed before the Munduruku were finally able to recover the *itiğ'a*. In December 2019, they again faced the long and difficult journey to Alta Floresta, under the guidance of their shamans—who had for many years been listening to disgruntled and sad spirits demanding to leave the museum where they were being held. Mobilizing warriors, men, women, and children from the upper and middle Tapajós and from the lower Teles Pires, they occupied the Natural History Museum. On Christmas Day 2019, they decided to rescue the *itiğ'a*. "We can no longer leave the spirits there. They complain about the cold, about the city, and they take revenge on us because we are not protecting them," explained one of the shamans to Loures and Moreira. The researchers also say that the Indigenous people spotted CHTP and EESM airplanes monitoring them during the five days they traveled along the Teles Pires River to Alta Floresta. They also spotted drones flying over the vicinity of the São Manoel dam (Loures and Moreira 2020).

In many ways, today the Munduruku are in the same position as the Ecuadoran Shuar, described by Jefferson Pullaguari in this volume:

> At present, we are left with no alternative but to continue adapting to local, national, and global economic transformations, under the banner of defending the few territories that have allowed us not to disappear as an ancestral Indigenous nationality and still remain in our custody—as we wait for the day when existing provisions of international and national laws on Indigenous peoples and nationalities finally translate into an equitable reality. (135)

COSMOPOLITICS OF DESTRUCTION

The seriousness of the violation of the Munduruku's sacred places and their *itiğ'a* is immeasurable for that people. If we try to translate our worldview to the *Pariwat* (non-Indigenous peoples), we center the Munduruku point of view in our conversations, so we together—Indigenous and non-Indigenous—can begin to have a more accurate understanding of the gravity of these offenses. Instead of seeing Karobixexe and Dekoka'a as (simply) geological formations, we must reconsider them ontologically. They are the abodes of spirits, places animated by nonhuman subjectivities, connected to each other since mythical times. This is a question of material and immaterial world heritage and intellectual property (Strathern 2009). In this sense (and following Stengers's proposition [2018]) we suggest that a cosmopolitical critique of "enterprises" such as hydroelectric plants is what is needed. For in addition to disrespecting the right to prior consultation, running over Munduruku traditions, and damaging the material and immaterial heritage (Stengers 2018) of that people, the violations promoted in the name of building dams have left Natives more susceptible to retaliation by the spirits. Let us explain.

There is a dynamic and subtle balance between human and nonhuman socialities, their spheres and spaces, in Munduruku cosmology. If the homes, objects, and memories of the spirits are maintained in one place and the circulation and lives of the Indigenous living are set off in another, this balance can be managed. Respecting the imperative of *not touching sacred places and objects* implies maintaining the necessary distance between the world of humans and that of spirits. Both are involved with the physical body of the land and susceptible to what happens to it; both are susceptible to each other's actions. If this imperative is followed to its logical end, then the spirits can become angry and cause accidents, victimizing the Munduruku. They do this since it is the Munduruku who have overseen the protection of sacred places and the care of the spirits.

> It is a time of death. The Munduruku will begin to die. They will have accidents and even the simplest of accidents will kill a Munduruku. Lightning will fall and kill Indians. The Indian will be working his garden patch and a branch will fall on his head. It's not for nothing that the branch fell on his head. A sharp point of the branch will pierce the Indian who goes hunting. And it is all because the government messed around with that sacred spot. (Torres and Branford 2017)

Two Munduruku women died of lightning strikes in 2019 in Alto Tapajós because of the violations of the sacred places and the *itig̃'a*. In our own ethnographic research along the Middle Tapajós, we also heard about "accidents" caused by spirits who were out for revenge. These included a child almost choking to death on a fish bone after certain clay containers, belonging to the *spirits of the fish*, were removed from the riverbed by miners. The child managed to save herself after being rushed to the shaman, who explained what had occurred. Reports of "accidents" like these and warnings like those mentioned above are common, not only among the Munduruku, but also among other Amazonian peoples.

Everything happens as if the worlds of the living and dead, the human and non-human, were mutually permeable and as if there was a reciprocal susceptibility between the Munduruku, the spirits, and the land. *Land* is understood here not only as the soil, subsoil, vegetation, *igarapés* (creeks and tributary streams), and river, but also the land as a home and the very bedrock of life for the beings that inhabit it. The land keeps the memories and marks of the past and of mythical times. The land is what the community establishes itself upon and from which relatives can nourish one another. The land bears fruit and thereby allows future generations to come into the world (Molina 2017; Coelho de Souza et al. 2017). It is even possible to state with some degree of certainty (considering both the accumulation of ethnological production in the South American lowlands and Indigenous discourses over the last decades) that the quality of a community's connection with the land and its cohabitants (the condition that what we call, somewhat allegorically, *reciprocal susceptibility*) is a general feature of Indigenous socialities.

Ailton Krenak (2020) tells us that "life is this crossing of the living organism with the earth in an immaterial dimension. . . . Think about life crossing mountains, valleys . . . life, which we have trivialized as if it were just a word." Indigenous thinking illuminates and expands unforeseen aspects of the concept and experience of life for us. In turn, shamanic initiation illuminates and expands the thinking of Indigenous peoples (Konepawa and Albert 2015). What are the consequences of this expansion for the way in which we face the "impacts" of "enterprises" such as the Teles Pires hydroelectric dam, or the *death projects* that are now advancing across the Tapajós? If life is lived by Indigenous people as in this crossing of which Ailton Krenak speaks, in which the diverse beings that inhabit the land and the land itself (and its rivers, and the rapids) in their multiple aspects are mutually implicated, any "model" of gauging impacts that dispenses with the Indigenous theory of life is at the very least ineffective (if not deliberately negligent). There are more beings and powers that could die or suffer damage from "enterprises" than dreamt of in our modern ontology, to paraphrase Shakespeare. Much more is at risk, and this risk is linked to chains of causality that are different from ours. This shift in perspective is fundamental. To not undertake it when evaluating "impacts" (by employing models in which there is no place for exiled spirits, for example) is to perpetuate a colonial relationship with the collectives impacted by "enterprises." It is to invoke a deeply colonial sovereign right to consider who (and what) shall die, and what (or who) should live.[7]

NOTES

1. This is a markedly complex issue in terms of its sociopolitical and economic dynamics in which it is involved and which it engenders. It is also deeply rooted the region's history. Analyzing it is thus beyond the scope of the present work. However, we point to an unmistakable sign of the problems involved with this activity at the present time: the proliferation of illegal gold mines in the region, many of which have even obtained illegal mining permits. The gravity of the issue has even mobilized the Federal Public Ministry.

2. The 1988 Federal Constitution, with regard to the duties of the Brazilian state, demarcates those lands traditionally occupied by Indigenous peoples and guaranteeing said peoples exclusive usufructuary rights to those lands (Cunha 2018; Rocha 2017). For archeological perspectives regarding Native occupation of the middle Tapajós, see Rocha 2017; Loures 2017; and Honorato de Oliveira 2015. Regarding the conflict around land ownership and the TI Sawre Muybu, see Loures 2017 and Molina 2020.

3. See, for example, the letter written by sixteen Indigenous peoples of the Xingu Indigenous Territory, represented by the Associação Terra Indígena do Xingu, along with two organizations from the Mebemgokrê people (Instituto Kabu and Instituto Raoni) and one from the Panará people, as well as the Associação Indígena Moygu (Ikpeng Community) and the Instituto Socioambiental (ISA). This letter was sent to several institutions linked to the project's potential financers: the China Construction Bank, the Chinese Embassy, and the Consumers Goods Forum, among others (Instituto Socioambiental 2018).

4. Italicized words are usually Native categories. Sometimes words are italicized for emphasis. The difference between the two usages should be self-evident.

5. On May 12, 2016, the Tribunal Regional Federal da 1ª Região ordered the undertaking of prior consultations with Indigenous peoples. This was considered to be a "posthumous consultation" by those who researched the case, given that sacred spaces had already been destroyed by the project in question and their effects (along with the dam's other impacts) were already being felt (Brasil de Fato 2016).

6. Cada acionista detém 33,333% da UHE São Manoel. A porcentagem da CTG é dividida com a EDP Brasil.

7. The allusion to Mbembe (2018) here is deliberate. It is in this sense that we have argued in favor of considering the damage promoted by hydroelectric projects and other *death projects* as genocide (Molina 2017).

REFERENCES

Agência Nacional de Águas. 2011. "Manifesto kayabi, apiaká e munduruku contra os aproveitamentos hidrelétricos no rio teles pires," Agência Nacional de Águas, 7 December 2011. http://www3.ana.gov.br/portal/ANA/noticias-antigas/manifesto-kayabi-apiaka-e-munduruku-contra-os.2019-03-15.0424022687.

Agência Nacional de Transportes Terrestres. 2020. "ANTT aprova Plano de Outorga da Ferrogrão." July, 9, 2020. http://www.antt.gov.br/salaImprensa/noticias/arquivos/2020/07/ANTT_aprova_Plano_de_Outorga_da_Ferrograo.html.

Aguiar, Diana. 2017. *A geopolítica de infraestrutura da China na América do Sul: um estudo a partir do caso do Tapajós na Amazônia brasileira*. Rio de Janeiro: Fase, Actionaid.

Alarcon, Daniela F., Brent Millikan, and Maurídio Torres, eds. 2016. *Ocekadi: hidrelétricas, conflitos socioambientais e resistência na Bacia do Tapajós*. Brasília e Santarém: International Rivers, Programa de Antropologia e Arqueologia da Universidade Federal do Oeste do Pará.

Amin, Mario Miguel. 2015. "A Amazônia na geopolítica mundial dos recursos estratégicos do século," *Revista Crítica de Ciências Sociais* 107 (September): 17–38.

Angelo, Maurício. 2020 "Mineradora inglesa Anglo American quer explorar terras indígenas na Amazônia." *Mongabay*, March 20, 2020. https://brasil.mongabay.com/2020/03/mineradora-inglesa-anglo-american-quer-explorar-terras-indigenas-na-amazonia/.

Barbosa de Oliveira, Frederico César. 2014. "Redes de comunicação espiritual e a burocracia do licenciamento ambiental no Rio Teles Pires." *Antropolítica Revista Contemporânea de Antropologia* 37: 157–81.

Brasil de Fato. 2016. "Tribunal ordena consulta prévia aos indígenas sobre instalação da usina Teles Pires." Brasil de Fato, December 5, 2016. https://www.brasildefato.com.br/2016/12/05/tribunal-ordena-consulta-previa-aos-indigenas-sobre-instalacao-da-usina-teles-pires.

Cardoso Rodrigues, Jondison. 2018. "O Arco Norte e as políticas públicas portuárias para o Oeste do estado do Pará (Itaituba e Rurópolis): apresentação, debate e articulações." *Revista NERA* 21, no. 42: 202–28.

Coelho de Souza, Marcela, et al. 2017. "T/terras indígenas e territórios conceituais: incursões etnográficas e controvérsias públicas projeto de pesquisa." *Entreterras*, [S.l.] 1, no. 1.

Cunha, Manuela Carneiro da. 2018. "Índios na constituição." *Novos estudos CEBRAP* 37, no. 3: 429–43.

De Assis, Raimundo, Jucier Sousa, and Osmar Fernando Alves da Silva. 2020. "A reprimarização no Brasil sob a ascensão da geopolítica chinesa no comércio exterior (2008–2018)/Reprimarization in Brazil under the rise of chinese geopolitics in foreign trade (2008–2018)." *Brazilian Journal of Development* 6, no. 3: 12121–39.

De Oliveira, Ariovaldo Umbelino. 2015. "A Amazônia e a nova geografia da produção da soja." *Terra livre* 1, no. 26: 13–43.

Escher, Fabiano, John Wilkinson, and Paulo Rodrigues Fernandes Pereira. 2018. "Causas e implicações dos investimentos chineses no agronegócio brasileiro." In *China: Direções Globais de Investimento*: 190–227. Rio de Janeiro: CEBC.

Governo Federal. 2020. "Em encontro com ministra Tereza Cristina, chineses prometem aumentar investimentos no Brasil." Governo Federal, October 7, 2020. https://www.gov.br/agricultura/pt-br/assuntos/noticias/chineses-prometem-a-ministra-tereza-cristina-aumentar-investimentos-no-brasil.

Honorato de Oliveira, Vinicius E. 2015. "Shatters Among Sherds: A Study of Lithic Assemblages of the Upper Tapajós River." Master's thesis, Institute of Archaeology, University College London.

Instituto Socioambiental. 2018. "Indígenas denunciam impactos da Ferrogrão aos seus possíveis investidores." March 19, 2018. https://www.socioambiental.org/pt-br/blog/blog-do-xingu/indigenas-denunciam-impactos-da-ferrograo-aos-seus-possiveis-investidores.

Kopenawa, Dani, and Bruce Albert. 2015. *A queda do céu: palavras de um xamã yanomami*. São Paulo: Companhia das Letras.

Krenak, Ailton. 2020. "A terra inabitável," YouTube, April 8, 2020. https://www.youtube.com/watch?v=6XoRg3nj1Ws.

Loures, Rosamaria. S. P. 2017. "Governo Karodaybi: o movimento Ipereğ Ayũ e a resistência Munduruku." Master's thesis, Universidade Federal do Oeste do Pará.

Loures, Rosamaria, and Fernanda Moreira. 2020. *A cosmopolítica Munduruku e o resgate das Itiğ'a Wuyjuyũ*. No prelo.

Torres, Mauricio, and Sue Branford. 2017. "A gente vai morrer no espírito também: Hidrelétricas avançam sobre terras e vidas Munduruku." *The Intercept Brasil*, January 26, 2017. https://theintercept.com/2017/01/16/hidreletricas-avancam-sobre-terras-e-vidas-munduruku/.

Mbembe, Achille. 2018. *Necropolítica. biopoder, soberania, estado de exceção, política de morte*. São Paulo: n-1edições.

Molina, Luísa. 2017. "Terra, luta, vida: autodemarcações indígenas e afirmação da diferença." Master's thesis, Universidade de Brasília.

Molina, Luísa. 2018. "As encruzilhadas das demarcações de TIs: 'interesse nacional,' etnocídio e genocídio." In *Índios, Direitos Originários e Territorialidade*, edited by Gustavo K. Alcântara, Lívia N. Tinôco, and Luciano M. Maia, 375–418. Brasília: Editora ANPR.

Molina, Luísa. 2020. "A subversão como método: repensando o genocídio a partir das terras e das lutas indígenas." In *Insurgências, ecologias dissidentes e antropologia modal*, edited by Jorge M. Villela and Suzane A. Vieira. Goiânia: Editora da Imprensa Universitária.

Moreno, Camila. 2015. *O Brasil made in China: para pensar as reconfigurações do capitalismo contemporâneo*. São Paulo: Fundação Rosa Luxemburg.

Munduruku, Ipereg Ayu. 2017. "Somos feitos do Sagrado!," *Movimento Ipereg Ayu* (blog), March 21, 2017. https://movimentoiperegayu.wordpress.com/2017/07/21/somos-feitos-do-sagrado/.

Oliveira, Rodrigo, and Flávia do Amaral Vieira. 2016. "Suspensão de liminar e usinas hidrelétricas: a flexibilização do licenciamento ambiental por via judicial." In *Ocekadi: hidrelétricas, conflitos socioambientais e resistência na Bacia do Tapajós*, edited by Daniela F. Alarcon, Brent Milikan, and Maurício Torres, 247–56. Brasília: International Rivers Brasil; Santarém: Programa de Antropologia e Arqueologia da Universidade Federal do Oeste do Pará.

Rocha, Bruna Cigaran. 2017. "Ipi Ocemumuge: A Regional Archaeology of the Upper Tapajós River." PhD thesis, Institute of Archaeology, University College London.

Rocha, Bruna Cigaran. 2020. "'Rescuing' the Ground from Under Their Feet? Contract Archaeology and Human Rights Violations in the Brazilian Amazon." In *Critical Perspectives on Cultural Memory and Heritage: Construction, Transformation and Destruction*, edited by Veysel Apaydin, 169–85. London: UCL Press.

Schutte, Giorgio Romano, and Victor Sant'Anna Debone. 2017. "A expansão dos investimentos externos diretos chineses. O caso do setor energético brasileiro." *Conjuntura Austral* 8, no. 44: 90–114.

Stengers, Isabelle. 2018. "A proposição cosmopolítica." *Revista do Instituto de Estudos Brasileiros* 69: 442–64.

Strathern, Marilyn. 2009. "Land: Intangible or Tangible Property?" In *Land Rights*, edited by Thomas Chesters, 13–38. Oxford: Oxford University Press.

Torres, Maurício, and Sue Branford. 2017. "'A gente vai morrer no espírito também': Hidrelétricas avançam sobre terras e vidas Munduruku." *The Intercept Brasil*, January 16, 2017. https://theintercept.com/2017/01/16/hidreletricas-avancam-sobre-terras-e-vidas-munduruku/.

Wegner, Rubia Cristina, and Marcelo Pereira Fernandes. 2018. "The Amazon and the Internationalisation of Chinese Companies." *Contexto Internacional*, 40, no. 2: 361–85. https://dx.doi.org/10.1590/s0102-8529.2018400200006.

Challenges for the Shuar in the Face of Globalization and Extractivism: Reflections from the Shuar Federation of Zamora Chinchipe

Jefferson Pullaguari

FOR US SHUARS, DEALING with colonization, the Western world, and globalization has been a real challenge. We find ourselves faced with the dilemma of maintaining our ancestral roots or leaving behind our origins and "modernizing" ourselves. The impact of colonization has been felt to such an extent that according to studies carried out by the Shuar Federation of Zamora Chinchipe (FESZCH), about 85 percent of our Shuar people have abandoned our most important customs and practices (Gnerre 2014)—our traditional clothing, language, gastronomy, and housing, for example. In this chapter, I offer a brief overview of the consequences of the colonization process for the Shuar people, particularly the development of large-scale mining in our territory. The strong ties developed between Ecuador and China in the nationalist government of Rafael Correa allowed China to invest in mining projects such as Mirador (in Zamora Chinchipe province) which, in theory, would resolve much of the country's poverty and benefit local and indigenous population. This was something never seen in Ecuador's history of extractivism. However, as I describe in this chapter, the negotiations and agreements between the Ecuadorean state and the Shuar organizations served mostly Chinese interests, while actively ignoring the legitimacy of Shuar leaders and the political organization. Today, we find ourselves in a situation like that described among the Munduruku people by Luísa Pontes Molina and Alessandra Korap

Munduruku in this volume: how can we be expected to give up our rights, lifeways, and sacred spaces in the name of development—particularly, a development that never seems to produce real benefits for us? As the Munduruku manifesto quote by Molina and Munduruku puts it, "What would the white man say if we built our villages on top of their properties, their sanctuaries, their cemeteries?" (122).

EARLY HISTORY OF COLONIZATION

To give a clear illustration of the evolution that has arisen in terms of our adaptation to different historical periods, it is necessary to return to 1890, five years before Salesian missionaries first entered our ancestral territories, when the people still drew their living from Nunkui (Mother Earth who provided us with food), Arutam (the Shuar god who provided protection and endowed those who paid tribute to the waterfalls with energy and other qualities), and Tsunki (the water god who provided food from the rivers). At that time, we Shuar maintained a harmonious and respectful balance in our interactions with the jungle, where our ancestors had always hunted and fished in a natural manner, only for what was needed and always with the permission of the deities that provided for us in abundance.

It was not until 1895, when Salesian missionaries began to contact us, that our ancestors began developing a curiosity around the fabricated objects used by the colonizers: their machetes, firearms, mirrors, combs, articles of clothing, and Western kitchen utensils, for example. It was this period that marked the "before, during and after" of our Shuar nation. My grandmother, Teresa Martin (daughter of Martin Ujukam, the last Shuar warrior to rule the southern territories of the Ecuadorian Amazon basin) recalled that during her childhood the Shuar maintained their ancestral worldview. They survived by eating *sajinos* (peccaries), *guantas* (spotted pacas), armadillos, deer, monkeys, fish, and any other animals her father could find on the land or in the rivers. Her mother maintained the *aja* (gardens) that provided tubers like cassavas, taros, potatoes, and sweet potatoes. With this diet, the Shuar were strong and healthy. Disease was almost unheard of, and the few that appeared were cured by the *uwijint* (shaman, witch doctor) using natural medicines. She also remembered that even the children were expected to contact the spirit of Arutam since, from an early age, they were raised to receive the strength and courage of the Shuar gods. This involved the taking of *natem* (ayahuasca), *guanto* (extract from the *Brugmansia* or angel's trumpet shrub) or wild tobacco juice, potions that allowed them to see the future and contact the spirits of their ancestors and gods in a ritual practiced at the waterfalls they believed were inhabited by Arutam.

When the *curas*[1] arrived, everything began to change, as they began to speak to our people about an all-powerful God that lived in the skies and punished those who worshipped other gods. These missionaries taught them the language they knew as Apach (Spanish) and traded machetes, rifles, Western food, and other trinkets for land, which allowed them to take over extensive territories where the same Shuar were forced to work on the construction of churches, schools, convents, and houses for the priests. Many children were separated from their families and taken to boarding schools, where they were taught to read and write, prohibited from speaking the Shuar language, and punished if they did. In a similar way, the arrival of mestizo settlers also imposed changes, as they stripped the Shuar of their clothing and ornaments, dressed them in Western clothing, and, under the pretext of improving their quality of life, taught them the value of money. During this period, we Shuar lost the freedom to practice our own customs.

Initially, relationships with the settlers were good, since they showed an interest in helping Shuar families. The relationship changed when the settlers began to take over our land under the ruse of illusory purchase. To make matters worse, the colonists—who taught Spanish to younger Shuar as a means of communicating with elderly leaders and other members of our upper echelons—were never interested in learning Shuar Chicham, the language of the Shuar.

At the behest of the state, the missionaries began to construct roads, which forced many Shuar to aggregate into various community settlements, whereas before the houses of each Shuar family were one or two kilometers apart. Wooden houses were built, side by side, with modest spaces set aside for meetings, religious, social and community services. Many Shuar children and adolescents were taken to Ecuador's cities, in a process of attempted assimilation that was both difficult and cruel, as they faced discrimination from a society that regarded them as wild animals. Few stayed in the cities. Most returned to their communities with sad memories and bitter news of a hostile, alien world.

AN INSIDIOUS ENEMY

Opening the door to our territories and extending a friendly hand to the Salesians, Franciscans, and other colonizers was one of the worst miscalculations ever committed by the Shuar people. What they thought was an honest cultural and experiential exchange ended up turning into a colonial process of domination and imposition by the larger society and state. This now continues in the form of extractivism. According to Kakarma Shiram,[2] "the Shuar opened their doors to their very extermination, in the sense of a mortality that was not physical but cultural." Similarly, in Brazil, as Molina and Munduruku point out in this volume in relation to the construction of megaprojects in the Munduruku territory, what for the state represents simply an area to extract resources, for local indigenous people it has everything to do with their lives, their cultural practices and their knowledge.

In the end, the reaching out to Shuar leaders and elders, the gifting of objects and trinkets, and even the promises to respect our cultural worldview all amounted to a deception perpetrated by an Ecuadorian state that regarded its Amazon basin as a region of infinite resources that had to be exploited to secure its place in the world economy (globalization), while also satisfying the interests of privileged individuals. Under the illusion of helping the Shuar, this insidious enemy opened a huge gap in society, further enriching those who already had power and plunging Indigenous nationalities (who were just coming to appreciate the ravages of this insertion in other parts of the world) into poverty. Before this, the Shuar were a people rich in territories. Our only poverty was a lack of Western savvy.

So why has globalization not been beneficial for us Shuar? As Kakarma Shiram told me, "We trusted those we shouldn't have trusted, a government whose purposes had nothing to do with equality or equity, but rather a hunger for power and status for those who administered it in the hopes of being included in the list of the world's richest, and that failed to appreciate the country's existing intercultural riches." Although it is true that globalization could not and cannot be stopped, since it is inevitable and irreversible, it is also true that the state could have administered many aspects of their domestic development in a different way, so that it could have more steadily and uniformly benefited Indigenous populations, without isolating or excluding them from national and global economic growth while maintaining respect for their cultures.

At present, we are left with no alternative but to continue adapting to local, national, and global economic transformations under the banner of defending the few territories that have allowed us not to disappear as an ancestral indigenous nationality and still remain in our custody. We wait for the day when existing provisions of international and national laws on Indigenous peoples and nationalities will finally translate into an equitable reality.

DILEMMAS FOR THE SHUAR IN THE FACE OF LARGE-SCALE MINING

For several decades, the Shuar population has had to take part in Ecuador's politics. Following the colonization of Ecuador's Amazon basin and a loss of the territory in the 1960s, the first political organizations emerged whose struggle focused on preserving Shuar territory and culture.

But it was not until the emergence of the Citizens' Revolution[3] that the Shuar directly approached an Ecuadorian president—in this case, a leader who presented himself as a Left-oriented militant who intended to guarantee the rights of Indigenous peoples and nationalities. The Shuar therefore supported the revolution's proposal to incorporate the rights of Indigenous nationalities and peoples into a new constitution. The Shuar breathed a sigh of hope when the Ecuadorian Constitution of 2008 was finally approved, in which Articles 56 and 57 fully guaranteed compliance with terms demanded by Indigenous people for many decades. However, as Emilia Bonilla discusses in this volume, the constitutional rights protected specifically by these articles and others regarding the rights of nature do not guarantee that Indigenous people can decide over the exploitation of resources in their territories, or even participate adequately in processes of prior consultation.

From 2007 until 2011, the Shuar population and FESZCH cooperated regularly with the Correa administration. As his government emphasized the formal recognition of community lands and the need to reduce the extreme poverty of the Shuar communities through the provision of basic services and community recreation spaces, as well as the signing of agreements to invest in human capital in different areas of the state, the Shuar experienced this as a time of harmony and enthusiasm. During this period, Correa showed interest in working for Shuar communities and maintained regular communication with the Shuar leaders of this province. In this sense, and because this period undoubtedly aroused the interest of leaders and other concerned Shuar in venturing into local and national politics to advocate for the development of their communities, it can be said that the Correa administration marked a "before and after" in the daily life of the Shuar nationality. The inclusion of young Shuar in some public institutions was the result of one of the agreements the Correa administration reached with FESZCH.

On the other hand, while we trusted Correa's public discourse, in which he clearly expressed his belief in the importance of environmental conservation and respect for Indigenous peoples, his cabinet (complying with the directives of Correa himself) was negotiating with transnational corporations at the so-called Ecuadorian Mining Dialog without the knowledge of the Indigenous voting base (although certain leaders were aware of this).

These dialogues would allow extractivist companies to operate on ancestral lands in exchange for benefits for Shuar communities. The mining companies and the Ecuadorian government offered to improve the quality of life of the Shuar by reducing their extreme poverty through commitments to create opportunities for unskilled labor, build infrastructure, strengthen organizations, protect the environment, and support the conservation of customs and traditions. In view of these promises, most Shuar leaders were inclined to grant the companies entry into the territories. Finally, because the state had a history of not treating Indigenous populations fairly, the feeling among Shuar was that this was an opportune time to demand reasonable compensation for the exploitation of resources in their territories.

However, nothing lasts forever. In 2011 arose the first incidents of friction between the government and Amazonian Indigenous populations, as well as of conflict within Indigenous groups because of disagreements over the mining issue (as the Correa administration had negotiated agreements with the transnationals behind the backs of these Indigenous populations). Moreover, while many Shuar people said no to mining, FESZCH had entered into cooperation and impact-benefit agreements with the transnational corporations and maintained close relations with these companies. The mining companies[4] accordingly viewed FESZCH as a shield against rejection by the ordinary people of Zamora Chinchipe. Nevertheless, a group of Shuar and their leaders were only barely able to thwart the intentions of the province's prefect, Salvador Quishpe, and some five hundred others to invade and burn down the Mirador camp as an act of protest. At the time, the mining company (whose then owners were Canadians) saw the Shuar as a strategic ally, so they did not hesitate to hold talks and sign agreements. These agreements, however, were not well received by the government, as it was operating under a policy of managing the project's royalties directly and centrally. This, in turn, provoked the Shuar leaders, who felt the royalties should have been channeled through (Indigenous) autonomous governments, as little or nothing had been done for the benefit of the communities. These series of disagreements marked the beginning of a breakdown and rupture of relations between the Correa administration and the Indigenous people of Ecuador's Amazon basin. In fact, as Julia Correa et al. argue in their chapter over the national Indigenous protests in October 2019, the Correa government had managed to neutralize and weaken the Indigenous movement in Ecuador through several mechanisms, one of which was the criminalization of Indigenous resistance. This is why there had not been any successful and massive Indigenous uprisings for almost a decade. The October protest became an opportunity for the Indigenous movement in Ecuador to articulate forces again.

THE MINING COMPANIES AND THE SHUAR: PERSPECTIVES AND REALITY

The following questions arise: Were the agreements and commitments established between FESZCH and the mining companies fulfilled? Why did relations between the mining companies and the Shuar people break down? What role did the Correa administration play? Were the voting bases really in agreement with the mining companies' entry into ancestral territories?

As the mining companies had effectively sold their publicity regarding fair treatment and responsible mining, the Shuar leaders had trusted, and persuaded their communities to trust, in their commitments to the Shuar's development and progress. For many, the rationale was that large-scale mining was going to happen no matter what, and that the best strategy was to negotiate with the companies. Thus, FESZCH reached an agreement with EcuaCorriente S.A. (ECSA, still under the ownership of Canadians) and received funds that were used to strengthen the organization and even allowed the construction of a modern building in the city of Zamora that would serve as headquarters and as a training center for Shuar youth. One of the latter states:

> We trusted the mining companies weren't playing with the Shuar people, since in the beginning they were helping the communities, at least in the Pangui area. ECSA started programs in communities like Etsa, Numpaim, and Yankur. It seemed like the company was really interested in seeing people lifted out of extreme poverty, since they were hiring Shuars from Santiago Paati, Certero, Pakints, and other communities outside of Pangui, like Ayui, Kukush, and Ankuash.
>
> Many of us who were opposed to the extractivism found ourselves the objects of hostility from colleagues who were in favor of mining, since at that point ECSA was already showing interest in the Shuar. Many were hired, and even members of my family joined the company. When they left, they agreed to tell us what the jobs were like and ended up telling us they were well paid, treated well, and that everything was great. So the news spread that the decision to allow entrance to the mining companies was the best decision our leaders had made. (Kakaram Shuar, personal communication)

Thus, ECSA, again a Canadian company at the time, was able to strategically divide our base by giving high-paying jobs to family members of Shuar leaders and even scholarships to their children to study in areas related to mining, with the promise of a guaranteed job during the mine's planned twenty-year extraction period. For the rest of the population, they organized projects like chicken farms and technical training programs:

> At that time, our colleague Rubén Naichap Yankur[5] was the one who had sat with the people from ECSA, in his capacity as president of the Shuar Federation. We only accompanied him for the signing of the agreements. It was always said that our communities were going to receive support from ECSA and that we should support the mining projects. Initially, it was clear that the support was reaching our communities, but when the Chinese took over, everything changed. Many of our people were even

fired from their jobs, and many of the development projects stopped receiving technical and economic support and ended up failing. It was from about that time that the Chinese started saying they were no longer giving us anything, because Correa had prohibited it. (René Jimpikit, personal communication)

And, in fact, things really did change with the arrival of the new project owners in 2011. Relations between the Chinese company and FESZCH (which had a new president) became tense, mainly because it no longer recognized the federation as an important player or as representing the Shuar communities. This was rationalized in terms of new government policies, which apparently prevented direct negotiations or agreements between mining companies and Indigenous organizations. Any issues related to royalties or the distribution of resources were to be negotiated directly with the government. Since the transfer of the mining concession to the Chinese company, the situation has been deteriorating to the point that people are conducting sit-ins and marches in protest against the policies of the mining company, which does not appear to require hardly any services of the Shuar workforce, whether skilled or unskilled. Testimonies like the following demonstrate the current unhappiness with the Chinese company:

With the gringos,[6] everything was different. With them, we could at least have conversations and reach agreements. But with the Chinese, the relations aren't good: all they do is yell. And our people, or I should say the very few who are still working, are treated badly. Their wages are low, the food is terrible, everything changed. There's no communication with the Chinese. There's no longer that "fair treatment" that was talked about. Now there are no projects or any support for our Shuar communities. The young Shuar who went to school on scholarships and who came back as professionals go around unemployed looking for work, and ECSA doesn't hire them because they say they don't have the right profile or experience. I can tell you right now that not even the president of our Shuar Federation is able to make agreements with them. (René Jimpikit personal communication)

I think they laughed at the Shuar people, and now the same people, who at that time looked at us with contempt for opposing ECSA, are supporting us. And we're counting on that support to rise up and defend our land. Now they realize that the mining companies only used our leaders to gain access to the land and curry popular support. They lie to the world, saying that everything's ok and that they have a friendly relationship with us Shuar, when this is not true. They say they invest millions of dollars for the benefit of the Shuar, but if you visit our communities you can see there's no such investment, and you can see that our communities continue to have the same needs and deficiencies as always. They say the government has our money and that we should complain to them, to get financing for our projects. (Kakaram Shiram, personal communication)

The people see that the positive relations they maintained with ECSA fell apart with the arrival of the Chinese, as so-called fair treatment no longer exists. The commitments and cooperation agreements, memorandums of understanding, programs, and projects never translated into reality. Our people are being exploited. Their working conditions are unacceptable, and the conservation and environmental protection policies are not being honored by this Chinese company, which, shielded by the Ecuadorian government, makes and breaks promises according to its own convenience. Nor has the Ecuadorian government done what is necessary to enforce its public policies in the territory for the benefit of Shuar centers and communities. Once again, the Shuar find themselves struggling alone to coexist in a society marked by selfishness, racism, and injustice.

FACING A FUTURE, DESPITE THE EXTRACTIVISM

With the Ecuadorian government defending extractivist interests and a current leader (president of FESZCH) who also supports mining, little or nothing can be done at this time to fight in defense of the ancestral territories currently under a mining concession and facing disaster.

Mineral extraction from the Mirador and Fruta del Norte mines has begun, and with this come new challenges for the Shuar nationality. Who is responsible for the well-being of the families that suffer the effects of the dust, particles, and debris spread by the trucks that pass through our communities transporting minerals, for the damage to the ecosystem, or for the animals that must look for a new home as their forest is being destroyed? The reality is that we Shuar were never prepared to withstand the impact of this extraction, which was presented to us as a simple affair that would not have consequences. In any event, today's panorama has proved otherwise, in part because factors like the health effects of the mining projects were never taken into consideration.

> Our children have to breathe the dust spread by the dump trucks and tractor-trailers that pass through here. Not just the dust from the ground, but from the loads. How do we know if these loads contain toxic minerals that might be carcinogenic to humans? They should have thought about all this before they started to take the gold and copper. Of course, since they're only interested in the *plata* [money], they're not taking any precautions to protect the health of the people who've always lived in this area. (René Jimpikit, personal communication)

> I think the mining companies should have thought more about the issue of the transportation of their materials, that they should have first focused on constructing a safe route, preparing spaces for roadways, asphalt, and many other things that were needed for this operation. Similarly, some kind of plan to minimize the impact the Shuar communities along their transportation routes were going to suffer. They should also have thought about how there would be people who would have to suffer, day after day, all the dust kicked up by their trucks, which, to make matters worse, are driven by irresponsible people who don't even notice our community members and even speed up as they pass by. Our children are suffering respiratory problems. And, for all we know, later people might even start dying from this dust. (Kakaram Shiram, personal communication)

The struggle in the face of capitalist forces that impose conditions and move the chess pieces of the world, according to their convenience, is and will continue to be a hard one. Our battle—to protect and keep alive ancient customs; to defend Li Nunke, our Mother Earth; to protect the water; to protect life; and to defend the legacy of the future generations that will want to know these majestic green mountains—is a war fought from a position of disadvantage, where the powerful carry the weapon of money.

We Shuar have been able to face the vicissitudes of colonization, acculturation, globalization, discrimination, mining, and the state, among others. Our history certainly does not lie when we say the Shuar are warriors, and that this strength has allowed us to overcome adversities. Despite the fact of a current fear of losing ancestral customs and traditions, we remain with nothing less than the hope and faith placed in Arutam that better days will come for our Indigenous nation.

NOTES

1. We use the term *curas* to refer to the Salesian missionaries who first entered our territories, as well as to the Franciscan missionaries who arrived later.

2. Pseudonym used to protect the identity of a Shuar woman from Pangui, whose family works for the Chinese company EcuaCorriente S.A. (ECSA).

3. Translator's note: The administration of former president Rafael Correa was conceived as the first stage of what Correa dubbed the *"Revolución Ciudadana"* (Citizens' Revolution), and Ecuadorians often refer to his administration with this phrase.

4. In Ecuador's Zamora Chinchipe province, there are currently two large-scale mining projects: Mirador, which is owned by ECSA (a Chinese company that purchased the interest of its Canadian predecessor), and Fruta del Norte, owned by Canadian corporation Lundin Gold Inc.

5. Rubén Naichap was president of FESZCH from 2009 to 2011.

6. Here, "gringos" refers to Canadians.

REFERENCES

FESZCH—Federación Shuar de Zamora Chinchipe. 2018. 'Plan estratégico del Pueblo Shuar de Zamora Chinchipe," Zamora.

Gnerre, Maurizio. 2014. "Los Salesianos y los Shuar construyendo la identidad cultural." In *Misiones, Pueblos Indigenas e Interculturalidad*, edited by Víctor Hugo Torres Dávila. Quito: Abya-Yala.

"Yes, We Do Know Why We Protest": Indigenous Challenges to Extractivism in Ecuador, Looking beyond the National Strike of October 2019

Julia Correa, Israel Chumapi, Paúl Ghaitai
Males, Jennifer Yajaira Masaquiza,
Rina Pakari Marcillo, and David Menacho

ON OCTOBER 6, 2019, Indigenous communities and rural organizations from different parts of Ecuador's Imbabura province made final preparations for their long march to Quito. This was the last communal gathering before leaving for the capital city: a moment of sadness and tears, *wawas* (young children) saying goodbye to their parents and grandparents, *runas* (men / Indigenous people) and their children taking a last look at the land of their birth without knowing if they would be coming back. And so, the *runas* departed to join a large uprising that returns them to the legacy of their forefathers.

ORGANIZATION OF INDIGENOUS PEOPLE

Chinese-supported infrastructural development caused the disruption of traditional lifeways and communities across South America. Native peoples have begun to fight back against the unthinking development that Gutiérrez, Carpio and Flores; Molina and Munduruku; and Pullaguari describe in their chapters in this volume as authoritarian, masculinist, and spectacular. In Ecuador, the Native response coalesced in a mass movement, resulting in a spectacular Indigenous revolt in October 2019.

On October 5, the National Confederation of Ecuadorian Indigenous Nationalities (CONAIE) called on all of Ecuador's Indigenous communities and rural organizations to march to the capital the next day. CONAIE and other local organizations were faced with the challenge of convening their bases in what would be the decade's largest mobilization of Indigenous people. The administration of former president Rafael Correa, as mentioned by Tuaza (2011), had worked directly with Indigenous communities to legitimize his authority and earn popular support while at the same time weakening their organization and movement. Likewise, CONAIE had ignored the communities' needs for some time: it concentrated on political issues and had lost the support of smaller organizations (Tuaza 2011). The October strike was therefore an opportunity to strengthen and reorganize Ecuador's Indigenous population. Focusing on the Indigenous protests and mobilization, this chapter addresses the consequences of China's presence and involvement in extractive projects in Ecuador and the implications of these for Indigenous peoples. We argue that the development of strong ties between Ecuador and China in the context of a populist and authoritarian government contributed not only to environmental destruction in the Amazon, but also to reinforcing inequalities and the disempowerment of minorities in a racist society.

In the northern part of Ecuador, local Indigenous organizations heeded agreements made in communal assemblies, chief among these the blocking of highways and streets. While it was not officially declared, it was also implicitly understood that community members would cooperate as a unit. In Cotachachi (a small town in northern Ecuador), for example, most leaders and younger adult men joined the march on Quito. The women maintained order and security within the communities. Communication was also vital: information about what was happening in Quito was transmitted to community leaders, who in turn transmitted it to the community, thereby maintaining unity. In the specific case of Cotacachi's Indigenous communes, their designated meeting place became a strategic location for communes throughout the region: the Panamerican Highway's northbound Cotacachi exit. Organization was maintained by communal leaders as well as by the leader and president of the Union of Rural Indigenous People of Cotacachi (UNORCAC), who expanded the struggle beyond the Indigenous universe: "I was no longer representing UNORCAC. I was representing the people, because it's not just us Indigenous people but rather the people in general who are united in these protests." At that point, the march of a united people began to take shape.

Meanwhile, in the south-central part of Ecuador, in the *kichwa* town of Salasaka, there was a peaceful march to the main government building of Tungurahua province. The main roads connecting Ecuador's altiplano and Amazon were blocked in this strategic area. The area's eighteen Indigenous communities organized to maintain this blockade twenty-four hours a day until October 5, 2019, when, due to the disorganization of the Indigenous Movement of Tungurahua (MIT), Salasaka entered into an agreement with Tungurahua's provincial and cantonal authorities (Consejo de Gobierno de Salasaka 2019). Nevertheless, in the capital, brothers and sisters from other towns continued their marches and protests. News of their situation was getting steadily worse. For this reason, a general assembly was convened on October 7 in which young people from Salasaka came to the podium, expressed their dismay at the situation, and inspired the town to join the protests in the capital. It was decided that five representatives from each neighborhood, along with members of the Government Council, would provide support in Quito. The rest of the people, with the help of the town's political lieutenant, would resume blocking the roads.

The organization of base populations was the most important factor in these cases. While there were some fractures, there was a much stronger cause: a shared experience of having been criminalized, invisibilized, violated, and persecuted, as well as compassion for those who were struggling on the "battlefield" at the time. The march on the capital began from different Indigenous communities throughout Ecuador. As one Indigenous leader narrates, "In the end, the people said, 'We're going.' And we went. We were obligated by the town's decision, but really never imagined what was waiting for us—that we would get there and they'd already be teargassing us."

> I am a *Runa Kichwa Salasaka* [Indigenous person from Salasaka]. Generation after generation I work the land, singing sorrows and dancing joys. From the depths of my memory, we have respected the difference that exists between your people and my people, many times with the disadvantage of having to confront your ignorance and receive your contempt. . . . I know you're waiting for us with fear because they've told you we're going to loot your stores, that I'm going to hurt you. But I ask myself after so much time, . . . when did I ever give you any reason to fear me?

So *Taitas* (fathers), *Mamas* (mothers), and *Wambras* (children) prepared themselves for a large mobilization in the city of Quito. They arrived in the capital to applause from the locals and a joyful welcome; to Indigenous songs and dances after a long march. But they were not received in this way in all parts, nor from all the people of the city.

MEDIA

"Recomiéndenles (a los indígenas) que se queden en el páramo."
(Advise them to stay in their [high-altitude] wastelands.)

—Statement made to reporters by Guayaquil's former mayor
in October 2019, as documented by a YouTube video
(*VA Television* 2019).

When news broke that Indigenous communities would support the mobilization convened by CONAIE, fear began spreading throughout Ecuadorian society. News reports from mainstream media sources emphasized incidents of looting, violence, and robberies allegedly committed by protesters (Revista Crisis 2019), reinforcing racist fears and narratives. This tendency was not just reflected in reports from the capital—it was visible in all parts of the country. Businesses closed and people locked themselves in their houses, clutching weapons to defend themselves in case "some Indian" broke in and tried to hurt them. While it is true that there was some looting and violence, with some of it attributable to protesters, these offenders were not connected to the official mobilization of Indigenous peoples.

No saben ni por qué protestan. (They don't even know why they are protesting.)

In their October 7 prime time programs, mainstream media sources like Teleamazonas highlighted the losses caused by the protests, insinuating that they were senseless.[1] The blocking of roads was treated as an injury to the nation's transportation network, affecting the public's ability to travel. People found themselves having to walk long distances or take longer, alternative routes to get to their destinations. They blamed this inconvenience on "the Indians" without considering the protests' legitimacy.

Combined with their failure to show abuses of military and police power, these media narratives had the effect of framing the Indigenous march as essentially criminal and violent. For this reason, social and alternative media played a crucial role, publishing photos, videos, live transmissions, and the testimony of protesters, demonstrating the raw reality of the protests. Community media also served an important role in telling the other side of the story: "As a witness, I listened on community radio to stories of deaths, injuries, and people fainting from exposure to tear gas. This made me sad, but also angry. I asked myself, 'Why aren't these stories appearing in the mainstream media?'" While community media cannot have a broad nationwide presence, during the National Strike of October 2019, it demonstrated how it can sometimes transcend its local role to keep an entire country informed.

VIOLENCE

We return to the arrival of the protesters to the capital, received on the one hand with applause and on the other with expressions of hate and rejection in the media. This occurred in the context of President Lenín Moreno's suspension of constitutional rights, which expanded the military and police's power to use force.

> Andrés Tugumbango (my uncle) says: "We ran because they were tossing tear gas bombs and shooting birdshot in all directions." A tear gas bomb hit Andrés in the stomach, and his scars are proof of this. That same night a young man was killed after being hit with a bomb. At this my father commented: "With their horses, the police were making us run, while they kept hitting us with tear gas bombs. The *guambrito* [young man] was running in a group that was ahead of us and was killed." That day, the number of injuries, disappearances, and arrests rose exponentially.

It is important to discuss the violence described in this testimony in more detail. As we can see, the peaceful protests did not last long, owing to the inflexible attitudes of both the state and the protesters. But the violent actions of the Indigenous people were not comparable to those of the nation's security forces. Each step or action of the Indigenous organizations was thwarted by a counteraction that was orders of magnitude more powerful. Community and independent media sources like *GKcity* and *Wambra EC* presented stories of the violence experienced by Indigenous people whose communities had declared "a suspension of constitutional rights in Indigenous territories" as a result of "the brutality of the military forces" (*Gkcity* 2019a). The state responded by stating "there are no

Indigenous territories," deploying armed forces to threaten the protestors. At this juncture, the Inter-American Commission on Human Rights clarified that "it is not appropriate for a state to use military forces to exercise domestic control over its security" and that the purpose of the military is to "serve, protect and guarantee domestic order" through "the elimination of enemy militaries."

As far as the arrests were concerned, *El Universo* newspaper reported that more than 80 percent were illegal detentions (*El Universo* 2019). According to GKcity's reports, if you were lucky, you only received bruises on your face and body or "cruel, inhuman or degrading treatment" (2019b). Trying to run or hide was futile. This was clearly demonstrated by the case of José Chaluisa, who died while trying to run. Chaluisa's father recounts that he saw his son "restrained by the neck. The police motorcycle stopped him and, without saying anything or cautioning him in a normal way, just stomped on him with his boots" (*Wambra* 2020).

There are eleven similar articles from alternative media source *Wambra*. In one of these, *Wambra* questions the state's explanations and discredits the claim that the deaths "occurred as part of the process of controlling the protests." Evidence and testimony demonstrate the contrary. The state exploited the "legitimacy" of its use of violence as well as its control over the justice system and mainstream media to evade responsibility for the harm and deaths it caused. As Maurera (2019, 144) explains, several international media sources such as *France24* recognized that the state had provoked the violence. *GKcity* explains this as demonstrating the state's failure to recognize the protests as "a social manifestation of discontent" through its rationalization that they were nothing more than "a politically motivated attempt to destabilize the government" (*Gkcity* 2019c).

The violence, however, was not only provoked by the state. Civilians who experienced interruptions in their academic, economic, and recreational activities also became violent. The protests revealed profound divisions and intolerance among mestizos in their attitudes toward Indigenous peoples. Expressions of racial hatred and contempt between different social groups aggravated an already polarized population (Izurieta 2020, 104). As a result of this polarization, "most mestizos and middle- and upper-middle-class people perceived Indigenous people as the enemy and developed attitudes of rejection toward them," which had the effect of exacerbating "the division and fracturing of an Ecuador that, for a long time, has suffered from a failed process of social cohesion" (106).

"RESOLUTION" OF THE PROTESTS

On October 13, after more than a week of strikes, protests, and violence, the state and CONAIE began talking. The dialogue was carried out in coordination with the United Nations and the Episcopal Conference of Ecuador and broadcasted on national networks. With the whole country watching, the state and CONAIE reached an agreement in which Decree 883 was abolished, putting an end to the protests. "The Indigenous movement has permanently disrupted a society that is exclusive, profoundly racist, ignorant of its own history, and refuses to acknowledge its own diversity" (Larrea 2004).

From the beginning of the twentieth century, Indigenous leaders like Dolores Cacuango and Tránsito Amaguaña have made their presence felt in national politics, planting the seeds of struggle. From the time of their first mobilization, Indigenous groups marched on the city of Quito to remind Ecuadorian society of their presence. The national strike of October 2019 took place twenty-nine years after the first mobilization of Indigenous peoples and fourteen years after the most recent mobilization in Quito. The recent October protests have made clear that Ecuadorian society has not overcome its everyday (but ignored and invisible) racism, which has again crudely and openly revealed itself. In this country, which considers itself plurinational and multicultural, it is important to understand the national strike in a broader context and to look beyond the events of the moment.

LOOKING BEYOND THE OCTOBER STRIKE

"La gente quiere todo regalado" (People want everything for free) was a common expression during the national strike, as though this were the only explanation for the protests. It would be simple to think superficially and explain the October protests as a reaction to the economic measures imposed by President Moreno. This chapter seeks to go beyond that sort of explanation. Having quickly surveyed the forms of violence employed during the strike, the role of the media, and how the Indigenous people organized themselves, we are now going to move to a broader analysis. For the remainder of the chapter, we will examine certain key policies and narratives of the two most recent presidential administrations in the context of structural racism, asking ourselves "What really caused the national strike of October 2019?"[2]

Before addressing this question, we would like to clarify some concepts and situate them in their historical context. The national strike, being a specific event from a specific historical period, emerged from a colonial framework. Colonization marked a change in the understanding of time and space in relation to Indigenous peoples and cultures, a change that is evidenced even in something as simple as the phrase "the discovery of America," which suggests a previously uninhabited continent (Muyolema 2001). Over time, this manner of thinking has developed in Ecuador in different ways. One was the hacienda system, which enslaved the Indigenous population. Another was in discourses regarding mixed races promoting the notion of "whitening" and seeking to homogenize the population. This had the effect of relegating Indigenous and African people to the status of undesirable "others" and excluding them from society (Stutzman 1981). A third manifestation of this thinking has been in the rejection and delegitimization of resistance and protest such as Indigenous uprisings and, most recently, the national strike of October 2019.

This reproduction of societal patterns can be understood as a propagation of the racial domination and subjugation characteristic of postcolonial societies. Given the way our history has been constructed, we must understand racism as a key aspect of our social structure. It is a "total social phenomenon" that pervades all levels of the structure, altering the reality of each individual according to his or her ethnoracial identity (De la Torre 2002). This total social phenomenon is what we call *structural racism*.

In this context, we will analyze in depth the policies and narratives of presidents Moreno and Correa and how we understand their links to the national strike of October 2019. We begin with the straw that broke the camel's back: Moreno's imposition of economic austerity measures. On October 1, 2019, President Lenín Moreno announced a package of economic reforms known as Decree 883, which imposed, among other things, the elimination of gasoline subsidies, the reduction of minimum salaries for temporary employment contracts, and the relaxing of tariffs on machinery and equipment (Pacheco 2019). These measures directly affected the most vulnerable sectors of the population and arose from a list of conditions imposed on Moreno by the International Monetary Fund in exchange for a three-year US$4.2 billion loan to alleviate Ecuador's national debt (Weisbrot 2019).

The mobilization of Indigenous people was not only responding to these economic measures, however. To understand the deeper motivations, we must go back in time to the beginning of the prior presidential administration. Rafael Correa, Moreno's predecessor, brought historical changes to Ecuador's politics. While there is much to say about his administration, we will focus on his politically progressive idealism, which was like that of other leaders in Latin America (Evo Morales, for example), and his close relationship with the People's Republic of China. This was a key aspect of his economic policy.

From the moment he assumed office, Correa demonstrated a left-leaning "post-neoliberal" focus, which he developed against the background of a national history dominated by neoliberalism, poverty, and a lack of public spending (Fernández-Salvador 2018, 81). Correa's nationalist discourse initially hinged on the ideas of *Sumak Kawsay* or *Buen Vivir*[3] and a vision of holistic development. However, as Emilia Bonilla discusses in this volume, political and economic interests were eventually given priority over these guiding principles (present both in the Constitution and in the National Development Plan), denying the right of Indigenous people to formally consent (or not) to extractive projects in their territory. While specific articles on the defense and protection of nature and Indigenous peoples were included in the Constitution of 2008, Correa's administration also initiated steps toward developing mining on a large scale as a means of fulfilling his promised plans for economic development and the elimination of poverty. In 2007, 2008, and 2009 there were protests and opposition to increased mining activities in Ecuador. The state nevertheless remained committed to projects that exploited the country's mineral wealth to "finance a model of solidary development" (Cisneros 2009, 16). Despite protesting voices, in 2009 a New Mineral Law was passed. This had the effect of conferring more power on the state and of silencing opponents. It was justified by claims that that this was the only way to assure a path of economic development and poverty reduction (Fernández-Salvador 2018, 83).

Intensified large-scale mining was largely driven by Chinese investment, which was the main source of funding for Ecuador's economic development. China's interest in Ecuador is primarily based on its natural resources, which are in protected wilderness areas and close to rural mestizo and Indigenous populations. The Correa administration nevertheless continued pursuing contracts with Chinese businesses and consortia for the construction of megaprojects, effectively reneging on its environmental promises and infringing on the collective rights of Indigenous communities (as discussed by Bonilla in this volume) and other nearby populations (Garzon 2019). Clear examples of these infringements can be seen in the communities of San Marcos in the Zamora Chinchipe province (Vallejo 2017) and Nankintz (in the province of Morona Santiago), both in the impact zones of mining projects (the Mirador and San Carlos Panantza projects, respectively) run by Chinese consortia.

Division and conflict within Shuar communities and organizations are also the consequences of the presence of mining companies and the development of large-scale mining in the province, as Shuar leader Jefferson Pullaguari discusses in this section. These conflicts, however, are rendered invisible by economic and political forces. As Méndez affirms (2012), the exportation of natural resources to China is a strategic source of financing and investment for Ecuador's infrastructure: schools, health care centers, roads, and hydroelectric power plants, among other things, which now constitute a symbol of modernity. Extractivism has therefore evolved into a national imperative (Arsel, Hogenboom, and Pellegrini 2016) and a precondition for meeting Ecuador's goals in economic development and well-being. However, the risks of mega-infrastructure and extractive projects to local and Indigenous populations have implications at different levels. These must be understood in a specific ontological context, as Luisa Pontes and Alessandra Korap discuss in this volume's chapter on Chinese megaprojects in the Tapajós–Teles Pires Basin in Brazil.

In this context, the possibility of a political relationship between the Correa administration and Indigenous organizations was lost (Pullaguari, this volume). Indigenous populations who opposed extractivism found themselves attacked by the state. They were criminalized and even persecuted. "Correa has described Indigenous groups and environmentalists in a disrespectful manner, as 'infantile' and as the greatest threat to his political agenda" (Arsel and Avila 2011). Here we can see one of Correa's most frequently employed strategies. Via a colonial understanding of modernity (Méndez 2012), he has focused on delegitimizing those who would criticize his developmental model. He accuses them of opposing development, technology, and progress. He then criminalizes, persecutes, and neutralizes opposing organizations (Cholango 2012). Those detained during the ten years of Correa's "Citizens' Revolution" included Ecuadorian union leaders, Indigenous people, students, and criminalized activists, all prosecuted under allegations of "terrorism." In most cases, Indigenous leaders have been detained on charges of assault and resistance, disorderly conduct, or interference with public utilities (Riofrío 2017). Earlier mobilizations like the 2012 March for Water were significantly weakened by the Correa administration's methods.

The national strike of October 2019 was a reaction to much more than Moreno's imposition of austerity measures. It was sparked by developmentalist discourses that are used to justify intensified extractivism, by the presence of Chinese mega-infrastructures, and by the silence imposed on Indigenous populations by Alianza País[4] during Correa's decade of power. The objective of this chapter is not simply to criticize Correa and Moreno, however, but rather to show that the motivations for the recent strike transcend these administrations. This is because, in spite of the differences between the two administrations and the different motives for protesting against either one, the same vulnerable populations have been harmed and/or criminalized. This is not about a specific political ideology, but rather about a racist system that has been present in Ecuador since colonial times.

CONCLUSIONS

In this chapter, we presented a distinct perspective on the national strike of October 2019 to demonstrate what was really happening beyond the screens of television and social media. We briefly analyzed some aspects of Correa's Citizens' Revolution to understand why Moreno's imposition of austerity measures was the straw that broke the camel's back, triggering the October protests. Finally, we have looked at certain political processes, each with its specific characteristics, as products of a historical and structural racism. Even so, as students we feel we are left with an emptiness: the need for a search that goes beyond merely understanding structural racism in a conceptual sense. It is for this reason that, from our points of view and personal experiences, as young Ecuadorian mestizos and Indigenous people, we have offered up our reflections. This is the first step along a possible path leading to change and not a proposed solution.

October 2019 was one of those moments that demonstrated Ecuador's structural racism, which has been constructed over centuries with few changes. Are we condemned to remain in this vicious circle? Historical moments like Indigenous uprisings have provoked questions about national society and forced people to change their perspective regarding the serious problems of inequality and discrimination that they carry inside themselves. The same society, however, has taken it upon itself to constantly delegitimize the protests. We, as part of this society, are inevitably learning, accepting, and interiorizing in one way or another these ways of dealing with real complaints and fair questions. For this reason, it is we who can and must unlearn all of this. We are accustomed to always blaming others, principally the Indigenous people themselves (viewing them as a problem to be solved); secondarily the government or system, without realizing that we are the ones who construct this system. The first step we need to take, therefore, is to recognize that we are part of this structural racism.

We have been shown the underlying realities of our society. The October protests, the COVID-19 pandemic, and even the Coca Codo Sinclair Hydroelectric Project's disasters brought to light inequalities in our society and showed us once again that it is always the most vulnerable groups who most suffer the impacts from these events while continuing to be made invisible: Indigenous people, rural mestizos, and Afro-Ecuadorians. For this reason, we recognize that it is imperative to legitimize the protest spaces where Indigenous peoples and others have succeeded in calling the non-Indigenous public's attention to ask them to "acknowledge our reality." Beyond this, we believe that even though the protests have earned an essential place in history for making this acknowledgement possible, the work should not only fall on those who choose to protest. It is necessary that mestizo populations also recognize Ecuador's racism and, above all, what it means to live with privilege in a racialized system. Proceeding from that recognition, these Ecuadorans must educate themselves, come to know other realities, and be prepared to renounce their privileges:

Somos los hijos del primer levantamiento. (We are children of the first uprising.) The protests have impacted us: young Indigenous and mestizo people, whether in primary school, high school, or university. As students, we follow the legacy that has been passed down to us. The struggle continues as we adapt to changes but also seek to make racism more visible. In October 2019, we experienced a new awakening in the face of an enormous ethnoracial rupture in Ecuador, and an opportunity to begin to speak, visibilize, and share.

NOTES

1. Teleamazonas, Prime Time News.

2. While this chapter focuses on the Indigenous population in describing the October protests, we would nevertheless like to clarify that there are other ethnoracial groups in Ecuador that experience similar realities (Afro Ecuadorians, *Montubios*, rural mestizos).

3. "*Sumak Kawsay* or *Buen Vivir* is a participative process that is constantly constructing itself and evolving. It is the path that leads to a full life in harmony with all the beings of Mother Earth." This Kichwa concept was adopted as a fundamental principle of the new Constitution of 2008 (CONAIE Administrator 2017).

4. Alianza País is the political party/movement founded by Rafael Correa. The current president, Lenín Moreno, is Correa's former vice president and also belongs to this party.

REFERENCES

Acción Ecológica, ed. 2015. "Informe sobre desalojos forzosos realizados por el estado ecuatoriano y La Empresa Minera China, Ecuacorriente (ECSA) en La Cordillera Del Cóndor Parroquia Tundayme." https://www.ocmal.org/informe-por-los-desalojos-forzosos-en-tundayme/.

Arsel, Murat, and Natalia Ávila. 2011. "State, Society and Nature in Ecuador: The Case of the Yasuní-ITT initiative." *NEBE Working Paper 2*, ISS/Hivos/USFQ/LIDEMA.

Arsel, Murat, Barbara Hogenboom, and Lorenzo Pellegrini. 2016. "The Extractive Imperative and the Boom in Environmental Conflicts at the End of the Progressive Cycle in Latin America." *Extractive Industries and Society* 3, no. 4: 877–79.

Assies, Willem, and Cletus Gregor Barié. 2003. *Pueblos indígenas y derechos constitucionales en América Latina: Un panorama.* Quito: Comisión Nacional Para El Desarrollo De Los Pueblos Indígenas y México Gobierno De La República, Banco Mundial Fideicomiso Noruego.

Bedoya, César. 2013. "Minería, movimientos sociales y respuestas campesinas. Una ecología política de transformaciones territoriales." *Íconos—Revista De Ciencias Sociales* no. 30: 125–27. doi:10.17141/iconos.30.2008.256.

Cholango, Humberto. 2012. "Los pueblos y nacionalidades de Ecuador frente al extractivismo." Conference paper, Universidad Politécnica Salesiana. Quito.

Cisneros, Paul. 2009. "El diálogo minero en el Ecuador: ¿Señales de una nueva relación entre comunidades, empresas extractivas y estado?" Facultad Latinoamericana De Ciencias Sociales, Observatorio Socio Ambiental.

CONAIE Administrator. 2017. "Con sus prácticas de vida los pueblos construyen milenariamente el Sumak Kawsay." *CONAIE*. May 24, 2017. https://conaie. org/2017/05/19/practicas-pueblos-y-nacionalidades/.

CONAIE Administrator. 2020. "Confederación De Nacionalidades Indígenas Del Ecuador." *CONAIE*. June 11. http://www.conaie.org/.

Consejo de Gobierno de Salasaka. 2019. "Soy Runa Kichwa Salasaka, de generación en generación vengo trabajando la tierra, cantando penas, danzando alegrías, desde lo profundo de mi memoria hemos respetado la diferencia que existe" Facebook post, October 5, 2019. https://www.facebook.com/413605409225188/ photos/a.413609809224748/475198196399242/?type=3&theater 2019.

Cortés, Alexis. 2012. "Modernización, dependencia y marginalidad: Itinerario conceptual de la sociología latinoamericana." *Sociologías* 14, no. 29: 214–35. doi:10.1590/S1517-45222012000100009.

De La Torre, Carlos. 2002. *El racismo en Ecuador: Experiencias de los indios de clase media*. Quito. ABYA YALA.

El Comercio. 2017. "Tres años de movilizaciones contra el gobierno de Rafael Correa." Editorial, August 17, 2017. https://www.elcomercio.com/actualidad/ ocho-movilizaciones-regimen-rafaelcorrea.html.

El Universo. 2019. "Mas del 80% de detenciones fueron ilegales y arbitrarias." October 17, 2019. https://www.eluniverso.com/noticias/2019/10/17/nota/7562600/ mas-80-detenciones-fueron-ilegales-arbitrarias.

Enlace Ciudadano. 2013. "Nro. 333 Desde La Maná, Cotopaxi." Presented by Rafael Correa. August 28, 2013. https://www.youtube.com/watch?v=NhQkR xgt7KU.

Enlace Ciudadano. 2015. "Nro. 410 Desde Pomasqui, Pichincha." Presented by Rafael Correa. August 7, 2015. https://www.youtube.com/watch?v=PR-DzX4-eyw.

Fernández-Salvador, Elena del Consuelo. 2018. "The Shuar and Large-Scale Mining in Zamora-Chinchipe, Ecuador: A Study of Ethnopolitics and the Struggle over Natural Resources." PhD dissertation, ISS-Erasmus University Rotterdam.

Garzón, Paulina. 2019. "Implicaciones de la relación entre China y América Latina. Una mirada al caso ecuatoriano." *Ecología Política* 56: 80–88.

GKcity. 2019a. "El ministro de Defensa desconoce la existencia de los territorios indigenas del Ecuador." October 7, 2019. https://gk.city/2019/10/07/ ministro-defensa-desconoce-existencia-pueblos-indigenas/.

GKcity. 2019b. "Organizaciones nacionales e internacionales preocupadas por vulneración de derechos humanos durante protestas Ecuador." October 7, 2019. https:// gk.city/2019/10/07/violacion-derechos-humanos-protestas-paro-nacional/.

GKcity. 2019c. "Lenin Moreno traslada el gobierno a Guayaquil, rechaza revisar las medidas y acusa al correísmo de la violencia." October 8, 2019. https:// gk.city/2019/10/08/lenin-moreno-traslada-sede-de-gobierno/.

Izurieta, Belén. 2020. "¿Qué pasó en Ecuador en octubre de 2019?" *El Outsider*: 99–106.

Larrea, Ana. 2004. "El movimiento indígena ecuatoriano: Participación y resistencia." *FLACSO*.

Lu, Flora, Gabriela Valdivia, and Néstor L. Silva. 2017. *Oil, Revolution, and Indigenous Citizenship in Ecuadorian Amazonia*. New York: Palgrave MacMillan.

Maurera, Sandra. 2019. "Paz, conflicto y violencia en Ecuador, 2019." *Revista de Cultura de Paz*: 133–48.

Méndez, Johan. 2012. "Eurocentrismo y modernidad: Una mirada desde la filosofía latinoamericana y el pensamiento descolonial." *Revista OMNIA* 18, no. 3: 49–65.

Muyolema, Armando. 2001. "De la 'cuestión Indígena' a lo 'indígena' como cuestionamiento. Hacia una crítica del latinoamericanismo, el indigenismo y el mestizaje." In *Convergencia de tiempos: Estudios subalternos/contextos latinoamericanos estados, cultural, subalteridad*, edited by Ileana Rodríguez, 327–63. Amsterdam: Editions Rodopi.

Pacheco, Mayra. 2019. "Decreto 883 establece que el alza de las gasolinas extra y ecopaís y del diésel regirá desde el 3 de octubre del 2019." *El Comercio*. October 2, 2019. https://www.elcomercio.com/actualidad/decreto-alza-gasolinas-diesel-subsidios.html.

Pequeño, Andrea. 2009. "Participación y políticas de mujeres indígenas en contextos latinoamericanos recientes." *FLACSO*.

Revista Crisis. 2019. "Insurrección 2.0. Los medios alternativos y el paro nacional." *Revista Crisis*.

Riofrío, Isabel. 2017. "Ecuador: Líderes indígenas piden 177 amnistías y 20 indultos para procesados durante el gobierno de Correa." *Mongabay*.

Stutzman, Ronald. 1981. "El Mestizaje: An All-Inclusive Ideology of Exclusion." In *Cultural Transformations and Ethnicity in Modern Ecuador*, edited by Norman E. Whitten, Jr, 45–94. Champaign: University of Illinois Press.

Tuaza, Luis Alberto. 2011. "Runakunaka Ashka Shaikushka Shinami Rikurinkuna, ña Mana Tandanakunata Munankunachu: Reflexiones sobre la crisis del movimiento indígena ecuatoriano desde las bases comunitarias." PhD dissertation, FLACSO.

Vallejo, Ivette, and Miriam García. 2017. "Mujeres indígenas y neo-extractivismo petrolero en la Amazonía centro del Ecuador: Reflexiones sobre ecologías y ontologías políticas en articulación." *Enfoques*: 1–43.

VA Television. 2019. "Nebot recomienda de forma racista y regionalista que los indígenas se queden en el Páramo." YouTube (video). https://www.youtube.com/watch?v=M5BoU73zJ2E.

Wambra. 2020. "Las muertes sin respuesta del paro nacional en Ecuador." January 8, 2020. https://wambra.ec/muertes-paro-ecuador/#:~:text=Cuatro.

Weisbrot, Mark. 2019. "The IMF Is Hurting Countries It Claims to Help." *The Guardian*. August 27, 2019. https://www.theguardian.com/commentisfree/2019/aug/27/imf-economics-inequality-trump-ecuador.

PART 3
GRASSROOTS PERSPECTIVES ON THE FRAGMENTATION OF BRICS

From Elusiveness to Ideological Extravaganza: Gender and Sexuality in Brazil-China Relations

Cai Yiping and Sonia Correa

AN EMERGING BILATERAL DISCOURSE

Gender and sexuality metaphors infuse the imaginaries of macroeconomic and political relationships between China and South America. They are pronounced when diplomats, scholars, and journalists talk about "inevitable marriage," "flirtation," or "courtship" between the two regions (Introduction, this volume, 3). This shift toward sexualized metaphors of intimacy marks an transformation in relations between China and South America, moving away from revolutionary Third Worldism toward bilateralism and possibly new relations of dependency. One example of this occurred in 2020 when Brazilian vice president Hamilton Mourão observed that Brazil's bond with China was an "inevitable marriage." As Zhiwei points out in his chapter in this volume (75), the word "inevitable" reflects the reality that China and Brazil are "indivisible." Moving from the geopolitical scale to local contexts, Queiroz, Praça, and Bitencourt (353–57) touch upon the sexual and gender aspects of the Brazil-China relationship, putting forth an integrated analysis of environmental racism and extractive patriarchy in their study of community mobilizations around a China-linked steel plant (CSA) in the Rio de Janeiro area, a metals firm recently bought by China: "Women are on the margins of the 'development' process created by CSA. Paid reproductive work, such as cleaning and cooking services, is almost their only opportunity to be included in the local labor market" (354).

In this context, our chapter zooms in on the bilateral gender/sexuality political and policy dialogues that have animated the most heated debates within and between China and Brazil: the policy platforms that have informed geopolitical sexualized imaginaries, as well as the systemic patriarchy and sexualized racism that structures power in both countries and in their transcontinental relationship. We frame the on-going global debates regarding women's and LGBTQI+ rights against the backdrop of the transformations that have taken place in both countries with regard to these issues, pointing toward ways in which they might develop.

Over the last decade, Brazil and China's economies have attracted global attention. Both are part of multilateral organizations (the United Nations [UN], World Trade Organization, Group 20, BRICS [Brazil, Russia, India, China, and South Africa], and so on), and Brazil is one of China's top destinations for direct investment and trading in Latin America and the Caribbean. Since the bilateral agreements made in 2000, finance and energy industries have expanded in both countries (Ministry of Foreign Affairs n.d.). Today, relations between Brazil and China are immersed in tensions caused by ideological attacks from Brazil's far-right nationalists against the Asian giant.

This chapter explores Brazil-China relations through the lens of gender, sexuality, and an analysis of UN conferences and legislative changes of the 1990s. The UN Conference on Environment and Development (UN-CED-Earth Summit) held in Rio de Janeiro in 1992 and the Fourth UN Conference on Women held in Beijing in 1995 had tremendous impacts on both countries. These events took place alongside two other major events: the International Conference on Human Rights (hosted in Vienna in 1993) and the International Conference on Population and Development (hosted in Cairo in 1994). Together, this cycle of conferences shaped policy and normative definitions, including intergovernmental agreements in relation to the concepts of gender and gender equality, women's and girls' rights, and sexual violence. Indeed, it was at the Fourth UN Conference on Women in Beijing that UN member states agreed to define sexual rights for the first time in history.[1] These conferences continue to be mentioned in periodical UN reviews, and definitions emerging from them have been translated into national laws, jurisprudence, and policy frameworks in many countries, including Brazil (Yiping and Dandan 2018).

Perhaps the best indicator of the impacts of the 1990s intergovernmental debates and agreements on these subjects was the reaction they sparked among conservative social and institutional actors, as well as among states that resisted them (Girard 2007). This reaction expanded beyond the UN's organizational boundaries. Since 2013, it has fueled antigender campaigns, often in opposition to abortion rights, which swept across Europe, Latin America, and the US (Kuhar and Patternote 2017; Case 2019). As a result of these mobilizations and their effects on national politics, and in sharp contrast with its past diplomatic behaviors, the Brazilian state became an advocate of regressive agendas.

In tracking the relations between Brazil and China, it is also worth noting that in the same 1990s UN conferences in which Brazil would play a very progressive role in relation to gender and sexuality, there existed ample room for civil society exchanges. For example, the parallel nongovernmental organization (NGO) events at UNCED and the Beijing Conference brought together civil society organizations (CSOs) and representatives from all over the world. However, although representatives from Chinese civil society were present in Rio in 1992, they were not visible. Three years later, the Beijing Conference and the Huairou Women's NGO Forum were attended by many Brazilian feminists. Once again, interactions with the Chinese women's organization were limited.

No consistent connections existed between Chinese and Brazilian civil societies regarding gender and sexuality before BRICS consolidated in the late 2000s. Consolidation along the China and Brazil axis began mostly through private companies and policy dialogue platforms—including those linked to BRICS itself—and through academic circuits (including economic and development policy and strategic studies). Chinese and Brazilian civil society actors also established rapports during the World Social Forums, though this was less common. Exchanges about gender and sexuality were even more scarce, although some interactions emerged between Brazilian and Chinese researchers and activists through Sexuality Policy Watch (SPW), the transnational research and action forum of the Brazilian Interdisciplinary AIDS Association. Relationships were strengthened in 2014 before and after the fifth BRICS Summit held in Fortaleza, when a parallel transnational civil society event was organized by Brazilian NGOs and social movements. After 2014, interactions evolved through the establishment of platforms aimed at infusing a gender perspective into BRICS (Oxfam Russia 2018).

Here, we investigate Chinese and Brazilian gender and sexuality exchanges between 2009 and 2015, paying attention to the SPW project, Emerging Powers, Sexuality and Human Rights. The chapter begins by revisiting the early grounds and outcomes of these interactions, providing a bird's-eye view of Brazilian and Chinese sexual political landscapes and the shifts that have occurred since then. Our concluding argument examines why it is difficult to establish durable connections between Chinese and Brazilian activists and researchers working within this domain.

BRICS AND SEXUALITY POLICY WATCH

The SPW was established as the Working Group on Sexuality and Social Policy in 2002, later changing its name. From the start, the SPW engaged in analyses and action-oriented research of transnational sexual politics that, since 2009, included China. The most significant of these projects was titled Emerging Powers, Sexuality and Human Rights (2012–2015). This included researchers and activists from Brazil, China, India, and South Africa, addressing the ways in which the emergence of BRICS interacted with gender and sexuality issues.[2] The project encompassed a parallel forum—the 2014 Fortaleza Summit—and presented its final outcomes at the 2016 AWID Forum in Brazil. While all these exchanges were fruitful in terms of making Chinese feminist and sexual politics better known to the Global South, they did not focus specifically on the Brazil-China relationship. However, the analyses developed by the Emerging Powers, Sexuality and Human Rights Project have mapped out a landscape of what was happening in Brazilian and Chinese sexual politics at around the time of the consolidation of BRICS.

When the project was initiated, BRICS was a buzzword among states, the press, funding agencies, international NGOs, and local CSOs.[3] In these quarters, many people expected the dawning of the BRICS to reshape the transnational balance of trade, the multilateral complex of governance (of financial institutions in particular), and development models. The BRICS concept was propelling imaginaries of a new postcolonial order led by the South. As usual in progressive development circles, topics of gender, sexuality, and related human rights were almost entirely absent. This blind spot inspired the SPW to engage with the new project. Most academic and civil society actors involved saw this as an opportunity for policy engagement, advocacy, and funding. While open to these possibilities, the project was designed to determine the place and meaning of gender and sexuality in a changing geopolitical order.[4]

It should be also noted that, in 2012 when research started, Brazilian gender and sexuality activists and researchers had good reasons to be concerned about how BRICS could negatively impact the UN and other intergovernmental negotiations on gender, sexuality, and human rights. The UNCED Rio+20 Conference—which had championed gender equality and sexual and reproductive rights in the UN since the 1990s—removed sexual rights from its conference's final documents. This was justified by Brazilian president Rousseff to preserve the geopolitical alliance of the countries of the Global South, some of which would have resisted this language (Nabulivou and Nayar 2012).

Two years later, starting with the Fortaleza BRICS Summit, Chinese and Brazilian feminists began to collaborate through other platforms, such as the 2016 BRICS Feminist Watch (BFW). This was formed to ensure the alliance would prioritize gender equality. The BFW actively engaged with the BRICS forum and the New Development Bank along with other CSOs to advocate for gender equality within political economy and development issues.

GENDER AND SEXUALITY POLITICS IN LATE TWENTIETH-CENTURY BRAZIL

As noted in the 2015 report "Emerging Powers, Sexuality and Human Rights: Fumbling Around the Elephant" (Corrêa and Khanna 2015), political agendas that center gender and sexuality have a very long history in Brazil. They encompass the remnants of colonization, "conservative modernization" characterizing postcolonial state formations, and the importance of sexuality in the twentieth-century construction of Brazilian national identities (Parker 2009). Contemporary gender and sexuality issues and policies were also, of course, affected by the redemocratization that followed the military dictatorship (1964–1989). The combined effects of rural–urban migration, women's education and incorporation into modern labor markets, a rapid expansion of public health and the social security system, and a robust telecommunications policy resulted in a rapid demographic transition and the related transformation of family structures, without which the gender and sexuality demands examined below could not have emerged and expanded.

During the 1960s and 1970s, urban and rural guerrilla movements, labor unions, and popular organizations (mainly connected to the Catholic Church) were the main poles of resistance to the Brazilian dictatorship. As redemocratization gained steam during the 1980s, different voices of resistance arose, and the lingua franca of human rights was incorporated into Brazil's political vocabulary. This assemblage comprised a wide and complex spectrum of political movements, including those claiming rights in the realms of gender, reproduction, and sexuality. Coinciding with the height of the redemocratizing mobilizations, the HIV/AIDS epidemic further fueled public expression of these claims (Parker et al. 1995).

Between the 1980s (when Brazil's new constitution was approved) and the late 2000s, gender/sexuality movements provoked sociocultural, legal, and public policy transformations (de la Dehesa 2010). These engagements began with women's rights and health and gender-based violence, later expanding to HIV/AIDS and LGBT rights. Gradually, conversations previously at the margins of society moved to the center of policy making (Vianna and Carrara 2007). In the 2000s, these political, legal, and policy issues would gain institutional attention, as the left-wing Workers' Party (PT) governments (2002–2016) opened space for and raised the visibility of agendas. They did this in conjunction with civil society, but also through the creation of solid executive bodies such as the National Secretary for Women's Policy and the National LGBT Policy. During the first cycle of the PT era (2002–2010), this policy commitment manifested in a series of state-funded national conferences on women's policies and in a LGBT conference held in 2008, hosted by President Lula, which gained international attention. This conference occurred amid a larger campaign of national and international visibility, epitomized by the mid-2000s parades where millions of people gathered in favor of LGBTQI+ rights.

It should also be noted that, as Brazil democratized, social and institutional formations were also impacted by the growth of fundamentalist Christian Evangelism and the deepening of Catholic conservative restoration. These religious strands have gained influence on social norms, lawmakers, and public policies through electoral politics and other means.[5]

Their emergence led to bartering between progressive politicians and the neoconservative religious actors installed in legislative bodies whenever gender, sexuality, and abortion rights come up. Additionally, laws and policies approved in the period under examination have not always been effectively applied. This indicates the frailty of policy commitments to LGBTQI+ and women's rights, reducing faith in the idea that state policies can protect the vulnerable. Since the mid-2000s, neoconservative religious forces have launched increasingly open and systematic offensives against gender and sexuality cultural changes and their related policy and legal gains.[6]

GROWING MOVEMENTS IN THE NEW DECADE

Brazilian movements for gender, sexual, and democratic rights faced considerable obstacles in 2010 (Corrêa 2020). During her presidential campaign, former candidate Dilma Rousseff was fiercely attacked because she had previously expressed favor for abortion rights. The electoral process was impacted by major controversies around the National Human Rights Plan, when sharp conflicts led to the decriminalization of abortion, removal of religious symbols from state buildings, and the creation of a Truth Commission to review the military dictatorship's human rights violations (Corrêa 2010). Following Rousseff's election, tensions shifted to the realm of LGBT rights. In early 2011, a set of educational videos produced by the Ministry of Education was criticized by members of the neoconservative religious caucus within Congress, including then-MP Jair Bolsonaro. Under pressure, Rousseff suspended the so-called Gay Kit (as it was labeled by its opponents).[7] Two years later, "gender ideology" became the target of a coalition comprising Catholics and Evangelicals that nationally and locally debated the 2014–2024 National Educational Plan. This assault subsequently unfolded into hundreds of state and municipal legal initiatives proposing to eliminate the term *gender* in local educational plans.[8]

Brazilian streets were unexpectedly taken over by huge crowds demanding redistributive policies in 2013. Demonstrators took aim at corruption and denounced the negative impacts of the megaevents planned for the 2014 World Cup and 2016 Olympics. Political analysts have interpreted these mobilizations as a turning point in Brazilian politics, arguing that the mode of governance that matured in the 1990s in the form of coalition presidentialism, based on a fragmented political system, was beginning to crumble.[9] Investigations carried out by the Truth Commission became public, causing unease among the military and propelling the repoliticization of the armed forces.[10]

Amid the mid-2000s corruption scandals and the 2008 economic crisis, the presidential elections opened a window of opportunity for increasingly popular conservative, nationalist, and right-wing mobilization. In a polarized election, Rousseff was reelected by a small margin. The defeated candidate raised suspicions about electoral integrity. By March 2015, the streets of Brazil were again overtaken by protests that repudiated corruption and called for the removal of Rousseff. Congress passed regressive provisions regarding abortion, the traditional family, and the "propagation of gender ideology" in education. Meanwhile, the expanding anti-Rousseff faction within Congress moved swiftly to impeach her (de la Dehesa 2013).

ANTIGENDER AS POLITICS BY OTHER MEANS

On April 17, 2016, millions watched the House vote for Dilma Rousseff's impeachment and were stunned to see most MPs affirming their faith in God, religion, and the family upon declaring their votes. This neoconservative religious climate revealed to wider audiences what had been unfolding for three decades in legislative debates on abortion, gender, and sexuality. The plenary session culminated with MP Jair Bolsonaro dedicating his vote to the military.

A year and a half later, in November 2017, philosopher Judith Butler visited Brazil and became the target of a virulent online campaign that depicted her as a "gender ideologue." This was followed by a public protest where an effigy portraying her as a witch was burned. The protest was small but represented an aggressive and public political performance against "gender ideology" that had previously been limited to religious circuits and policy debates. The "burning of Butler" gathered a heterogeneous assemblage of secular and religious actors that orbited around an "ecumenical" core composed of neoconservative Catholics and Evangelicals. This group expanded, becoming increasingly bellicose when the 2018 presidential campaign took off. In addition to the use of illegal messaging and accessing of personal digital data, Bolsonaro's campaign strategy was based on the dissemination of propaganda against "gender ideology." One of the most widely shared narratives in this stream of fake news were tales of the distribution of the "Gay Kit" by his opponent, Fernando Haddad, when the latter had been Minister of Education in 2011.

A study performed by AVAAZ in partnership with Idea-BigData shows that 83.7 percent of voters who received these materials believed them to be true (Pasquini 2018). "Gender ideology" cohered sexual morality and political corruption while "Marxist communism" simultaneously incited political panic, reviving deep anti-Communism sentiments in Brazilian society (Corrêa and Parker 2019). Since Bolsonaro's election, antigender rhetoric systematically peppered public authorities' speech. Attacks on gender and sexuality in education grew, and strict antigender guidelines were incorporated in human rights and foreign policy frameworks. Brazil is entrenched in antigender stances that are deeply embedded in statecraft.[11]

GENDER AND SEXUALITY POLITICS IN "RISING CHINA"

The Bolsonaro regime continued pushing anticommunist panic. Accusations targeted the PT and its legacy, as well as ex-president Lula. However, they also aimed at Venezuela, Cuba, Argentina, and, more intensively, at China. The Asian giant was persistently portrayed as an evil communist state rivaling Trump's US. In the parlance of government ideologues, China is depicted as antithetical to the Western Judeo-Christian values and that Brazil needs to be "saved from disaster" (Gonçalves 2021). In early 2019, key figures of Bolsonaro's inner circle viciously lambasted right-wing MPs who traveled to China for a commercial cooperation tour. In 2020, the surge of COVID-19 and the subsequent Chinese vaccine diplomacy further fueled open ideological assaults. The minister of foreign affairs called COVID-19 the "Communavirus," and the federal government tried to block an agreement between the Chinese company Sinovac and the state of São Paulo to produce vaccines in Brazil. The COVID-19 crisis also set the stage for new relationships between the two countries, however. State governors, in opposition to Bolsonaro, began to negotiate for vaccines and other medical products. Chinese development cooperation supported a number of nonstate COVID-19 emergency programs, including those conducted by labor unions.

Meanwhile, there was intensified state control and surveillance and revived cultural conservatism in China (e.g., the reactivation of Confucian values to ensure social harmony and the women's role in the family) (Corrêa and Khanna 2015). Simultaneously, rapid transformations of Chinese sexual identities, norms, and practices emerged within public discourse. This is sharply reflected in sexuality research, which is leaving behind its previous roots in sexology (Yingying 2019). Various issues related to gender and sexuality, women's rights, and development in China are now raising concern among policy makers, researchers, women's rights advocates, and CSOs. This list includes (but is not limited to) gender-based violence, misogyny, and discrimination against women, the LGBTQI+ community, and gender nonconforming people. Chinese scholars and activists understand how the complexity of antigender, antisex, and anticommunism politics in the global context shapes and is shaped by local gender and sexuality politics.

Market forces and commercialization play an important role in the realm of gender and sexuality politics in the PRC. China is one of the world's largest manufacturers of erotic and contraceptive products. The National Sex Culture, Adult Products, and Health Care Products Expo has been held in Guangzhou since 1999. Activities organized by LGBTQI+ groups, young feminists, and sexuality educators have increased the visibility of sexuality and gender issues. These movements are often inspired by global trends in terms of their framing, strategy, and actions, but this does not automatically lead to sustained organizational or institutional transformation. The heated debates and discussion can be observed on social media platforms and mainstream media, which reflect the growing anxieties and panic over declining fertility and rising divorce rates (which are often blamed on women's rights and economic independence, and the influence of the West). Resistance to "sexual liberation" within Chinese society culminated in the voices of prominent local groups like "antipornography network" or "antisex aunties." The latter was known for publicly assaulting and denouncing sex education programs at the 2014 Sex Culture Expo held in Xi'an (Lele 2021). Ironically, one of the antipornography volunteer groups was initiated by the sex shop owners who pledged a respect for love and the family and denounced extramarital sex. These women are usually Evangelical Christians and may represent a larger, transnational antigender movement.

Legislation in China has not created a clear path toward gender equality. The Chinese government officially suspended the thirty-five-year-old one-child policy in 2013 (Gu, Mao, and Hu 2019). In 2015, an anti–domestic violence law was finally adopted after nearly two decades of efforts by women's organizations, researchers, and women's rights lawyers. Civil society applauded these changes. However, feminists remain concerned about the 2021 civil code, which established a thirty-day cooling-off period for couples who want to dissolve their marriages, although this clause does not apply to families with a history of domestic violence or extramarital affairs (Yan 2020). A new overseas NGO law was approved in early 2017 to regulate the activities of foreign NGOs in China. It required foreign organizations to register with the Ministry of Public Security and have an official Chinese sponsor organization. These measures regulate relationships between Chinese and foreign NGOs, especially those advocating for human and women's rights, LGBTQI+ issues, labor rights, and environmental protection (Batke 2020).

In sharp contrast to this restrictive regulation—along with the "China rising" geopolitical narrative of the last decade—the government expanded its commitment to gender equality and women's development at the global level. China and UN Women cohosted meetings to commemorate Beijing+20 in 2015 and Beijing+25 in 2020. On these occasions, President Xi Jinping reaffirmed that gender equality is state policy and that China's financial support to UN Women and developing nations was meant to accelerate the implementation of the Beijing Platform for Action and Sustainable Development Goals (SDG 5) on gender equality and women's empowerment (Xi Jinping 2020). Most importantly (and for the first time in the context of the newly launched "China's International Development Cooperation in the New Era" policy), gender equality is one of the priority areas for China's future international development cooperation (State Council Information Office 2021). However, scholars raised concerns that without meaningful participation of women's CSOs and human rights advocates, the agenda might not be implemented (Shieh 2021).

Despite restrictions on foreign NGOs in China, Chinese NGOs are now "going out" (or "going global") as part of the new phase of the Belt and Road Initiative. The Chinese government encouraged NGOs to play a wider role in global issues, such as humanitarian relief and poverty alleviation, climate change, counterterrorism, and food security. It sees the initiative as an agent for "soft power" and as a tool for global governance (China Daily 2016). The Chinese state is also moving away from a government-oriented approach toward foreign aid. The draft guidelines of the China South-South Cooperation Fund were written to support other developing countries in fulfilling the objectives of the 2030 sustainable development agenda. In a global environment in which financial support for civil society is shrinking, this policy shift will affect many countries such as Brazil.

WILL BRAZIL AND CHINA CONNECT ON GENDER AND SEXUALITY?

Since the mid-2000s, China's impact on the Brazilian political economy has been expanding. The concrete connections between the two countries remain quite vague, however, even regarding economic development. Consistent and precise analyses of China and its expanding investments reveal that Brazilian territories/regions are unevenly affected (Queiroz, Praça, and Bitencourt, this volume). This vagueness is more pronounced in relation to matters of gender and sexuality. One of the videos reporting on the Civil Society Forum (held in parallel with the 2014 Fortaleza BRICS Summit) featured gender activists that spoke about the potentially detrimental effects of BRICS, which mostly meant Chinese investments, and their threat to both bodies and territories—an elusive affirmation. On the Chinese side of the equation, information on Brazil can hardly be found in the media (except during the BRICS Summits). Perceptions of Brazil among the Chinese public have been limited to football, samba, and Carnival. However, Chinese CSO representatives who attended the World Social Forum or Rio+20 Summit in Brazil were impressed by Brazil's vibrant social movements and their critical attitude toward government. As we have seen, gender and sexuality political and policy landscapes in Brazil and China have been transformed since 2012. Exchanges, dialogues, and relations have expanded in various domains.

In terms of state-led dynamics, China established a new frame for development that is open to civil society. On the Brazilian side, the rightward shift created a scenario in which China is now squarely plotted in the maze of antigender ideology and politics. Even so, this overlap is never mentioned in the swarm of analyses that have proliferated since 2019 that examine the constant attacks of the Bolsonaro administration against China. The rather unexpected ideological nexus now linking Brazil, China, and gender/sexuality politics (through "communism") may, however, inspire the renewal and amplification of exchanges between researchers and activists engaged with these political and conceptual domains in the two countries.

For Chinese scholars and activists engaging in gender and sexual politics, there is no better way to understand and resist the resurgence of conservative traditional gender norms and values (and to disclose the subtle and complicated linkage between antisex and antipornography groups) than to learn from Brazilian colleagues who have frontline experience. There has been growing collaboration between CSOs in China and other South countries that have received Chinese investments and development aid. With this comes a focus on monitoring the social and environmental impacts on human rights (including gender rights) in local communities.

Cooperation between Brazil and the PRC with regard to gender and sexual politics has become more imperative in this context. Patterns of Chinese development assistance need to be looked at closely and critically, as they may impact upon this work in unexpected ways. It would also be productive to explore the vague links established between "gender ideology," communism, and the realities of gender and sexuality in China. But there are also challenges to be faced. While the trajectory and lessons of past interactions have fertilized a terrain upon which a new cycle of exchanges can grow, dialogue must increase and diversify so that such an endeavor might become fruitful, inspirational, and sustainable.

NOTES

1. The first part of Paragraph 96 of the Beijing Platform of Action ensures human rights of women include their right to exercise their sexuality, free from discrimination, coercion, and violence. But in the years that followed, this language would be redrafted in the UN Human Rights Surveillance Committees and Special Procedures reports. It now reads: "All persons have the right to exercise their sexuality free from discrimination coercion and violence while ensuring that no harm is infringed upon the rights of others."

2. SPW's second round of global research (2008–2010) sponsored regional dialogues that opened the opportunity for a first engagement with Chinese researchers (Corrêa, de la Dehesa, and Parker 2014). In 2013, while the Emerging Powers project was still underway, SPW conducted two training programs on sexuality research for Global South activists and researchers, in which three young Chinese women participated. Lastly, in 2018 the final report of a last cycle of global research was launched, which includes a chapter on Chinese contemporary sexual politics authored by Huang Ying-Ying (Corrêa and Parker 2019).

3. Local civil society mobilization around BRICS was uneven across the five countries. It gradually became very intense in Brazil and gained traction in South Africa. It was not strong in India and rather weak in Russia and China, which were primarily represented by think tanks and researchers.

4. The outcomes of the project, which include two reports and a series of videos documenting the Civil Society Forum, were organized in parallel to the fifth BRICS Summit in Fortaleza (Waisbich 2016).

5. The "return of the religious" in neoconservative expressions is not exclusively Brazilian. But the impact of religious neoconservatism on lawmaking and public policy is notable and mainly due to growing Evangelical influence since the 1980s. On their side, ultra-Catholic forces resort to both well-established methods of direct influence on high-level policy makers and members of the Church.

6. This can be illustrated by two key events of those years. In 2005, a Tripartite Commission was created by the executive branch to reform punitive abortion laws. When it presented its results, the corruption scandal (the Mensalão) of the PT government erupted, leading the executive branch to retreat from the proposal. Subsequently, an antiabortion caucus was established at the House. This was also followed by the 2007 Conference of Latin American Bishops that hosted Pope Benedict XVI and other ultra-Catholic organizations, which began propagating attacks against "gender ideology."

7. When informing the public about the decision, Rousseff declared that her government would not "impose" sexual orientation on public school students.

8. The national survey performed by the Professores contra o Escola sem Partido identified 106 law provisions either presented or approved at state and municipal levels. Until 2020, 17 other antigender law provisions had been tabled at the House, none of which has yet been approved. These provisions keep proliferating even when the Supreme Court has already decided only a few of those that had been approved, considering them to be unconstitutional.

9. The definition of coalition presidentialism was crafted by political scientist Sergio Abranches (1988) In 2018, Abranches adjusted the original frame in the following terms: "The multiparty coalition is an essential requirement of governance in the Brazilian model. Not all multiparty presidential regimes are so dependent on a majority coalition. In Brazil, coalitions are not contingent, they are imperative. No president has ruled without the support and respect of a coalition. It is a permanent feature of our versions of coalition presidentialism."

10. Regarding the repoliticization of the military, another trend to be taken into account is that from the mid-1990s onward, the Army has been increasingly called to intervene in territories affected by the unresolved crisis of public security, in particular in Rio de Janeiro.

11. The other main examples are Hungary and Poland. There was also much convergence between the Bolsonaro antigender agenda and the Trump administration's policy guidelines.

REFERENCES

Abranches, Sérgio. 2018. *Presidencialismo de coalizão: Raízes e evolução do modelo político brasileiro*. São Paulo: Companhia das Letras.

Abranches, Sergio. 1988. "Presidencialismo de coalizão: O dilema institucional brasileiro." *Dados* 31, no. 1: 5–9.

Batke, Jessica. 2020. "The New Normal for Foreign NGOs in 2020." China NGO Project. https://www.chinafile.com/ngo/analysis/new-normal-foreign-ngos-2020.

Case, Mary Anne. 2019. *Trans Formations in the Vatican's War on "Gender Ideology."* Chicago: University of Chicago Law School, Chicago Unbound.

China Daily. 2016. "China's NGOs Urged to Play Bigger Role on Global Issues." April 19, 2016. http://www.chinadaily.com.cn/china/2016-04/19/content_24676002.htm.

Corrêa, Sonia. 2010. "Abortion and Human Rights in Brazil -Part II." Sexuality Policy Watch. https://sxpolitics.org/abortion-and-human-rights-in-brazil-part-2/5184.

Corrêa, Sonia S , ed. 2020. *Anti-gender Politics in Latin America. Summaries of Country Case Studies*. Rio de Janeiro: Associação Brasileira Interdisciplinas de Aids (ABIA). https://sxpolitics.org/GPAL/uploads/E-book-Resumos-completo.pdf.

Corrêa, Sonia, Rafael de la Dehesa, and Richard Parker. 2014. "Sexuality and Politics: Regional Dialogues from the Global South—Volume 2," Sexuality Policy Watch. https://www.sxpolitics.org/sexuality-and-politics/volume2.html.

Corrêa, Sonia, and Isabela Kalil. 2020. "The Case of Brazil: A Perfect Catastrophe?" In *Anti-gender Politics in Latin America. Summaries of Country Case Studies*, edited by Sonia Corrêa, 47–65. Rio de Janeiro: Associação Brasileira Interdisciplinas de Aids (ABIA). https://sxpolitics.org/GPAL/uploads/E-book-Resumos-completo.pdf.

Corrêa, Sonia, and Akshay Khanna. 2015. "Emerging Powers, Sexuality and Human Rights: Fumbling around the Elephant?" SPW Working Papers, no. 11 (June).

Corrêa, Sonia, and Richard Parker. 2019. *SexPolitics: Trends & Tensions in the 21st Century—Contextual Undercurrents*. Rio de Janeiro: Sexuality Policy Watch.

de la Dehesa, Rafael. 2010. *Queering the Public Sphere in Mexico and Brazil: Sexual Rights Movements in Emerging Democracies*. Durham, NC: Duke University Press.

de la Dehesa, Rafael. 2013. *The End(s) of Activism? Sexual Rights and the Brazilian Workers Party*. Fletcher Forum. http://www.fletcherforum.org/2013/09/30/deladehesa/.

Girard, Françoise. 2007. "Negotiating Sexual Rights and Sexual Orientation at UN," in *Sex Politics: Reports from the Frontlines,* edited by R. Parker, R. Petchesky, and R. Sember. Sexuality Policy Watch. http://www.sxpolitics.org/frontlines/home/index.php.

Gu, Baochang, Zhuoyan Mao, and Mengyun Hu. 2019. *An Ongoing Journey: Review of ICPD+25 in China*. Beijing: China Population and Development Research Center and UNFPA China.

Kuhar, Roman, and David Patternote, eds. 2017. *Anti-Gender Campaigns in Europe: Mobilising Against Equality*. London: Rowman & Littlefield.

Lele, Hu. 2021. "Anti-sex Aunties" Should Not "Anti-sex" with Violence." *People*. http://opinion.people.com.cn/n/2014/1118/c1003-26048516.html.

Gonçalves, Marcos Augusto. 2021. "Derrota de Trump prenuncia ataque inédito e violento da direita radical, diz Benjamin Teitelbaum." A review of *The War for Eternity* by Benjamin Teiltebaum. *Folha de São Paulo*, January 15, 2021. https://www1.folha.uol.com.br/ilustrissima/2021/01/derrota-de-trump-prenuncia-ataque-inedito-e-violento-da-direita-radical-diz-benjamin-teitelbaum.shtml.

Ministry of Foreign Affairs of the People's Republic of China. n.d. " China and Brazil." https://www.fmprc.gov.cn/mfa_eng/wjb_663304/zzjg_663340/ldmzs_664952/gjlb_664956/3473_665008/.

Nabulivou, Noelene, and Anita Nayar. 2012. "DAWN Speaks Truth to Power at Rio+20! DAWN." Dawnnet. https://dawnnet.org/sites/default/files/articles/dawn_analysis_rio20.pdf.

Oxfam Russia. 2018. "Feminist Watch and Advancing Feminist Agenda in International Development in the Context of BRICS." https://en.oxfam.ru/news/575/.

Parker, Richard G. 2009. *Bodies, Pleasures, and Passions: Sexual Culture in Contemporary Brazil*. Nashville, TN: Vanderbilt University Press.

Parker, Richard, Renato Quemmel, Katia Guimares, Murilo Mota, and Veriano Terto Jr. 1995. "AIDS Prevention and Gay Community Mobilization in Brazil." *Development—Journal of the Society for International Development* 2: 49–53.

Pasquini, Patrícia. 2018. "90% dos eleitores de Bolsonaro acreditaram em fake news, diz estudo." Uol, Folha De S.Paulo. https://www1.folha.uol.com.br/poder/2018/11/90-dos-eleitores-de-bolsonaro-acreditaram-em-fake-news-diz-estudo.shtml.

State Council Information Office of the People's Republic of China. 2021. "China's International Development Cooperation in the New Era."

Shieh, Shawn. 2021. "China's White Paper and the BRI: Can We Expect China to Deliver on the SDGs?" Business and Human Rights Resource Center (March). https://www.bhrrc.org/en/blog/chinas-white-paper-and-the-bri-can-we-expect-china-to-deliver-on-the-sdgs/.

Vianna, Adriana, and Sergio Carrara. 2007. "Sexual Politics and Sexual Rights in Brazil: A Case Study" In *Sex Politics: Reports from the Frontlines*, edited by R. Parker, R. Petchesky, and R. Sember. Sexuality Policy Watch. https://www.sxpolitics.org/frontlines/book/pdf/capitulo1_brazil.pdf.

Waisbich, Laura Trajber. 2016. "Diverse Voices: A Brief Account on the Civil Society Spaces at the Margins of the 8th BRICS Summit in India." Sexuality Policy Watch. https://sxpolitics.org/diverse-voices-a-brief-account-on-the-civil-society-spaces-at-the-margins-of-the-8th-brics-summit-in-india/16206.

Xi Jinping, H. E. 2020. "Statement Made by President of the People's Republic of China, High-level Meeting on the Twenty-fifth Anniversary of the Fourth

World Conference on Women." October 1, 2020. www.fmprc.gov.cn/mfa_eng/wjdt_665385/zyjh_665391/t1821556.shtml.

Yan, Alice. 2020. "New Law Requires 30-Day Cooling-Off Period before Chinese Couples Can Divorce." *South China Morning Post*, May 31, 2020. https://www.scmp.com/news/china/society/article/3086837/new-law-requires-30-day-cooling-period-chinese-couples-can.

Yingying, Huang. 2019. "Sexuality Research and Sex Politics in 21st Century of Mainland China." In *Sex Politics: Trends & Tensions in the 21st Century—Contextual Undercurrents—Volume 2*, edited Sonia Correa and Richard Parker. Rio de Janeiro: Sexuality Policy Watch.

Yiping, Cai, and Zhang Dandan. 2018. *Body, Sexuality and Reproduction in a Changing Context. Development Alternatives with Women for a New Era.* DAWN. https://sxpolitics.org/trendsandtensions/uploads/volume2-2019-26042019.pdf.

The Refraction of Chinese Capital in Amazonian Entrepôts and the Infrastructure of a Global Sacrifice Zone

Gustavo Oliveira

AGROINDUSTRIAL TRADE is so central to Brazil-China relations that it continues unabated despite the shift in Brazilian geopolitical orientations during the administration of President Jair Bolsonaro. Despite anti-China rhetoric, the Bolsonaro government did continue to cater to agribusiness interests, encouraged further exports to China and even brokered the sale of Brazilian state-owned companies and infrastructure to Chinese companies (Senra 2019), illustrating the "pragmatism" with which political elites in both China and Brazil pursue economic ties perceived to be natural and inevitable (as Zhou, Camoça, Hendler, Rodríguez, and Aguiar explain in this volume). Here, I draw upon ethnographic fieldwork and theoretical frameworks of global political ecology to examine how Chinese capital is refracted through Brazilian actors to expand export-oriented infrastructure in the Amazon, turning Amazonian entrepôts into a global sacrifice zone.

These entrepôts are the linchpins of a combined strategy of Brazilian and transnational elites to facilitate the expansion of Brazilian agroindustrial exports. The agroindustrial boom that covered the Brazilian Cerrado with soybeans encounters a bottleneck in the road-based export channels through southeastern Brazil. Consequently, agribusinesses have pushed both left-wing and right-wing governments for infrastructure investments in the Amazon Basin, dubbed Arco Norte, the "northern arch" of export-oriented infrastructure. Between 2010 and 2018, soy and maize exports through the Arco Norte expanded from 6 to 30 million tons per year, doubling its share of total Brazilian exports from 14 percent to 28 percent (ANTAQ 2019). At the very heart of the Arco Norte is the Tapajós-Amazon waterway linking the ports of Barcarena and Miritituba (Pará state), operated mainly by Brazilian and transnational companies like Amaggi, Bunge, Cargill, Louis Dreyfus, and the leading Chinese agribusiness trading company COFCO.

This infrastructure is usually discussed in terms of "corridors," emphasizing *flows* of capital, energy, and commodities through railroads, power lines, and waterways (as Aguiar, Camoça and Hendler, and Thomaz et al. do in their chapters in this volume). Instead of discussing these ports in Barcarena and Miritituba as a "corridor," however, I insist on characterizing them as entrepôts, which brings attention to the social and material relations present in those locations. Moreover, while mainstream narratives, including many chapters in this volume, concern themselves with China's "impacts" upon Brazil, and the latter's "dependence" upon raw commodity exports to China, I reject such country-level and unilateral frameworks to focus on how such projects are *coproduced* by various actors across multiple scales and through complex socioecological transformations that cannot be reduced to "impacts" or "dependence" (Oliveira et al. 2020; Oliveira and Myers 2021). Thus, while some colleagues struggle to attribute "impacts" to China's investments in Brazil (Camoça and Hendler, for example, conclude in their chapter that "the importance of Chinese actors in this process, especially COFCO, is less clear in its effects," 265), I demonstrate how Chinese operations in the Arco Norte unfold in such a way that Chinese capital and corporate control become refracted through Brazilian public and private actors. This enables Chinese firms to circumvent socioenvironmental resistance, promoting continuities in Chinese investment strategies despite shifts in Brazilian politics. An ethnographic vignette illustrates how port construction in the Amazon is embroiled in socioeconomic, environmental, and ethnic conflicts in the region. I argue that the shifts in global political economy triggered by the US-China trade war and the COVID-19 pandemic increase the importance of these Chinese-backed projects in Amazonian entrepôts, which cannot be reductively attributed to Chinese capital or actors, even as these entrepôts are transformed into socioecological sacrifice zones where environmental degradation, poverty, drug trafficking, and sexual violence are increasingly concentrated.

REFRACTION OF CHINESE CAPITAL IN AMAZONIAN ENTREPÔTS

For an ethnographic understanding of how Chinese capital "lands" in the Amazon, I trekked between corporate offices in Beijing, Hong Kong, Brasília and São Paulo, and finally from the major city of Belém at the mouth of the Amazon River to the fluvial ports of Barcarena and Miritituba. The China Oil and Foodstuffs Corporation (COFCO) is China's leading state-owned agribusiness trading company, headquartered in Beijing and operating as the central government's primary instrument for wielding agribusiness for geopolitical power. In early 2015 COFCO International (the subsidiary created to "digest" recently acquired transnational agribusiness companies, particularly Nidera and Noble) inaugurated a new office in Hong Kong.[1] Although these Nidera and Nobel companies were headquartered in the Netherlands and Hong Kong respectively, and operate across Argentina, Australia, Ukraine, and a handful of other countries, a COFCO executive reassured me their operations in Brazil were "the most important" for their global acquisition strategy.[2] Nidera and Noble were rising stars in Brazilian agribusiness, making gains from their trading desks in São Paulo against the well-established giants from the US through an "asset-light" strategy that prioritizes strategic partnerships for just-in-time logistics over the vertical integration of their leading competitors. As most port infrastructure in Brazil's southeast was already dominated by those firms, the Arco Norte was their best chance to expand market share. When COFCO's executives launched negotiations for the acquisition of Noble and Nidera, they learned that both companies were independently contracting with a new logistics operator for a major new waterway project in the Amazon basin. This synergy consolidated COFCO's decision to acquire both companies as its strategy for tapping Brazilian soy exports.[3] Thus, without directly investing in the construction ports or the navigation of barges, COFCO effectively gained control over a leading logistics operator by incorporating Noble and Nidera.

I circulated amidst São Paulo's high-rises during 2014 and 2015 to follow up on these global acquisitions. Directors at Noble and Nidera introduced me to the president of another company, Hidrovias do Brasil S/A (HBSA, or "Brazil's Waterways") which they had contracted for the operation of soy exports through the Tapajós-Amazon waterway. My interviews with these executives revealed the manner in which Chinese capital refracts through Brazilian actors. COFCO learned about both Noble and Nidera's contracts with HBSA before any of these companies knew that COFCO was negotiating for their purchase and effectively merging HBSA into an exclusive service provider. "I thought I would be getting two different clients, so there could be a power balance with my company," lamented the president of HBSA, "but just as we signed the contracts they announced both Noble and Nidera are getting incorporated into COFCO."[4] "So you ended up effectively as a subsidiary of COFCO as well?," I asked. He sighed in dismay. "Exactly."[5] When the HBSA-constructed ports in the Amazon were inaugurated in 2015, they were technically owned and operated by a Brazilian company, receiving loans from the Brazilian national development bank. Their operational capital, management strategy, trade flows, and price-setting mechanisms were effectively COFCO's, however. Thus, despite the refraction of corporate control, there is no ambiguity for COFCO's executives when talking about "our investments" in the Arco Norte, and the strategic gains and profits they expect from "our logistics infrastructure" in Brazil, even while they leave operations "in the hands of our Brazilian teams."[6]

This refraction takes place through Brazilian *public* actors as well, who provide political cover and continuity to projects at risk of popular opposition due to negative socioecological impacts, and the perception of Chinese "takeovers" of Brazilian resources and strategic assets. After all, the expansion of logistics infrastructure on the Tapajós-Amazon rivers is promoted by the Brazilian federal and Pará state governments, which respectively finance and expedite licensing operations for infrastructure construction in the Arco Norte. "Our waterways and ports are the best way for Brazil to expand exports," explained a director at the Pará state government's Department of Economic Development. "So if the Chinese are going to guarantee markets and give working capital to one of our companies to operate this waterway, we support that. We promote that!"[7]

Indeed, as Pedlowski, Felipe and Costa, and Thomaz et al. also show in their chapters in this volume, local governments and Brazilian corporations expedite the construction and operation of entrepôts while sacrificing public health, security, and environmental sustainability in their rush to build the Arco Norte.

GOLDEN DUST ACROSS THE TAPAJÓS RIVER

Itaituba is a small town on the Tapajós, a tributary of the Amazon. The new COFCO-controlled port sat across the river in the small community of Mirituba. I had flown in earlier that week, and that afternoon I was sitting at a cheap plastic table underneath a mango tree along the river, downtown, to meet with Silva,[8] who ordered up beer, manioc, and fried fish for us to nibble while we talked. Silva explained that this was his favorite spot to meet friends when he came back from school in Santarém, the larger city downstream where the Tapajós flows into the Amazon. "Itaituba still doesn't have enough educational opportunities for its youth," Silva lamented, "so we are all still alligator-students: we have to go up and down the river if we are lucky enough to go to college." Silva's work as community organizer interlinks Catholic nongovernmental organizations (which play an important role advancing socioecological justice in the Tapajós and Amazon basin, as Camoça and Hendler show in their chapter in this volume) with the Munduruku, the Indigenous nation that has lived on these riverbanks since before the arrival of white settlers (as Molina and Munduruku's chapter in this volume shows). At the time, the Munduruku were campaigning for demarcation of their territory, curtailing illegal logging and mining, and halting construction of the São Luis hydroelectric dam a few kilometers upriver, which threatened to flood their land and disrupt the river ecosystem upon which they have depended for countless generations. Interestingly, since most Brazilian infrastructure construction companies were sidelined due to their involvement in massive corruption scandals, the China Three Gorges Corporation stepped in to bid for its concession (Aguiar 2017, see also Rodriguez's chapter in this volume).

Demarcation of Munduruku territory and opposition to the dam were the main political issues in the region. Silva encouraged social movements to organize against the ports as well. "You see all that yellow dust there across the river?" Silva gestured to the soy dust spewing from the ports as they loaded barges. "That dust isn't just over the water, it also mixes with the red dust the trucks kick up on the road all the way up to 'the 30,' [see below] and it gets in everyone's lungs in Mirituba. If the kids there don't get run over by all the trucks, they're gonna grow up with lung problems from breathing this dust day-in, day-out."

Silva's role as a community organizer is crucial, as he understands his Indigenous community's spirituality, ontology, and epistemology, and effectively connects it to the political economic materiality that can be grasped by the rest of Brazilian and international society. To illustrate, the Munduruku's spiritual ontology maintains that the destruction of their sacred places by infrastructure construction creates imbalances between the spiritual and human world that cause calamities and "accidents" (as Molina and Munduruku explain in this volume). Silva shows how this is not "mere superstition," as many outsiders dismiss it, but an apt description of the actual increase in roadside accidents, as young children become trampled by the soy trucks barreling down to the new ports in Miritituba, polluting the air in ways that increase "incidental" deaths from chronic health conditions.

Yet these are only the most visible negative effects of the new ports in Miritituba. The more insidious problems of sexual violence and drug trafficking concentrate a little further away, where the trucks bringing soy from the highlands south of the Amazon park for "triage" as they waited their turn to unload. "The 30" that Silva mentioned is the largest truck stop in the region, located 30 kilometers away from the ports in a community called Campo Verde. But there are smaller wait-stations located as close as 1 and 5 km away from Miritituba. "We pressured the mayor to rewrite zoning to make sure the trucks would stay away from residential areas," Silva continued, somewhat dismayed. "But the municipal council was against it because they say all the revenue from the ports is going to the Itaituba side and the only thing that is going to be left for the people in Miritituba is whatever business they can get from the truckers."

Popular sentiments in Itaituba/Miritituba were either optimistic about the expected benefit from the ports or defeatist about their negative impacts. "The most we can do is mobilize people for some compensation from ATAP," Silva continued, referring to the association of companies operating the new ports. "They paid for a new sports court and go around with these educational programs, training people to work in construction and teaching the kids about red-yellow-and-green. But the mayor never actually installed a stop light in Miritituba and ATAP doesn't train the *truck drivers* to slow down when they come into town! So, it's as if it's our own fault if we suffer with this so-called development!" According to Silva, the municipal government and the companies do not promote the well-being of people in the region, just their own revenues and profits. "The rest is all just a farce."

A key architect of this "farce" was Fernando,[9] a consultant hired by HBSA and other companies to work on the socioenvironmental licensing and corporate social responsibility programs of the new ports. The next day I returned with Fernando to Itaituba from a visit to the HBSA port on a private speedboat used by some of the port managers. Most people live on the Itaituba side of the river, especially the better paid managers who stay in large company-owned houses along the banks of the river, where the "nicer" shops and restaurants are located. Fernando was not from the region and did not actually live in Itaituba. Like other white-collar workers at the ports, he flew in Tuesdays and out Thursdays when he had to conduct business. We sat at a sturdy wooden table in a restaurant, drinking caipirinha before Fernando ordered a pizza for dinner. Seeing me as a fellow outsider in this place, he vented about the poor quality of the food, drink, and service. (Admittedly, the pizza was not that good.) "This is the problem with this place," he told me. "People here don't have any sense! Poorly educated, lacking capacity . . . really, it's an ignorant mass of people."

Fernando's sentiments wavered between pity and disgust for the poor people of Itaituba/Miritituba, but it was against the local government that he directed most of his vitriol. "All I want is to get that goddamn 'New Miritutuba' out of there," Fernando explained, referring to the expansion of small businesses and residences toward the newly constructed ports across the river, "that's a fucking huge liability" for the companies he represented. "Instead, they want us to fund social infrastructure there and the municipal government won't rezone it. What's more, we can only operate on the condition we make these social investments. But the municipal government doesn't take any responsibility to run them!" The sports center and fire station they funded, for example, received no staff from the municipal government for their operation. "Soon after inauguration, everything was looted and messed up!" In a way, Fernando knew those initiatives were basically a farce. "When this thing is fully operational, we're talking about unloading forty thousand tons of soy per day, an average three thousand trucks in the triage lots every fucking day. *That* is where the real socioenvironmental impact is!" But, he admitted, "I can't do anything about that without local and state government enforcement. What am I going to say to the bar owner there? 'If you see a truck driver with an underage girl, you have to kick him out'!? The guy is making money off this! It is the state that has to step in. The municipality has zero capacity to deal with this shit!" But again, residents were not merely victims of poor government in Fernando's eyes: "You take a girl like that, her mom was a whore in the *garimpos* [mining camps], her grandma was a whore during the timber boom, and her great-grandmother was a whore during the rubber cycle. How do you expect her not to be a whore now? Her parents even make them go [do sex] work in the triage lots!"

In Fernando's eyes, the ports are the first good thing to happen in the region. "The history of this place began when the military came in to put down the Cabanagem revolt, you know?" Fernando asked rhetorically. "Then came the rubber cycle, then the timber cycle, and finally the gold cycle," Fernando continued, "so for these people, it has always been like this, rubber soldiers, gold miners, everyone just wants to get rich easy extracting the wealth from the place, without investing anything for the long term." It is true that white settlers founded Itaituba as a military garrison in the struggle to suppress the Indigenous and *mestiço* revolt against the Empire of Brazil during the 1830s, and that the political economy of the region has been marked by the boom-and-bust cycles of rubber (1870–1940s), timber (1950–1960s), and gold extraction (1970–1980s). Yet while analysis of Brazilian political economy in terms of "cycles" of extractivism usually critiques the comprador elite to whom Fernando is dedicated (Prado Jr. [1942] 2011), Fernando himself drew upon that framework to lament the local impediments to seizing the opportunity that the ports provide for the region. "These people turn to me and talk about the 'cycle of the ports,' and I gasp. I mean, port is not a cycle! But how can you change these people?" Disheartened, I glanced across the river at the yellow dust rising from the ports and barges. I asked Fernando what he thought about that. "That dust? That's the new gold dust of this region. But unlike the *garimpos* [artisanal gold mining], this one is here to stay."

INFRASTRUCTURE OF A GLOBAL SACRIFICE ZONE

I have argued elsewhere that eco-modernism promotes intensification of soy production over the Cerrado to curtail deforestation in the Amazon and effectively sacrifices the latter to "spare" the former (Oliveira and Hecht 2016). Here, I argue a similar mechanism is at play in sacrificing the socioecology of Amazonian entrepôts for the benefit of transnational agribusiness. This sacrifice is quite tangible. It is materially predicated upon the infrastructure of entrepôts themselves. In Barcarena, for example, vibrations from the construction of the HBSA port caused significant structural damage to several homes in the neighboring community, rendering them uninhabitable to the present day.[10] There and in Miritituba, the increased flux of trucks has aggravated various social ills. Since the new ports came into operation in 2014, high homicide rates have been maintained, there has been an increase in deaths from road accidents (particularly children run over by trucks), and a surge of drug trafficking and sexual violence (Portal da Transparência da Segurança Pública 2021). Multiple scholars find clear evidence that this is associated with the new ports' operations (Rodrigues 2018; Maciel et al. 2019). Underage prostitution and sexual violence against children have also become significantly worse, albeit underreported in official statistics (Oliveira 2020). Felipe and Costa, and Thomaz et al. share similar findings in their chapters in this volume on other entrepôts.

The mainstream narrative about Chinese infrastructure investments in the Amazon is that benefits can be maximized and risks mitigated by governments imposing strict regulations, as Chinese state-owned financiers and infrastructure construction companies tend to respect local laws (Gallagher et al. 2019; see also the chapters by Saggioro Garcia and Pereira, Waisbich, and Rodríguez in this volume). This overlooks how Chinese capital is refracted through local public and private actors who have political and economic interests that do not necessarily align with the socioenvironmental well-being of the people most directly affected by new infrastructure projects. This is true not only with regard to the socioecological impacts of infrastructure construction and operation but also, more fundamentally, to the ideas of development, modernization, and global integration that undergird these projects. Infrastructures that connect sites of natural resource extraction with global markets, rendering places like Barcarena and Miritituba mere entrepôts through which capital and goods flow, leave behind socioecological ills that outweigh gains from employment, commerce, and taxation. Deepening our analysis beyond government-to-government relations and macroeconomic descriptions of investment projects (upon which Garcia and Pereira, Rodríguez, and Zhou tend to focus in their chapters in this volume), we reveal why such projects propel the elites and midlevel technocrats who assemble them, while marginalizing others, increasing social inequality, and aggravating environmental degradation. Such a critique is needed now more than ever, as shifts in global political economy triggered by the US-China trade war and the COVID-19 pandemic increase the importance of Chinese-backed infrastructure projects in Amazonian entrepôts.

Sacrifice zones are not made without resistance, however, and social struggles have gained important victories. In 2016, the federal Public Prosecutor's Office transferred responsibility for environmental licensing of ports on the Tapajós from the state to the federal government, halting further construction because previous projects were licensed individually without considering the compounded interaction of their impacts (MPF 2016). That triumph for local environmentalists was soon followed by a victory for the Munduruku, whose campaign successfully reversed the environmental license of the Chinese-backed São Luis do Tapajós hydroelectric dam (Aguiar 2017). But both victories may be temporary, and they do not reverse the damage that has already been done.

The Bolsonaro administration encouraged further infrastructure investments in the Amazon, pressuring the federal environmental agency to loosen regulations (based upon the perverse rationale that the rivers are already "anthropic" due to the existing ports, so they no longer require environmental protection) and extending the period for renewed environmental impact assessments for several hydroelectric dams on the Tapajós into 2021 (Reuters 2020). Given the deep economic crisis Brazil now faces alongside the COVID-19 pandemic, and the depleted coffers of the Brazilian national development bank and infrastructure construction companies (which lost contracts and paid huge fines due to the anticorruption crackdown of recent years), Chinese companies are leading contenders for new infrastructure projects in the Amazon. And despite Bolsonaro's anti-China rhetoric, state governments actively solicit Chinese investors. In November 2019, for example, the Pará state governor personally led a delegation of the China Communication Construction Company to meet with the federal minister of the economy, signing memoranda of understanding for over US$1.7 billion in infrastructure investments in his state (Menezes 2019). Chinese capital is thus likely to continue its refraction into Amazonian entrepôts, building the infrastructures of a global sacrifice zone.

NOTES

1. Personal interview with a COFCO International senior executive, Hong Kong, March 26, 2015.

2. Personal interview with a COFCO International senior executive, Hong Kong, March 26, 2015.

3. Personal interview with a COFCO International senior executive, Hong Kong, March 26, 2015.

4. Personal interview, São Paulo, May 15, 2015.

5. Personal interview, São Paulo, May 15, 2015.

6. Personal interview with a COFCO International senior executive, Hong Kong, March 26, 2015.

7. Personal interview, Belém, July 27, 2015.

8. This character, an amalgam of three different individuals occupying a similar structural position as described in this vignette, was created to maintain the anonymity of those individuals. All quotes are paraphrased from real statements documented in the author's field notes.

9. Once again, this character is an amalgam, created to maintain the anonymity of two individuals in similar structural positions. All quotes are paraphrased from real statements documented in the author's field notes.

10. Field site visit and personal interviews with community members and HBSA contractors who admitted to this negative impact, Barcarena and Brasília, August 2015.

REFERENCES

Aguiar, Diana. 2017. *A geopolítica de infraestrutura da China na América do Sul: Um estudo a partir do caso do Tapajós na Amazônia brasileira.* Rio de Janeiro: Fase/Actionaid.

ANTAQ (National Agency of Waterway Transports). 2019. "Aumenta participação do Arco Norte no escoamento da soja e do milho para exportação" (Arco Norte increases its share of soy and maize exports). http://portal.antaq.gov.br/index.php/2019/02/20/aumenta-a-participacao-do-arco-norte-no-escoamento-da-soja-e-do-milho-para-exportacao/

Gallagher, Kevin, et al. 2019. *China and the Amazon: Toward a Framework for Maximizing Benefits and Mitigating Risks of Infrastructure Development.* Washington, DC: Inter-American Dialogue.

Maciel, Franciclei, Júlio Schweickardt, Jessé Maciel, and Izaura Costa. 2019. "Política de desenvolvimento, ambiente e saúde na Amazônia: Uma análise da região do Tapajós." (Development policy, environment, and health in the Amazon: An analysis of the Tapajós region). *Revista Brasileira de Estudos Urbanos e Regionais* 21, no. 1: 155–72.

Menezes, Carol. 2019. "Governo garante início da Ferrovia Pará em 2021, obra de R$ 7 bilhões. Cooperação com a China no Pará é o maior investimento de infraestrutura no Brasil." (Government guarantees launch of Pará Railway in 2021, a 7 billion BRL construction project. Cooperation with China in Pará is the largest infrastructure investment in Brazil.) *Agência Pará*, November 12, 2019. https://agenciapara.com.br/noticia/16323/.

MPF (Federal Public Prosecutor's Office of Brazil). 2016. "MP pede suspensão do licenciamento de portos em Itaituba (PA)" (Public prosecutor suspends licensing of ports in Itaituba, Pará). Press release, February 16, 2016. http://www.mpf.mp.br/pa/sala-de-imprensa/noticias-pa/ministerio-publico-pede-suspensao-do-licenciamento-de-portos-em-itaituba-pa.

Oliveira, Assis da Costa. 2020. "Fronteira Tapajós e direitos das crianças: Impactos sociais de grandes empreendimentos econômicos" (Tapajós Frontier and the rights of children: Social impacts of large-scale economic investments). Civitas 20, no. 1: 53–64.

Oliveira, Gustavo de L. T., and Susanna B. Hecht. 2016. "Sacred Groves, Sacrifice Zones, and Soy Production: Globalization, Intensification and Neo Nature in South America." *Journal of Peasant Studies* 43, no. 2: 251–85.

Oliveira, G. de L. T., Galen Murton, Alessandro Rippa, Tyler Harlan, and Yang Yang. 2020. "China's Belt and Road Initiative: Views from the Ground." *Political Geography* 82: 102225.

Oliveira, G. de L. T., and Margaret Myers. 2021. "The Tenuous Co-Production of China's Belt and Road Initiative in Brazil and Latin America." *Journal of Contemporary China* 30, no. 129: 481–499. DOI: 10.1080/10670564.2020.1827358.

Portal da Transparência da Segurança Pública. 2021. Governo do Para. http://sistemas.segup.pa.gov.br/transparencia/.

Prado, Caio Jr. (1942) 2011. *Formação do Brasil contemporâneo* (Formation of contemporary Brazil). São Paulo: Companhia das Letras.

Reuters. 2020. "Estudos sobre hidrelétricas no Tapajós têm prazo prorrogado até 2021 pela Aneel" (Studies for hydroelectric dams in the Tapajós have deadline extended until 2021 by the National Agency for Electric Energy). *Reuters*, May 25, 2020. https://economia.uol.com.br/noticias/reuters/2020/05/25/estudos-sobre-hidreletricas-no-tapajos-tem-prazo-prorrogado-ate-2021-pela-aneel.htm.

Rodrigues, Jondison. 2018. "O Arco Norte e as políticas públicas portuárias para o Oeste do estado do Pará (Itaituba e Rurópolis): Apresentação, debate e articulações" (The Northern Arch and the public policies for ports in the west of Pará state [Itaituba and Rurópolis]: Presentation, debate, and articulations). *Revista NERA* 21, no. 42: 202–28.

Senra, Eduardo. 2019. "Um ano após reclamar que China 'compraria o Brasil,' Bolsonaro quer vender estatais e commodities em visita a Xi Jinping." (One year after complaining that China 'would buy Brazil,' Bolsonaro wants to sell [Brazilian] state-owned companies and commodities during his visit to Xi Jinping.) *BBC*, October 23, 2019. https://www.bbc.com/portuguese/brasil-50161509.

"The Bank We Want": Chinese and Brazilian Activism around and within the BRICS New Development Bank

Laura Trajber Waisbich

CHINESE CAPITAL THAT is flowing into Latin America and, particularly, Brazil rarely follows a simple path. Its processes "are obfuscated by the manner that Chinese capital and corporate control are refracted through various Brazilian public and private actors. This refraction enables Chinese firms to circumvent socioenvironmental resistance, promoting continuities in Chinese investment strategies despite shifts in Brazilian domestic politics" (Oliveira, this volume, 179). Meanwhile, China itself asserts that its "Stepping Out" into the world is, as Zhou Zhiwei portrays it, the start of a new era "abandoning the zero-sum game thinking of the Cold War" and carrying out "mutually beneficial cooperation with various types of countries in the world." In the case of Brazil, this can be described as a "marriage" (this volume, 75). As readers will have remembered from the introduction of this volume, however, marriages are not necessarily egalitarian. Will the flow of Chinese capital into the Global South usher in a new era of egalitarian prosperity and the death of neocolonialism? Or will it be a colonialism reborn? The answer to this question depends upon the sensitivity of the financial structures promoting this new wave of development to local and transnational critique and oversight.

This chapter looks specifically at how the checks and balances over financial power are (or are not) being constructed in and around what has been envisioned as one of the major institutions that will be responsible for financing the new Global South in the context of China's Stepping Out policy: the BRICS (Brazil, Russia, India, China and South Africa)-led New Development Bank (NDB).

In May 2020, Brazilian Marcos Troyo was elected president of the NDB, created by the BRICS countries in 2014 and headquartered in Shanghai, China. Troyo was appointed by Brazil to occupy the position, succeeding Indian K. V. Kamath in the bank's rotating presidency. Troyo's appointment symbolically marked the end of the NDB's first life cycle, as well as the end of an initial cycle of social activism and mobilization surrounding the construction of the bank.

This chapter analyzes the dynamics of mobilization and partnerships between Chinese and Brazilian civil society organizations (CSOs) around the NDB between 2013 and 2020. I see these as an example of transnational activism within the framework of the so-called internationalization of China. The chapter provides an overview of the areas and themes in which Chinese civil society has sought to influence the Chinese state and Chinese companies operating abroad. I argue that this activism has grown (especially with regard to environmental issues) and that it is based on collaborative interactions with the state that seek to improve China's internationalization, not openly confront it. This chapter is thus a critical analysis of joint mobilization and attempts at dialogue with the bank and its shareholder members in a context of scarce material expression and visibility for the projects the NDB finances.

EMERGENT FORMS OF ACTIVISM AND SOCIAL PARTICIPATION IN THE MARCH OF CHINESE INTERNATIONALIZATION

As Rodríguez has pointed out elsewhere in this volume, China's internationalization is one of the most significant geopolitical and economic phenomena in the world today. Although begun in the 1990s (with the Going West and Going Out policies), the phenomenon intensified during the Xi Jinping Era (2012–) with the launch of the Belt and Road Initiative (BRI). The internationalization process includes a growing flow of foreign direct investments from China to different areas of the globe and the establishment of a set of public instruments to support the internationalization of

Chinese companies (especially state-owned ones) through export credits, overseas project financing, capitalization, and so on. At the same time, China seeks to expand its presence and activism within the G20 and the United Nations' development system (Mao 2020) and to build new global financial institutions, such as the Asian Infrastructure Investment Bank (AIIB) and the NDB itself.

It is in this context that China's growing presence in the world becomes of interest to Chinese society. This interest has manifested itself in the emergence of specialized nonstate media focused on business (such as *Caixin Globus*) or on environmental issues (*China Dialogue*), promoting a national debate about China's internationalization process (Ma 2018). This interest in China's Stepping Out has also grown on social media networks among the urban middle class who are increasingly active in blogs and microblogs (Ma 2019).[1]

The involvement of nongovernmental organizations (NGOs), voluntary associations, and foundations working internationally on issues of international development and humanitarian aid (Hsu, Hildebrandt, and Hasmath 2016) is growing in parallel with China's international presence. In recent years, political activism by NGOs, especially those focused on the environment, has also intensified, monitoring the impacts of Chinese internationalization and influencing the policies and practices of state and parastatal actors. Among the most active of these institutions are the Greenovation Hub (GHub), Green Watershed, and the Global Environmental Institute and Chinese branches of international NGOs such as the World Wildlife Fund, Greenpeace, Friends of the Earth, International Rivers, World Resources Institute, Oxfam, Asia Foundation, and the Ford Foundation.

Following the model of "embedded activism" (Ho and Edsmond 2008), these entities have taken on a dual role. On the one hand, they collaborate with the state and with Chinese companies operating abroad; on the other, they critically engage with and attempt to control "from below" China's actions beyond its borders. As in the domestic sphere, environmental and sustainability issues are most evident in this field, galvanizing a greater number of Chinese organizations, acting in the "politically acceptable" field of environmental activism (Barbieri 2018). This approach focuses on China's "ecological footprint" (Yeophantong 2020) and acts to pressure government actors and companies. Its efficacy is undergirded by the importance given by the Chinese Communist Party to environmental issues during the Xi Era (particularly the emphasis on Ecological Civilization and Green Economy).

ENVIRONMENTAL ACTIVISM WITHIN THE BRI: OUTLINES AND LIMITS

Working on environmental issues within the framework of the BRI allows Chinese and China-based organizations to forge connections with transnational networks that are interested in the role and impact of Chinese investments around the globe, be these activism networks or multistakeholder networks (e.g., UN agencies, multilateral banks, foundations, research centers). As described by scholars of social movements (Keck and Sikkink 1998; Della Porta and Tarrow 2005), these networks provide resources and opportunities (political, symbolic, and material) for Chinese organizations (or those based in China) to act in domestic and transnational spaces. An example of this pattern can be seen in the case of the Green BRI initiative, which has allowed Chinese entities to move their activism into the transnational realm. The initiative itself is of interest to the Chinese government, being managed by the government in partnership with national and international actors, including research centers (such as the International Institute of Green Finance) and NGOs (such as GHub). According to Wencai Zhang, director-general for international economic and financial cooperation at the Chinese Ministry of Finance, "President Xi made it very clear that we want to promote a high-quality BRI. . . . More will be done to ensure quality infrastructure and encourage companies and Chinese banks to adopt internationally accepted standards, including socioenvironmental standards" (Saldinger 2019).

Taking advantage of this opening, Chinese and China-based organizations started to track China's internationalization through this embedded environmental activism and constructive dialogue approach. This dialogue presupposes the adoption of arguments that resonate with government institutions and companies, such as the rhetoric of improving China's global image and working to "reduce and avoid social and financial risks" of projects (GHub 2019). It is with this discursive arsenal that these actors seek to influence socioenvironmental policies and regulations for Chinese investments abroad, as well as practices for monitoring and assessing the risks/impacts[2] of Chinese development projects. On the other hand, they seek to work with companies that are operating internationally, given that many of these companies still have little international experience and value partnerships with civil society in matters of socioenvironmental analysis or community dialogue (Jiang 2019). Guided by notions of "learning" and "improvement," Chinese CSOs situate themselves as mildly critical partners, helping shape certain practices, as was the case with Global Environmental Institute's involvement in the campaign that led to the suspension of the construction of the Myitsone hydroelectric plant in Myanmar (Yeophantong 2020). Lack of such engagement in the case of Brazil may be at least partially responsible for the apparent lack of Chinese concern with the impacts of projects such as those detailed by Oliveira; Molina and Munduruku; Queiroz, Praça, and Bitencourt; and Pedlowski in this volume. That Brazilian organizations have difficulties in reaching out to their Chinese counterparts in these situations may also be partially due to the fact that not much is actually known about China in Brazil (Queiroz, Praça, and Bitencourt; and Longobardi, this volume).

This is a "possible activism," in which the entities involved have a certain political space to advocate for the official adoption of "international standards"[3]of transparency, prior consultation, and socioenvironmental safeguards, finding increasing openness to this type of input. Given the governmental rhetoric regarding the Green Agenda, advocacy entities can dialogue with the state and begin to act as partners in achieving these objectives, helping to translate rhetoric into practice and pointing out inconsistencies. An example is the case of China funding and/or building thermoelectric plants in other countries (Hao 2019).

Countless CSOs recognize that the repertoire of constructive dialogue or even advice on corporate social responsibility are viable forms of engagement, but are not always sufficiently critical. For some groups, this is a pragmatic option in that it improves instruments, seeks to control damage, and promotes long-term incremental reform. For others, it is a belief in the legitimacy of the interface with the state and of institutionalized dialogue. The same sort of tension occurred in Brazil during the government of the Workers' Party (2003–2016) at the Brazilian National Development Bank Forum for Dialogue with Civil Society (2014–2016). The justification presented for engagement was that it was possible and desirable to critically dialogue with the government and seek to improve practices and policies

(Cardoso, Borges, and Rodriguez. 2015).[4] A similar option for institution-alized critical-constructive engagement can also be seen in the case of the NDB, discussed below.

This model of activism contains tensions. Mobilization requires that Chinese CSOs acquire deep technical knowledge of the world of development finance, of the roles of the banking system and financial regulators, and of the modus operandi of state-owned companies. This is a nonnegligible challenge for organizations originally specialized in environmental issues, not to mention for grassroots organizations. Such activism also requires organizations to be (re-)positioned as "partners" in improving practices. This makes it impossible to delve deeper into issues considered to be "more sensitive," such as the social impacts of investments on ethnic minorities and Indigenous peoples, or involuntary resettlement.[5] Furthermore, it is a challenge to act politically in a context where political participation remains limited to issues perceived as nonthreatening to the regime's political stability (Zhang 2017). The trend in the Xi era has been to eliminate past gains with regard to transparency and participation at the local level (Stromseth, Malesky, and Gueorguiev 2017), especially after the approval of the new legal framework for NGOs (Kuhn 2018) in 2018. At the same time, the political space for constructive dialogue on environmental issues and climate change has expanded during the same period.[6]

It is upon these bases that we need to comprehend the additional challenge of consolidating networks and coalitions with partners in the countries and territories in which Chinese investments are materializing and that might, when necessary, create or reinforce opposition and resistance, especially with regard to Chinese projects that have serious socioenvironmental impacts. Some of the so-called success stories in resisting Chinese (co-)funded projects, such as the Lamu coal power plant in Kenya, appear to have adopted a national and transnational campaign model, allying with Northern actors, putting pressure on the partner government or other financers, and relying very little upon Chinese organizations (Olander 2019).

Although there are examples of campaigns that have also involved Chinese actors, such as the Myitsone hydroelectric plant in Myanmar (mentioned above), this sort of activism is a new frontier, given the growing importance of Chinese financing around the globe and the need that local communities have to understand Chinese sectoral and governmental guidelines and the Chinese legal system (Zhang 2017). The participation of Chinese entities in transnational activism networks may even strengthen efforts to transform the current socioenvironmental guidelines into more robust mechanisms that guarantee and protect the rights of populations affected by projects. This has direct implications on the possibility of future joint action within the framework of Chinese investments in Latin America, given that this is an even less consolidated frontier of expansion in China's "going out."

ACTIVISM IN THE NEW DEVELOPMENT BANK (2014–2020)

It is in this context that the study of an existing partnership between entities based in China and in other countries, including Brazilian groups, can illustrate the possibilities and challenges of joint activism in matters of foreign policy and international development. This is the case of the BRICS-led bank, the NDB, which has been the object of transnational social mobilization since its creation.

CSOs' interest in the bank began with the official announcement in 2012 that the BRICS countries intended to create a new multilateral financial institution. Interest grew as governments moved forward with the design and establishment of the NDB in 2014. Many of the groups following the BRICS' agenda (especially in India, Brazil, and South Africa—known as the IBSA countries) saw the bank as an opportunity to influence the direction of the then still very much ethereal BRICS partnership (Pomeroy et al. 2016). Some organizations were also interested in development financing issues and saw activism around the NDB as a means of influencing the direction of this new institution from its beginnings. Furthermore, because the bank has "new" in its name and a commitment to financing "sustainable infrastructure" in the Global South (NDB 2017), many organizations believed they had a unique window of opportunity for influence. Others, more critical, opposed the bank from the beginning, denouncing it as an instrument of BRICS subimperialism and critiquing its model of extractive and uneven (Bond and Garcia 2015).

This plurality of understandings of the bank ended up generating coalitions of activists that were equally diverse, following the lines designated by Bond and Garcia (2015) as the "BRICS-from-Below" and "BRICS-from-the-Middle." The first was composed of grassroots organizations and more radical social movements, the second of professionalized CSOs and more conciliatory research centers. These differences have materialized over time in different choices with regard to building and participating in spaces for independent dialogues (the so-called Peoples' Forum on BRICS) or socio-state (Pires and Vaz 2014) interfaces (the so-called Civil BRICS) in the context of the annual BRICS Summits. Similar differentiation occurred in activism with the NDB. A CSO coalition consolidated an international network of "incidence and dialogue" with the bank, but this did not prevent other groups' more contentious strategies, such as carrying out street protests against the NDB in Johannesburg (2018) and Cape Town (2019) (Waisbich Forthcoming). Although these divisions cannot be taken as total or static, this panorama helps us to situate and differentiate Chinese participation in the networks. While entities from the IBSA countries were involved in both groups, Chinese entities remained largely absent from the broader mobilizations that took place during the summits and only began to act once the bank became a target.

During this first cycle of activism, joint advocacy actions targeting the bank happened mainly through the BRICS Working Group (GT-BRICS) within the International Coalition for Human Rights in Development.[7] Since the creation of the NDB, the network has focused on a dialoguing with the bank on such topics as access to information, socioenvironmental policy, gender, and social participation. In its early years, the Working Group sought to influence the construction of NDB policies in these areas (Coalition for Human Rights in Development 2017), as well as on-site monitoring of the NDB's projects and tracking their potential impacts (Thompson and De Wet 2018). So far, however, few projects financed by the bank have gained the material expression and visibility necessary for this type of action.

WHILE WAITING FOR THE CRISIS: CHALLENGES OF MAINTAINING A LOW-INTENSITY ACTIVISM

In the context of the transnational activism of the BRICS Working Group, only one project was monitored: a road project in the state of Madhya Pradesh, India, monitored by the feminist collective BRICS Feminist Watch. The study sought to analyze the on-site functioning of the bank's socioenvironmental policy and conducted an independent analysis of risks and impacts (BRICS Feminist Watch 2018). So far, no action of this sort has been carried out in Brazil by the Brazilian organizations most involved in the issues the bank's projects touch upon, such as Conectas, Inesc, Oxfam Brasil, REBRIP, Action Aid Brasil, Articulação SUL, Ecologia e Ação and Ibase. At the same time, the NDB's additional contributions to a set of investments for the extension of the port of Durban in South Africa created protests in the wake of long-standing challenges to the project (Bond and Mottiar 2018).

The number of Chinese entities in the BRICS Working Group remained low, and was limited mainly to three entities: GHub, Green Watershed, and Oxfam Hong Kong.[8] Although the participation of Chinese entities has grown since the Working Group began its formal dialogue with the bank and meet with its representatives (twice at the bank headquarters in Shanghai, in 2017 and 2018, and other times on the margins of the bank's annual meetings in Delhi, Shanghai, and Cape Town), the number remains low, particularly when compared to the number of representatives from the IBSA countries or to the number of Chinese entities watchdogging the AIIB. In a clear allusion to the potential "boomerang effect" of transnational activism (Keck and Sikkink 1998), environmental groups emphasize that their work with the NDB and AIIB generates opportunities to move forward on agendas such as socioenvironmental safeguards and to bring them back home, given that these instruments are more consolidated in multilateral banks than they are in the Chinese banks and corporations now operating internationally.

So far, the impact on the NDB has generated few concrete results other than the establishment of the dialogue itself. The low number of entities mobilized in all the countries involved contributes to a limited "critical mass" of social pressure on the NDB and in the shareholder countries. The bank has politely remained open to dialogue but has shown little response to the demands for more information about funded projects and for clear commitments in the areas of gender and climate change. The low impact of transnational mobilization is also a result of an exhaustion of the mode of engagement based on policy dialogue in more abstract terms. A historical analysis of the World Bank shows that transnational campaigns based on "paradigmatic" and "controversial" cases had greater effects on the bank and on its shareholders, contributing to reforms in the bank's operational model (Fox and Brown 1998). In the case of the NDB, however, problematic cases capable of creating mass mobilizations have not yet occurred. The bank sought to finance less ambitious and low-risk projects in its first years of operation (Waisbich and Borges 2020), and civil society so far has few instruments for pressuring the bank and its shareholders, or for generating national mobilizations, reinforcing the lack of critical mass. The NDB and its operations remain largely invisible on the ground, given the delays in completing the operations it has already approved, as well as its business model of financing via intermediaries such as national development banks and private companies.

Finally, there has been a series of domestic political and economic crises in the three IBSA countries in recent years, and these crises have redirected activism toward domestic issues, accelerating a process of demobilization of the monitoring of foreign policies by CSOs, including within the framework of the BRICS/NDB. The network has thus been left an orphan, given that the Chinese entities did not take the lead either. Taken together, these problems affected the initial enthusiasm of the few groups that had mobilized, and mobilization has slowed down, particularly from 2019 on. This situation, however, can be reversed if any project financed by the NDB becomes paradigmatically problematic.

CONCLUSION

This chapter has sought to bring to light the dynamics of transnational social mobilization of Chinese groups around the internationalization of China. Based on the case of the BRICS-led NDB and the partnership forged between Chinese and Brazilian organizations (as well as their Indian and South African counterparts), the article discusses the existing spaces for building dialogue and creating critical impact on the Chinese project in its environmental and multilateral dimensions.

Although limited, activism on the part of highly professionalized Chinese environmental organizations has grown in recent years in parallel with the expansion of Chinese investments in the Global South and the ecological rhetoric of the Xi Era. Spaces for participation within China were partially expanded because the Communist Party, financial institutions, and companies realized the usefulness of civil society's knowledge and expertise for improving certain practices and mitigating financial and reputational risks arising from failed projects. At the same time, organizations took advantage of the existing interface to consolidate an agenda for a more environmentally friendly policy and regulation frameworks within China and to try to convert the party's green rhetoric into practice in Chinese investments abroad. Although the gap between guidelines and practices remains substantial, the guidelines are nonnegligible in terms of their potential for building channels for dialogue and influence, albeit in very moderate terms.

Following a similar model of critical-constructive dialogue, transnational activism with the NDB continues to be mostly latent, waiting for crises and controversies that may allow national groups opportunities for more concrete mobilization. The strategies and repertoires adopted during the bank's first years focused on providing inputs to its governance and policies. These are no longer adequate, however, given the end of the bank's cycle of construction and the low responsiveness of the bank, but also given the relatively little material impact that NDB investments have so far had.

However, while project monitoring has not become a new modus operandi for CSOs' engagement with the bank, the NDB provides elements for us to reflect upon the potential and challenges of transnational mobilization in the case of Chinese investments (either at the bilateral level, or in the case of other multilateral arrangements, such as the Green BRI or AIIB). The first of these is the need to expand the network of Chinese-based organizations working on China's Stepping Out, as these can navigate local actors and institutions that external organizations cannot. The second is the need to connect Chinese CSOs with a more diverse group of social actors in partner countries in the Global South, strengthening transnational networks capable of creating distinct pressure points on the increasingly complex financing arrangements involving public, private, and multilateral actors. Under this new South-South financing paradigm, these pressure points are located not only in Chinese banks and companies but also in national governments in other countries in the South that bid for projects, as well as the national parliaments and courts that oversee them.

NOTES

1. Interview with a representative of an international NGO headquartered in Beijing, November 2018.

2. His includes the directives of the Ministries of Commerce and the Environment in 2013 regarding Environmental Protection, External Investments and Cooperation,

and the directives regarding Green Credit published by bank regulators and the recommendations of the Committee of Green Finances of China.

3. Interview with a representative of a Chinese NGO, February 2019.

4. Interview with a representative of a Brazilian NGO, Rio de Janeiro, October 2018; interview with a representative of a Brazilian NGO, São Paulo, August and September 2018.

5. Interview with a representative of a Chinese NGO, February 2019.

6. Interview with a representative of a Chinese NGO, February 2019.

7. https://rightsindevelopment.org/our-work/brics/

8. Although in dialogue with a broader group of Chinese entities and groups with offices in China such as Greenpeace, World Wildlife Fund, Friends of Earth, and the Global Environment Institute, which are also active in addressing issues of Chinese development finance abroad and China's projects with the AIIB.

REFERENCES

Barbieri, Mariana Delgado. 2018. "Sociedade civil e crise ambiental: Atuação do movimento ambientalista no processo de modernização e urbanização da China contemporânea." BRICS Initiative for Critical Agrarian Studies (BICAS) Working Paper. Brasília: UnB.

BRICS Feminist Watch. 2018. "Gender Monitoring of the New Development Bank. Major District Roads, Madhya Pradesh, India. Key Findings." Nova Déli: BRICS Feminist Watch.

Bond, Patrick, and Ana Garcia. 2015. *BRICS: An Anti-Capitalist Critique*. London: Pluto.

Bond, Patrick, and Shauna Mottiar. 2018. "Terrains of Civil and Uncivil Society in Post-Apartheid Durban." *Urban Forum* 29, no. 4: 383–95.

Cardoso, Alessandra, Caio Borges, and Maria Elena Rodriguez. 2015. *Política socioambiental do BNDES: Presente e futuro*. Brasília: INESC.

Coalition for Human Rights in Development. 2017. *The BRICS New Development Bank Strategy. A Civil Society Perspective for Truly Sustainable Infrastructure and Transformative Development Cooperation*. https://rightsindevelopment .org/wp-content/uploads/2017/04/Folheto-The-BRICS-Sustainable2.pdf.

Della Porta, Donatella, and Sidney Tarrow. 2005. *Transnational Protest and Global Activism*. Lanham, MD: Rowman & Littlefield.

Fox, Jonathan, and L. David Brown. 1998. *The Struggle for Accountability: The World Bank, NGOs, and Grassroots Movements*. Cambridge, MA: MIT Press.

GHub. 2019. *Environmental Risk Management Manual for China Overseas Investment*. https://www.ghub.org/en/environmental-risk-management-manual-for-china-overseas-investment/.

Hao, Feng. 2019. "Can Chinese Aid Steer Asia toward Clean Energy?" *China Dialogue* (blog), November 29, 2019. https://chinadialogue.net/en/energy/11699 -can-chinese-aid-steer-asia-toward-clean-energy/.

Hsu, Jennifer Y. J., Timothy Hildebrandt, and Reza Hasmath. 2016. "'Going Out' or Staying In? The Expansion of Chinese NGOs in Africa." *Development Policy Review* 34, no. 3: 423–39.

Ho, Peter, and Richard L. Edmonds, eds. 2008. *China's Embedded Activism: Opportunities and Constraints of a Social Movement*. Routledge Studies on China in Transition 30. London: Routledge.

Jiang, Xiheng. 2019. "Green Belt and Road Initiative Environmental and Social Standards: Will Chinese Companies Conform?" *IDS Bulletin* 50, no. 4: 47–68.

Keck, Margaret E., and Kathryn Sikkink. 1998. *Activists beyond Borders: Advocacy Networks in International Politics*. Ithaca, NY: Cornell University Press.

Kuhn, B. 2018. "Changing Spaces for Civil Society Organisations in China." *Open Journal of Political Science* 8: 467–94.

Ma, Tianjie. 2018. "How Should the Chinese Media Approach Belt and Road Reporting?" *Panda Paw Dragon Claw* (blog). July 18, 2018. https://pandapawdrag onclaw.blog/2018/07/18/how-should-the-chinese-media-approach-belt-and -road-reporting/.

Ma, Tianjie. 2019. "Anxieties of Development. Emerging Voices in Chinese Social Media." *Chublic Opinion* (blog). February 9, 2019. https://chublicopinion .com/2019/02/09/anxieties-of-development-emerging-voices-in-chinese-social -media/.

Ma, Tianjie. 2020. "Chinese Firms Struggle to Fund Renewables Projects Overseas." *China Dialogue* (blog). April 9, 2020. https://chinadialogue.net/en/ energy/11952-chinese-firms-struggle-to-fund-renewables-projects-overseas/.

Mao, Ruipeng. 2020. "China's Growing Engagement with the UNDS as an Emerging Nation: Changing Rationales, Funding Preferences and Future Trends." Discussion paper. Bonn: German Development Institute.

New Development Bank. 2017. *NDB's General Strategy 2017–2021*. Shanghai: New Development Bank.

Olander, Eric. 2019. "Kenya Tribunal Blocks Chinese-Financed Coal Power Plant." *China in Africa Podcast*. Johannesburg.

Pomeroy, Melissa, Alex Shankland, Adele Poskitt, Kaustuv Kanti Bandyopadhyay, and Rajesh Tandon. 2016. "Civil Society, BRICS and International Development Cooperation: Perspectives from India, South Africa and Brazil." In *The BRICS in International Development*, edited by In Jing Gu, Alex Shankland, and Anuradha Chenoy, 169–206. London: Palgrave Macmillan UK.

Pires, Roberto R. C., and Alexander C. N. Vaz. 2014. "Para além da participação: Interfaces socioestatais no governo federal." *Lua Nova: Revista de Cultura e Política*: 61–91.

Saldinger, Adva. 2019. "China's Belt & Road Initiative out-Lends MDBs, Sees Itself as 'Global Public Good.'" *Devex*. https://www.devex.com/news/china-s-belt -road-initiative-out-lends-mdbs-sees-itself-as-global-public-good-95873.

Stromseth, Jonathan, Edmund Malesky, and Dimitar D. Gueorguiev. 2017. *China's Governance Puzzle: Enabling Transparency and Participation in a Single-Party State*. Cambridge: Cambridge University Press.

Thompson, Lisa, and Pamela T. De Wet. 2018. "BRICS Civil Society Initiatives: Towards the Inclusion of Affected Communities in Collective Development?" *Third World Thematics: A TWQ Journal* 3, no. 5–6: 745–64.

Yeophantong, Pichamon. 2020. "China and the Accountability Politics of Hydropower Development: How Effective Are Transnational Advocacy Networks in the Mekong Region?" *Contemporary Southeast Asia* 42, no. 1: 85–117.

Waisbich, Laura Trajber. Forthcoming. "Negotiating Foreign Policy from Below: Voice, Participation and Protest." In *Broken Promises? Rethinking Political Values and Resistance in Post-colonial Developmental States*, edited by Fiona Anciano and Joanna Wheeler. London: Berghahn.

Waisbich, Laura Trajber, and Caio Borges. 2020. "The BRICS' New Development Bank at the Crossroads: Challenges for Building Development Cooperation in the Twenty-First Century." In *International Development Assistance and the BRICS*, edited by Jose A. Puppim de Oliveira and Yijia Jing, 149–87. Singapore: Springer Singapore.

Zhang, Chun. 2017. "China Needs Urgent Oversight of Investments' Social and Environmental Footprint." *Diálogo Chino* (blog). https://dialogochino.net/en/extractive-industries/10158-china-needs-urgent-oversight-of-investments-social-and-environmental-footprint/.

Río Blanco: The Big Stumbling Block to the Advancement of China's Mining Interests in Ecuador

The Yasunidos Guapondélig Collective

ON JUNE 1, 2018, Ecuadorian judge Oswaldo Paúl Serrano Arízaga granted a protective injunction[1] filed by several communities from Molleturo on the grounds that their constitutional right to free, prior, and informed consultation from the Ecuadorian government had been violated, thereby suspending the operations of a nearby Chinese-controlled mining project.

Coming after twenty-four years of resistance to the advance of metal mining in this rural parish of Ecuador's Azuay province, this judgment constitutes a historic victory. However, we believe this could not have been achieved without the participation of the village of Río Blanco, which—in less than a year—went from being "pro-mining" to being the community that most contributed to the protests, paving the way for the aforementioned court ruling. We believe Rio Blanco's unexpected shift was a response to the following factors:

The relationship the area's residents had with the mining project, previously in the hands of a Canadian company, changed when the project was taken over by a Chinese company.

The development of ties between activists from Cuenca and Río Blanco[2] following the decision of the Yasunidos Guapondélig collective to set

aside prejudices and join forces with local communities, without imposing any individual agenda.

After discussing China's strong presence in Latin American economies
and particularly in Ecuador, this chapter narrates community efforts to
resist mining activities. This and other extractive and mega-infrastructure
projects have been taken over by Chinese companies as part of China's
strategy of becoming a major partner in Latin America, especially with
those governments associated with neodevelopmentalist tendencies
(Waisbich; Rodríguez; Vásconez; Thomaz, Martins, and Magalhães; and
Fernández-Salvador and Vitieri, this volume). Put simply, "Latin America
is positioned in the world market as a major supplier of raw materials,"
both minerals and agricultural products (Rodríguez, this volume, 337).
Highlighting the comprehensive character of its influence, Rodríguez
continues:

> On the demand side, China is currently the third largest consumer of gas
> and the second largest consumer of petroleum, while concentrating more
> than 30 percent of the global demand for raw materials such as copper,
> soy, iron, and steel. China is an essential trading partner for Latin Amer-
> ica. But the relationship between China and Latin America is not lim-
> ited to raw materials. Project financing and direct investment by Chinese
> companies are also important in the region and becoming more so. Only
> twenty years ago, financial relations between China and Latin America
> were practically nonexistent; now they are enormous. (337)

Rodríguez also points out that, within this general context, no two Latin
American countries have attracted more Chinese investment than Brazil
and Ecuador. Here, we focus on Ecuador, discussing the relations between
China and that country. We also recount how Río Blanco community
members united with activist collectives from the city of Cuenca in order
to successfully confront the neodevelopmentalist behemoth created by the
Ecuadoran state and subsidized by China.

ECUADOR-CHINA RELATIONS

In January 2020, Ecuador and China celebrated forty years of bilateral
relations as "integral strategic partners." By early 2019, binational trade

totaled almost US$6 billion. To date, more than ninety Chinese companies are doing business in Ecuador. Likewise, Ecuador is the first Latin American country to be admitted as a member of China's Asian Infrastructure Investment Bank (*El Universo* 2020). Over the last twenty years, these relations have intensified in the diplomatic, economic, political, and strategic spheres, thanks to the rise of the Asian giant as a global capitalist power and its investments in the geopolitical South (Sacher 2017). China's increased presence in Latin America coincided with a wave of neodevelopmentalist governments (Svampa 2011; Reyes and Chun Lee 2017) and other perceived favorable characteristics of the region.

In the Sino-Latin American relationship, four stages or phases have been identified: increased trade since 1990, increased financing since 2007/2008, increased Chinese direct investment since 2007/2008, and increased Chinese involvement in infrastructure projects since 2013 (Dussel 2018). According to the most recent ECLAC[3] report (2019), in 2018 China was among the largest investors in the region (along with Europe and the United States), with the Asian nation primarily focused on the acquisition of extractive and agrobusiness companies, power generation, basic services, and infrastructure. The Andean region has attracted substantial Chinese direct foreign investment in mega-mining, with a combined investment in Peru-Ecuador of US$15.720 billion during the 2005–2015 period. This represents two-thirds of the total direct foreign investment directed toward this extractive sector of the two Andean countries (Sacher 2017). It should be noted, however, that there is a deep structural imbalance in China's trade relationship with Latin America, marked by a growing trade deficit. Because Latin American exports tend to have limited added value or technological significance, this has the effect of reinforcing a long-standing "center-periphery" trade structure, which in turn prevents the region from overcoming the colonial stereotype of being a supplier of raw materials to more developed countries (Machado Aráoz 2018).

China's recent Belt and Road Initiative (BRI) seeks even more economic involvement with Latin America and the Caribbean (LAC). It not only reflects the Asian giant's strategic interest in the area, but also betrays its aspirations to incorporate the region into a twenty-first-century version of the Maritime Silk Road. Together with China's establishment of free trade agreements with several LAC countries, the BRI clearly points to a continued coordination of economic and development strategies designed to increase China's footprint in the global economy (by mid-2019, a total of eighteen countries had signed a memorandum of understanding joining them to the BRI). Importantly, these trade agreements have serious impacts on LAC countries in terms of investment, agriculture, ancestral knowledge, health, and biodiversity (Ecuador Decide 2020). They accelerate the concentration of both capital and labor markets (Cajas-Guijarro 2018). Presently, Ecuador maintains a free trade agreement with the European Union and plans to consider similar agreements with China and the US.

For the 2005–2016 period, Ecuador—surpassed only by Venezuela and Brazil—ranked third among LAC countries in terms of its total Chinese debt (US$17.4 billion) (Niu 2018). Historically, the issue of foreign debt has been one of Ecuador's greatest problems, serving as an means of domination since the era of Latin America's independence movements. China emerged as a financing alternative when it restructured Ecuador's foreign debt in 2009 during a global economic crisis. In subsequent years, however, the debt has skyrocketed. While Chinese credit in Ecuador has not been tied to letters of intent or "structural adjustment" programs, as has been the case with International Monetary Fund loans, it has been linked to the construction of infrastructure (for example the Coca Codo Sinclair hydroelectric plant, the largest in the country) and the extraction of natural resources (petroleum and mining), often under conditions that require Ecuador to select Chinese companies for the construction or operation of these projects (Acosta and Cajas-Guijarro 2018).

Unfortunately, despite Ecuador's recent economic boom (due to a rise in commodity prices) and talk about upgrading its productivity, the country has not seen meaningful structural changes, but rather a process of deindustrialization and economic suppression, owing largely to its over-reliance on large-scale mining as an economic pillar—with twenty-seven active projects as of 2017 (Sacher 2017). Reyes Herrera's chapter in this volume discusses the dynamics of the relation between China and Ecuador in those periods that witnessed economic boom (the reformism of Rafael Correa's administration) and bust (in the postreformist period of Lenín Moreno's administration).

CHINESE MINING IN RÍO BLANCO, MOLLETURO: BACKGROUND

Chinese capital is behind the development of several Ecuadorian mining operations, including the Río Blanco and Mirador projects. As discussed in the introduction to this volume, the common narrative behind Chinese investments in infrastructure and extractive projects is that, if adequately regulated, economic benefits may well surpass the risks and the damage these cause to local populations. However, as several authors in this volume show (Van Teijlingen and Hidalgo Bastidas; Vasconez), Chinese projects have been criticized for having a high impact on the environment and on the well-being of people. Project Mirador, which inaugurated the country's era of mega-mining, showcases the myriad irregularities, alleged constitutional rights violations, and patterns of repressing and criminalizing social protest that have been identified since the Chinese company arrived.[4] Considering this, extractive projects have to face local resistance struggles, many of which have even been successful in stopping resource extraction and environmental damage. This was the case of the Munduruku people, who campaigned against the São Luis do Tapajós hydroelectric dam and got the environmental license for the project revoked (Oliveira, this volume, 187). It is also the case of Río Blanco, which we will discuss next.

The medium-sized Río Blanco project, located in the Andes of the southern province of Azuay, traces its origins to 1994 when the British company Rio Tinto–Zinc Corporation (RTZ) began operations in the parish of Molleturo. In 1998, RTZ sold its concession to San Luis Minerales S.A., a subsidiary of Canadian-owned International Minerals Corporation. The project remained in an advanced exploration phase until 2013, when the concession was sold to Ecuagoldmining South America S.A., a subsidiary of Chinese-owned Junefield Mineral Resources Holdings Ltd. (Junefield). As the project had enjoyed the government's full approval since 2008, upon taking over the concession, the new owners began outlining plans for extraction.

Although the Río Blanco project has provoked socioenvironmental conflict since the late 1990s (Quizhpe-Parra 2020), this escalated substantially after Junefield took over the concession. This is mainly due to certain changes in the project's relations with local communities in conjunction with the government's pro-mining policy orientation.

AN URBAN ECOLOGICAL MOVEMENT ARRIVES IN THE VILLAGE OF RÍO BLANCO

For years, the local communities' environmentalist struggles had been concentrated in Molleturo's eponymous parish seat where, since 2013, an organized group of women called Defenders of Pachamama (Mother Earth) have maintained a persistent campaign demanding "páramos libres de minería" (highlands free of mining). On the other hand, the communities surrounding the project (Río Blanco and Cochapamba) had been considered allies of the mining company, a situation that led to clashes with the town of Molleturo.

In December 2016, amid these confrontations, a resident of Cochapamba concerned about divisions within the community over the mining project contacted the Yasunidos Guapondélig collective (2016)[5] and alerted us to recurring conflicts among residents of this supposedly pro-mining community. Although neutral on the mining issue, he was interested in reducing the level of fragmentation within the community, which had reached a point where people were confronting each other at Sunday church services. He invited us to participate in a debate that would present the arguments of pro- and anti-mining speakers, with the idea of creating healthier dialog in the community. As neither the mining company nor the government agreed to participate, the event was never held, but the collective help set up a youth camp that met in Cochapamba and also in Paredones, a nearby archaeological site.

Despite earlier warnings that we could not approach Cochapamba or Río Blanco without risking attacks, the collective began visiting the area. During our first visit, we drove up to the mining project's gated entrance in Río Blanco village. It was raining heavily, and a guard prevented us from entering. We found ourselves stranded in a notoriously pro-mining community that just four months earlier had hosted Ecuador's vice president to announce, among other lofty remarks (Paspuel 2016), the inauguration of the mine's extraction phase.[6]

Without many options, we got out of the vehicle and knocked on the door of the house in front of the sentry box. Don[7] Leonidas cautiously let us enter his room to shelter us from the rain. There, as we drank the hot tea he offered us, we began to answer his wary questions. As the conversation progressed, he gradually admitted not only that was there division within his village over the mining project but also that the project had already impacted the local environment (water had been extracted from the land and a lagoon had already dried up). These comments obviously contradicted the belief, widely held among activists, that Río Blanco's support for the mining project had been unanimous. As he recounted one disenchantment after another, we ended up spending the entire night in his room. The next day we left our contact information and offered to support sharing his testimony in Cuenca or anything else he might need.

A few days later, we received a call from Don Leonidas's sister, Magdalena, who said that there was a group of university students visiting the mining project. Eager to show them the drying up of local springs (which had left several houses, including her mother's, without water), she wanted the group to also learn about the community's real attitudes toward the project. We made an appointment with Magdalena to collect her testimony regarding the springs so that we could share it with local media.

DISAPPOINTMENT WITH THE NEW CHINESE MINING COMPANY

After receiving us at her home, Magdalena showed us a wastewater treatment pool the mining company had built near her patio, which frequently gave off unpleasant odors. She also told us about the drying up of the springs, that even her mother never recalled happening before. She made clear she believed this was due to mining operations that had diverted some of the groundwater.

With nostalgia, she recalled the arrival of the first mining company, "la RTZ,"[8] more than twenty years earlier when she was a teenager—in particular, the kindness of its staff and the projects for gardening and farming *cuyes*[9] that they implemented with the community. She added that after RTZ was replaced by the "Canadian San Luis Minerales,"[10] the project's relations with the village had deteriorated.

But, in Magdalena's opinion, the problems became more serious with the arrival of Junefield. As she recounted, community projects either ended or only benefited a few families. The project began making unilateral decisions:

closing roads or building the wastewater-treatment pool next to her house. The community's primary school, which also served as a community center, no longer had Internet access, and their secondary school had been closed.

While not opposed to mining, Magdalena had hoped the social projects would resume, although she was unaware that providing (apparent) benefits to communities as a means of coopting leadership and weakening their social fabrics is a common corporate tactic. After this visit, we agreed to organize a meeting with the community to discuss actions that could remedy their problems.

STRENGTHENING TIES WITH THE CITY OF CUENCA

The meeting took place in Río Blanco's community school. We started by clarifying the reason for our presence, namely, to defend human rights, the autonomy of rural communities, and the environment, making clear that we wanted to support and accompany the community without the condescending expectation of "saving" anyone. We also assured them that, although we considered the mining project to be detrimental, in no way would we impose this idea or do anything that would deepen existing conflicts in the community. After this introduction, we enjoyed a fluid, entertaining, and open dialog with the attendees, who agreed they were struggling with a strong division, yet longed for their lost cohesion. As we closed the meeting, they asked us for a workshop on organizational strengthening and labor law so they could defend themselves against the company that hired several of their members, as the working conditions seemed unfair to them.

When we conducted the workshop, it became evident that the people of Río Blanco valued economic autonomy, recognized their women's ability to work with fabrics and make handicrafts, and appreciated the scenic beauty of their highland environment. The option of developing a community tourism project excited everyone.

Back in the city, we focused on the logistics of assembling the first group of tourists who would visit Río Blanco (San Antonio de Rio Blanco 2017). The community took care of the rest. They welcomed us, fed us, and shared stories of the highlands as we toured waterfalls, lagoons, and mountains and enjoyed beautiful landscapes. The gastronomic experience was also very satisfying. A portion of the funds collected were distributed among the members of the community group formed for the tourism project. Part of the remainder was used to create a small common fund to promote two ventures: community tourism and agroecology.

The community rediscovered its ability to organize. They continued to coordinate new dates for tourism events, with different families contributing food from their gardens, horses for the tours, rooms for guests, and other items. They planned the construction of a communal house to receive tourists, as well as the expansion of new and better routes for hiking and horseback riding.

In view of this renewed cooperation, the community found the strength to organize around other issues, holding the mining project accountable for the closure of roads, social divisions, and environmental damage. In August 2017, the community decided to hold a sit-in, blocking the entrances to the mining camp. They maintained this protest for two months, resulting in the first stoppage of the mine's activities and delays in the extraction of minerals. This was the first substantial demonstration of the community's determination to prevent the project from taking control of the territory. These protests ended up receiving considerable national attention, with the mainstream media's coverage of the government's use of force to stop the community's efforts. Thus, the Río Blanco community began to receive more support and solidarity from Cuenca, as well as from the rest of the country.

At the same time, the struggle for water protection was consolidating in Cuenca. An important space for coordination emerged in the form of the Water Council, which joined social organizations, communities, academia, and local authorities. The strength of this platform helped water protection become a priority issue in the media and local politics. While the national government was forced to turn its attention to the robust movement developing in this southern part of the country, it nevertheless maintained a strategy of turning it into a mining district.

The sit-in ended when an agreement was reached with the governor of Azuay,[11] who promised to address the community's demands directly with Ecuador's president and, in the meantime, to order a pause in the mining project's activities. This agreement, however, was never fulfilled, and the company resumed its activities.

In May 2018, the mainstream media's announcement that the Río Blanco project had produced its first output of mineral materials provoked a new uprising among the local communities, who again interrupted the project's activities and demanded the withdrawal of the Chinese company in control of the concession. On this occasion, the government's response was immediate. Around three hundred soldiers and members of the national police's special forces were deployed to repress the protest, despite it having been carried out within the communities' legitimate right to resistance[12] and despite warnings from the Office of the Ombudsman[13] on the dangers of the disproportionate use of force.

The military and police presence resulted in a confrontation that ended with the burning of the mining project's camp, the arrest of four people (who were later found innocent), and the persecution and criminalization of forty-three people, who are still being investigated by the prosecutor general.[14]

Almost immediately afterward, urban organizations and interested citizens raised voices in opposition to this state violence, denouncing it to national and international human rights organizations. At the same time, an effort was organized to provide support for the community members under investigation and to address the impact of this military intrusion on the communities.

The fact that most of the members of these local communities opposed the mining project, which had been imposed without any regard for their constitutional right to prior consultation, was made public. Meanwhile, the efforts of urban activist organizations effectively framed this crisis in the public discourse in terms of its environmental and social urgency, fostering widespread public sympathy for what was perceived to have been a serious violation of constitutional rights.

These public sentiments were vindicated in June 2018, when a civil court issued a preliminary injunction,[15] finding a violation of the communities' right to free, prior, and informed consultation and ordering the suspension of mining activities in the Río Blanco area, as well as the demilitarization of the conflict. This ruling in favor of communities[16] marked the first time that an Ecuadorian community has been able to legally suspend the operations of a foreign-operated metal mining project.

While the government appealed the decision, the provincial court that heard the appeal affirmed the initial decision in favor of the communities, ratifying the suspension of the mining project (Guambaña 2018). To assist the communities, Cuenca's Water Council gathered leaders from several social, political, academic, community, and local government sectors to attend the appellate hearing and give testimony that contradicted the government.

To date, the project's operations remain suspended. However, the government and the company that owns the concession continue to insist on reopening it. On October 3, 2018, the Ministry of Energy and Nonrenewable Natural Resources and the Office of the Prosecutor General filed an extraordinary protective action[17] with the Constitutional Court of Ecuador in Quito, challenging the provincial court's ruling. Should the government win this new appeal, the provincial court's decision (ratifying the project's suspension) would be reversed, thereby opening the door to renewed mining activities. While the Constitutional Court has taken the government's petition under advisement, it has yet to set any hearings on the matter.

CONCLUSION

Because it is a deeply expropriating activity (Machado Aráoz 2018), industrial mining not only monopolizes territories and displaces their inhabitants but also destroys the economy and the social fabric of local communities (Dávalos 2013). The introduction of organizational and economic strategies as an alternative to extractivism made it possible to correct some of the divisions within the Río Blanco community. Their resistance strategy—strengthened by interactions with urban activists—quickly spread throughout the territory like a mighty river.

The alliance between the Río Blanco community and the city of Cuenca created conditions for a historic judicial ruling that, to date, has succeeded in suspending the mining project's operations. While the community assumed the role of initiating and maintaining active resistance at the project site, supporters in Cuenca were able to publicize their activities, as well as the government's disproportionate response. The determination of these groups has been driven by a common discontent with the imposition of a mining project that threatens a territory common to both populations: the Río Blanco highlands, not only home to the homonymous village community, but also part of El Cajas National Park, one of the city of Cuenca's natural treasures.

NOTES

1. Ecuador's constitution guarantees procedural recourse to protective injunctions, which are issued to prevent or curtail violations of human or environmental rights.

2. The village of Río Blanco, located within parish of Molleturo, lies about thirty-eight miles west of Cuenca, Ecuador's third most populous city.

3. ECLAC (*CEPAL* in Spanish) refers to the Economic Commission for Latin America and the Caribbean, a Chile-based U.N. organization that promotes economic and social development in the region.

4. CEDHU 2010; Sacher 2017; Solíz 2018; Granizo 2019.

5. A Cuenca-based environmentalist collective, we have achieved notoriety in the press and social media for our activities and proposals as water defenders. See our Facebook page at: https://www.facebook.com/yasunidoscuenca2014/.

6. In response to this discouraging event, and despite the apparent hopelessness of seeing any reversal of this decision, as a collective we had published an open letter explaining the environmental and social disaster the mine's exploitation would produce.

7. In Spanish, "don" is used as a term of respect, but unlike "señor" (Mr.) it is mainly used as a prefix to a person's first name (for example "don José") or nickname ("don Pepe").

8. She was referring to the Anglo-Australian mining giant then known as Rio Tinto–Zinc Corporation, which the people of Río Blanco remember by its initials.

9. *Cuy* is the Kichwa word for guinea pig, a family of rodents domesticated in the pre-Columbian era from various species native to the South American Andes. Beyond having ritual significance in Indigenous cultures, they have historically been an important source of food—and are still commonly eaten in the Andean regions of Colombia, Ecuador, Perú, and Bolivia.

10. At the time San Luis Minerales S.A., an Ecuadorian company, was operating in Río Blanco as a subsidiary of Canadian-owned International Minerals Corporation.

11. While governors act as local authorities, they are nevertheless part of the national government's executive branch and essentially represent the president in the different provinces.

12. Article 98 of Ecuador's constitution defines and protects the right to resistance.

13. The Defensoría del Pueblo del Ecuador (Office of the Ombudsman) is an autonomous agency of the national government, whose purpose is to protect human and environmental rights.

14. The Fiscalía General del Estado (Office of the Prosecutor General) is another autonomous national agency, whose purpose is to investigate and prosecute violations of Ecuador's criminal laws.

15. Ecuadorian courts may issue orders imposing *Medidas Cautelares* (literally "precautionary measures," equivalent to a preliminary injunction or temporary restraining order) for the purpose of preventing, impeding, or interrupting any threatened or ongoing violation of legal rights.

16. Case No. 01333201803145. Protective Injunction Petition No. 03145-18 (eSATJE 2018).

17. Petition No. 2546-18-EP.

REFERENCES

Acosta, Alberto, and John Cajas-Guijarro. 2018. "La deuda eterna contraataca: cómo el correísmo nos regresó al pasado." In *El Gran Fraude: ¿Del correísmo al morenismo?* Quito: Montecristi Vive.

Cajas-Guijarro, John. 2018. *Los capos del comercio. Concentración, poder y acuerdos comerciales en el Ecuador: un preludio.* Quito: Plataforma por el Derecho a la Salud/ Fundación DONUM/FOS.

Comisión Ecuménica de Derechos Humanos (CEDHU). 2010. *Intervención minera a gran escala en Ecuador y vulneración de derechos humanos.* Federación Internacional de Derechos Humanos, FIDH. Caso Corriente Resources.

Constitución de la República del Ecuador, Montecristi, Manabí. 2008. *Registro oficial 449 del 20 de octubre del 2008.*

Dávalos, P. 2013. "No podemos ser mendigos sentados en un saco de oro: Las falacias del discurso extractivista." In *El correísmo al desnudo*, edited by A. Acosta et al., 190–215. Quito: Montecristi Vive.

Dussel, E. 2018. "Chinese Infrastructure Projects in Mexico: General Context and Two Case Studies." In *Building Development for a New Era. China's Infrastructure Projects in Latin America and the Caribbean*, edited by E. Dussel, A. Armony and S. Cui, 58–76. Mexico City: Red Académica de América Latina y el Caribe sobre China.

ECLAC/Comisión Económica para América Latina y el Caribe. 2019. *La inversión extranjera directa en América Latina y el Caribe.* https://repositorio.cepal.org/bitstream/handle/11362/44876/1/S1900582_es.pdf.

Ecuador Decide. 2020. "Mejor sin TLC." https://www.redecuadordecide.org/.

El Universo. 2020. "Ecuador y China llegan a 40 años de relación como socios estratégicos integrales." January 16, 2020. https://www.eluniverso.com/noticias/2020/01/16/nota/7694277/ecuador-china-llegan-40-anos-relacion-como-socios-estrategicos.

eSATJE. 2018. "Consulta de Procesos" [Case Search]. http://consultas.funcionjudicial.gob.ec/informacionjudicial/public/informacion.jsf .

Granizo, Paola. 2019. *El campo minado de la salud. Megaminería a cielo abierto en la Amazonía sur del Ecuador y sus impactos sobre la salud.* Quito: Plataforma por el Derecho a la Salud/ Fundación DONUM/FOS.

Guambaña, Johnny. 2018. "Tribunal de Azuay ratifica fallo que suspende actividad minera del proyecto Río Blanco." *El Universo*, October 2018.

Machado Aráoz, Horacio. 2018. *Potosí, el Origen: Genealogía de la minería contemporánea.* Quito: Editorial Abya-Yala.

Monini, Salvatore, and Luca Serafini. 2017. "The Relationship between Ecuador and China: A Dangerous Alliance?" *Working Paper Series.* http://www.sustainability-seeds.org/papers/RePec/srt/wpaper/0818.pdf.

Niu, H. 2018. "La iniciativa de la franja y la ruta y la cooperación financiera China-Latinoamérica." In *La franja y la ruta: iniciativa china de cooperación con*

América Latina y Caribe, edited by Jiang Shixue and Fortunato Mallimaci, 252–61. Ushuaia: Ediciones UNTDF.

Paspuel, Washington. 2016. "El proyecto Río Blanco generará 611 000 onzas de oro en 11 años." *El Comercio,* August 11, 2016.

Quizhpe-Parra, Carlos. 2020. "La commoditización de las subjetividades: la minería en la provincia del Azuay, Ecuador y los casos de los proyectos Río Blanco y Loma Larga." Master's thesis, Facultad Latinoamericana de Ciencias Sociales, FLACSO Sede.

Reyes, Milton, and Po Chun Lee. 2017. "La relación China-Ecuador en el siglo XXI: elementos relevantes para la discusión." *Working Papers.* Instituto de Altos Estudios Nacionales.

Sacher, W. 2017. *Ofensiva megaminera en los Andes. Acumulación por desposesión en el Ecuador de la "Revolución Ciudadana."* Ediciones Abya-Yala: Quito.

San Antonio de Rio Blanco. 2017. "Río Blanco Camping Fest!" Facebook (event), May 26–27, 2017. https://www.facebook.com/events/461004967583275/.

Solíz, F. 2018. *"Extractivismos: criminalización de las resistencias locales de la década perdida."* In *El Gran Fraude: ¿Del correísmo al morenismo?* Quito: Montecristi Vive.

Svampa, M. 2011. *Pensar el desarrollo desde América Latina.* http://www.maristellasvampa.net/archivos/ensayo56.pdf.

Yasunidos Guapondélig Collective. 2016. "Carta abierta a la Ciudadanía de Cuenca, a propósito de la inauguración de la explotación del proyecto minerorío blanco." Open Letter, August 11, 2016. https://fr.scribd.com/document/320901072/Carta-abierta-a-la-ciudadania-de-Cuenca-a-proposito-de-la-inauguracion-de-la-explotacion-del-proyecto-Rio-Blanco.

Protectionism for Business, Precarization for Labor: China's Investment-Protection Treaties and Community Struggles in the Latin American and Caribbean Region

Ana Saggioro Garcia and Rodrigo Curty Pereira

CHINA HAS GAINED IMPORTANCE as an economic partner of Latin America and the Caribbean (LAC) over the past two decades. By 2019, China became the region's second largest trading partner, only behind the United States, with a total trade of US$307.4 billion in 2018 (Ray and Wang 2019, 2). The Asian country is also an important source of credit for the region, having provided more than US$140 billion to Latin American governments and public companies since 2005 (Gallagher and Myers 2019, 1). China became the main investor in terms of mergers and acquisitions in LAC in 2017 (CEPAL 2018, 40) and, in following years, remained among the top three investors, behind the US and Europe (CEPAL 2019, 44). Despite China's economic strength, the Asian giant is still considered to be in many ways a developing nation. For this reason, some analysts about Chinese relations with the Global South are quite optimistic. These see the Asian country as possibly overcoming the neoliberal practices normally attributed to the Global North (Vadell, Lo Brutto, and Milk 2020). Other readings, however, point to the fact that trade and Chinese foreign direct investment (FDI) in LAC are concentrated in primary sectors, reproducing an economic pattern of dependence in Latin America (CEPAL 2018; Stallings 2020; Spilak and Ghiotto 2019).

This chapter seeks to evaluate these two readings about China-LAC relations, highlighting processes of crony protectionism and labor precarization that tend to fall into the gap that opens up between these two dominant readings and the polarized political perspective each represents. We start with the critical theory of Robert W. Cox (1981), who understands the phenomena of international relations based on historical structures and the study of particular social forces. Along these lines, we ask how economic relations between China and the LAC region have been organized in terms of material capacities, ideas, and institutions since the 2000s. What are the main actors or social forces that are involved?

As many chapters in this volume note, the twenty-first-century world is marked by China's rise, challenging US hegemony and creating new dynamics in the Global South. Since the early 2000s, the LAC region witnessed an increasing flow of Chinese investment, trade, and credit. Maria Elena Rodríguez for example, observes that "China is currently the third largest consumer of gas and the second largest consumer of petroleum, while concentrating more than 30 percent of the global demand for raw materials such as copper, soy, iron, and steel," all resources that can be found in abundance in the Global South and, in particular, South America. China, in other words, "is an essential trading partner for Latin America" (Rodríguez, this volume, 337).

China ceased to be a minor economic player in the region in the 1990s, becoming the main trading partner of several Latin American and Caribbean countries, an important source of FDI and credit from 2010 on (CEPAL 2018; Stallings 2020; Ray and Wang 2019; Myers and Gallagher 2020a; Dussel Peters 2020). This was accompanied by the creation of multilateral forums (such as the New Development Bank, detailed by Waisbich in this volume), bilateral treaties, visits by Chinese leaders (as Brancoli and Guerra's chapter details) and official documents for Chinese policies in the region (such as the "white papers" discussed by Rodríguez, this volume, 337–38) (The State Council 2016). In these spaces, narratives about the growing Chinese presence have focused on South-South cooperation and particularly on growth and mutual development.

In this chapter, we first present the material outlines of China-LAC relations, expressed in Chinese trade, investment, and credit flows, as well as the main sectors and countries these flows are directed toward. We also point out the main Chinese companies and banks acting in this context. We then analyze official narratives regarding China-LAC relations, as well as the socioenvironmental impacts and conflicts surrounding Chinese investments.

We seek to highlight the social and narrative forces in dispute within the historical structure. We conclude that relationships between China and Latin America are enormously important considering the current geopolitical disputes and Latin American infrastructure needs. At the same time, these relationships can create or reinforce contradictions in the territories where Chinese projects are implemented. It is up to Latin American countries to seek to break their dependence on natural resources exportation to shape a more socially just and sustainable post-COVID-19 world.

COMMERCE, CREDIT, AND DIRECT INVESTMENT

Trade between China and the LAC region has grown since 2005 as a result of the rise in commodity prices and Chinese demand for natural resources (Menezes and Bragatti 2020; Stallings 2020). The rising Chinese economy has demanded minerals, metals, and fossil fuels to enable its growth, and LAC export sectors benefit from this. Additionally, the rising Chinese middle class has started to consume more meat, which has also increased the demand for soy for animal feed (Menezes and Bragatti 2020, 42–49).

Brazil, Chile, Venezuela, and (more recently) Peru, Suriname, and Trinidad and Tobago all have a trade surplus with China (CEPAL 2018, 40; Ray and Wang 2019, 3). According to ECLAC data (2018, 41), the Central American countries—and particularly Mexico—have a trade deficit. LAC's exports to China are mostly primary products. In 2017, these accounted for 72 percent of the region's total trade to China, while representing only 27 percent of the region's trade with the rest of the world. Just five products alone accounted for 70 percent of the region's exports to China in that year: soybeans, copper ore, iron ore, refined copper, and oil (42). Imports, on the other hand, have been concentrated among low-, medium-, and high-technology manufactured products, accounting for 91 percent of LAC imports from China in 2017 (CEPAL 2018, 41).

According to UNCTAD (2020a, 4), China is still behind the US and Europe in terms of investments in LAC. Chinese investments have grown, however, reaching US$134.770 billion between 2000 and 2019, according to Dussel Peters (2020, 6). Annual flows of Chinese FDI in LAC have fluctuated with commodity prices, reaching a measure of stability in the period from 2013 to 2019 at an average of US$12.412 billion per year.[1] In 2011, China was responsible for 13.64 percent[2] of total investments in the region. More recently, it has been responsible for an annual average of 8 percent.[3] China also protects its LAC investments through bilateral investment treaties with fifteen countries and three free trade agreements containing provisions on investments (UNCTAD n.d.).

Chinese FDI in LAC is concentrated in a few countries. Brazil is the main recipient, having received US$48.70 billion in Chinese investments between 2000 and 2019. It is followed by Peru, Chile, Argentina, and Mexico (Dussel Peters 2020). According to CEPAL (2019, 45), China concentrated its interests in acquiring agrobusinesses and extractive industries, in energy generation, basic services (provision of water, gas, and electricity), and infrastructure.[4] According to data from the China Global Investment Tracker, 74 percent of Chinese investments in LAC between 2005 and 2019 were directed to natural-resource-intensive sectors: agriculture, energy, and mining. The energy sector (which includes investments in oil, gas, and renewable energy) was responsible for more than half of that (American Enterprise Institute and Heritage Foundation 2020).[5]

Chinese capital's preference for investments in natural resources and energy is notorious, as is the complementarity of these investments with the Latin American products most imported by China. The only exception seems to be the agricultural sector, which represents only 4 percent of Chinese FDI in LAC, despite the importance of soy for the Asian country. We believe that in relations with LAC countries, China seeks to meet strategic needs that correspond to projects for Chinese development. Menezes and Bragatti (2020, 449) explain this tendency as an effect of the Chinese global strategy of "Stepping Out," in which companies seek to invest in natural resource and energy markets to guarantee the provision of the food and raw materials for the Chinese economy.

Significantly, Chinese investments are concentrated in five state-owned companies responsible for one-third of China's total investments in LAC since 2000. These are State Grid (which invested US$15.52 billion (11.5 percent of the total), China Three Gorges (CTG, US$11.02 billion, 8.2 percent), Sinopec (US$10.89 billion, 8.1 percent), China National Petroleum Corporation (CNPC, US$5.63 billion, 4.2 percent), and China National Offshore Oil Corporation (CNOOC, US$4.46 billion, 3.3 percent) (Dussel Peters 2020, 10). All these companies operate in the energy sector. Sinopec (n.d.), CNPC (n.d.) and CNOOC (n.d.) are focused on oil and gas production (CTG Brasil n.d.).

State Grid (n.d.) and CTG have investments in renewable energy (mainly hydroelectric) and in electricity transmission.

Another key aspect of China-LAC relations are the loans from Chinese development banks to countries in the region. According to Gallagher and Myers (2019, 1), the amount of credit granted by just two Chinese banks (China Development Bank and Export and Import Bank of China) to Latin American countries since 2005 was over US$140 billion, exceeding the loans made by the traditional financial institutions active in the region such as the World Bank and the Inter-American Development Bank. According to these authors, Chinese credit has been contracted mainly by four LAC countries: Argentina, Brazil, Ecuador, and Venezuela. Venezuela has taken out 17 loans totaling some US$2.2. billion: fully 45 percent of the loans made. As for the other countries, Brazil has taken out US$28.9 billion in loans, Ecuador US$18.4 billon, and Argentina US$17.1 billion. These loans are concentrated in the energy and infrastructure sectors.

NARRATIVES AND CONFLICTS

As Sino-Latin American economic relations have intensified, the governments involved have created cooperation mechanisms. The China Forum and the Community of Latin American and Caribbean States (China-CELAC Forum) is one of the main platforms for cooperation between China and the LAC countries (MFA of China 2016, 2020). This organization is important because it brings together China and the thirty-three member countries of CELAC[6] in a single discussion forum. The forum has also been used by Chinese leaders to announce investment funds, cooperation plans, and estimates of direct investments and trade with LAC countries. It is a meeting place for government representatives, financial institutions, and representatives of companies from China and LAC (MFA of China 2016, 5).

In this sense, the forum has become one of the main promoters of cooperation between member countries. Below, we analyze speeches by Chinese president Xi Jinping in two meetings of this institution (the Meeting of Leaders of China and the CELAC in Brasília in 2014; the Ministerial Meeting of the China-CELAC Forum in Beijing in 2015), in addition to two official documents from the Chinese government for LAC: the China-CELAC Cooperation Plan (2015–2019) and the LAC policy paper published in 2016.

Xi Jinping's speeches at the meetings of the China-CELAC Forum notably emphasize the concept of the Forum as a South-South cooperation initiative that aims to achieve "common development goals" (MFA of China 2016, 64). On both occasions, the "1 + 3 + 6" cooperation strategy was addressed. This consists of the implementation of a single cooperation plan, through three economic mechanisms (trade, investment, and credit), in six strategic sectors: energy and natural resources, infrastructure construction, agriculture, manufacturing, scientific and technological innovation, and information technologies (66–68).

In all the documents analyzed, the idea that China-CELAC cooperation aims to promote "inclusive growth and sustainable development" was heavily supported (MFA of China 2016, 66; State Council 2016). In the 2016 Chinese government policy for LAC, the 3x3 cooperation model, was added. This consists of building transport, electricity, and information routes and expanding three financing channels: funds, loans, and insurance. In that same document, priority areas for China-LAC cooperation are outlined and the idea of South-South cooperation as a win-win proposition is promoted.

The documents we analyzed recognize the need to diversify trade and investments in the region, increasing the export of high value-added products and services and strengthening Latin American countries' industrial capacity. They also emphasize, however, the "strong complementarity in economic structure and development strategy between China and Latin America" (MFA of China 2016, 66), defending the need to maintain trade in Latin America's "traditionally competitive" products.

As we have shown, this reveals an emphasis on primary and natural resource sectors in the region. These sectors, in turn, are permeated by socioenvironmental conflicts involving Chinese companies in LAC. We were able to identify fifty-seven cases of socioenvironmental conflicts, with a clear concentration in the energy (44 percent), mining (37 percent), and infrastructure (10 percent) sectors. We note that there is also a strong correlation between these sectors and the main targets of Chinese FDI.

What caused these conflicts? What are the narratives of the local communities affected by them? To answer these questions, we used thematic analysis methodology (Caulfield 2020; Herzog, Handke, and Hitters 2019) to identify "potential" and "real" causes. Potential causes are those possible causes of conflict pointed out by affected communities in their narratives, normally attributed to projects that have not yet been implemented but which have a great chance of causing damage to the environment and to the communities themselves. The real causes, in turn, are those that have already occurred in already implemented projects. We have been able to distinguish the causes and sort them into four categories: environmental, socioenvironmental, labor violations, and human rights violations.

The main causes of potential conflicts involve areas of natural conservation or high biodiversity, the pollution of bodies of water, and operations in Indigenous or traditional communities' territories. A case in point is the Grand Interoceanic Canal Project in Nicaragua. This mega-infrastructure project envisages the construction of a 286-km-long canal across Nicaragua to allow the transport of cargo from the Caribbean Sea to the Pacific Ocean and vice versa (EJAtlas 2018b). The concession was obtained by the Hong Kong Nicaragua Canal Development Investment Company. The project was initially challenged by peasant and Indigenous communities because of the immense impact it would have on the entire nation and on Lake Nicaragua, the largest source of fresh water in the country and a region of great cultural significance for Nicaraguans. These social forces claimed that the canal's construction would heavily impact biodiversity in protected areas and displace Indigenous and traditional communities across the country. Technical feasibility studies were called for. So far, however, the project shows no significant progress (*Deutsche Welle* 2019). Nevertheless, in 2019 Nicaraguan president Daniel Ortega declared that his government is still planning to build the canal.

Failure to conduct consultations with the impacted populations and inadequate environmental impact studies constitute one of the main real causes identified by this study in terms of the creation of socioenvironmental conflicts with Chinese companies. Fifteen conflicts occurred in part due to a lack of adequate prior consultation, while seventeen projects were accused of not correctly conducting or publicizing environmental impact studies. Other common real causes are the pollution of bodies of water, compensation for displacement or unjust environmental damage, and preference for more sustainable alternatives.

Gold mining in Río Blanco in Ecuador, by Ecuagoldmining (a subsidiary of the Chinese company Junefield Mineral Resources) gave rise to a conflict that brought together all the above causes and others as well (EJAtlas 2019b). The groups that oppose the mine accuse the company of not having carried out the environmental impact study in consultation with the affected communities, in breach of Ecuador's legislation. They also argue that the Río Blanco mine is close to the head of several rivers and that mining and the opening of roads to export gold has polluted these.

In our research, we also tried to identify the main actors or social forces involved in these conflicts. With regard to Chinese companies, we found that they were often acting in conjunction with European and North American companies, contradicting the South-South cooperation narrative mentioned above. Our study reveals that some Chinese companies are involved in more than one case of socioenvironmental conflict. These companies are without exception in the energy and mining sectors. Sinohydro and CTG are construction companies, but they operate in the hydroelectric sector and (in the case of CTG) are responsible for the generation of energy in some of their projects. Three of these companies are among those that invest the most in the region: CNPC, CTG, and Sinopec.

Sinohydro, a state-owned multinational specialized in the construction of hydroelectric plants, is involved in conflicts in Bolivia, Chile, Ecuador, Honduras, Peru, and Venezuela. One of the most controversial cases involves the Aguas Zarca Hydroelectric Project in Honduras. In this case, the Lenca Indigenous peoples opposed the construction of hydroelectric plants and dams on the Gualcarque River, Indigenous sacred territory (EJAtlas 2018b). There was much resistance to the project on the part of these communities. The Honduran government responded by persecuting the opposition's leaders. The case culminated in the internationally notorious assassination of opposition leader Berta Cáceres (Blitzer 2016). Sinohydro abandoned the project in 2012 due to the escalation of these conflicts (EJAtlas 2018b).

CNPC and Sinopec are two large Chinese state companies operating in the oil and gas sector. Three conflicts involve two companies' joint ventures in Ecuador: Andes Petroleum and PetroOriental. The greatest amount of opposition was mobilized in the case of Andes Petroleum's acquisition of exploration rights in Blocks 74, 79, and 83 in Sápara and Kichwa Indigenous territory (Amazon Watch 2019). These are part of the Yasuní National Park, located in Ecuador's Amazon region (EJAtlas 2018b). The Indigenous communities were opposed to oil exploration because of its potential for contamination and deforestation in a region of high biodiversity and because of the impacts that extractive activity would have on the social fabric of the Native groups. Protests were organized, and the Ecuadoran government responded by criticizing and criminalizing these movements. Resistance was conducted through protests, popular campaigns, pressure on the Chinese embassy in Ecuador, lawsuits denouncing the lack of prior public consultation, and struggles for control of the airstrips in the territory (Amazon Watch 2019).

Our study of socioenvironmental conflicts involving Chinese companies in Latin America and the Caribbean has also allowed us to identify some of the subordinate or resistant social forces. These actors are particular to each conflict and national context. Among the main resisting social forces are environmentalists, Indigenous communities, social justice organizations, and local residents. Environmental groups include national and international organizations. These groups act both in association with the communities directly affected by the projects and independently. In the case of a conflict involving CNPC and Sinopec in the Sápara and Kichwa Indigenous territories, Amazon Watch supported Indigenous resistance by publicizing and defending the struggle of these peoples. In the case of the Condor Cliff—Barrancosa Hydroelectric Complex in Argentina, several environmental groups formed a coalition (Río Santa Cruz Sin Represas) that led the campaign against dam construction, carrying out protests and suing the companies involved in the project (EJAtlas 2019a).

The category "social justice promotion organizations" includes those nongovernmental organizations dedicated to reducing social inequalities and guaranteeing civil, political, and economic rights. In the cases we studied, we found that these generally support the communities directly affected by Chinese projects. One example is the Landless Rural Workers Movement (MST), which worked in partnership with local communities to prevent iron mining and the construction of a pipeline by Sul-Americana Metais (controlled by the Chinese Honbridge Holding) in Grão Mogol in Brazil (EJAtlas 2018a). Indigenous communities have also been consistent actors in the conflicts we studied. These groups have the internationally recognized right to be consulted with regard to economic activities in their territories (ILO 1989). What we have labeled "residents" are local communities that do not enjoy any special status guaranteed by international conventions.

CONCLUSION

We have sought to highlight the different narratives surrounding economic relations between China in LAC, showing the socioenvironmental conflicts resulting from projects by Chinese companies in the region.

Using Robert W. Cox's (1981) historical structure method, we have sought to highlight material capabilities in terms of China's investment, trade, and credit in LAC, the institutions involved, and the ideas and narratives regarding China–Latin America relations. These tend to either emphasize South-South cooperation and inclusive and sustainable growth or push for the exploitation of natural and primary resources, resulting in socioenvironmental conflicts.

We understand that China has consolidated itself as one of LAC's main economic partners, being to a large extent responsible for the growth of the region's economies over the past two decades. Relations with China support Latin America in strengthening the region in the face of its historic US influence, positioning LAC in the current global geopolitical dispute. On the other hand, China-LAC relations often suppress the infrastructure needs of Latin American countries. We also find that these relationships display several contradictions. China seeks to respond to its strategic demands in terms of energy and natural resources, inserting itself in accumulation processes that generate negative impacts on the populations in the territories where projects are implemented.

In this sense, it is worth mentioning that the development model historically adopted by Latin American countries (particularly their dominant classes and governments) is based on the extraction of natural and energy resources that are sold to foreign markets. In this context, Latin American nation-states have often not guaranteed their national sovereignty and the social, environmental, and human rights of their populations. Social struggles and resistance are important in pressuring states in this direction. We live in a changing world in which China will play an increasing role. Change has been accelerated by the COVID-19 pandemic. Latin America and the Caribbean need to gain prominence to shape the postpandemic world and break with historic relations of dependence on the export of commodities, reversing the traditional international division of labor. So far, this division of labor has mostly been reinforced in LAC relations with China.

NOTES

1. Authors' calculations based on data from Red ALC-China (2020).

2. Authors' calculations based on data from Red ALC-China (2020) and UNCTAD (2020b).

3. Average value for the 2017–2019 period (Dussel Peters 2020).

4. According to CEPAL (2019), the United States and Europe showed a more diverse investment portfolio in the region, being more based in fusions and acquisitions in high tech (Internet, software, and telecommunications).

5. Authors' calculations based on data from the American Enterprise Institute and Heritage Foundation (2020).

6. At the moment the forum was created, CELAC had as members Antigua and Barbuda, Argentina, the Bahamas, Barbados, Belize, Bolivia, Brazil, Chile, Colombia, Costa Rica, Cuba, Dominica, Ecuador, El Salvador, Granada, Guatemala, Guyana, Haiti, Honduras, Jamaica, Mexico, Nicaragua, Panama, Paraguay, Peru, The Dominican Republic, Santa Lucia, St. Christopher and Nevis, Saint Vincent and the Grenadines, Surinam, Trinidad and Tobago, Uruguay, and Venezuela (MFA 2016, 5).

REFERENCES

Amazon Watch. 2019. "Indigenous Opposition Forces Andes Petroleum out of Controversial Rainforest Oil Block." *Amazon Watch*, November 6, 2019. https://amazonwatch.org/news/2019/1106-indigenous-opposition-forces-andes-petroleum-out-of-controversial-rainforest-oil-block.

American Enterprise Institute and the Heritage Foundation. 2020. "China Global Investment Tracker." https://www.aei.org/china-global-investment-tracker/.

Blitzer, Jonathan. 2016. "The Death of Berta Cáceres." *New Yorker*, March 11, 2016. https://www.newyorker.com/news/news-desk/the-death-of-berta-caceres.

CEPAL. 2019. *La inversión extrajera directa em América Latina y el Caribe*. Santiago: United Nations Publication.

CEPAL. 2018. *Explorando nuevos espacios de cooperación entre América Latina y el Caribe y China*. Santiago: United Nations Publication.

Caulfield, Jack. 2020. "How to Do Thematic Analysis." *Scribbr*, June 19, 2020. https://www.scribbr.com/methodology/thematic-analysis/.

CNOOC. n.d. "Operations: Brazil." https://cnoocinternational.com/en/operations/americas/brazil.

CNPC. n.d. "CNPC in Brazil." https://www.cnpc.com.cn/en/Brazil/country_index.shtml.

Cox, Robert W. 1981. "Social Forces, States and World Orders: Beyond International Relations Theory." *Journal of International Studies, London* 10, no. 2: 126–55.

CTG Brasil. n.d. "Negócios." https://www.ctgbr.com.br/negocios/.

Dussel Peters, Enrique. 2020. *Monitor de la OFDI China en América Latina y el Caribe 2020*. Ciudad de México: Universidad Autónoma de México.

Deutsche Welle. 2019. "Ortega revive proyecto de canal interoceánico en Nicaragua." August 14, 2019. https://www.dw.com/es/ortega-revive-proyecto-de-canal-interoce%C3%A1nico-en-nicaragua/a-50019224.

EJAtlas. 2020a. "The Global Atlas of Environmental Justice." https://ejatlas.org/.

EJAtlas. 2020b. "Andes Petroleum Oil Proposal in Sápara Indigenous Territory in Amazon Rainforest, Ecuador." https://ejatlas.org/conflict/andes-petroleum-oil-proposal-in-sapara-indigenous-territory-in-amazon-rainforest-ecuador.

EJAtlas. 2020c. "Incinerator of Urban Solid Waste in Barueri, São Paulo, Brazil." https://ejatlas.org/conflict/incinerator-of-urban-solid-waste-in-barueri-sao-paulo-brazil.

EJAtlas. 2019a. "Represas del río Santa Cruz, Argentina." https://ejatlas.org/conflict/represas-del-rio-santa-cruz1.

EJAtlas. 2019b. "Rio Blanco, Molleturo, Azuay, Ecuador." https://ejatlas.org/conflict/rio-blanco-molleturo-azuay-ecuador.

EJAtlas. 2018a. "Iron Ore Mining and Mineroduct, Grão Mogol, Minas Gerais, Brazil." https://ejatlas.org/conflict/iron-ore-mining-and-mineroduct-grao-mogol-minas-gerais-brazil.

EJAtlas. 2018b. "Proyecto Hidroeléctrico Agua Zarca, Honduras." https://ejatlas.org/conflict/proyecto-hidroelectrico-agua-zarca-honduras.

Gallagher, Kevin P., and Margaret Myers. 2019. China-Latin America Finance Database. Washington, DC: Inter-American Dialogue.

Herzog, Christian, Christian Handke, and Erick Hitters. 2019. "Analyzing Talk and Text II: Thematic Analysis." In *The Palgrave Handbook of Methods for Media Policy Research*, edited by Hilde Van Den Bulck, Manuel Puppis, Karen Donders, and Leo Van Audenhove, 233–47. Basingstoke: Palgrave Macmillan.

ILO. 1989. "Convenção n° 169, de 27 jun. 1989." Geneva: ILO, 1991. https://www.ilo.org/dyn/normlex/en/f?p=NORMLEXPUB:12100:0::NO::P12100_ILO_CODE:C169.

Martínez, O. B. 2014. "La geopolítica petrolera China en Ecuador y el área andina." *Tensões Mundiais* 10, no. 18: 255–73.

Menezes, Roberto Goulart, and Milton Carlos Bragatti. 2020. "Dragon in the 'Backyard': China's Investment and Trade in Latin America in the Context of Crisis." *Brazilian Journal of Political Economy* 40, no. 3: 446–61.

MFA of China. 2016. *Basic Information about China-CELAC Forum*. Beijing: Ministry of Foreign Affairs of China.

MFA of China. 2020 "Ministerial Meetings." *China-CELAC Forum*, March 6, 2018. http://www.chinacelacforum.org/eng/zyjz_1/bjzhy/t1539906.htm.

Myers, Margaret, and Kevin Gallagher. 2020a. *Scaling Back: Chinese Development Finance in LAC, 2019*. Washington, D.C.: Inter-American Dialogue.

Myers, Margaret, and Kevin Gallagher . 2020b. "China Latin America Finance Database." https://www.thedialogue.org/map_list/.

Ray, Rebecca, Kevin P. Gallagher, Andres Lopez, and Cynthia Sanborn. 2015. *China in Latin America: Lessons for South-South Cooperation and Sustainable Development*. Boston: Boston University.

Ray, Rebecca, and Kehan Wang. 2019. *China-Latin America Economic Bulletin 2019 Edition*. Boston: Boston University.

Red ALC-China. 2020. "América Latina y el Caribe: OFDI china a nivel de empresa (2000–2019)." https://www.redalc-china.org/monitor/informacion-por-pais/busqueda-por-pais/80-america-latina-y-el-caribe.

Sinopec. n.d. "Quem somos." https://www.repsolsinopec.com.br/quem-somos/nossas-atividades/.

Slipak, Ariel, and Luciana Ghiotto. 2019. "América Latina en la Nueva Ruta de la Seda: El rol de las inversiones chinas en la región en un contexto de disputa (inter)hegemónica." *Cuadernos del CEL* 4, no. 7: 26–55.

Stallings, Barbara. 2020. *Dependency in the Twenty-First Century? The Political Economy of China-Latin American Relations.* Cambridge: Cambridge University Press.

State Council of the People's Republic of China. 2016. "Full text of China's Policy Paper on Latin America and the Caribbean." http://english.www.gov.cn/archive/white_paper/2016/11/24/content_281475499069158.htm.

State Grid. n.d. "Sobre." https://www.stategrid.com.br/pagina-inicial/sobre/.

UNCTAD. 2020a. *World Investment Report: International Production Beyond the Pandemic.* New York: United Nations Publications.

UNCTAD. 2020b. "Foreign Direct Investment: Inward and Outward Flows and Stock, Annual." https://unctadstat.unctad.org/wds/TableViewer/tableView.aspx?ReportId=96740.

UNCTAD. n.d. "International Investment Agreements Navigator: China." https://investmentpolicy.unctad.org/international-investment-agreements/countries/42/china.

Vadell, Javier, Giuseppe Lo Brutto, Alexandre Cesar Cunha Leite. 2020. "The Chinese South-South Development Cooperation: An Assessment of Its Structural Transformation." *Revista Brasileira de Política Internacional* 63, no. 2: 1–22.

PART 4

LOGISTICS REGIMES AND MINING

A Mine, a Dam, and the Chinese-Ecuadorian Politics of Knowledge

Karolien van Teijlingen and Juan Pablo
Hidalgo-Bastidas

IT WAS CROWDED IN TUNDAYME on July 18, 2019. The streets of the village in the foothills of the Cordillera del Cóndor, a mountain range in the Ecuadorian Amazon, are normally nearly empty. But that day, there was a coming and going of armored cars, government vehicles, and lots of police. They headed to the mining project located outside the village, where a stage had been set up. The reason for the festivities was the inauguration of the Mirador mining project, which—after twenty years—was finally ready to produce its first grams of copper and gold.

The Mirador project is not just another mine in Latin America: it is Ecuador's very first large-scale mine, the flagship project of the country's aspirations to become Latin America's next mining frontier. "Today is a historical and fundamental day for the consolidation of the mining sector and the development of Ecuador," the minister of nonrenewable resources said in his inaugural speech. The Mirador mine, run by Ecuacorrientes S.A. (hereafter ECSA) and owned by the China Railway Construction Corporation Limited and Tongling Nonferrous Metals Group Holding, is also the first and largest Chinese investment in Ecuador's mining sector. This makes it a key project in the context of the growing Ecuador-China relations, described by David Mosquera Narváez and the Yasunidos Guapondélig Collective in their chapters in this volume. Mirador is furthermore a controversial project. Long before the mine was inaugurated, it was criticized by environmental organizations, local communities, human rights lawyers, and mining engineers. Their latest critique concerns the mine's design, which they say is fraught with errors and incorrectly executed. The experts assure us that the question is not *if* but *when* a major catastrophe will take place.

What the consequences of poor designs may look like was recently illustrated by another Chinese-built project in Ecuador, the Coca Codo Sinclair hydroelectric dam (hereafter CCS). In her chapter in of this book, Sigrid Vásconez narrates the environmental disaster that resulted from the construction of this dam. Built on inadequate and poorly surveyed soil, the dam caused the riverbed to erode and eventually collapse. To hydrologists and geologists, this event was no surprise: they had warned of poor studies and inadequate dam design. As was the case with the Mirador mine, these criticisms were ignored. The rest is history.

This chapter takes these two events as a starting point for reflection on the impact of large-scale Chinese investments in Ecuador. We ask what role Chinese operators have played in the politics of knowledge generation around these projects against the backdrop of the emerging geopolitical "marriage" between China and Ecuador and the disintegration of the Amazon biome. How did Chinese actors gather knowledge on the possibly catastrophic effects of their projects, and what role did officials of Ecuador's government play in approving the projects? How did they respond to criticism from environmental organizations and communities? Finally, what can we expect for the future of Chinese-Ecuadorian knowledge politics in the context of Ecuador's renewed dependency on China following the COVID-19 pandemic?

CHINA AND ECUADOR: A SOUTH-SOUTH LOVE AFFAIR

When the charismatic, self-proclaimed post-neoliberal Rafael Correa was elected president of Ecuador in 2007, one thing was clear: the World Bank and the International Monetary Fund—institutions that influenced the country's economic policy in the 1980s and 1990s—would no longer have it their way. Employing popular anti-imperialism, Correa defaulted on foreign debts, expelled the World Bank's country manager, and unilaterally renegotiated terms of payment. This move cut off Ecuador's access to finance, but Correa didn't care. He had found a new and powerful ally across the Pacific. China filled the void left by the World Bank and

International Monetary Fund, becoming Ecuador's single largest lender (Hogenboom 2017). Chinese investors and companies found their way into the Ecuadorian oil, energy, and mining sectors. These investments were welcomed by Correa, as Narváez (this volume) points out, for his administration had declared these sectors to be "strategic" pillars of its progressive development strategy.

Relations between Ecuador and China were promoted as South-South cooperation. As discussed in the introduction to this volume, this represented an ostensibly more equal relationship than the one with the imperialist North. In this "brotherhood," China was portrayed not only as a great source of finance, but also as Ecuador's big brother leading the way. China had ample experience in what Ecuador sought to achieve: modern infrastructure, mining, renewable energy, and technological innovation (Vice President of Ecuador n.d.). Cooperation was therefore permeated with promises of knowledge and technology transfer that would lead to Ecuador's "take off" as a modern, industrialized nation (Redacción Económica 2016). This transfer would take place "on the job" through collaboration on projects. Ecuador would gain infrastructure as well as the knowhow to be able to stand on its own two feet.

Despite abundant references to an egalitarian South-South partnership, relations between China and Ecuador were anything but equal. Ecuador was (and continues to be) dependent on China's checkbook and demand for primary resources. Meanwhile, Ecuador lacked the know-how and experience not only to implement large-scale projects but also to regulate them. These unequal power relations had a significant impact on how Chinese projects in Ecuador were carried out and on how environmental and social risks were studied, assessed, and considered. This inequality became visible in the Mirador mining project and the CCS dam, as these were the two crown jewels of China-Ecuador relations.

THE MIRADOR MINE: DEEP PITS AND HIGH DAMS

The Mirador mining project, which transformed the lush green mountains of Tundayme into an industrial enclave, has been controversial from the start. Although less successful than the communities around the Río Blanco project (see Yasunidos Guapondélig Collective, this volume, 208), local communities, environmental movements, and human rights organizations from Quito have protested the project for about two decades due to its impacts on the Amazon's ecosystems and for invading Indigenous and peasant land. Recently, voices from the mining sector joined this critique. E-Tech International—a group of US-based mining engineers that independently assesses technical reports and environmental impact studies—issued a scathing report on the Mirador mine (Emerman 2015). The engineers focused on the tailings facilities, the large basins where mining waste is stored in perpetuity. These are the weak spots of large-scale mines (Uranium Wise n.d.), and in cases of failure, impacts are devastating. In January 2019, for example, the dam of a tailings facility of a mine near Brumadinho in Brazil collapsed, and a wave of toxic mud engulfed the valley downstream, killing 290 people.

E-tech's engineers foresee a similar disaster in Tundayme if ECSA continues its operations according to plan (Emerman 2018). The company wants to build the highest tailings dam on Earth. Although one would expect that such an enormous dam would comply with safety regulations, that does not seem to be the case at Mirador. According to E-Tech, the designs of the dam that needs to keep mining waste in place for thousands of years are based on erratic data regarding local seismic activity and rainfall, the two main risk factors that have contributed to dam failures in the past (Roche and Baker 2017). The planned dams are also too steep when compared to international standards and will be built with inadequate, likely contaminated, material. To make things worse, the dam that is being built does not even follow the initial design. In practice, the slope of the dam is steeper than planned, and it uses a building method that is prohibited in many countries as too risky (Emerman 2018).

If E-tech's engineers are right and the dam collapses, the consequences will be disastrous. The tailings facility will store some 450 million cubic meters of waste containing heavy metals and acids. Tundayme is located 1 kilometer downstream and will probably be covered by meters of sludge in a matter of minutes. So will the Churuwia Indigenous territory and the numerous Indigenous and peasant that families that live nearby. E-tech calculates that waste contamination might make it as far as Peru (Emerman 2015), affecting the ecosystems of one of the most pristine parts of the Amazon rainforest.

Interestingly, ECSA's technical reports and environmental impact assessments (EIA) ignore or minimize these risks. These documents are required to obtain an environmental license and are considered essential to decision making with regard to safeguarding the environment. In the case of Mirador, the risk for water contamination with heavy metals and acid drainage was mentioned but assessed as "insignificant" (van Teijlingen 2019). In a similar vein, impacts of a possible collapse of the tailings facilities were deemed to be local, affecting only 10 km of the river downstream. In its public relations, ECSA reiterated its environmental responsibility while claiming it would use minimal quantities of water. Criticisms were thus ignored and the company did not respond to the findings. In fact, it immediately began to build the tailings facility.

Even more interesting is the way in which Ecuadorian authorities have dealt with the contradicting claims regarding the Mirador project. According to former president Correa, in the "New Mining Era" Ecuador would only allow "responsible mining." Putting these words into practice has been a major challenge. The Ministry of the Environment is underfunded, resulting in low capacity and insufficient expertise to review environmental impact studies.[1] The ministry is unable to carry out independent research: all decisions were based on data and test results provided by ECSA. As large-scale mining is new for Ecuador, bureaucrats lacked internal policies and guidelines on how to judge environmental impacts. In fact, most of these guidelines were written *after* ECSA was granted permits.

Moreover, within the Ecuadoran government, there was a growing consensus that this new industry would allow Ecuador to "develop" and that therefore "la minería va porque va"—mining must continue because it must. This authoritarian cry for mining was particularly strong for Mirador since it was the keystone of growing China-Ecuadorian relations. In an internal meeting on the project, Chinese officials stated that Mirador was quid pro quo for other Chinese investments in Ecuador (Andrews 2012, 47). There was a fierce internal lobby directed at the Ministry of the Environment and the Water Secretariat to issue licenses, even though the project did not comply with regulations. Bureaucrats from these ministries reported that officials from the Mining Ministry visited them every week to demand approval, while ECSA representatives would casually stop by to hand out presents.[2]

In their discussion of mining disasters in Canada, Morgenstern, Vick, and Van Zyl point out that these are often the result of "human errors" (2015). Looking at how both ECSA and the Ecuadorian government dealt with the controversies around the Mirador, however, there might be more to blame. A combination of Ecuador's dependency on China, an authoritative "extractive imperative" (Arsel, Hogenboom, and Pellegrini 2016), and little capacity to assess impacts transformed the EIAs and environmental licenses for this project into mere administrative hurdles. The fact that the inauguration described in the introduction took place while the Ministry of the Environment had not even issued the environmental license illustrates this disregard. Although warned of "human errors," government and company representatives never responded to criticisms. As a result, Ecuador will soon host the highest pile of mining waste on the planet: a potential future disaster of gigantic dimensions.

COCA CODO SINCLAIR AND THE TALE OF THE UNTAMABLE RIVER

> Respect for land and water and rivers has been an essential part of the experience and culture of our peoples. The river is a living entity, which is born, grows, develops, and when properly used, multiplies, constituting a source of progress and development. . . . Coca Codo Sinclair symbolizes on the one hand the constructive action of man, led by the technique and engineering, but above all it constitutes an example of what it means to use water responsibly, respect for nature and care for our only planet. (Tele Ciudadana 2016)

The CCS had a long history before becoming a concrete project. It began in the 1970s, during the surge of the developmental State in Ecuador. According to Teräväinen, the first studies were carried out in 1976, suggesting a project of 859 MW (2019). A bigger project would have had a much too socioenvironmental and economic risk, since its site was located only a few kilometers away from the Reventador volcano. In fact, an eruption of Reventador interrupted project studies in 1990.

In 2007, Rafael Correa's "Citizens' Revolution" brought the project back to life, presenting it as the hydroelectric sector's crown jewel. As discussed by Vasconez in this volume, this project was also controversial. The CCS's environmental impact assessments were conducted between 2007 and 2008 over five months. They were approved in record time: one week (Teräväinen 2019). The project's technical studies were obsolete and did not include a survey of the hydraulic characteristics of the river downstream or of the San Rafael waterfall. The latter was excluded from the study because engineers deemed it useless to study what was downstream of the CCS. After all, there was no CCS-related infrastructure there, so this area was "beyond" the scope of the project (*El Comercio* 2020a).

Despite these deficiencies, the construction of one of the biggest hydroelectric plants of Ecuador started in 2010. In greenlighting construction, Jorge Glas, the former Ecuadorian vice president and the minister of strategic sectors, disregarded the recommendations of earlier studies, contracting for a project of 1,500 MW, double the original recommended capacity (Pallares 2020). According to a former CCS general manager, senior government officials pushed for the construction of the project because "a new study would have taken several years, and they did not want to delay things" (Casey and Krauss 2018). Correa's stubbornness in building this dam was related to geopolitical and ideological issues, as well as to the masculine bravura that has been highlighted by Gutiérrez Guevara, Carpio, and Flores in this volume (60). After all, Correa had promised to modernize and transform Ecuador's energy matrix, damn the cost.

Like many of the strategic projects of the Citizens' Revolution, the CCS had backing from China (Hidalgo Bastidas 2020), which provided financial "support": 85 percent of the CCS was funded by the Export-Import Bank of China (nearly US$1.7 billion). The rest (15 percent) was the Ecuadorian counterpart, with a total project cost of US$2.3 billion. Together with other loans, Ecuador owes almost US$19 billion to the Asian giant. In exchange, Correa's government gave up the country's natural resources for decades to come. While the Export-Import Bank provided finance, Ecuador was required to hire Chinese companies. Eventually, the state-owned Chinese company Sinohydro was contracted to build the CCS. China and Ecuador's discursively "equal" partnership had the explicit aim of enhancing Ecuador's knowledge and technical capacities. In practice, however, things worked out differently. The CCS was constructed through a "turnkey contract." This meant that Sinohydro was given full responsibility to plan and build the project while Ecuador would receive the keys to the plant once it was ready.

The main role played by the Ecuadorian government was to facilitate the work by approving the environmental impact assessment in record time and by providing the project with its environmental license despite its high environmental and geological risks. In practice, China kept the know-how to itself while Ecuador was left with a risky project and enormous international debt.

Once the project was inaugurated in 2016, the economic, technical, and socioenvironmental problems and criticism did not stop. First, alleged corruption related to the project and China-Ecuador relations began to surface as several senior government officials were sentenced or investigated (Plan V 2018). Second, the collapse of the San Rafael waterfall in February 2020 and the rupture of the country's main oil pipeline in early April brought the CCS back to the front pages. According to experts from the Ecuadorian National Polytechnic University, the waterfall's collapse was caused by a lack of studies regarding the river's hydraulics downstream from the CCS. Before the project was built, the Quijos River was characterized by a high sediment load. The project design therefore included a sand trap that diminished the level of sediment in the water before it entered the turbines. This sand trap made the river "hungry" for sediments and seeking to find a new equilibrium. To do so, the river started to "eat" its own bed and banks, a process called *regressive erosion*.

Despite numerous warnings by environmental studies and experts, the government and the Chinese construction company did not take seriously the words of the former minister of electricity and renewable energy during the CCS's inaugural speech. The river revealed itself to be a "living entity" requiring respect. The Ecuadorian government's technocratic dream and Chinese ambitions to become the new strategic ally of Latin America resulted in disaster. The worst part is that this story of an untamable river has not yet ended. Eventually, the process of regressive erosion might reach the CCS dam and bring down the US$2.3 billion crown jewel, responsible for 30 percent of the country's energy (Torres 2020).

In response to the disaster, the Ecuadorian government initially referred to what happened as a "natural" phenomenon—implicitly negating a relation between the CCS and the erosion. Warnings by experts that the oil pipeline and eventually the CCS project were in danger were ignored. When the pipeline broke during the 2020 COVID-19 pandemic, press releases by the government focused on the economic losses this represented (see Vásconez, this volume). Clean-up of the spill proceeded slowly and could not prevent contamination from reaching Peru in a matter of days. Even as experts and the media confirmed the relation between the CCS and the rapid erosion of the river, the government remained silent. The only thing it did was to contract geo-hydrological studies—thirty years too late.

The government's silence is likely motivated by another ongoing disaster—the COVID-19 crisis—and the still unequal China-Ecuador relations as described by Reyes Herrera in this volume. Just like President Correa, President Moreno understands that Chinese loans are a lifeline for Ecuador's postpandemic recovery. Open critique of the "big brother's" main projects in Ecuador might not be appreciated in this context. Interestingly, Sinohydro and Chinese officials themselves did show some introspection when CCS came under criticism in 2018. A Chinese diplomat said, "We did not pay enough attention to environmental issues" (Casey and Krauss 2018). In the face of current affairs, however, the Chinese government joined the Ecuadorian government in silence, limiting public communications to donations of face masks to Ecuadorian hospitals.

CHINA-ECUADOR RELATIONS AND THE POLITICS OF ENVIRONMENTAL KNOWLEDGE

In a colorful advertisement published right after the inauguration of the Mirador project, ECSA praises itself for "raising a new paradigm for the growing mining industry" of Ecuador. Due to its sustainable environmental and social practices and great efforts to transfer knowledge, the advertisement reads, Ecuador is now entering a new "copper age." In a similar vein, the CCS dam was promoted as a landmark project for the energy transition of the country. Here too, transfer of knowledge and technology was at the top of the agenda. However, what kind of "paradigm" and knowledge practices did these projects bring to Ecuador?

The cases we discussed to offer preliminary answers to this question were the Mirador copper mine (located in the Southern Ecuador Amazon) and the Coca Codo Sinclair hydroelectric project (in the northern Amazon). Both provide a gloomy picture of what Chinese-owned or -built, "strategic" resource projects have brought to Ecuador. Our analysis has focused on the way in which environmental impacts were studied, assessed, and considered, leading us to question these projects' "politics of knowledge"—that is, the struggles concerning "whose knowledge matters, where, when, and why" (Goldman, Nadasdy, and Turner 2011, 132).

Both Mirador and the CCS were marked by controversies about the studies and data that undergirded their design. In both cases, alternative claims by communities, civil society, critical engineers, or researchers related to environmental impacts were denied or brushed off as politically motivated nonsense. The critiques remained unanswered by the Ecuadoran government and the Chinese companies involved, and the controversial projects were implemented. Over the last months, we have seen the first indications of where such problematic politics of knowledge lead. The dramatic collapses of the Quijos River near the CCS—and possibly much worse disasters in the future—are by no means "natural" phenomena. They are human made, shaped by the power relations in which they are embedded.

Some of these power relations can be explained by the strategic value of the Mirador and CCS projects for both the Ecuadoran government's political agenda and its growing but unequal relations with its main financer, China. This dependency placed high pressure on officials to enable the projects, rushing environmental studies and licensing processes. In fact, like the community consultations discussed by Bonilla in this volume, the EIAs were often seen as bureaucratic hurdles instead of opportunities to ensure better environmental and social performance. In this context, the transfer of knowledge and technology to Ecuador was minimal.

Due to the poor management of the COVID-19 pandemic, Ecuador is entering a severe economic and social crisis. The government is facing a major budget deficit. Although Ecuador has improved its relations with the International Monetary Fund and World Bank over the last years, it is also turning to China for financing. In 2020, the Minister of Finance announced a loan of US$2.4 billion by two Chinese banks (*El Comercio* 2020b). This will further deepen the unequal relationship between the two nations, creating more pressure to extract Ecuador's natural resources to pay off the debt. The effects will go beyond the economic and social spheres analyzed by Delgado del Hierro in this volume. The combination of a need for finance and a weakened state will probably unleash a race to the bottom in terms of environmental safeguards, in which economic interests will further invade the politics of environmental knowledge. We therefore fear that the gloomy scenario that we describe is unlikely to soon change for the better.

NOTES

1. In 2018, the Ministry of the Environment declared a "state of emergency" due to the amount of environmental impact assessments it was unable to progress.

2. Informal conversations with anonymous informants from the Ministry of the Environment and Water Secretariat, 2015.

REFERENCES

Andrews, Craig B. 2012. "Getting to Yes: The Practitioner's Guide to Negotiating Mining Investment Agreements. Lessons from Ecuador." Working Paper 90. Research School of Accounting and Commercial Law, Victoria University of Wellington. http://www.victoria.ac.nz/sacl/centres-and-institutes/cagtr/work ing-papers/WP90.pdf.

Arsel, Murat, Barbara Hogenboom, and Lorenzo Pellegrini. 2016. "The Political Economy of the Extractive Imperative: Social Conflict, Development and the State in Latin America." *Extractive Industry and Society* 3 (4): 880–87.

Casey, Nicholas, and Clifford Krauss. 2018. "It Doesn't Matter If Ecuador Can Afford This Dam. China Still Gets Paid." *New York Times,* December 24, 2018. https://www.nytimes.com/2018/12/24/world/americas/ecuador-china-dam .html.

El Comercio. 2020a. "Especialistas investigan el impacto del socavamiento del río Coca en la central Coca Codo." April 23, 2020. https://www.elcomercio.com/ actualidad/impacto-socavamiento-rio-coca-codo.html.

El Comercio. 2020b. "Ecuador recibirá créditos de China por USD 2 400 millones entre junio y octubre del 2020; la próxima semana arranca renegociación de bonos." May 29, 2020. https://www.elcomercio.com/actualidad/ecuador-credi tos-china-economia-deuda.html.

El Universo. 2016. "Ecuador y China inauguran hidroeléctrica Coca Codo Sinclair." Photograph taken at November 18, 2016. https://www.eluniverso.com/ noticias/2016/11/18/nota/5909182/ecuador-inauguro-hidroelectrica-coca -codo-sinclair-financiada-china.

Emerman, S. 2015. *Overview of Two Studies on the Riverine Transport of Tailings from a Possible Tailings Dam Breach at the Mirador Mine in Southeastern Ecuador.* Santa Fé, NM: E-Tech International.

Emerman, S. 2018. *Evaluación del diseño y de la construcción de las presas de relaves para la Mina Mirador, Zamora Chinchipe, Ecuador.* Spanish Fork, UT: Malach Consulting.

Goldman, Mara J., Paul Nadasdy, and Matthew D. Turner. 2011. *Knowing Nature: Conversations at the Intersection of Political Ecology and Science Studies.* Chicago: University of Chicago Press.

Hidalgo Bastidas, Juan Pablo. 2020. *Agua, poder y tecnología. Megaproyectos hídricos y movimientos sociales en Ecuador*. Quito: Abya-Yala/Justicia Hídrica/CEDLA-UvA.

Hogenboom, Barbara. 2017. "Chinese Influences and the Governance of Oil in Latin America the Cases of Venezuela, Brazil, and Ecuador." In *Geopolitical Economy of Energy and Environment*, edited by Mehdi Amineh and Guang Yang, 172–211. Leiden: Brill.

Morgenstern, N., S. Vick, and D. Van Zyl. 2015. *Report on Mount Polley Tailings Storage Facility Breach*. Province of British Columbia: Independent Expert Engineering Investigation and Review Panel.

Pallares, M. 2020. "Coca Codo Sinclair: ¿pagará la China por el inminente desastre?" *4Pelagatos*, April 23, 2020. https://4pelagatos.com/2020/04/20/coca-codo-sinclair-pagara-la-china-por-el-inminente-desastre/ 2020.

Plan V. 2018. "La grieta de usd 2000 millones de Coca Codo Sinclair." https://www.planv.com.ec/investigacion/investigacion/la-grieta-usd-2000-millones-coca-codo-sinclair 2018.

Redacción Económica. 2016. "La alianza con China se enraíza." *El Telégrafo*, October 5, 2016. https://www.eltelegrafo.com.ec/noticias/economia/8/el-presidente-chino-xi-jinping-visitara-ecuador.

Roche, C., K. Thygesen, and E. Baker, eds. 2017. *Mine Tailings Storage: Safety Is No Accident. A UNEP Rapid Response Assessment*. Nairobi: United Nations Environment Programme and GRID-Arendal.

Teräväinen, Tuula. 2019. "Negotiating Water and Technology—Competing Expectations and Confronting Knowledges in the Case of the Coca Codo Sinclair in Ecuador." *Water* 11, no. 3: 411.

Tele Ciudadana. 2016. "Inauguración del proyecto hidroeléctrico Coca Codo Sinclair" August 14, 2020. https://www.youtube.com/watch?v=GowoOqe-ths.

Torres, Wilmer. 2020. "Erosión: se necesitan USD 12,3 millones para proteger a Coca Codo Sinclair." *Primicias*, June 15, 2020. https://www.primicias.ec/noticias/economia/millones-para-obras-de-mitigacion-erosion-rio-coca/ n.d.

Uranium Wise. n.d. "Chronology of Major Tailings Dam Failures." https://www.wise-uranium.org/mdaf.html.

van Teijlingen, K. 2019. "Mining in the Land of Buen Vivir: The Politics of Large-Scale Mining, Development and Territorial Transformation in the Ecuadorian Amazon. " PhD dissertation, University of Amsterdam.

Vice President of Ecuador. n.d. "Vicepresidente Jorge Glas llegó a China para cumplir una intensa agenda de actividades." https://www.vicepresidencia.gob.ec/vicepresidente-jorge-glas-llego-a-china-para-cumplir-una-intensa-agenda-de-actividades/

Rafael Correa's Administration of Promises and the Impact of Its Policies on the Human Rights of Indigenous Groups

Emilia Bonilla

THE NEED TO FINANCE FORMER president Rafael Correa's development ambitions led Ecuador to make China its main strategic partner during 2007–2017. The consequences of this decision have been explained by Delgado del Hierro and van Teijlingen and Hidalgo Bastidas in this volume (Martín-Mayoral 2009). As the latter two authors put it, in practice, Chinese development projects kept technological know-how for the Chinese while leaving Ecuador with risky projects, environmental disasters, and international debt (van Teijlingen and Hidalgo Bastidas, 235).

But Chinese-backed megaprojects don't just run rough-shod over the environment. As Camoça and Hendler; Molina and Munduruku; Pullaguari; Queiroz, Praça, and Bitencourt; and Pedlowski demonstrate in this volume, they also trample the rights and lifestyles of the peoples whose lands they are built upon. This is particularly the case when it comes to South America's Indigenous populations.

By 2008, eight Chinese investment projects in Ecuador had violated the rights of Indigenous peoples. Of these, six were operating in protected areas. The most frequent violations involved the right to prior consultation and communal rights to ancestral lands (Centro de Derechos Económicos y Sociales 2018).

This chapter argues that these violations were attributable to the Correa administration's handling of the Ecuador-China relationship. First, the administration's promises to Indigenous sectors are contrasted with its conduct. We then examine discrepancies between the 2009 Mining Law and the 2008 Constitution. Finally, we discuss the impact of the administration's extractivist policies on Indigenous rights in two cases of national relevance.

AN ADMINISTRATION OF PROMISES (2007–2017)

In 2006, Rafael Correa opened his presidential campaign with the promise of a "Citizens' Revolution" (Ospina Peralta 2011). Conceived as a popular response to the evils of neoliberalism, this vindicated social and Indigenous struggles and a new kind of government inspired by respect for nature, where the state would assume a more central role in all sectors of the economy (Pasquel Valladares and Boelens 2019, 302).

In 2007, Correa convened a Constituent Assembly to draft a new constitution in conformity with the Citizens' Revolution platform in line with the principle of *Sumak Kawsay*,[1] which envisions a country where all people "effectively enjoy their rights, and exercise responsibilities within the framework of interculturality, respect for their diversity, and harmonious coexistence with nature" (EC 2008). The new constitution's Article 71 recognized the *environment* as having judicially protected rights. The assembly also expanded the rights of Indigenous peoples. Article 57 recognized and guaranteed the collective rights of Ecuador's Indigenous peoples in accordance with international human rights instruments.

While the new constitution guarantees respect for nature and Indigenous peoples, the government's conduct demonstrated otherwise. Under the mask of "Socialism for the Twenty-First Century," politics, corruption, and opportunism were prioritized over rights (Restrepo Echavarría 2017). Contrary to his promises, Correa changed his position on the inviolability of nature, explaining that it should be protected but that this had to be balanced against benefits that extractive industries could offer the economy (Vališková 2016, 74).

The administration also promised changes in the productive and energy matrix. This project, implemented in 2013, advocated for overcoming the state's dependence on oil and raw materials. Accordingly, it proposed an "increase in productive capacity [and the] promot[ion of] a culture of knowledge among Ecuadorians" as well as the strengthening of national industries (Díaz Rodríguez 2019, 380) within a framework of environmental sustainability. This project was hampered by the country's dependence on fossil fuels, poor infrastructure, and the high costs of process migration (Ciccozzi 2019, 16). The government thus reverted to the exploitation of hydrocarbons as well as an increase in foreign debt and economic dependence on countries like China.

The strengthening of ties with China facilitated the introduction of Chinese companies into Ecuador, resulting in environmental problems and social conflicts, including the violation of Indigenous groups' rights to ancestral lands. While Chinese companies adopted Correa's discourse of offering benefits to Indigenous communities, they have left behind a record of abuses, persecution, and criminalization (Vališková 2016).

The Correa administration abandoned the principle of *Sumak Kawsay* embodied in its National Plan for Good Living (Ciccozzi 2019), particularly insofar as the plan had promised to promote and protect Indigenous and environmental rights. High concentrations of natural resources are found in Indigenous peoples' territories, and hydrocarbon and mining concessions in these areas have resulted in the destruction of homes, violations of Indigenous autonomy, and the delegitimization of Indigenous authority, as Pullaguari and others analyze in this volume. In short, the Correa administration's conservationist discourse was largely superficial: its objective was to promote its platform and obtain resources and support from foreign actors.

THE CONSTITUTION OF 2008 AND THE LAW OF MINING OF 2009

In 2009, the Mining Law was enacted to promote responsible and sustainable industry while attracting foreign investors (Alston 2018, 83). In pushing for the law, the Correa administration once again relied on a populist discourse that stressed the importance of mining for Ecuador's development.

The enactment of the law violated the constitutional rights of Indigenous peoples, particularly in terms of their right to prior free and informed consultation, since they did not participate in the drafting process. According to Article 57 of Ecuador's constitution, the government must carry out a prior consultation with Indigenous peoples before commencing any activity that involves nonrenewable resources "found on their lands and that may affect them environmentally or culturally."

In 2009, the Confederation of Indigenous Nationalities of Ecuador filed a lawsuit alleging the Mining Law was unconstitutional. Ruling on the matter, the Constitutional Court resolved to regulate the consultation processes, despite the fact that there are already standards regarding this included in the principles of the IIHR (Inter-American Institute of Human Rights) (EC 2010). However, since this ruling did not address the question of unconstitutionality, the mining law remains in force.

ECUADOR-CHINA RELATIONS

The Correa administration's need to finance its promises complemented China's need for fossil fuels. Conditions were thus ripe for a strong relationship. When oil prices fell in 2014, China became Ecuador's most important trading partner and main source of financing, as discussed by Delgado del Hierro and Reyes Herrera in this volume. This led the Ecuadorian government "to pay for its state infrastructure development projects and social development expenses with Chinese loans and investments" (Aidoo 2017).

According to data from 2015, fluctuations in oil prices and Ecuador's urgent need for financing led the Correa administration to allocate 90 percent of national oil production to Chinese companies, ignoring the principles of *Sumak Kawsay* (Ciccozzi 2019).

In 2009, President Correa had promoted the Yasuní-ITT[2] initiative to prohibit the extraction of oil lying beneath the Yasuní National Park in Ecuador's Amazon basin. To support this conservation plan, the international community was asked to donate US$3.6 billion. Claiming that contributions had been insufficient, Correa withdrew from the initiative in 2013 and allowed exploitation in Yasuní (Alston 2018, 85). Subsequent oil exploitation in this national park not only brought environmental consequences but also violated the rights of the Indigenous populations that inhabit the area, which include the Taromenane and Tagaeri peoples (Land Is Life 2019).

CORREA'S EXTRACTIVIST POLICIES AND THEIR IMPACT ON INDIGENOUS RIGHTS

In 1977, Ecuador ratified the American Convention on Human Rights (ACHR), expressing its consent and commitment to comply with its provisions and adopting three human rights obligations: to respect human rights, to guarantee human rights and to adopt nondiscriminatory measures in support of these obligations under articles 1 and 2 (OAS 1969). The Inter-American Court of Human Rights (IACHR) held that the ACHR also protects the individual and collective rights of Indigenous peoples (Ruiz-Chiriboga and Donoso 2017). These rights are also protected by the United Nations Declaration on the Rights of Indigenous Peoples and the Convention on Indigenous and Tribal Peoples in independent countries (ILO 1989).

While Ecuador's extractivist boom dates back to the 1970s, this analysis concludes that the Correa administration's extractivist policies violated the human rights of Indigenous groups and nationalities, particularly their rights to prior, free, and informed consultation and communal rights to ancestral territories. We will now turn to two examples of these violations: the exploitation of Blocks 14 and 17 of the Yasuní National Park and the Mirador Project.

RIGHT TO PRIOR, FREE, AND INFORMED CONSULTATION AND COMMUNAL RIGHTS TO ANCESTRAL LANDS

The United Nations Declaration on the Rights of Indigenous Peoples obliges states to consult with Indigenous peoples and guarantee their participation in initiatives or decisions that affect their rights or lands (UN General Assembly 2007). States are obligated to incorporate into their legal systems and institutions standards that guarantee the right to prior consultation through reliable channels of dialog (IACHR 2012, 166–67).

Consultation is mandatory "in the realization of development or investment plans or projects or the implementation of extractive concessions in indigenous or tribal territories" (CIDH 2019, 283), especially where natural resources may be affected. For this reason, Indigenous peoples must be given a leading role in the decision-making process through good faith dialog and the seeking of mutual benefit (285).

The Inter-American Court interpreted Article 21 of the ACHR as protecting the links that Indigenous peoples have with their lands, natural resources, "and the intangible elements that emerge from them" (IACHR 2012, 145). In this sense, there is a spiritual bond that "must be recognized and understood as the fundamental basis of their cultures, their spiritual life, their integrity and their economic survival" (IACHR 2001, 149). States are obligated to respect these spiritual ties, according to relevant Indigenous uses, customs, and beliefs (ILO 1989).

YASUNÍ NATIONAL PARK

The Tagaeri and Taromenane are Indigenous peoples who live in voluntary isolation in the Ecuadorian Amazon basin. In 1999, their territory was designated as the Tagaeri Taromenane Protected Zone (TTPZ), defined in 2007 as overlapping the southern part of the Yasuní National Park (De Marchi, Pappalardo, and Ferrarese 2013). However, some argue this delimitation was made to accommodate the interests of foreign companies without taking into account the needs of the zone's inhabitants. Additionally, it has been reported that while the Correa administration was actively promoting the Yasuní-ITT initiative, it was also conducting secret negotiations with a Chinese bank to exploit the area in exchange for financing (Plan V 2016).

"So that the exploration or extraction of natural resources in ancestral territories does not imply a denial of the subsistence of the Indigenous people," the Inter-American Court held that states must implement a variety of processes in order to guarantee Indigenous rights. These include the right to prior consultation and sharing of benefits, the necessity of conducting environmental impact studies, and the implementation of mechanisms minimizing environmental impacts. Failure to adhere to any of these requirements constitutes a violation of Indigenous peoples' property rights as recognized in Article 21 of the ACHR.

In view of these standards, Ecuador's failure to consult with Indigenous peoples amounted to a serious legal and constitutional oversight. President Correa arbitrarily subrogated his consent to exploitation in the TTPZ, ignoring Article 57 of Ecuador's 2008 Constitution, which provides that "the territories of the peoples in voluntary isolation are irreducible and inviolable ancestral possessions."

Similarly, Ecuador ignored mechanisms that limit the territories for resource exploitation. For example, the Correa administration granted a concession to the Chinese company PetroOriental S.A. to exploit 49.6 percent of Block 17 and 1.2 percent of Block 14 of the national park, both of which overlap with the TTPZ (De Marchi, Pappalardo, and Ferrarese 2013, 34), thereby contravening Article 407 of the Constitution, which prohibits all extractive activities "in protected areas and in areas declared as inviolable." Under both constitutional principles, themselves based on international law, the Tagaeri and Taromenane peoples' rights to prior consultation and ancestral territories were therefore violated. The Ecuadorian government also breached the inviolability that derives from their voluntary isolation in the TTPZ, which could be regarded as ethnocide under Article 57.

THE MIRADOR PROJECT

In 1999, the Canadian company Corriente Resources bought a concession within the Mirador Project for mineral exploration work. Because its plans did not include the extraction of minerals, in 2010 the company sold the concession to China Tongling Nonferrous Metals Group Holdings and China Railway Construction Corporation (Leifsen et al. 2017, 16).

Between 2012 and 2015, Ecuador's national police violently evicted residents from the area (Plan V 2019). Inhabitants tried to open a dialog with Chinese companies to denounce the abuses, only to be met with intimidation and violence (Van Teijlingen and Warnaars 2017, 132). Even President Correa acknowledged these police measures, but argued that they had been peacefully conducted and that reports to the contrary were a campaign mounted to discredit his government (Plan V 2019).

These arbitrary evictions and disproportionate uses of force led to the violation of the rights of the inhabitants. In 2014, these people were identified and acknowledged it "as an Indigenous Shuar community . . . under the name Comunidad Amazónica de Acción Social Cordillera del Cóndor Mirador[3] [CASCOMI]" (Van Teijlingen and Warnaars 2017, 134).[4] The purpose of this designation was to allow the community to benefit from rights specific to Indigenous peoples under article 57 of the constitution. In view of the Inter-American Court's ruling on the legitimacy of extractivism in these territories (IACHR 2012, 157), failure to consult with CASCOMI regarding mining activity at Mirador was a clear violation of the constitution.

Chinese companies operating on the project have used intimidation and unconstitutional legal mechanisms to obtain land ownership. Irregular purchases, for example "arbitrary demands for mining easements, filing civil lawsuits against families without formal property titles" (Colardelle and Jarrín 2018, 16). Thirty-two families lost their homes after being violently evicted (Plan V 2019).

Since 2006, environmental impact studies have been carried out in the area. These were superficial, uninformative, and limited (Liefsen et al. 2017, 22). While the government tried to establish procedures to prevent environmental damage, these have not been effective. In 2015 activities at the mine were briefly suspended "due to a lack of measures to avoid contamination of rivers by runoff waters and sedimentation generated during the construction phase" (Liefsen and Benham Hogan 2017, 217), only to be resumed without the implementation of corrective measures. The Correa administration's handling of the Mirador Project violated an Indigenous community's rights to prior, free, and informed consultation, and ancestral territories.

CONCLUSION

Despite the inclusion of guarantees for Indigenous peoples in the 2008 Constitution, the Correa administration and Chinese companies engaged in actions and coercive behavior in violation of these rights. In a reversal of its *Sumak Kawsay* narrative, the administration promoted development discourse as an argument for exploiting natural resources in protected areas. The violations committed in the Yasuní National Park and the Mirador Project are two examples of this.

Beyond violating constitutional rights, the Correa administration's conduct was contrary to its duties under the ACHR to respect and guarantee Indigenous rights and to adopt measures in support of these obligations. Despite several layers of legal protections, the government's extractivist policies focused only on economic and developmental ambitions, leading to actions that have criminalized the Indigenous peoples it swore to protect.

While this study has focused on the Correa administration's handling of the Yasuní National Park and the Mirador Project, it should be noted that these were not isolated events. Similar violations have occurred throughout Ecuador's history, in other projects, and with the participation of companies of various nationalities. Sadly, they continue to be repeated.

The road ahead for Indigenous land rights is uncertain. The public is beginning to wake up and denounce the government's false promises, especially during the current COVID-19 panic. Sadly, "corruption" is today's most common characterization of the government. Hopefully one day this can be replaced by "hope" and "justice."

NOTES

1. "*Sumak kawsay*," a Quechua phrase that can be translated as "life in fullness."

2. "ITT" refers to Ishpingo, Tiputini, and Tambococha, three nearby petroleum exploration sectors.

3. The name translates to "Mirador Condor Ridge Amazonic Community for Social Action."

4. Historically, the area was exclusively Shuar. Since 1950 it has been "a space shared between Shuar communities, rural mestizos, and Andean Quechua groups," (Leifsen and Benham Hogan 2017, 12).

REFERENCES

Aidoo, Richard, Min Ye Pamela L. Martin, and Diego Quiroga. 2017. "Las huellas del dragón: la diplomacia petrolera de China y sus efectos en la política de desarrollo sostenible en Ecuador y Ghana." *International Development Policy* 8, no. 1. https://doi.org/10.4000/poldev.3337.

Alston, Eric. 2018. "Ecuador's 2008 Constitution: The Political Economy of Securing an Aspirational Social Contract." *Constitutional Studies* 3: 69–99.

Centro de Derechos Económicos y Sociales. 2018. "El impacto de los capitales chinos en Ecuador." November 5, 2018. https://cdes.org.ec/web/el-impacto-de-los -capitales-chinos-en-ecuador/.

Ciccozzi, Elena. 2019. "El Buen Vivir a la prueba del neoextractivismo. Ambigüedades del progresismo ecuatoriano y continuidad con el neoliberalismo." *Crisol* 9. http://crisol.parisnanterre.fr/index.php/crisol/article/view/170.

CIDH. 2019. *Derechos de los pueblos indígenas y tribales sobre sus tierras ancestrales y recursos naturales: normas y jurisprudencia del sistema interamericano de derechos humanos.* December 30, 2019. OEA/Ser.L/V/II. Doc. 56/09.

Colardelle, Claire, and Sofía Jarrín. 2018. "Examen periódico universal, tercer ciclo de evaluación de las obligaciones extraterritoriales de la República Popular de China desde sociedad civil: Casos de Argentina, Bolivia, Brasil, Ecuador y Perú." *FIDH and CICDHA.* http://cdes.org.ec/web/wp-content/uploads/2018/10/ Informe-Regional_CICDHA.pdf.

De Marchi, Massimo, Salvatore Pappalardo, and Francesco Ferrarese. 2013. *Zona intangible Tagaeri Taromenane (ZITT): ¿Una, ninguna, cien mil? Delimitación cartográfica, análisis geográfico y Pueblos Indígenas Aislados en el camaleónico sistema territorial del Yasuní.* Padua: Cleup.

Díaz Rodríguez, Natacha Pahola De las Mercedes, Mora Pisco, Lilia Lourdes, Durán Vasco, and Marco Edmundo. 2019. "Las bases del cambio de la matriz productiva en Ecuador (2006–2016)." *Revista Universidad y Sociedad* 11, no. 4: 377–84.

EC, Constitutional Court of Ecuador. 2010. "Sentencia." Case Nos.: 0008-09-IN, 0011-09-IN (consolidated), March 18, 2020.

EC. 2008. *Constitución de la República del Ecuador.* Official Publication 449, October 20, 2008.

EC. 2009. *Ley de Minería*. Official Publication, Supplement 517, January 29, 2009.

IACHR. 2001. "Sentencia de 31 de agosto de 2001 (Fondo, Reparaciones y Costas)." *Comunidad Mayagna (Sumo) Awas Tingni v. Nicaragua*. August 31, 2001.

IACHR. 2012. "Sentencia de 27 de junio de 2012 (Fondo y Reparaciones)." *Pueblo Indígena Kichwa de Sarayaku v. Ecuador*. June 27, 2012.

ILO. 1989. International Labor Organization, *Convention on Indigenous and Tribal Peoples in Independent Countries*. June 27, 1989.

Land Is Life. 2019. "Estrategia regional de protección para pueblos aislados, pueblos indígenas en aislamiento en la Amazonía y Gran Chaco." *Informe regional: territorios y desarrollo—IR*. Quito: Ediciones Abya Yala.

Leifsen, Esben, and Benham Hogan. 2017. "Desposesión por contaminación: La gobernanza de un desastre ambiental de evolución lenta." In *La Amazonía Minada: Minería a gran escala y conflictos en el Sur del Ecuador*, edited by Karolien van Teijlingen, Esben Leifsen, Consuelo Fernández-Salvador, and Luis Sánchez-Vázquez, 209–35. Quito: USFQ, Ediciones Abya-Yala.

Leifsen, Esben, Luis Sánchez-Vázquez, Karolien van Teijlingen, and Consuelo Fernández-Salvador. 2017. "Una ecología política del proyecto minero." In *La Amazonía Minada: Minería a gran escala y conflictos en el Sur del Ecuador*, edited by Karolien van Teijlingen, Esben Leifsen, Consuelo Fernández-Salvador, and Luis Sánchez-Vázquez, 11–43. Quito: USFQ, Ediciones Abya-Yala.

Martín-Mayoral, Fernando. 2009. "Estado y mercado en la historia de Ecuador: Desde los años 50 hasta el gobierno de Rafael Correa." *Nueva Sociedad* 221: 120–82.

OAS. 1969. *American Convention on Human Rights*. November 22, 1969.

Ospina Peralta, Pablo. 2011. "Corporativismo, estado y revolución ciudadana: el Ecuador de Rafael Correa." In *Culturas políticas en la región andina*, edited by Christian Büschges, Olaf Kaltmeier and Sebastian Thies, 85–116. Madrid: Iberoamericana Vervuert.

Pasquel Valladares, Andrea Carolina, and Rutgerd Boelens. 2019. "(Re)territorializaciones en Tiempos de 'revolución Ciudadana: Petróleo, Minerales y Derechos de la Naturaleza en el Ecuador." *Estudios Atacameños* 63: 301–13.

Plan V. 2016. "De China, con infinito amor." November 21, 2016. https://www.planv.com.ec/historias/sociedad/china-con-infinito-amor.

Plan V. 2019. "La otra historia de mirador." July 24, 2019. https://www.planv.com.ec/investigacion/investigacion/la-otra-historia-mirador.

Restrepo Echavarría, Ricardo. 2017. "Sovereign Democratic Transformation in Ecuador (2007–2016)." *Review of European Studies* 9, no. 4: 20–33.

Ruiz-Chiriboga, Oswaldo, and Gina Donoso. 2019. "Sección especial, jurisprudencia de la Corte IDH sobre los pueblos indígenas y tribales fondo y reparaciones." In *Comentario Convención Americana sobre Derechos Humanos*, edited by Christian Steiner and Marie-Christine, 1131–202. Bogotá: Fundación Konrad Adenauer.

UN General Assembly. 2007. *United Nations Declaration on the Rights of Indigenous Peoples*. September 13, 2007. A/RES/61/295.

Vališková, Barbora. 2016. "Análisis de la posición ideológica del gobierno ecuatoriano en el contexto de la movilización indígena antiextractiva," *Cuadernos del CENDES* 33, no. 91: 65–91.

Van Teijlingen, Karolien, and Ximena Warnaars. 2017. "Pluralismo territorial e identidades en el conflicto minero en la cordillera del Cóndor." In *La Amazonía Minada: Minería a gran escala y conflictos en el Sur del Ecuador*, edited by Karolien van Teijlingen, Esben Leifsen, Consuelo Fernández-Salvador, and Luis Sánchez-Vázquez, 103–40. Quito: USFQ, Ediciones Abya-Yala.

China Oil and Foodstuffs Corporation in the Tapajós River "Logistics Corridor": A Case Study of Socioenvironmental Transformation in Brazil's Northeast

Alana Camoça and Bruno Hendler

THIS CHAPTER ANALYZES the socioenvironmental impact of the construction of the logistical corridor in the basin of the Tapajós River Basin, a 1,200-mile-long Brazilian tributary of the Amazon River. We analyze the role of the China Oil and Foodstuffs Corporation (COFCO) in the construction of the corridor, focusing on two processes: land acquisition by agribusiness in the Mapitoba region (an acronym for the border area between the Brazilian states of Maranhão, Piauí, Tocantins, and Bahia); and the search for alternative routes for agribusiness product transportation in Brazil's center-west. We focus on the influence of COFCO, an exporter of grain produced in Brazil through the operations (and acquisition) of local businesses and partners. COFCO is also a large-scale investor in the Tapajós logistics corridor. Our research reveals the socioenvironmental impacts caused by COFCO's operations.

Logistical challenges comprise bottlenecks that limit China's consumption of Brazilian products. As Gustavo Oliveira puts it in his chapter in this volume, "the main bottleneck of the agroindustrial boom that covered the Brazilian Cerrado with soybeans are the road-based export channels through southeastern Brazil. Consequently, agribusinesses have pushed both left- and right-wing governments alike to invest in new infrastructure in the Amazon basin. Dubbed the Arco Norte, or 'northern arc' the export-oriented infrastructure megaproject will supposedly remove Brazil's transport bottlenecks" (179).

Diana Aguiar also touches upon this problem in her chapter, with regard to the planned construction of railroad links between the Cerrado and the ports of the Brazilian Amazon, and the key role Chinese financing plays in this: "The soy barons know that without Chinese investments, many of these infrastructure projects are much less likely to get off the ground." (Aguiar, this volume, 323).

Molina and Munduruku have demonstrated in their chapter what these "death projects" mean to the Indigenous ways of life and cosmopolitical views of the world. Likewise, the chapters by Oliveira, and Felipe and Costa illustrate the on-the-ground impacts faced by traditional populations throughout the soy transport corridor as this megainfrastructure is put into place. Costa describes how new ports, geared to ship soy, have devastated the communities and landscapes she has known all her life:

> One day I was coming here [to Cajueiro]. I took a van and the boy said "We are going to enter the port." When that van went into the port, I cried out. I couldn't [contain] myself. When I saw that beach where I grew up. . . . Today everything is covered in iron. It is a mat; it is ore; a chunk of stuff. They ended it all." (270)

This chapter, while in dialogue with these other studies, takes a step back to a wider view. Our aim is to give the reader a more holistic picture of the impacts of these projects. The hypothesis we present below is that a dependent variable of these processes is the construction of logistical corridors for the export of agricultural production through the Tapajós River Basin and that these contribute to irreversible socioenvironmental impacts in the region. Our chapter examines the effects of Chinese demand for Brazilian products, as well as Chinese interests (and investments) in the purchase of Brazilian land through the acquisition of companies that operate in the region or through partnerships with companies that have invested in increasing their transportation capacities. Our emphasis here is on the activities of COFCO and their partners.

AGRIBUSINESS IN CENTRAL-WEST BRAZIL AND THE NEW
AGRARIAN FRONTIERS

Primary product exportation has historically been relevant for the generation and concentration of wealth in Brazil. This fact has been reflected in the way the country has been economically inserted into the three historical phases of international food regimes (Escher and Wilkinson 2019). In the first, which lasted from the end of the nineteenth century until the 1930s, Brazil mainly exported coffee, but also sugar, cotton, rubber, leather, cocoa, mate, and tobacco (Costa 2000, 175). In the second regime, which lasted from 1945 to the mid-1980s, the country saw industrialization in its southeast, which brought greater variety to its exports. However, even at the height of industrialization, primary products maintained their primacy in Brazilian exports (Almeida 2007).

Due to its geographic location, agribusiness in the Brazilian center-west has specific challenges affecting its profitability: competition from production in more traditional regions, such as the Brazilian south and southeast; the region's distance from the main centers of domestic consumption; the distance of the center-west from the main export outlets, given that it is Brazil's only entirely landlocked region; and the region's lack of infrastructure, which intersects with the previous challenges.

The main characteristic of agribusiness in the center-west is the large size of land properties established there. The average contains 322 hectares, while in the north of Brazil the average is 112 hectares and in the rest of the country it does not exceed 60 hectares. The *Atlas of Economic Complexity*[1] shows that agricultural products have accounted for about 35 percent of Brazil's exports since 1995.[2] It is noteworthy that 30 percent of this total is made up of soy and derivatives, 12 percent is composed of sugarcane and derivatives, 7 percent of chemical wood pulp, 6 percent of poultry, and 4 percent of coffee and corn. Given the relevance of soy, it is important to note that according to Censo Agro, production in the center-west of Brazil is not as competitive as that in the south and southeast.

From the 1990s onwards, growing foreign demand for commodities pushed the agricultural frontier into two other regions of Brazil: the southern Legal Amazon (the north of Mato Grosso and the south of Pará and Rondônia) and the Mapitoba region. In the transition from the second to the third international food regime, the Brazilian state lost prominence to large corporations (national and foreign) in transforming geographical space through an unprecedented vertical integration of production and circulation of goods.

Agribusiness competitiveness in the international market has been stimulated in the Arco Norte through this process, creating profits for banks, investment funds, and multinational corporations (Rodrigues 2018, 213). It has expressed itself in policies favoring the interests of a fraction of Brazil's hegemonic class, with strong connections to multinational corporations and newly hegemonic countries such as China (211).

A GRAIN AT A TIME: BRAZILIAN AGROBUSINESS AND COFCO

Over the last decades, Brazil-China commerce has intensified. In 2019, China became the destination for 26 percent of Brazil's exports, reaching an annual value of US$63.4 billion (MDIC 2020). In 2018, 53 percent of these exports were of agricultural products and 42 percent of minerals, petroleum, and their derivatives. Economic interdependence between Brazil and China gained more strength in the following decade, with an influx of investments by the Chinese. These have been concentrated in the agricultural sector due to the Asian country's search for food security and its policy of internationalizing of companies, which became official in 2001 with China's "Going Out Strategy" (Escher and Wilkinson 2019, 672–73). Chinese firms like ChemChina, Anhui Longping High-Tech Seeds, Hunan Dakang Pasture Farming Co/Pengxin, and COFCO are some of the most important recent investors in Brazil.

COFCO is a Chinese state-owned company founded in 1952. Headquartered in Beijing, it is the largest Chinese state-owned company in the grain sector. Much of the company's investment in Brazil are *brownfields*, with the purchase of warehouses and other facilities. In 2014, COFCO acquired the Dutch grain trader Nidera (US$1.2 billion) and Noble Agri (US$1.5 billion), both with operations in Brazil (Escher and Wilkinson 2019, 674–75). At the same time, the Chinese company has increased its grain storage capacity in the state of Mato Grosso.

COFCO has expectations for growth in both soy and sugarcane production in Brazil. It is estimated that while the company exported 8.5 million tons of soy and corn in the 2016/17 harvest, in the 2018/19 this quantity rose to 9.2 million tons. A map from the 2018 Trase Report (a global platform monitoring commodity production chains), shows the origin of COFCO's soybeans in 2016, demonstrating these overwhelmingly come from the two new agricultural frontiers of the center-west/Legal Amazon and Mapitoba (Trase 2018a).

According to this data, US multinationals Archer Daniels Midland (ADM) and Cargill, the Dutch Bunge, the French Louis Dreyfus (collectively known as the ABCD group) and the Brazilian corporation Amaggi create the highest risk of deforestation among the main soybean exporters in Brazil (2006–2016). COFCO contributes little to the total index of deforestation (2018b). According to Sena (2020) and Aguiar (Aguiar 2017), the number of ports along the Tapajós has grown in response to agribusiness expansion, greatly intensified by Chinese demands. This is because the cost of transportation from the center-west is 35 percent lower for ports in the north than for ports in the south/southeast (Escher, Wilkinson, and Pereira 2017, 22). In the case of China, shipping from the north reduces costs by allowing routes through the Panama Canal.

One of the main investors in Brazilian ports has been the China Communications & Construction Company (CCCC). After acquiring 80 percent of Concremat, CCCC made investments in the ports of Miritituba, Vila do Conde, and Itaqui, as well as in the cargo terminal of the port of Maranhão (Escher, Wilkinson, and Pereira 2017, 19; Escher and Wilkinson 2019). The footprint of this state-owned company can be indirectly traced through contracts with companies such as Hidrovias Brasil, which operates along the Tapajós with a Cargo Transshipment Station (CTS) in Miritituba and a Private Use Terminal (PUT)[3] in Vila do Conde (HBSA 2020). The Arco Norte route is currently growing the fastest in terms of Brazil's soy transport infrastructure. According to Antaq (2019a), the region's percentage of total participation in the transport of soy and corn doubled in eight years. The movement in the port of Santarém is particularly noteworthy, with 8.7 million tons shipped in 2018, of which 8 million were corn and soy.

One of the biggest bottlenecks for export flows to the north is the lack of road and rail infrastructure to reach the ports. Lack of investment and the Brazilian government's relatively recent logistical strengthening projects have attracted interest from Chinese investors. These programs operate through privatization and concessions for transnational capital through foreign direct investment. This has also been the case for already existing projects, such as the Logistics Investment Program (LIP) of the Rousseff government and the Investment Partnership Program (IPP) of the Temer government (Escher, Wilkinson, and Pereira 2017, 23). Under Jair Bolsonaro, privatization, land concession, and collusion with agricultural elite interests led to the dismantling of Brazil's environmental inspection and control bodies.

Two of the projects worth mentioning are Ferrovia Paraense, a railroad that would connect southeastern Pará to the port of Barcarena, and Ferro-grão, a railroad that would run from Mato Grosso (where COFCO has an office) to the town of Itaituba. In the case of Ferrogrão, bidding is scheduled to begin in 2020. Meanwhile, news items have been popping up in the media about the possible interest of the Chinese state-owned company[4] and even of Hidrovias do Brasil (Aguiar 2017) in this project.[5]

According to a report by Ibase (Rodrigues 2017), Itaituba has been one of the major recipients of investments for intermodal waterway and road infrastructure, due to its geographic position, its relative remove from the city center, lack of waiting for transport ships at its docks, and its low level of surveillance by the municipal and state environmental agencies. The need to expand transportation of agricultural production to the north of Brazil has caused local conflicts and socioenvironmental problems, not only in Itaituba but in several other regions in Pará, such as Santarém. We will present these in the following section

LOGISTIC ADVANCES AND SOCIOECONOMIC AND ENVIRONMENTAL PROBLEMS IN THE TAPAJÓS

According to Aguiar (2017), the grain logistics corridor in the north of Brazil has been expanding, generating negative impacts in the Tapajós River basin in the Amazon. Much of this expansion is being driven by the growing demands of the Chinese market. One of the impacts is the increase in land prices, pushing traditional communities out of their territories. Aguiar's analysis of land titles demonstrates predatory squatting, as well as the destruction of archaeological sites.

Land purchases made by companies have created "friction between antagonistic territorialities—of the State, capital and subordinate/insurgent groups" so "that the territorialization of one determines the annihilation of the other as such and its [subsequent] transformation" (Aguiar 2017, 40). According to Rodrigues (2018 220) the formation of new export corridors in the *Arco Norte* contributes to internal differentiation of land use, land speculation, and the financialization of the territory; an increase in deforestation as a result of the expansion of the agricultural frontier; the deterritorialization of traditional peoples; an increase in territorial conflicts between miners, landowners, and Indigenous and traditional peoples; and the violation of social and ethnic rights.

In an interview with the authors of this article, Catholic Father Edilberto Sena, president of the Amazon News Network (RNA), a member of the Tapajós Livre Movement, a disciple of the Liberation Theology, and a resident of Santarém, made several criticisms regarding logistical development and the construction of hydroelectric plants in the Tapajós region. The priest emphasized the role of multinational corporations in port building and other logistics projects in the north, especially in the state of Pará. According to Father Edilberto, corporations like Cargill have settled into the region without bringing benefits to local populations (Sena 2020).

In an opinion article published on his personal blog, Father Edilberto emphasizes the environmental impacts of agribusiness logistics, reporting on how the Tapajós River has become cloudy, poisoned by mercury and by the pesticide-filled[6] soy that falls into the river during transportation. The soy is eaten by the fish that serve as an important food source for the region's population. Although there are no studies supporting his claims, Edilberto believes that cancer has significantly increased among the local population since the construction of Cargill's port in Santarém in the early 2000s.

Another consequence of logistical expansion is the increasing difficulty residents encounter in using the river due to the purchase of riverside land by companies and the increased risks of accidents for small vessels due to increased shipping. Finally, the paving of BR-163, the planned ports between Santarém and Itaituba, and the Ferrogrão project have stimulated invasions of Indigenous lands by *garimpeiros*[7] and predatory land squatters,[8] as well as the purchase of land from the local population by farmers and large investors at very low prices (Sena 2020).

China's main presence along the Tapajós is focused on the possible construction of hydroelectric plants, as was the case with Chinese investments along the Teles-Pires (Aguiar 2017, 24). Although Chinese investments are not yet very visible in the region, there is the possibility that they will grow (Sena 2020).

Deforestation is another problem resulting from the expansion of grain cultivation. According to the Trase Report (Trase 2018b, 10), of all the commodities that generate environmental risks, the most traded on international markets is soy (grain, oil, and paste). In 2016, Brazil, Argentina, and Paraguay together produced almost 50 percent of world's soy in an area totaling approximately 56 million hectares. As a commodity that generates substantial environmental risk, soy is an important player in the region's territorial dynamics. Thirty-seven percent of soy expansion in the Mapitoba in recent years was accomplished through direct elimination of native vegetation. According to the Trase Report, "just six big companies in the soy market (Bunge, Cargill, ADM, Louis Dreyfus, COFCO, and Amaggi) were responsible for 57 percent of soy exports from Brazil in 2016. Buyers of soy from these six companies can be associated with at least two thirds of the total deforestation risk associated with soy expansion over the last decade" (2018b).

Between 2001 and 2017, soybean production expanded by 310 percent in Mapitoba alone and was responsible for 14 percent (approximately four million hectares) of all new soy planting in Brazil. The Chinese market was one of the major catalysts of this process, with 70 percent of Brazilian soy exports to China coming from Mapitoba. COFCO is responsible for 6 percent of all soy exports, being the seventh largest exporter in the region (Lazzeri 2019). With revenues of US$3.98 billion, soybeans were the main Brazilian export in 2019. About 76 percent of this value was generated by sales to China.[9]

The struggle of the region's peoples against investments in infrastructure and deforestation is not recent. In an interview given in 2020, Father Edilberto Sena mentioned the support of NGOs such as Greenpeace International in the early 2000s, which helped make heard the region's residents' complaints about the socioenvironmental impacts of agribusiness in the Amazon, impacting the image of many brands. In view of this, trading companies were pressured to implement sustainability measures.

In July 2006, the Soy Moratorium pact was signed, in which the Brazilian Association of Vegetable Oil Industries (ABIOVE) and the Association National of Cereal Exporters committed to not sell soy from areas that had been deforested within the Legal Amazon (ABIOVE 2020). Initially, the proposal was supposed to last two years, but the moratorium has been renewed annually and is now more than ten years old.[10] However, this has not prevented deforestation in the Amazon because, according to a report presented in 2018 by the Soy Working Group, only 1.2 percent of deforestation in the Amazon was caused by soy planting.[11] Deforestation continues to occur due to the actions of land grabbers, loggers, and the growing logistics projects linked to soy production.

In a newspaper report published in *O Estado Net* in Santarém, criticizing the expansion of soy, Father Edilberto wrote:

> The pigs and chickens Europe and China get fed [on soy], while the people of the Amazon watch the ships pass by and are left [in their toxic] dust. Not even the export taxes remain within the state. The soy producers who came from the center-west and south to our region mostly look at us as lazy and as lacking any vision for improving our lives. This is because we do not cut down five hundred, a thousand, and more hectares to plant soybeans. Arrogant, they are little interested in our culture. There are those who even despise *tacacá* [a north Brazilian soup] and only drink their *chimarrão* [yerba mate]. They arrived here in the region and began clearing and cutting down forest, later poisoning the land and the streams with pesticides. They do not show respect for the forest or for the neighbors of their large estates.[12]

According to the National Institute for Space Research (INPE), despite the reduction of deforestation in the Legal Amazon since 2008, it started to increase again in 2014. The state of Pará leads the way in accumulated deforestation (1988–2019) accounting for 34.12 percent of the total with 152,165 km^2. Mato Grosso is in second place with 32,77 percent and 146,142 km (INPE 2020).

The current scenario is therefore one of advancing agribusiness, expanding deforestation, poisoned ecosystems, and intensifying land conflicts. The demand of the Chinese market since the 2000s has played an important role in these processes. However, although Chinese capital has had some recent relevance in these questions, their aggravation is more due to the Brazilian economic elites and European and North American investors and companies, which have gained strength since the 1990s (particularly the ABCD group). These groups have been much more important than the Chinese in the socioenvironmental impacts of agribusiness in Brazil.

CONCLUSIONS

We propose that there is a causal relationship between prosperity, the advance of agribusiness in the center-west/Legal Amazon and Mapitoba regions (independent variables), and negative socioenvironmental impacts on the Tapajós River Basin (dependent variable). This is due to Brazil's insertion in the second and third international food regimes via grain production and export, with an emphasis on soy. The impacts identified in the text are varied: deforestation, river poisoning, land conflicts, and real estate speculation. Furthermore, these impacts have worsened not only with the advance of the agricultural frontier, but also with the construction of transportation corridors, transforming the geography and deteriorating the means of subsistence and quality of life of local peoples.

The intervening variable (the importance of Chinese actors in this process, especially COFCO) is less clear in its effects. On the one hand, the demands of the Chinese market have been decisive for the expansion of agribusiness in Brazil. On the other, the weight of Chinese investment is considerably less than that of companies that have been operating in Brazil for a longer period, who have historically generated the greater amount of socioenvironmental impact in the Tapajós River Basin. However, the data collected and presented here also shows that the entry of COFCO and other Chinese companies in Brazil tends to further accentuate these processes.

NOTES

1. https://atlas.cid.harvard.edu/.
2. The Atlas of Economic Complexity's data begins in 1995.
3. According to Aguiar (2017, 41), Law12.815 of 2013 regulated the establishment of port terminals for private use in the country and "paved the way for the boom in ports for the export of commodities via the state of Pará, especially along the Tapajós and lower Amazon rivers, aiming to overcome the 'contradiction' of Brazil's having the most competitive production in the world 'in-country' while confronting the world's most precarious logistical exportation infrastructures."
4. https://relatorioreservado.com.br/noticias/cofco-compra-seu-bilhete-para-a -ferrograo/.
https://epocanegocios.globo.com/Economia/noticia/2019/09/cofco-planeja-in vestir-mais-no-brasil-mas-sera-seletiva.html.

5. https://forbes.com.br/last/2019/08/apos-investir-us-12-bi-hidrovias-do-brasil
-explora-opcoes-de-expansao-diz-cfo/.

6. In 2019 alone, 474 pesticides were approved for use in Brazil. 26 of these
were new and 448 were generic pesticides. https://g1.globo.com/economia/agro
negocios/noticia/2019/12/28/numero-de-agrotoxicos-registrados-em-2019-e-o
-maior-da-serie-historica-945percent-sao-genericos-diz-governo.ghtml.

7. Illegal miners.

8. https://blogdopadresena.wordpress.com/2019/10/31/analise-de-conjuntura-na
cional-com-foco-na-amazonia/.

9. https://summitagro.estadao.com.br/china-se-consolida-como-principal-des
tino-de-exportacao-da-soja-brasileira/.

10. https://www.noticiasagricolas.com.br/noticias/soja/246832-moratoria-da-so
ja-e-absurdo-mas-assunto-do-setor-privado-diz-ministra.html#.XtUKwsB7nbo.

11. https://www.mma.gov.br/informma/item/14566-noticia-acom-2018-01-2792
.html.

12. https://www.oestadonet.com.br/noticia/10109/santarem-355-anos-nao-somos
-preguicosos-por-edilberto-sena/.

REFERENCES

ABIOVE. 2020. "Sustentabilidade e Moratória da Soja." https://abiove.org.br/
    sustentabilidade/.

Aguiar, Diana. 2017. *A geopolítica de infraestrutura da China na América do Sul:
    um estudo a partir do caso do Tapajós na Amazônia brasileira*. Rio de Janeiro:
    Fase, Actionaid.

Almeida, Paulo R. de. 2007. "As relações econômicas internacionais do Brasil dos
    anos 1950 aos 80." *Revista Brasileira de Política Internacional*. 50, no. 2: 60–79.

Antaq (Agência Nacional de Transportes Aquaviários, Anuário). 2019a. "Aumenta
    participação do Arco Norte no escoamento da soja e do milho para expor-
    tação. Agência Nacional de Transportes Aquaviários." http://portal.antaq.gov.
    br/index.php/2019/02/20/aumenta-a-participacao-do-arco-norte-no-escoamen
    to-da-soja-e-do-milho-para-exportacao/.

Antaq (Agência Nacional de Transportes Aquaviários, Anuário). 2019b "Diretor
    da ANTAQ fala sobre a importância do Arco Norte em audiência no Senado.
    Agência Nacional de Transportes Aquaviários." http://portal.antaq.gov.br/in
    dex.php/2019/06/18/diretor-da-antaq-fala-sobre-a-importancia-do-arco-norte
    -em-audiencia-no-senado/.

Antaq (Agência Nacional de Transportes Aquaviários, Anuário). 2020. Agência Na-
    cional de Transportes Aquaviários. http://web.antaq.gov.br/anuario/.

Bernstein, Henry. 2015. "Food Regimes and Food Regime Analysis: A Selec-
    tive Survey." Paper presented at the Land Grabbing: Perspectives from East
    and Southeast Asia Conference, Chiang Mai University, Thailand, June 2015.
    https://www.iss.nl/en/research/research-networks/land-deal-politics-initiative/
    land-grabbing-perspectives-east-and-southeast-asia-conference-papers.

CNT. 2019. *Pesquisa CNT de rodovias*. 2019. Brasília: SEST SENAT, 2019.

COFCO Intl. 2017. *Atendendo à demanda do amanhã*. *COFCO International Relatório de Sustentabilidade de 2017—Executive summary*. www.cofcointerna tional.com/sustainability/.

Costa, Wilma P. 2000."Economia primário-exportadora e padrões de construção do Estado na Argentina e no Brasil." *Economia e Sociedade* 14: 175–202.

Domingues, Mariana Soares, and Célio Bermann. 2012. "O arco de desflorestamento na Amazônia: da pecuária à soja." *Ambient. soc.*, 15, no. 2. https://doi .org/10.1590/S1414-753X2012000200002.

Escher, Fabiano, and John Wilkinson. 2019. "A economia política do complexo Soja-Carne Brasil-China." *Revista de Economia e Sociologia Rural*, 57, no. 4: 656–78.

Escher, Fabiano, John Wilkinson, and Paula Pereira. 2017. "Drivers and Implications of Chinese Investments in Brazilian Agribusiness: Actors, Strategies and Market Dynamics of the Corporate Food Regime." Paper presented at the 5th International Conference of the BRICS Initiative for Critical Agrarian Studies, Moscow, October 13–16, 2017. https://www.iss.nl/media/61740.

HBSA. 2020. Projetos logísticos hidrovias Brasil operação norte. http: //hbsa.com .br/projetos-logisticos.

Hiratuka, Célio, and Fernando Sarti. 2016. "Relações econômicas entre Brasil e China: análise dos fluxos de comércio e investimento direto estrangeiro." *Revista tempo do mundo* 2, no. 1.

INPE. 2020. Plataforma Terra Brasilis, Instituto Nacional de Pesquisas Espaciais. http://terrabrasilis.dpi.inpe.br/en/home-page/.

Lazzeri, Thais. 2019. "Demanda chinesa por soja ligada a 223 mil hectares de desmatamento no Brasil." *Diálogo Chino*. https://dialogochino.net/pt-br/pt/25843 -demanda-chinesa-por-soja-ligada-a-223-mil-hectares-de-desmatamento-no -brasil/.

Lima, Thiago, and Alexandre C. Leite. 2016. "Estrangeirização de terras: um questionamento à cooperação na ordem econômica internacional contemporânea?" *Monções: Revista de Relações Internacionais da UFGD* 9.

MDIC. 2020. Comexvis. Ministério da Indústria, Comércio Exterior e Serviços, Ministério da Economia. http://comexstat.mdic.gov.br/pt/comex-vis.

Medeiros, Carlos A., and Marcos Cintra. 2015. "Impacto da ascensão chinesa sobre os países latino-americanos." *Revista de Economia Política* 35, no. 138: 28–42.

MTPA (Ministério dos Transportes, Portos e Aviação Civil). 2017. *Corredores logísticos estratégicos: Complexo de soja e milho*. Volume 1. Brasília: MTPA.

Rodrigues, Jondison C. 2017. "Portos no Rio Tapajós: o arco do desenvolvimento e da justiça social?" Rio de Janeiro: Relatório Ibase.

Reed, Sarita, and Vinicius Fontana. 2019. "Demanda chinesa por soja empurra rota do agronegócio para Amazônia." *Diálogo Chino*. https://dialogochino.net/pt-br/ infraestrutura-pt-br/23265-demanda-chinesa-por-soja-empurra-rota-do-agro negocio-para-amazonia/.

Rodrigues, Jondison Cardoso. 2018. "O arco norte e as políticas públicas portuárias para o oeste do estado do Pará (Itaituba e Rurópolis): apresentação, debate e articulações." *Revista Nera* 42, no. 21.

Schallengerger, Erneldo, and Iara E. Scneider. 2010. "Fronteiras agrícolas e desenvolvimento territorial—ações de governo e dinâmica do capital." *Sociologias* 25, no. 12.

Sena, Edilberto. 2020. Entrevista concedida a Alana Oliveira e Bruno Hendler. Via Skype, May 31, 2020.

Trase, Anuário. 2018a. *Sustentabilidade das cadeias de produção: risco de desmatamento na exportação da soja Brasileira. Executive Summary.* http://resources.trase.earth/documents/TraseYearbook2018_Pt.pdf.

Trase, Anuário. 2018b. *Sustentabilidade das cadeias de produção: Risco de desmatamento na exportação de soja brasileira, Transparência para Economias Sustentáveis, Instituto Ambiental de Estocolmo e Global Canopy.* https://yearbook2018.trase.earth/.

Deforestation, Enclosures, and Militias: The Logistics "Revolution" in the Port of Cajueiro, Maranhão

Sabrina Felipe and Lucilene Raimunda Costa

PENSIONER LUCILENE RAIMUNDA COSTA, 62, has recurring dreams from when she was a child. "I always dream about Itaqui. Itaqui was an incredibly beautiful community; Boqueirão beach was beautiful, with immense dunes and rich vegetation: lots of cashews, *murici*, *guajuru*, guava, many birds. Plenty of fish, shrimp. [In the dream] I see the beach, the people, my grandmother's house, the backyard." The Itaqui of Lucilene's dreams, in the rural periphery of São Luís, the capital of Maranhão, no longer exists. Throughout Lucilene's childhood and adolescence in the 1970s, and her later in adulthood in the 1980s, she witnessed the dunes, vegetation, fruit trees, animals, and all the natural wealth of the community be systematically eliminated to make way for the Porto do Itaqui, currently managed by EMAP (Empresa Maranhense de Administração Portuária) (n.d.), a state-owned public company, and the Ponta da Madeira Maritime Use Terminal (MUT), a private port of the Vale SA transnational mining company (Vale n.d.).

Lucilene's dreams materialize today in the images of what was done to the Itaqui of her childhood. "[In the 1970s] I saw that bucket line carrying all the sand from those beaches, from those dunes, to that port. It is something that still bothers me today. One day I was coming here [to Cajueiro]. I took a van and the boy said, 'We are going to enter the port.' When that van went into the port, I cried out. I couldn't [contain] myself. When I saw that beach where I grew up. . . . Today everything is covered with iron. It is a mat; it is ore; a chunk of stuff. They ended it all."

Lucilene's situation is increasingly being faced by Indigenous, *quilombola*, and other traditional populations throughout the Brazilian north due to megaprojects tied to the development of Tapajós exportation corridor (described by Camoça and Hendler in this volume). The Munduruku, whose lands these projects have invaded, call them "death projects," as they destroy entire cosmologies and ways of living through radical alterations to the geography and ecology. Molina and Munduruku describe their effects on the Munduruku, in this case, the dynamiting of geographical structures that were sacred in indigenous cosmology. As one Munduruku elder describes it: "We had this sacred place and when I die I would go there. But as the government is now dynamiting everything, we will end even in spirit. We will die in spirit, too" (Molina and Munduruku, this volume, 122).

In the same vein, Gustavo Oliveira's interlocutors in the small riverine town of Itaituba describe the environmental impacts port building have had on their community:

> "You see all that yellow dust there across the river," Silva gestured toward the soy dust spewing from the ports as they loaded barges. "That dust isn't just over the water. It also mixes with the red dust the trucks kick up on the road all the way up to 'the 30,' and it gets in everyone's lungs here in Miritituba. If the kids here don't get run over by all the trucks, they're gonna grow up with lung problems from breathing this dust day-in, day-out." (Oliveira, this volume, 182)

All along the Tapajós Corridor, people are waking up to find that lands and communities that they've known for centuries—sometimes millennia—have been changed beyond recognition. In some cases (as we shall see below), this "wake up" has been literal.

Lucilene was born in Itaqui, the region where her family had lived since the 1960s. Lucilene and her family members were pushed out of Itaqui as the port works progressed over the years. In the end, none of her people remained there:

> Itaqui, Camboa dos Frades, and Cajueiro were extensions of our families. Camboa dos Frades just had my grandfather's family. And here [Cajueiro] there were also many who were in my family. They had a settlement. We

lived in Cajueiro and my grandfather lived . . . my grandfather was a nomadic type: he spent time in Cajueiro, time in Camboa, time in Itaqui.

After they were removed from Itaqui, the family migrated to the Anjo da Guarda neighborhood, the same destination as other families pushed out by the port. From Anjo da Guarda, Lucilene then moved to Cajueiro, where she has lived for twenty-nine years.

Cajueiro is formed by five nuclei: Morro do Egito, Guarimanduba, Andirobal, Parnauaçu, and Cajueiro itself. In this territory, "approximately 350 families live by fishing, collecting shellfish, family farming and small-scale animal breeding. The community's territory is in the rural area of São Luís Island, where the Rio dos Cachorros, Limoeiro, Taim, Porto Grande, Vila Cajueiro, Portinho, Ilha Pequena, Embaubal, Jacamim, Amapá and Tauá-Mirim communities are also found" (Alves et al. 2018).

An important regional historical landmark is Morro do Egito. In 1864, the Tambor de Mina *terreiro*, the "Terreiro do Egito Ilê Nyame," was founded by Massinocô Alapong, also known as Basília Sofia, an African woman from Cumassi on the Gold Coast (now Ghana). The sacred trees used in African-Brazilian spiritual obligations remain in place today (Movimento Defesa da Ilha 2019).

Lucilene sees today's destruction of Cajueiro as a replay of the destruction of her home in the 1970s. The threat of eviction is coming closer, once again for the construction of a port:

> Since approximately the late 1980s, Cajueiro has been threatened with compulsory displacement in order to accommodate a steel production complex in the area. This has created a feeling of insecurity among groups in Cajueiro and in the other communities that make up the territory. (Alves et al. 2018)

As of 2014, the Porto São Luís Private Use Terminal company (formerly WPR São Luís Gestão de Portos e Terminais S/A, run by Walter Torre Junior, president of the WTorre group of São Paulo) began its siege of Cajueiro, claiming to own part of its lands where the company intends to build a port. The majority shareholder in this project is the Chinese infrastructure transnational China Communications Construction Company (CCCC), which intends to invest R$ 1.7 billion in the venture (*O Imparcial* 2017).

They [company agents] started going there [Cajueiro] before 2014, but it started in 2014. The [company] got there and started saying that it owned the area. They put guards there, then they started buying up some pieces [of land] from people. Others they just took: they said the area was theirs, people were afraid of losing it and sold for anything.

This report is by Maria da Glória, a fifty-nine-year-old merchant whose house in Cajueiro was demolished by the company on August 12, 2019. A report published by the *Intercept Brasil* (TIB) on February 17, 2020, narrates one of the most dramatic moments in the violations committed by CCCC, MUT, and the state of Maranhão against residents of Cajueiro:

> Maria da Glória, 59, left her beans and meat ready in the 'fridge and went to pick up her 11-year-old grandson at school. Once back home, all she needed to do was heat up the food and have lunch. When Maria and her grandson got home, shortly after noon, they found no food, nor the refrigerator, nor the dishes, nor most of the furniture and utensils that had been in the house. Almost all the things contained in the house where Maria da Glória lived with her husband and grandson (in the Cajueiro community in the rural area of São Luís, Maranhão) had been placed in a moving truck by dozens of men paid by the company Private Maritime Use Terminal (MUT) Porto São Luís Company. . . . In front of the house, accompanied by her grandson and watched over by men from the Maranhão Military Police Shock Battalion, the resident of Cajueiro saw her last pieces of furniture being placed in the moving truck. Then, with no reaction but a silent cry, she watched the driver of a backhoe demolish her home in less than five minutes. Maria da Glória's house was one of 22 destroyed that day. (Felipe 2020)

According to the same report, "Monday August 12, 2019, became nationally known (Barbosa 2019) for the violence with which the Maranhão Military Police's Shock Battalion acted in the name of the repossession writ granted by Judge Marcelo Oka (Bourshceit 2019) at the request of MUT Porto São Luís."

> Pepper spray was used by police against the residents of Cajueiro, including children, the elderly, and women—one of them pregnant (Diálogo Chino 2019). On the same Monday, at around 10 pm, the Shock Battalion again cracked down using tear gas and rubber bullets (G1 MA 2019)

on about forty people, including residents of Cajueiro and supporters of the community, who were peacefully camped in front of the Palácio dos Leões, headquarters of the state government, protesting the violence of the removals. The secretary of state public security, Jefferson Portela, personally accompanied the policemen during the operation (Diego 2019). (Felipe 2020)

Just over a month after that episode, Lucilene had part of her yard destroyed by the port companies:

> When the houses were knocked down on August 12, 2019, my yard was included in the repossession writ. Only they didn't do it on August 12, because they weren't able to. I didn't even know it was going to happen. On September 19, when I thought I was going to a conciliation hearing [with the company], they came here with a document, showed me that they were going to realign the fence (that fence that there) because they had won repossession in court. As I didn't understand much of it, I didn't think they were going to do it soon. Then on Monday the 23rd, when I was going to see [a doctor in São Luís], I went to see [lawyer Caroline Rios] of Justiça nos Trilhos, and she told me that I should talk to the public defender who was also part of this case. But when I arrived [at home, in Cajueiro] they had already cut down [the fruit trees in the yard]. There was no time. They are so cowardly that they came in through the bottom! They claimed that I had moved the fence into their area in order to get more compensation. I never did that! The old fence posts are still there. Then they came and blew it up.

On this occasion, MUT and the CCCC destroyed numerous groves and patches that Lucilene had planted and spent years tending. According to the pensioner, the companies had previously destroyed a babassu palm grove that she had protected on part of the land. "I filed against them in court [over the felling of the palm trees]. The judge decided the case for them, saying that I was an invader."

MARANHÃO: RICHES PASS THROUGH BUT POVERTY REMAINS

Other logistics and energy infrastructure projects threaten traditional communities in Maranhão. These include the duplication of the BR 135 highway, which passes through dozens of *quilombola*[1] communities; the expansion of the Alcântara Launch Center (CLA), which threatens to remove *quilombolas* from that municipality; and power lines driven through fragile ecosystems, also in *quilombola* territories (*Intercept Brasil* 2020).

These projects show that Maranhão has been designated as a territory for the extraction and export of commodities, a designation that comes at a high price for the communities that have lived on these lands for centuries.

> Arco Norte, a strategic plan of the federal government that has the support of state and municipal governments and the private sector, is one of the great impulses for the make-over of Maranhão as a transit territory. The plan aims to increase the flow of commodities from north-central Brazil and other regions to the international market—especially to China—by lowering transport costs. The plan includes an infrastructure of ports, railways, highways, and stations that already exist or are to be built in states in the north and northeast of the country, such as Rondônia, Amazonas, Amapá, Pará, and Maranhão. (Felipe 2020)

Such projects contribute little in terms of local wealth, says Professor Horácio Antunes de Sant'Ana Júnior, coordinator of the Development, Modernity and Environment Study Group at the Federal University of Maranhão:

> These are projects to produce wealth for export; projects that work in enclave format and therefore do not leave much [for local communities] and have a very strong tendency to confirm what we have seen since the dictatorship. They are projects that promote very large production and accelerated wealth, but a wealth that promotes misery through the destruction of local ways of life, local landscapes, and the disruption of communities (Lima 2013).

FROM CHEAP LABOR TO CALLING THE SHOTS

China today plays a central role in the reconfiguration of Maranhão as a territory for the exploitation and transportation of commodities and a destination for investment (Borges 2019) in infrastructure. CCCC appears as a spearhead (*Exame* 2019a) in this process, with acquisitions of Brazilian energy (*Gazeta do Povo* 2017), engineering, and infrastructure companies.

Since the late 1990s, China has understood the process of globalization and is creating large changes in the world's economy. This is the conclusion of "The Infrastructure Geopolitics of China in South America," (Aguiar 2017) a study carried out by researcher Diana Aguiar:

> Today, China not only exports industrial goods with little or no added value (as it has done in the past), but Chinese banks and their construction and services companies travel the globe to put their money, their (increasingly sophisticated) goods and its expertise in highly technical services such as civil engineering. All of this is happening while China is becoming the destination of most of the mineral, energy, and agricultural commodities produced in the world: goods that are indispensable for sustaining the growth of that nation.

HEGEMONIC PLANS

According to lawyer Guilherme Zagallo, China's ventures look to long-term strategic issues, both from the point of view of the state and from the perspective of a dispute for economic hegemony with the United States. For Zagallo, China is beginning a period of consolidation of neocolonialism in Latin America and Africa:

> China literally has a capital reserve of trillions of dollars (Exame 2019b). It has capital in a volume that Western companies do not have or are not interested in employing because they are focused on short-term quarterly profits. China does not yet have a nominally higher GDP than the US or the military power of the Americans, but they have made total investments (with emphasis on military investments) in volumes higher than the Americans. If this growth is maintained, in a few years they will inevitably replace the Americans as the world's main economy, dictating the global rules on the basis of the worst of two regimes: the centralized, non-democratic economy of Chinese socialism and the unbridled ambition and unlimited greed of Western capitalism, which does not see global warming and denies proven facts.

WITH THE FORCE OF THE STATE

Although the CCCC port in Cajueiro is a private project, the government of the State of Maranhão has played an essential role in its implementation.

The preliminary licenses for the port were signed by the State Secretariat for Environment and Natural Resources under the Flávio Dino government. The Federal Police and Public Defense Ministries and the Maranhão State Public Defender's Office have all pointed out that these licenses are irregular. Among other things, they ignore a grant in 1998 made by the Maranhão government (through Iterma—Instituto de Colonização e Terras do Maranhão) to the residents of Cajueiro, guaranteeing usufruct title to families in the community.

In addition, "the property titles presented by the company interested in the area are under investigation for suspected land grabbing. The WPR—today the MUT—tried to prevent examination of those documents, claiming that the Judiciary would waste time on a 'useless' process. The company's request was denied by the courts. The criminal investigation remains under wraps" (Felipe 2020). Two expropriation decrees that guarantee the port's construction area were also signed by the Flávio Dino government, the first in March 2018 and the second in April 2019.

According to Article 64, Item III, of the Constitution of the State of Maranhão, it is the sole competence of the state governor to "sanction, promulgate, and make public the laws, as well as to issue decrees and regulations for their faithful execution" (Dino 2020). After the publication of the report by *The Intercept Brazil*, Governor Dino affirmed that he has no responsibility for the expropriation of the lands in Cajueiro, as this was the result of a judicial decision and "the government does not interfere in judicial decisions."

"It is the state government that signed the expropriation process that will allow the judge to declare that the lands can be seized," says Professor Horácio Antunes de Sant'Ana Júnior. "This is an attempt by the state government to deny responsibility for the process: casting it as a purely legal decision is an attempt to distort reality,"

On March 11, 2020, the government of the State of Maranhão reversed itself in relation to the second expropriation decree, signing another decree annulling the previous one that had expropriated part of Cajueiro (*O Estado* 2020). The justification for annulment of the decree was a recommendation from the 31st Specialized Prosecutor's Office for the Defense of Public Assets and Administrative Probity of the State Prosecutor's Office. It aimed at "avoiding legal action with consequent legal uncertainty."

However, after filing a writ for a restraining order, MUT–Porto São Luís managed to acquire an injunction in June 2020, granted by Judge Ricardo Duailibe, validating once again the initial decree of expropriation that had been subsequently annulled. The Maranhão state government has not yet appealed this decision as of August 2020.

TURNING POINT: FROM THE COMMUNITIES TO CHINA

Upon assuming his first term as governor in 2015, Dino opened dialogue with residents of Cajueiro who opposed the construction of the port. One of the first actions of his government was to revoke the expropriation decree signed on the penultimate day of the prior Roseana Sarney government, suspending the license that has been granted pending further studies.

"Suddenly, in 2016, these meetings [between government and community] end . . . and, to everyone's surprise, without prior notice, in 2016 the prior license is reconfirmed by the state government, without having any public audience," recalls Professor Horácio Antunes de Sant'Ana Júnior.

According to the professor, the turning point for the Dino government with regard to the Cajueiro port project happened when the Chinese company Acom and the then-WPR began talks with the state government regarding possible investments for the port project:

> At the end of 2016 and the beginning of 2017, information began popping up that WPR, today's MUT, was in the process of negotiating with the Chinese. . . . These negotiations were now mainly being intermediated by the vice governor [Carlos Brandão], who participated in various Maranhão business missions to China.

On the night of April 6, 2017, Dino went to São Paulo to be present for the signing of the investment agreement between CCCC and WPR. "I am happy that Maranhão was chosen to host such an important investment and I commend the entrepreneurial capacity of WPR," he declared on the occasion (*O Imparcial* 2017).

DEVELOPMENT: A PURE AND CLEAN DISCOURSE

If the expansion of Chinese enterprises (or the transportation and exportation infrastructure that favors them) is not good for the traditional communities of Maranhão, it is a positive factor as Flávio Dino considered running for the presidency in 2022.

> Flávio Dino sees himself as one of the main figures in the fight against Bolsonarism, which is a necessary, fundamental struggle, no doubt. He needs capital to counteract the restrictions that will come from federal budget blocks and retention of federal funds, as have already been threatened (Jornal do Comércio 2019). In the context of the national political ascension of a broad front against Bolsonarism and against twenty-first-century fascism, how can you achieve an economic structure that will support this struggle?

The question is from lawyer Rafael Silva, legal advisor to the Pastoral Land Commission (CPT / Maranhão), an organization that has been following the Cajueiro case since 2014. The contributions of Chinese capital in Maranhão (and, with them, promises of employment, investment, and development) strengthen the Dino government and, by extension, Dino's strategy for launching a presidential bid against Bolsonaro in 2022.

Bolsonaro and Dino have very different worldviews. Bolsonaro delves deeply into the logic of prejudice and hatred, the elimination of the Other, nationalism, and the construction of internal enemies. Meanwhile. Dino's worldview is anchored on legal, technical, and institutional bases, seeking to rescue democracy and supporting the judiciary. Nevertheless, both Bolsonaro and Dino have the same sort of discourse when it comes to development. "Chinese capital has an entry here," reflects Rafael Silva.

> While it increasingly opens its maw to cause more destruction, it raises the flag of development, which is presented as a pure and clean discourse. This is an official narrative, which has enormous legal support. It can count on the support of the judiciary, which will not politically oppose it, because the judiciary also believes in this logic, in this sort of discourse.

Caught between these two opposing worldviews, which have the same horizon of capitalist development, are the original and traditional peoples of Maranhão. For most of them, whether under an imagined Dino or Bolsonaro government, development has meant forced displacement, loss of land, the elimination of ancestral ways of life, and the threat of death. "Who among us is not going to be against Bolsonaro?" asks Rafael Silva.

And who of us will be the traitor who will attack the one who can face him? We stay in a place where we consciously know we will be wiped out, too. The big question that is being asked by the social movements, the popular struggle, is this: Who is going to be put together to be wiped out? Cajueiro is being wiped out.

IMPACTS FELT BY THE PEOPLE, BUT IGNORED BY COMPANIES AND THE GOVERNMENT

A year after her expulsion from the house where she had lived in Cajueiro, Maria da Glória says that none of her family has returned to the region. They do not want to relive the pain of the destruction of their home.

Maria da Glória's eleven-year-old grandson, who had just arrived home from school, witnessed the collapse of the house surrounded by the Military Police's shock battalion. He suffered psychological impacts. "In the beginning it was bad. Every weekend, I had to go with him to some beach, somewhere, because he packed his bag saying he was going to Cajueiro," says Maria da Glória. "He was very shaken."

Maria da Glória, her husband, and grandson returned to live in a house they own in the Anjo da Guarda neighborhood, where their daughter and son-in-law live with a newborn child. The elderly couple continues to work in a small cafeteria they have in the neighborhood. The house they built in Cajueiro was on a plot of land of about two thousand square meters. There, Maria da Glória grew coffee, annatto, acerola, lemon, tanja, sapodilla, avocado, coconut, manioc, graviola, guava, cashews, and pineapples. On the day her family was evicted, she was unable to remove anything.

Lucilene says that the residents expelled from Cajueiro are "spread out" in the Vila Maranhão and Anjo da Guarda neighborhoods, just like the people who were earlier expelled from Itaqui. According to Lucilene, some of these people continue to return to Cajueiro to fish and collect fruits.

The dreams that Lucilene has of the Itaqui of her childhood draw on the same feeling that she today expresses in relation to the Cajueiro that she knew and lived in before the destruction caused by the Sino-Brazilian venture:

I miss everything. There were three babassu palms, lined up at the entry to the town of Andirobal. I thought those palm trees were beautiful, that the sunset behind the palms was incredibly beautiful. I would pass them, and Brother Carlos would come by. He would go fishing and I would go to my mother's house. The palm leaves were swinging as if to say good-bye. They had already destroyed everything around them. I looked at them and said "Brother Carlos, the palm tree seems to be saying goodbye to us." He looked up and asked, "What is this? The other morning when I came in [from Andirobal], the palms were there. When I came back, they were gone. Many former residents continue to return to Cajueiro, either to guarantee some food through fishing and fruit gathering, or to try to maintain some sense of belonging. It is as if we have lost a loved one. It's not just losing our land: it's losing a lot more. It's like I lost a loved one. What it was, right? I miss that when I pass by there, that beautiful horizon. But they are no longer. . . . I miss them, I miss the whole thing."

NOTE

1. Communities descended from escaped, liberated, or rebellious slaves.

REFERENCES

Aguiar, Diana. 2017. *A geopolítica de infraestrutura da China na América do Sul.* Rio de Janeiro: ActionAid Brasil, FASE, Recife, APOIO. https://fase.org.br/wp -content/uploads/2017/06/A-geopolitica-de-infraestrutura-da-china-na-Amer ica-do-Sul.pdf.

Alves, Luciana Railza Cunha, and Christiane de Fátima Mota. 2018. *Comunidade do Cajueiro: não é o território que é nosso. Nós é que somos o território,* Boletim Cartografia da Cartografia Social: uma síntese das experiências 14 (April 2018). Manaus: UEA. Edições.

Barbosa, Catarina. 2019. "PM age com violência em despejo para construção de megaporto no Cajueiro (MA)." *Brasil de Fato.* https://www.brasildefato.com .br/2019/08/12/pm-age-com-violencia-em-despejo-para-construcao-de-porto -no-cajueiro-ma/.

Borges, Raimundo. 2019. "Vice-governador fala sobre investimentos da China no MA, eleições de 2020 e de 2022." *O Imparcial.* https://oimparcial.com.br/polit ica/2019/05/vice-governador-fala-sobre-investimentos-da-china-no-ma-elei coes-de-2020-e-de-2022/.

Bourshceit, Aldem. 2019. "No Maranhão, juiz autoriza destruição de casas em co-munidade afetada por megaporto." *InfoAmazonia.* https://infoamazonia.org/ pt/2019/05/portugues-no-maranhao-juiz-autoriza-destruicao-de-casas-de-co munidade-afetada-por-megaporto/#!/story=post-19448.

Diálogo Chino. 2019. "Mulher grávida é agredida por policiais em protesto de mora-dores de Cajueiros contra reintegração de posse forçada." https://www.youtube .com/watch?v=zhgYCywzbhI.

Diego, Emir. 2019. "Polícia Militar do Maranhão age com truculência com moradores do Cajueiro." https://www.youtube.com/watch?v=COcbQPsGxmE&feature=emb_title.

Dino, Flávio. 2020. "Todas as acusações contra o citado projeto privado tem sido apresentadas ao Judiciário. . . ." Twitter, February 21, 2020, 10:52 am. https://twitter.com/FlavioDino/status/1230928318226214912.

Empresa Brasileira de Administração Portuária. n.d. Porto do Itaqui. http://www.emap.ma.gov.br/emap/a-emap.

Época Negócios. 2018. "FMI diz que China poderá ser maior economia do mundo em 2030." https://epocanegocios.globo.com/Economia/noticia/2018/07/fmi-diz-que-china-podera-ser-maior-economia-do-mundo-em-2030.html.

Exame. 2019a. "O tamanho do apetite chinês no Brasil." https://exame.com/blog/primeiro-lugar/o-tamanho-do-apetite-chines-no-brasil/.

Exame. 2019b. "Reservas internacionais da China sobem a US$ 309 trilhões em fevereiro." https://exame.abril.com.br/economia/reservas-internacionais-da-china-sobem-a-us-309-trilhoes-em-fevereiro/.

Fachin, Patrícia, and Wagner Fernandes de Azevedo. 2019. "China ascende nas áreas econômica e militar, mas não projeta sua cultura pelo mundo. Entrevista especial com Marcos Reis." *Instituto Humanitas Unisinos.* http://www.ihu.unisinos.br/159-noticias/entrevistas/593121-china-ascende-nas-areas-economica-e-militar-mas-nao-projeta-sua-cultura-pelo-mundo-entrevista-especial-com-marcos-reis.

Felipe, Sabrina. 2020. "Negócios da China: como a grana da China desaloja pobres no Maranhão—com aval de Flávio Dino." *The Intercept Brasil.* https://theintercept.com/2020/02/17/governo-flavio-dino-china-maranhao/.

Gazeta do Povo. 2017. "China investiu R$ 60 bilhões na compra de empresas brasileiras em menos de três anos" https://www.gazetadopovo.com.br/economia/nova-economia/china-investiu-r-60-bilhoes-na-compra-de-empresas-brasileiras-em-menos-de-tres-anos-1ci5a0367h96bpv44bdw8rw8o/.

G1 MA. 2019. "Manifestantes do Cajueiro são expulsos da frente do Palácio dos Leões em São Luís." Globo. https://g1.globo.com/ma/maranhao/noticia/2019/08/13/manifestantes-do-cajueiro-sao-expulsos-da-frente-do-palacio-dos-leoes-em-sao-luis.ghtml.

The Intercept Brasil. 2020. "Negócio da China." https://www.instagram.com/p/B81VYgBJiF7/.

Jornal do Comércio. 2019. "Jair Bolsonaro ameaça retaliar governadores do nordeste." https://www.jornaldocomercio.com/_conteudo/politica/2019/08/696662-jair-bolsonaro-ameaca-retaliar-governadores-do-nordeste.html.

Lima, Luciana. 2013. "Construção de rodovias no governo militar matou cerca de 8 mil índios." *Último Segundo iG.* https://ultimosegundo.ig.com.br/politica/2013-09-25/construcao-de-rodovias-no-governo-militar-matou-cerca-de-8-mil-indios.html.

Movimento Defesa da Ilha. 2019. "Manifestantes do Cajueiro são expulsos da frente do Palácio dos Leões em São Luís." https://g1.globo.com/ma/maranhao/noticia/

2019/08/13/manifestantes-do-cajueiro-sao-expulsos-da-frente-do-palacio-dos
-leoes-em-sao-luis.ghtml.

O Estado. 2020. "Governo do Estado anula decreto que desapropriou o Cajueiro."
https://imirante.com/oestadoma/noticias/2020/03/17/governo-do-estado
-anula-decreto-que-desapropriou-o-cajueiro/.

O Imparcial. 2017. "Chineses investem R$ 1,7 bilhão em porto privado em São
Luís." https://oimparcial.com.br/noticias/2017/04/chineses-investem-r-17
-bilhoes-em-porto-privado-em-sao-luis/.

Vale. n.d. "V.Doc—Contando histórias," Sem data. http://www.vale.com/hotsite/
PT/Paginas/v-doc/ponta-da-madeira.aspx.

PART 5
HYDROELECTRICS
AND RAILROADS

Hungry and Backward Waters: Events, Actors, and Challenges Surrounding the Coca Codo Sinclair Hydroelectric Project in Times of COVID-19

Sigrid Vásconez D.

THE COCA CODO SINCLAIR hydroelectric project (CCS), emblematic of former Ecuadorian president Rafael Correa's administration, was financed by the Chinese government and constructed by Sinohydro, a Chinese state-owned hydropower company. The project, which commenced in 2016, was built despite serious questions from nonprofit environmental and human rights organizations. Doubts about the social and environmental impact of the project were never addressed by the government. Complicating matters, after the change of government in 2018, evidence of corruption emerged. Nevertheless, given the project's magnitude, these questions were relegated to a forgotten drawer. All of this changed, however, with the implosion of the nearby San Rafael waterfall on February 2, 2020. This triggered a series of events that have brought the project back into the public arena.

Both the questions and the recent postimplosion events will be explored in this chapter. The events will be discussed within a political economy framework, where Chinese investment takes on a different character in the atmosphere of the COVID-19 pandemic and the serious economic crisis now facing Ecuador. Furthermore, this juncture is understood as part of a larger process in which China actively developed strong ties with the Global South, becoming a primary funder and contractor of infrastructure projects such as CCS. Considering this current panorama, public policy challenges (especially given Ecuador's debt with China) become critical. This chapter offers observations regarding these challenges. Finally, it explores how scientific questions regarding the appropriateness of the project entered public discourse through a confluence of scientists and journalists mobilized by the recent implosion. The effects of these questions are being discussed amid the obligatory confinement of much of the Ecuadorian population due to the COVID-19 pandemic.

COCA CODO SINCLAIR PROJECT: A BRIEF HISTORY PRIOR TO COVID-19

It is important to understand that the CCS has long been an apple of the Ecuadorian government's eye. The idea was first proposed in the late 1950s and early 1960s, when what was then the Ecuadorian Electric Power Institute carried out studies of the hydroelectric potential of the Quijos and Coca Rivers at a site known as Codo Sinclair (Sinclair Elbow), named in honor of the US geologist who identified it in 1927. Despite new studies in the 1970s, the exploitation of the potential of the Coca River remained hypothetical for more than twenty years.

In 2008, one year after being inaugurated to his first term as president of Ecuador, Rafael Correa reactivated plans for the CCS project. Correa touted the CCS as the best option for achieving energy sovereignty, allowing Ecuador to step into the future (*El Universo* 2018). Argentinian president Cristina Kirchner, one of Correa's ideological colleagues in the twenty-first-century socialism movement (21CS), attended and participated in the ceremony, signing an agreement for HidroCoca, a joint venture between the public entities Energía Argentina (ENARSA) and Ecuador's Thermopichincha (*El Universo* 2018). This collaboration did not last long, however, as ENARSA withdrew from the agreement in 2009 (*El Comercio* 2009), taking approximately US$1.9 billion in financing and leaving Ecuador without a partner.

The forging of political alliances was one of the key elements of the developmentalist vision championed by 21CS countries at the time. This saw the state as the central driver of the economy, particularly through infrastructure projects. While a structural analysis of the ideological vision of ALBA member-states[1] is beyond our scope, it is important to note that another common denominator among these countries was their opposition toward US policy and Washington-based international agreements. These ideological elements permeated the Correa administration's agenda. Moreover, 21CS's left-leaning alignment coincided with an increase in China's involvement in Latin America.

As the Ecuadorian government sought financing for the CCS, rhetorical construction of the project continued. The government's message was repetitive and penetrating: the CCS and other energy and extraction megaprojects were the key to transforming Ecuador's production matrix and achieving energy sovereignty. This messaging effort, which excluded dissident voices, persuaded most Ecuadorians that the CCS was a necessity.

Thanks to high oil prices during the 2007–2014 period, the Correa administration was able to complete many infrastructure projects. These were termed "strategic investments," a category that was protected under Ecuador's new constitutional framework. In the bidding and negotiation for these projects, strategy merged with ideology. Most of them were developed through alliances with companies from ideologically aligned countries. This strategy opened the door to the contracts from which serious corruption cases later arose (e.g. the Odebrecht cases, the Panama Papers scandal) (Plan V 2016).

In 2010, two years after the announcement of the CCS's reactivation, the Correa administration entered into an agreement with China for the construction of the project. This would be financed with a US$1.682 billion loan from China Eximbank (Export-Import Bank of China) with a very high interest rate (Casey and Krauss 2018). Years later, when the dam was finally completed, the total cost of the project had risen to US$2.3 billion, with the difference also financed through a Chinese loan. At the time it began involvement with the CCS project, China, through various state-owned companies, initiated other investments in Ecuador's strategic sectors, and Ecuador entered the Beijing Consensus. In this volume, David Mosquera Narváez's chapter examines the nature of the relations between China and Ecuador from 2007 on. According to Mosquera, China was beginning its "Stepping Out" strategy in Latin America just as Ecuador was ready to receive credit for projects.

CONSTRUCTION OF THE PROJECT AND INITIAL
QUESTIONS

Before building the CCS, Sinohydro presented environmental impact studies (EIS) and an environmental management plan (EMP) for the Quijos River and Coca River basin. Several universities and a variety of environmental organizations and groups (both local and national) sought to participate in these studies. Academic experts observed a lack of updated hydrological and rainfall data in Sinohydro's EIS and EMP (López 2008). Daniela Rosero of Cornell University published a study of the basin's ecological flow[2] using current data. He noted a discrepancy between these data and the results of the EIS and EMP, which were based on the standard averages stipulated in the government's project guidelines (Rosero 2020). In its assessment of the CCS's environmental impacts, Sinohydro's studies failed to incorporate key aspects of the Coca River's ecological vulnerability (current accurate data regarding the basin's pluvial regime, the project's likely impact on the same, and a proper assessment of ecological flow).

Given the project's magnitude, this lack of adequate study can be seen as negligent. In the wake of the February 2020 waterfall implosion, which disrupted the Coca River's natural flow, the river's continuing upstream erosion processes have led to ecological disaster. Accordingly, the absence of accurate studies for the river will be a determining factor in the effort to define damage mitigation efforts. As Carolina Bernal of Ecuador's National Polytechnic School has commented, the CCS was constructed using incomplete geological and hydrological data (Bernal 2020). The lack of accurate data will impair efforts to formulate meaningful projections as to whether the river's erosion will result in even more damage to the river basin. Criticisms regarding poor studies and inadequate designs have also been made in relation to the Mirador mining project located in the southern Amazon region. In their chapter, van Teijlingen and Hidalgo Bastidas discuss the politics of environmental knowledge in both the Mirador and CCS cases. These authors ask important questions about how both projects were approved by government officials in the context of Chinese-Ecuadorean relations.

In addition to environmental issues, labor problems (*La Hora* 2012), accidents, and delays (*El Universo* 2014) were reported during the CCS's construction. In this context, Rui Jie Peng also presents a chapter in this volume, arguing that flexible labor reform and policies that prioritize capital accumulation have accentuated inequalities between Chinese and Ecuadorean workers in transnational workplaces such as the CCS. According to the government, these situations "were always smoothly resolved." When faced with any problematic observations regarding the project's construction, the government simply reaffirmed existing narratives about the project and the importance of Ecuador's alliance with China, minimizing the importance of environmental and human rights concerns raised by organizations such as Ecological Action and CEDHU (Ecumenical Commission on Human Rights) and journalists.

COMPLETION OF THE CCS AND THE NEW ADMINISTRATION

In November 2016, months into the campaign in which two members of Correa's administration, Lenín Moreno and Jorge Glas, ran for president and vice president, the CCS project was completed. The inauguration ceremony was attended by Chinese president Xi Jinping, who took the opportunity to seal new financial support for Ecuador through the Sino-Ecuadorian investment fund. This was on the order of US$10 billion and aimed at Ecuador's energy and extraction sectors (Plan V 2016).

The amounts, terms, and interests of China's investment in loans to Ecuador were only revealed years later, well into the Moreno administration. This occurred largely due to an agreement with the International Monetary Fund that demanded transparency in public finance (International Monetary Fund 2019).

The role of Chinese investment in the CCS project entered into public debate in the wake of the February 2, 2020, implosion of the San Rafael waterfall. The resulting disruption of the river's watercourse caused erosion on an enormous scale. Infrastructure damage has included pipeline ruptures, which have caused oil and gasoline to spill into the river, affecting downstream population and ecosystems.

THE WATERFALL IMPLOSION

Since February 2020, different questions about the CCS have arisen and, with them, new actors. This new wave of inquiry emerged thanks to the fact that the Coca River's erosion disaster coincided with the COVID-19 pandemic.

The implosion of the San Rafael waterfall, whose 490-foot drop had made it the tallest in the country, was immediately reported by the mainstream media. The reporting, however, lacked scientific analysis. *El Universo*, one of the country's main newspapers, published the following headline: "Due to rains, the San Rafael waterfall, the tallest in Ecuador, suffered an implosion that affected its course" (*El Universo* 2020a).

The mainstream media's initial treatment of the event provoked a group of scientists to expose concerns through social media that the probable cause of the phenomenon was a loss of the Coca River's hydrostatic equilibrium due to the CCS project. This hydrostatic imbalance hypothesis is based on a phenomenon called "hungry waters," which is caused by the loss of sediments (Kondolf 1997). In the CCS project, sediments are extracted in the hydroelectric plant's intake. With reduced sediments, the river's downstream erosive capacity increases, accelerating, in turn, erosion of the riverbed.

Observing this scientific debate on social media, a group of environmentalists convened a meeting between scientists and journalists approximately two weeks after the implosion. A direct channel of communication was created for sharing information and to allow a free exchange of scientific interpretations, providing information that journalists could use in reporting on the disaster.

As a result, reports appeared in specialized (Paz Cardona 2020) and alternative digital media (Basantes 2020b) and there was at least some coverage in the mainstream media (Orozco 2020). This constituted a new element in the public debate surrounding the CCS project.

A PANDEMIC, EROSION, PIPELINE RUPTURES, AND FORCE MAJEURE

Two months after the waterfall implosion, erosion on the Coca caused the rupture of three crude oil pipelines (Basantes 2020b). As a result, Ecuador's oil sector declared a state of force majeure (*El Telégrafo* 2020).

At the time, Ecuador was in a state of emergency due to the COVID-19 pandemic, with the population under mandatory quarantines. Confinement favored the dissemination of news and allowed scientific questions about the disaster to enter the public discourse (Basantes 2020b). This represented criticism that had not been seen before. Questions revolved around possible errors in the construction the CCS project in an area with multiple seismic[3] and volcanic vulnerabilities (the project sits at the foot of the active El Reventador volcano), a very high level of rainfall, and unstable soils (Bernal 2020). In the wake of the pipeline ruptures and with the support of environmental, human rights (Amazon Frontlines, CEDHU) and Indigenous organizations (the Confederation of Indigenous Nationalities of Ecuador's Amazonian Region) began suing the Ecuadorian State (Paz Cardona 2020).

In early June 2021, the oil sector declared a state of force majeure due to the danger of new pipeline ruptures (Paz Cardona 2020). While bypass and detour plans are currently being drawn for the pipelines, the force majeure situation is likely to continue into the foreseeable future.

According to scientists from Ecuador's National Polytechnic School and the Universidad San Francisco de Quito, as well as specialists from the US Geological Survey, erosion will only stop when the river encounters a knickpoint: a geomorphological fold made of hard stone (Torres 2020). Lack of accurate studies will complicate the process of determining the location of this knickpoint. There is the possibility that the erosion will reach the CCS's hydroelectric intake, located 11 miles upstream from the implosion site. Should this occur, the plant's functionality could be affected.

ECONOMIC AND GEOPOLITICAL REPERCUSSIONS

The state of force majeure meant that the country stopped transporting and refining petroleum, forcing the Esmeraldas refinery to shut down for emergency maintenance. During this month-long interim, petroleum prices around the world fell sharply because of decrease in demand during the COVID-19 pandemic (*El Comercio* 2020).

Barely one month later, on May 20, 2020, because of the volatility in world oil prices, the Ecuadorian government issued a decree allowing domestic gasoline to be sold at closer to true market prices (*El Universo* 2020b). With this decision, Ecuador abolished a fuel subsidy program that had been in place since the 1970s, something no prior administration had ever done. This occurred while the country was under lockdown due to COVID-19, reducing the possibility of any kind of social conflict. The decree took effect in July 2020. The liberalization of fuel prices will have long-term domestic impacts and also affect the petroleum presale contracts Ecuador maintains with China. A portion of Ecuador's debt is paid through petroleum shipments under a fixed preset price (Casey and Krauss 2018). Even though it is economically unfeasible to produce petroleum during such a severe market downturn, Ecuador will have to continue doing so to comply with its obligations. In view of this situation, the Moreno administration entered negotiations with China in June 2020. While not much is presently known about these talks, it is assumed that Ecuador is attempting to renegotiate its debt and improve the terms of its presale arrangement. While there are reports of a positive tone to the negotiations, Ecuador's Achilles's heel will be the effective penalty-cost of each barrel of petroleum that is exported as payment against its debt. For a detailed discussion of the negotiations between Ecuador and China and the resulting foreign debt, and an analysis of the impact of the economic crisis, see Delgado del Hierro's article in this volume.

Renegotiation is taking place in the context of the COVID-19 pandemic, in which China is seen as the source of the virus. Under global scrutiny, China is attempting to gain ground by supporting developing countries in which it has investments, thereby giving rise to a new diplomacy that may signify a change in the conditions of the Beijing Consensus, as Li Zhang's and Pedro Vásquez's articles in this volume describe in the context of Brazil (Gil 2020). In the wake of the COVID-19 pandemic, many countries will face serious limitations in their abilities to pay China. Because this is a completely unprecedented situation, it is unclear how China and its debtor nations will respond. Nevertheless, it does provide context for understanding China's current diplomacy, particularly as it finds itself in a series of confrontations with the US.

While the present chapter will not attempt to expand this geopolitical analysis, the opportunity to negotiate more favorable terms with China appears propitious for Ecuador. Nevertheless, maneuvering room will be limited if Ecuador cannot develop an alliance with other countries in similar situations, or end up placing itself first-in-line in these negotiations.

As it finds itself trapped in a storm of geopolitical struggles, Ecuador will have to develop an intelligent strategy, something that would seem almost impossible for a Moreno administration currently exhausted by the COVID-19 pandemic and the general crisis of being daily hit with corruption scandals.

WHAT'S NEXT FOR THE COCA CODO SINCLAIR?

In Ecuador's debt negotiations with China, the CCS will surely not be addressed. Although the contractual terms are unknown, news from the negotiations suggests that Ecuador will not be able to demand compensation if the project is severely affected by the Coca River's erosion, even though this does appear to be directly attributable to real deficiencies in Sinohydro's hydrological and geological studies. It would appear China no longer has any effective responsibility for the CCS.

To begin facing the current threat to the CCS, the government, through the Electric Corporation of Ecuador, has sought technical support from the US through various federal agencies: the US Geological Survey and the Environmental Protection Agency, among others. This reflects warmer relations with the US and suggests a new geopolitical alignment.

Options for mitigating threats to the CCS are still being developed; the future of the hydroelectric project appears uncertain. What is apparent is that scientific calls for greater depth and rigor in the planning and design of infrastructure projects are being taken more seriously. In various forums and groups that have proliferated in the wake of the disaster, plans are being formulated to better analyze the suitability of future projects, such as the one proposed for the Zamora-Santiago River, currently in the planning stage. The difficulty will be the extent to which scientific actors are able to influence political decisions. The history of the CCS project demonstrates this challenge.

CONCLUSIONS

The emergence of new discourses from the scientific front regarding the CCS and the influence these have had on current public debates would not have been possible were it not for some unfortunate coincidences. If the regrettable happenstance of the waterfall implosion, the resulting regressive erosion of the Coca River, the rupture of oil pipelines, and other events had not occurred during the COVID-19 lockdown, the influence of a new wave of scientific discourse would certainly have been less. These coincidences generated a new alliance of scientists and journalists. Today, the CCS is no longer regarded by the media from a public management perspective limited to questions about corruption. A more technical approach has been added to the public sphere, demanding a commensurate government response. This multisector space of coordination is clearly an innovation.

The decision to construct the CCS project in an area prone to a confluence of so many risks is now being seriously questioned, as is the decision to locate so much of the project's infrastructure in the same area. This could potentially result in changes in Ecuador's energy planning policy. It would be premature to count on this, but at least the conversation has begun and has already provoked important responses.

NOTES

1. ALBA refers to the Caracas-based Alianza Bolivariana para los Pueblos de Nuestra América (Bolivarian Alliance for the Peoples of Our America). While Argentina and Uruguay have shared many of ALBA's principles, neither of these two countries ever formally joined the alliance.

2. The term *ecological flow* refers to the minimum quantity and quality of water flows required to sustain a river's functionality and ecological value.

3. The epicenters of the March 5, 1987, Ecuador earthquakes were located near the present site of the CCS's hydroelectric intake.

REFERENCES

Basantes, A. C. 2020a. "La rotura del OCP revela el efecto de construir en zonas de alto riesgo." *GK*, May 3, 2020. https://gk.city/2020/05/03/rotura-ocp-ecuador-riesgo/.

Basantes, A. C. 2020b. "Ecuador: la rotura del oleoducto OCP revela el impacto de construir en zonas de alto riesgo." *Mongabay Latam*, May 4, 2020. https://es.mongabay.com/2020/05/ecuador-rotura-oleoducto-ocp-petroleo/.

Bernal, C. 2020. "Hidrosedimentología del Río Coca." Expert panel presentation: Efectos de las represas en los ecosistemas acuáticos: el caso de la represa Coca Codo Sinclair en la Cuenca del Río Napo, by the Acquatic Ecosystems Study Group, School of Biological Sciences, Universidad Central del Ecuador, Webinar, June 10, 2020. https://www.youtube.com/watch?v=a6wpnqjZXw4.

Casey, Nicholas, and Clifford Krauss. 2018. "It Doesn't Matter If Ecuador Can Afford This Dam. China Still Gets Paid." *New York Times,* December 24, 2018. https://www.nytimes.com/2018/12/24/world/americas/ecuador-china-dam.html.

El Comercio. 2009. "Enarsa deja el Coca-Codo Sinclair." September 14, 2009. https://www.elcomercio.com/actualidad/enarsa-deja-coca-codo-sinclair.html.

El Comercio. 2020. "Petróleo de Texas, referente para Ecuador, cierra en negativo a USD -37,63 USD el barril por primera vez." April 20, 2020. https://www.elcomercio.com/actualidad/desplome-precio-petroleo-texas-covid19.html.

La Hora. 2012 "Sinohydro admite problemas laborales en Coca Codo." December 15, 2012. https://lahora.com.ec/noticia/1101437711/sinohydro-admite-problemas-laborales-en-coca-codo- 2012.

International Monetary Fund. 2019. 'IMF Press Release 10/72.' March 11, 2019. https://www.imf.org/es/News/Articles/2019/03/11/ecuador-pr1972-imf-executive-board-approves-eff-for-ecuador.

Gil, T. 2020. "Coronavirus: cómo China gana presencia en Latinoamérica en medio de la pandemia (y qué implica para la región y el mundo)." *BBC*, April 14. https://www.bbc.com/mundo/noticias-internacional-52238901.

Kondolf, G. M. 1997. "Hungry Water: Effects of Dams and Gravel Mining on River Channels." *Environmental Management* 21: 533–51.

López, V. 2008. "No solo '. . . Una forma inteligente de sembrar el agua para cosechar energía' Implicaciones del Proyecto Coca Codo Sinclair para la Amazonía Ecuatoriana." EcoCiencia-Proyecto Fortalecimiento a Gobiernos Locales. Text prepared based on a presentation made by Janet Ulloa, for the 5th Forum on Water Resources, Portoviejo, May 7, 2008. http://www.flacso.org.ec/docs/CocaCodoSinclair.pdf.

Orozco, M. 2020. "El Coca-Codo puede esfumarse en el río." *El Comercio*, April 13, 2020. https://www.elcomercio.com/blogs/economia-de-a-pie/analisis-columnista-coca-codo-esfumarse.html.

Paz Cardona, A. J. 2020. "Ecuador: demandan al Estado y a empresas petroleras por derrame de crudo en los ríos Coca y Napo" *Mongabay Latam*, April 30, 2020. https://es.mongabay.com/2020/04/derrame-de-petroleo-rio-coca-indigenas-demandan-a-ecuador/.

Plan V. 2016. "Coca Codo, la joya de la corona se inaugura con sobrecostos y largos retrasos." November 14, 2016. https://www.planv.com.ec/investigacion/investigacion/coca-codo-la-joya-la-corona-se-inaugura-con-sobrecostos-y-largos.

Pallares, M. 2020. "Coca Codo Sinclair: ¿pagará la China por el inminente desastre?" *4pelagatos*, April 10, 2020 .https://4pelagatos.com/2020/04/20/coca-codo-sinclair-pagara-la-china-por-el-inminente-desastre/.

Rosero, D. 2020. "Caudales ecológicos estimados y operación de la Coca Codo Sinclair," Expert Panel Presentation: Efectos de las represas en los ecosistemas acuáticos: el caso de la represa Coca Codo Sinclair en la Cuenca del Río Napo, presented by the Aquatic Ecosystems Study Group, Department of Biological Sciences, Universidad Central del Ecuador, Webinar, June 10, 2020. https://www.youtube.com/watch?v=o-_ivYeMBOQ.

El Telégrafo. 2020. "Energía declara el estado de fuerza mayor por ruptura de SOTE y OCP." April 11, 2020.https://www.eltelegrafo.com.ec/noticias/economia/4/energia-ruptura-sote-y-ocp.

Torres, W. 2020. "Infraestructura vial, petrolera y eléctrica, en riesgo por erosión del río Coca." *Primicias*, May 18, 2020. https://www.primicias.ec/noticias/economia/infraestructura-vial-petrolera-electrica-riesgo-erosion-rio-coca/.

El Universo. 2008. "Construcción de Coca Codo Sinclair se iniciará en 60 días." March 31, 2008. https://www.eluniverso.com/2008/03/31/0001/9/94A66CCBB0864D5987E0D53B2318706D.html.

El Universo. 2014. "Trabajadores de proyecto Coca Codo Sinclair reclaman mejores condiciones laborales." December 15, 2014. https://www.eluniverso.com/noticias/2014/12/15/nota/4349296/trabajadores-proyecto-coca-codo-sinclair-paralizan-temporalmente.

El Universo. 2018. "Alecksey Mosquera, condenado a 5 años por lavado de activos en caso Odebrecht." April 11, 2018. https://www.eluniverso.com/noticias/2018/04/11/nota/6708445/mosquera-condenado-5-anos-odebrecht.

El Universo. 2020a. "Por lluvias, cascada San Rafael, la más alta de Ecuador, sufrió implosión que afectó su cauce." February 20, 2020. https://www.eluniverso.com/noticias/2020/02/03/nota/7722261/lluvias-cascada-san-rafael-mas-alta-ecuador-sufrio-implosion-que.

El Universo. 2020b. "Ahora los precios de combustibles se ajustarán por bandas." May 20, 2020. https://www.eluniverso.com/noticias/2020/05/20/nota/7846095/subsidios-combustible-comercializacion-precios-internacionales.

Electrification of Forest Biomes: Xingu-Rio Lines, Chinese Presence, and the Sociotechnological Impact of the Belo Monte Hydroelectric Dam

Laís Forti Thomaz, Aline Regina Alves Martins, and Diego Trindade d'Ávila Magalhães

NEGATIVE CONSEQUENCES OF INVESTMENTS in infrastructure have gained greater visibility following Brazil's decision to abide by international environmental protection and human rights standards. This has become crucial for those Brazilian regions with greater biodiversity and a larger presence of traditional communities. The Brazilian state has the responsibility to mitigate the environmental and social impacts of these projects. Civil society and traditional communities also need to participate in the process so that these actions are effective.

Camoça and Hendler, Molina and Munduruku, and Felipe and Costa have demonstrated in this volume how Brazil's need to meet Chinese demands in the area of soy exports led to the Brazilian state ignoring or disregarding civil society and local community needs in the planning of mega-development projects in which Chinese financing plays a significant role.

But it is not just commodity production and export that is creating massive development enterprises. The growing need for electricity in Brazil led to the creation of dams and other energy-generation and transmission projects. As Maria Elena Rodríguez points out in her chapter, Chinese investments have played a significant role in making these plans become reality: "Chinese FDI has previously been concentrated in agriculture, mining, and petroleum. Recent years, however, have seen increasing investments in the energy and electricity sector. When analyzing confirmed Chinese investments since 2003, sector by sector, one begins to see a clear and growing preference for the energy sector is observed" (341).

Like the soy exportation projects being developed along the Tapajós Corridor, much of this new energy infrastructure is being installed in environmentally and culturally sensitive regions of Brazil, particularly in the Amazon. Molina and Munduruku have detailed the impacts of one such project in this volume, highlighting the callousness of both the state and its private-sector allies in their treatment of sacred Indigenous lands. But while energy production and transmission in the Amazon is linked to development projects in the region, it mostly seeks to meet the demands of Brazil's industrialized southeast.

Below, we will look at the impacts of what is perhaps Brazil's most controversial hydroelectric project, highlighting a little-known collateral effect: the need to build transmission lines to carry the electricity it generates from the Amazon to Brazil's power-hungry southeast.

The Belo Monte Hydroelectric Plant is located near the city of Altamira on the Xingu River, a tributary of the Amazon River in the northern region of Brazil. It is the fourth largest hydroelectric plant in the world, supplying 10 percent of Brazil's energy demands. Its first turbine spun up in 2016. On November 27, 2019, the dam was officially inaugurated after the activation of its eighteenth and last turbine (Vilela 2019; Norte Energia 2020). This increased the northern region's importance in meeting the demands of the southeast and south, which are the country's largest energy consumers. The distance between Belo Monte and the south required overcoming technical and financial challenges in building an efficient high-voltage electric grid connecting the north to the southeast.

Belo Monte generated controversies about its social and environmental consequences. Its construction led to changes in the flow of the river. This impacted the local flora and fauna and forced out resident populations, including traditional Indigenous and riverside communities, who had to move from the territories that kept their natural and cultural heritage alive. The work limited activities such as river travel and fishing due to the interruption of the river's flow and the reduction of its fish population caused by hillside demolitions during the project. During the construction of the hydroelectric plant and its transmission lines, which generated local jobs, communities reported serious and social problems such as violence, drugs, prostitution, and human trafficking (*Diálogo Chino* 2016; Peduzzi 2013).

As Rodríguez, and Saggiorio Garcia and Curty Pererira have pointed out in this volume, China has made enormous investments in Brazil's energy sector through the state-owned company State Grid. This company has been operating in Brazil since 2010 through State Grid Brazil Holding (SGBH). With financing from the National Bank for Economic and Social Development (BNDES), it has led the task of overcoming the technical challenges of building the lines enabling electricity to flow from Belo Monte to southeast Brazil.

Our chapter looks at the participation of social actors in the decision-making process regarding the collateral effects of the construction of the second stretch of the Belo Monte line: the Xingu-Rio transmission line (the Xingu-Rio TL). It also analyzes the progress of the project's environmental compensation (EC) payouts. The Xingu-Rio Transmissão Elétrica (XRTE) concessionaire (part of SGBH), the Brazilian Institute of the Environment and Renewable Natural Resources (IBAMA), and management bodies of the Conservation Unit (CUs) all took part in addressing the environmental agenda surrounding this project. This included public hearings with the Fundação Cultural Palmares (Palmares Cultural Foundation—FCP) and the *quilombola* community of Malhadinha (TO). The sources we consulted include journalistic materials, company reports, documents from public hearings, technical opinions, and minutes of meetings made available by IBAMA and FCP via the Access to Information Law.

STATE GRID BRAZIL HOLDING'S ACTIVITIES

State Grid Corporation of China (State Grid) is a Chinese state-owned energy company founded in Beijing in 2002. It is the world's largest electric utility, holding second place in the Fortune Global 500 ranking for 2018. Its coverage extends to 80 percent of China, serving 1.1 billion consumers. The company arrived in Brazil in 2010 via SGBH.

Brazil-China energy cooperation is deep and extensive. Eight of fifteen bilateral agreements between the two countries from 2006 to 2017 are in the energy sector (Xavier et al. 2018, 65–67). In 2018, out of the twenty-nine confirmed Chinese investment projects in Brazil, thirteen were for energy generation, transmission, and distribution (CEBC 2019, 12). Among these,

SGBH's investments stand out. In 2017, the company became the controlling shareholder of CPFL Energia, the largest private group in Brazil's electricity sector with investments of US$1.8 billion (Montoya and Kaltenecker 2019). In 2018, the company's investments reached US$6 billion, and it became the leader in the electric sector in Brazil (Cohen 2019a).

Much of SGBH's resources are invested in the transmission line from Belo Monte. The first stage of the project, called the Xingu-Estreito line, allows the power to flow from the plant to Minas Gerais, through Tocantins and Goiás. SGBH also operated on the second stretch of the line, the Xingu-Rio TL, through its subsidiary XRTE. Like the Xingu-Estreito TL, the Xingu-Rio TL uses ultra-high-voltage technology with a direct current of 800 kV and a transmission capacity of 4 gigawatts: more than a third of the 11.2 gigawatts of Belo Monte's capacity.

This TL cost R$8.7 billion with part (R$5.2 billion) financed by the BNDES. It was inaugurated in 2019 and runs for 2,539 km with 4,448 towers from Anapu (PA) to Paracambi (RJ). The company points out that 139 km were added to the initial project to bypass conservation areas and thus reduce the TL's environmental impact. In fact, the company claims that its environmental analysis was carried out before the engineering analysis, specifically so that environmental issues could be considered. By November 2017, IBAMA (2017) had initially identified 78 municipalities the Xingu-Rio TL would run through, along with 188 CUs in the area covered by the project. By 2019, the number of municipalities affected by the Xingu-Rio TL had climbed to 81 (Cohen 2019b).

IBAMA AND ENVIRONMENTAL COMPENSATION

As pointed out above, the project changed its construction plans to minimize its environmental impact, increase energy efficiency, and transfer technology to Brazil. However, as it crosses three complex biomes (the Amazon, the Cerrado, and the Atlantic Forest) the very magnitude of Xingu-Rio TL raises questions about its impacts. Generally, a company like XRTE prepares environmental impact studies taking into consideration the fact that it will have to pay EC for its activities. IBAMA issues technical opinions regarding projects, and distribution of the EC is based on technical notes and projects from management units of protected areas (CUs). The Chico Mendes Institute for Biodiversity Conservation

(ICMBio) is the governing body of federal CUs, while subnational environment departments are the governing bodies of the CUs belonging to states or municipalities. IBAMA and the Federal Environmental Compensation Committee (FECC) assess the projects the governing bodies place before them, then each body is authorized to negotiate their own environmental compensation compromise agreement with the company. Signing an agreement enables the application of resources for implementing projects.

In March 2016, SGBH sent its environmental impact report to IBAMA. This was rejected because IBAMA allegedly claimed that the draft of the reference agreement, which guides preparation of the report, did not include consultation with the management bodies of seven CUs (protected areas). Furthermore, these CUs were not mentioned in the project description sheet (Borges 2017; Godoi and Freire 2017). The environmental impact report was presented in June 2016, containing information about the transmission lines and the regions affected by them. Regarding the choice of the line routes (three alternatives were presented), the report highlights the following as selection criteria:

> Ease of access; avoid interference in urban areas, population groups, settlements, aerodromes, mining, industries; avoid interference with vegetation and Conservation Units; avoid interference with caves; avoid interference with indigenous lands and *quilombola* communities. (Sistema de Transmissão Xingu-Rio 2016, 20)

The report also lays out the environmental protection areas (EPA) affected by the project: the Rio Guandu, Mário Xavier National Forest, Gandu-Açu, Boqueirão da Mira, and da Serra da Cambraia. XRTE presented nineteen environmental programs for controlling, mitigating, and compensating for the project's impacts.

From September 26 to 30, 2016, IBAMA (2016) held nine public hearings to present the environmental impact study and report regarding the Xingu-Rio transmission system and to discuss it with stakeholder communities, which were Seropédica (RJ), Monte Alegre de Goiás (GO), Andrelândia (MG), Porto Nacional (TO), Itutinga (MG), Itaporã do Tocantins (TO), Unaí (MG), Curionópolis (PA), and Novo Repartimento (PA) (IBAMA 2016). At Seropédica's hearing to discuss the Guandu EPA and Mário Xavier National

Forest, Silvia Martins, a representative of a group of farmers in the Ribeirão das Lajes microbasin region, stressed that this type of project should listen to communities to better mitigate impacts. In turn, the environmental director of Concremat (the company hired by SGBH to carry out the environmental licensing for the line), Josefina Kurtz, said they had sought to reduce the impacts on traditional communities and the environment during planning (Comitê Bacia Hidrográfica Guandu 2016).

The environmental license for the project was only granted by IBAMA on February 23, 2017. This occurred after attempts by Cai Hongxian, XRTE's CEO, to pressure then minister of mines and energy Fernando Filho and the National Energy and Electricity Agency for the license to be quickly released so work on the lines could continue (Borges 2017).

In summary, in the XRTE/CMAT report (Sistema de Transmissão Xingu-Rio 2017), the company states that the southwestern region of Minas Gerais will not be significantly impacted by the project in terms of its flora, herpetofauna, bird populations, and mastofauna. However, on earlier occasions, the company indicated that the region had already suffered impacts caused by the project. In the Pará region, the company claimed that their actions would not significantly affect the flora, since "the landscape is already highly fragmented, [and there would be] little impact from the point of view of connectivity and diversity of plant species" (74).

On November 18, 2017, IBAMA presented Technical Opinion No. 48/2017, which contained R$35,265,231.95 for environmental compensations. This represented 0.5 percent of the project's listed value of R$7,053,046,390.00. It was included in the calculation of the degree of Impact. According to IBAMA, "The amount of environmental compensation listed here is considered to be exceptional for the purposes of the project." Thirty percent of that amount (R$10,579,569.58) could be applied by ICMBio in CUs in any region, even outside the project's impact area if expenditures could be justified. The Technical Note No. 100/2018 / DCOMP / DILIC, from April 13, 2018, defined the affected CUs, but only on April 25 did IBAMA approve the EC amounts.

We examined 168 documents which the Xingu-Rio TL board of directors prepared between September 27, 2017 and April 24, 2020 (IBAMA 2017). These document the most important actors in the project's environmental compensation plan: IBAMA, FECC, ICMBio, and the state and municipal environmental secretariats. We analyzed maps, EC projects, specific actions for each project, and costs for each action, as well as references between the original EC proposals and the application of resources by the XRTE project.

We highlight three pieces of information from the ongoing process at IBAMA. First, most of the resources funded the creation of CUs, land tenure regularization, the acquisition of vehicles and equipment, and the preparation of management plans. The governing body that will receive most of the EC funds was ICMBio, which will manage R$23,275,447.16 of the more than R$35 million. According to the XRTE-ICMBio CCAF (Comite de Compensação Ambiental Federal [Federal Environmental Compensation Commission]), this institution (the ICMBio CCAF) will spend these funds by 2022. We emphasize that this was the only CCAF that was signed and registered up to April 24, 2020. Other management bodies have been authorized to negotiate and launch their CCAFs with XRTE: Santa Rita do Jacutinga (MG), Canaã dos Carajás (PA), Nova Iguaçu (RJ), and Rio de Janeiro (RJ).

In August 2020, the Goiás State Environmental Secretariat, responsible for the state's CUs, reported that land tenure regularization depends on the conclusion of negotiations with private landowners (IBAMA 2017) and on the evaluation of their properties. It also depends on the issuance of property titles and the final decisions of ongoing judicial proceedings. The secretary sent a letter on April 8, 2020, to explain why it did not apply national standards for prioritizing EC projects. It claimed that some of the designated CUs already had resources for regularization and management, so they could use additional funds for other activities. It also pointed out that there are two additional compensation plans in progress: one for the Xingu-Estreito project by Belo Monte Transmissora de Energia and another for compensation from Cerradinho, Açúcar e Energia SA.

It is worth mentioning the only CU that is not covered by the XRTE EC plan. The Municipality of Natividade (TO) requested the inclusion of the Monumento Natural da Serra de Natividade CU. This CU was created more than a year after XRTE evaluated the eligibility of affected CUs for receiving EC.

COMPENSATION PAID TO THE MALHADINHA QUILOMBOLA COMMUNITY

In XRTE and CMAT's environmental impact report (Sistema de Transmissão Xingu-Rio 2016), thirty-three affected *quilombola* communities certified by the FCP were identified. However, SGBH claims that only the Quilombola Malhadinha Community in Tocantins would suffer any direct interference and thus needed to be compensated. This was achieved by building a factory to process fruit pulp and a meeting space for the *quilombola* association (State Grid Brazil Holding 2019).

To enable compensation for the project's social impacts, XRTE held workshops with the residents of Malhadinha. According to the FCP, on April 12, 2017, a meeting was held to present and deliver the Quilombola Basic Environmental Project (QBEP) of the Xingu-Rio Transmission System. A week later a second hearing was held involving forty-nine people, including FCP representatives, Malhadinha residents, the Concremat Environmental Consultancy, and XRTE, as well as representatives from the Quilombola Communities of Tocantins (COEQ-TO). In the minutes of this event, we found that there were still many questions about the project:

> Mrs. Maria Aparecida of COEQ-TO said that the presentation was superficial, that it is necessary to have more clarity and greater detail regarding the foreseen impacts and planned actions, presented in a language that was accessible for the community. She also emphasized that the material presented was delivered very close to the date of the hearing. (Fundação Cultural Palmares 2017)

In this hearing, community concerns are evident. The health of community residents was also considered, and XRTE said that it would monitor employees from outside the community. At this stage, the company, together with the Secretariat of Family Agriculture, committed itself to helping the community acquire the Quilombola Seal (a certificate of origin issued by the FCP that attributes cultural identity to *quilombola* products). Environmental Education and Heritage Education Programs were also envisaged, the latter to guarantee the community's cultural heritage. Although criticized, the QBEP was approved by the majority (eighteen votes) of those present from the community.

FCP employee Tiago Cantalice held a consultation on March 20, 2019, with the community to evaluate the execution of the Quilombola Basic Environmental Project (Fundação Cultural Palmares 2019). Sixty-six members of the community attended this meeting. Discussions involved how the community could organize itself to utilize the pulp produced by the new factory. In the minutes of the meeting, the FCP representative explained the importance of SEBRAE (Brazilian Support Service for Small and Micro Enterprises) in training the community, in addition to requesting that "the company [XRTE] support the community to connect to consumers (including city governments) and to identify outlets for the fruit pulp produced in the Malhadinha community."

> Tiago believes that a long-term partnership between XRTE and the community is essential; one offering technical assistance and even financing in its initial years (money for agroecological technical monitoring and the purchase of some inputs, among other things). . . . Tiago pointed out that it would be interesting to adopt solar energy generation systems, to relieve the community with regards to electricity costs and ensuring greater reliability for the electricity system, as power outages are common.

Both the Quilombola Seal and the QBEP were discussed at this meeting. In general, the community reported that they were satisfied with XRTE's performance, citing that in addition to the *quilombolas*, two Indigenous territories were identified by XRTE in Pará, the Parakanã, and the Trincheira-Bacajá. However, a study by the company found that these communities were "outside the limits of the studies required by Interministerial Ordinance 60/2015 " (Sistema de Transmissão Xingu-Rio 2016, 60). In the 2017 report, the company repeated that no Indigenous communities were identified within the limits, stating that the project had avoided interfering in the settlements.

CONCLUSIONS

This chapter has focused on the electric transmission line from Belo Monte, in Pará, to Rio de Janeiro, constructed by the Chinese company State Grid Brazil Holding (SGBH) through its concessionaire, Xingu-Rio Transmissão Elétrica (XRTE). We have shown how the *quilombola* community of Malhadinha (TO) formulated its demands on XRTE, as well as the involvement of Fundação Cultural Palmares (FCP) in the negotiations regarding social compensations to be paid to this community. We have also presented the processes of preparing proposals for environmental compensation (EC) by the governing bodies of conservation units (CUs), in dialogue with the Brazilian Institute for the Environment and

Renewable Natural Resources (IBAMA), for later negotiation and signature of a compensation agreement by XRTE.

In this sense, we have presented the discussions regarding the concerns of the municipalities affected by the project. We showed IBAMA's decision to grant the license and establish approximately R$35 million in compensations for the CUs. This amount was deemed "exceptional," according to a technical opinion by IBAMA experts, which allows us to infer that the XRTE project intended to agree to an adequate amount of compensation for its environmental and social impacts.

Based on the material made available by IBAMA, the attributions, competencies, and accumulated experience of the governing bodies of ICMBio's federal CUs contributed to the speed with which the term of commitment with XRTE was signed, enabling the application of resources for project execution. The internal difficulties of municipal and state agencies, as well as negotiations with private owners in the CUs, have affected the EC process, but these cannot be inferred as compromising its successful conclusion.

With regard to social compensations, the only traditional community to receive compensation was Malhadinha. The study identified that, in addition to the fruit pulp processing plant and a meeting space, requests from residents regarding physical infrastructure, logistics, and training were included in compensation. The records of the meetings with the community show the apparent contradiction between the construction of a transmission network that crosses a community suffering from a lack of energy, and this was pointed out. However, there are contractual impediments and technical limitations preventing XRTE from meeting these demands. The socioenvironmental impacts of the project and the compensation for these did not change the preexisting need for proper public policies. Socioenvironmental compensation is not expected to replace the state's role in addressing sanitation, electricity, Internet access, and other social needs.

REFERENCES

Assembleia Legislativa de Minas Gerais. 2018. *Autoridades pedem novos estudos sobre linha de transmissão.* April 17, 2018. https://www.almg.gov.br/acompanhe/noticias/arquivos/2018/04/17_minas_energia_meio_ambiente_eletrodo_sul_minas.html.

Borges, André. 2017. "Chineses pedem 'intervenção' de ministro em licença ambiental de linha de transmissão." *Estado de São Paulo,* January 11, 2017. https://

economia.estadao.com.br/noticias/geral,chineses-pedem-intervencao-de-ministro-em-licenca-ambiental-de-linha-de-transmissao,10000099372.

CEBC. 2019. *Conselho Empresarial Brasil-China. Investimentos Chineses no Brasil 2018: o quadro brasileiro em perspectiva global.* Rio de Janeiro: CEBC.

Cohen, Sandra. 2019a. "A gigante chinesa que energiza o Brasil." *State Grid Brazil Holding* June 11, 2019. https://www.stategrid.com.br/a-gigante-chinesa-que-energiza-o-brasil/.

Cohen, Sandra. 2019b "Como a State Grid se tornou a líder do setor elétrico brasileiro." *Revista Época*, July 12, 2019. https://epocanegocios.globo.com/Empresa/noticia/2019/07/como-state-grid-se-tornou-lider-do-setor-eletrico-brasileiro.html.

Comitê Bacia Hidrográfica Guandu. 2016. *Audiência Pública discute instalação de empreendimento na APA-Guandu*, September 28, 2016. https://www.comiteguandu.org.br/noticias.php?id=473.

Diálogo Chino. 2016. "Transmissão de energia de Belo Monte retira vegetação nativa no Brasil." September 8, 2016. https://dialogochino.net/pt-br/infraestrutura-pt-br/7249-transmissao-de-energia-de-belo-monte-retira-vegetacao-nativa-no-brasil/.

Fundação Cultural Palmares (FCP). n.d. "Agenda Quilombola 2017–2019." http://www.palmares.gov.br/?page_id=44590.

Fundação Cultural Palmares (FCP). 2017. *Ata da Fundação Cultural Palmares sobre a 2a Oitiva realizada na Comunidade Machadinha, referente ao Sistema de Transmissão Xingu-Rio, concernente a Linha de Transmissão em Corrente Contínua 800kV Xingu.* April 19, 2017.

Fundação Cultural Palmares (FCP). 2019. *Ata da Fundação Cultural Palmares sobre a Consulta junto à Comunidade Quilombola Machadinha Execução do PBAQ do Sistema de Transmissão Xingu-Rio.* March 20, 2019.

Godoi, Maurício, and Wagner Freire. 2017. "Belo Monte: State Grid pede ajuda do MME para destravar licenciamento de linhão." *Canal Energia*, January 12, 2017. https://canalenergia.com.br/noticias/38662177/belo-monte-state-grid-pede-ajuda-do-mme-para-destravar-licenciamento-de-linhao.

Grandes Construções. 2018. "Belo Monte, uma odisseia ainda longe do fim. Especial Sobratema-Belo Monte." June 25, 2018. http://www.grandesconstrucoes.com.br/Materias/Exibir/belo-monte-uma-odisseia-ainda-longe-do-fim.

Instituto Brasileiro do Meio Ambiente e dos Recursos Naturais Renováveis (IBAMA). 2016. "IBAMA realiza audiências públicas sobre sistema de transmissão Xingu-Rio." September 12, 2016.

Instituto Brasileiro do Meio Ambiente e dos Recursos Naturais Renováveis (IBAMA). 2017. *5 Brasília.* November 18, 2017.

Instituto Brasileiro do Meio Ambiente e dos Recursos Naturais Renováveis (IBAMA). 2018. *Ata da Sexagésima Oitava Reunião Ordinária do Comitê de Compensação Ambiental Federal (FECC).* April 25, 2018. https://www.gov.br/IBAMA/pt-br/centrais-de-conteudo/68-ro-FECC-pdf/view.

Montoya, Miguel Angel, Daniel Lemus, and Evodio Kaltenecker. 2019. "The Geopolitical Factor of Belt and Road Initiative in Latin America: the cases of Brazil and Mexico." *Latin American Journal of Trade Policy* 2, no. 5.

Norte Energia. 2020. "A História de Belo Monte—cronologia." Brasília. https://www.norteenergiasa.com.br/pt-br/HEP-belo-monte/historico.

Peduzzi, Pedro. 2013. "Apreensão de crack aumenta 900% em município próximo a Belo Monte." *Agência Brasil.* February 15, 2013. http://memoria.ebc.com.br/agenciabrasil/noticia/2013-02-15/apreensao-de-crack-aumenta-900-em-municipio-proximo-belo-monte.

Sistema de Transmissão Xingu-Rio (XRTE/CMAT). 2016. *RIMA—Relatório de Impacto Ambiental.* https://document.onl/download/link/sistema-de-transmissao-xingu-rio-rima-relatorio-de-de-transmissaosistema.

Sistema de Transmissão Xingu-Rio (XRTE/CMAT). 2017. *Estudos Socioambientais da área dos eletrodos de terra: Anapu—Pará e Minduri—Minas Gerais.*

State Grid Brazil Holding (SGBH). 2019. *Sistema de Transmissão Xingu-Rio.* YouTube, April 9, 2019. https://www.youtube.com/watch?v=RhSetRLvVEo.

Théry, Hervé, and Neli Aparecida de Mello-Théry. 2016. "O sistema elétrico brasileiro." *Confins* 26. https://doi.org/10.4000/confins.10797.

Vilela, Pedro Rafael. 2019. "Belo Monte liga última turbina e inicia operação completa." *Agência Brasil,* November 27, 2019. https://agenciabrasil.ebc.com.br/politica/noticia/2019-11/belo-monte-liga-ultima-turbina-e-inicia-operacao-completa.

Xavier, Philipe Pedro Santos, Elia Elisa Cia Alves, Andrea Quirino Steiner, and Fabíola Faro Eloy Dunda. 2018. "Brazil-China Energy Cooperation: Did BRICS Change Anything?" *JCIR* Special Issue (2018): 53–73. https://journals.aau.dk/index.php/jcir/article/view/2265/1787.

Vanity Projects, Waterfall Implosions, and the Local Impacts of Megaproject Partnerships

Consuelo Fernández-Salvador
and Maria Amelia Viteri

RAFAEL CORREA'S GOVERNMENT BEGAN construction of the Coca Codo Sinclair (CCS) dam in 2009. As Vásconez, and van Teijlingen and Hidalgo Bastidas discuss in this volume, the project was imagined in the 1970s, but only started construction fifteen years later (López 2009, 2). Working with the Chinese state Sinohydro Corporation, the construction of the project on geologically unsuitable land brought changes in the surrounding area, especially in the area of direct impact: El Chaco canton[1] and its administrative parishes. While there was concern regarding the environmental impacts of the CCS, the project raised expectations among local populations for economic growth and job opportunities, while also encouraging migration from all over the country.

The construction period between 2009 and 2016 saw the area thriving in terms construction-spurred economic activity. As heavy equipment became part of the everyday landscape, the construction sites and infrastructure work started to take shape, altering the landscape. Similarly, expectations of economic development, land speculation, and commercial investments increased among local residents, who believed the project to be a source of hope and opportunity.

Political imaginaries that romanticize mega-infrastructure projects abound around the world. This chapter, however, understands these projects as linked to colonial heteronormative state formations (Viteri and

Picq 2014), where epistemological framings of South-South cooperation are embedded in colonial, post-, and decolonial imaginings. In Ecuador, these imaginaries took shape within a political discourse that favored an extractive-based development model as a strategy for poverty reduction and redistribution (Davidov 2013; Bebbington and Humphreys 2011). In this context of neoextractivism and developmentalism (Gudynas 2009; Arsel 2012), investment in large infrastructure projects was key for the government of Rafael Correa between 2007 and 2017, as analyzed by Reyes Herrera and Delgado del Hierro in this volume.

We illustrate the central socioeconomic effects of these imaginings in local communities impacted by the dam. We reflect on the marginality and invisibility of Amazonian populations as manifested in the policies (or lack thereof) that have been exacerbated by the current pandemic. Our analysis is based on literature review as well as field work conducted in the CCS and Mirador projects (Fernández-Salvador 2018).

RISING AND FALLING EXPECTATIONS

Large infrastructure projects such as the CCS raise expectations at the national and local level. The project was supposed to start a transition to clean and noncontaminating energy production and to double the country's electrical capacity, generating 1500MW daily (Garzòn 2018, 84). To this end, the government signed a contract with Sinohydro Corporation, a Chinese state company, which would build the project.

A rise in business and economic activities and an influx of migrant workers characterized the period of construction between 2009 and 2016. This was accompanied by displays of wealth in and around the project, including four temporary external campsites and the construction of a system of transmission towers and lines. Besides the activities surrounding the CCS, other strategic projects such as oil extraction in the province contributed to the implementation of about one hundred development programs by the Ecuador Estratégico (Ecuador Estratégico n.d.) state company. As was the case in other provinces of the Amazon region, the modern, sophisticated, and highly technological schools (known as *millennium schools*) built by Ecuador Estratégico were considered to be emblematic projects by the Correa government (van Teijlingen and Fernández-Salvador Forthcoming; van Teijlingen and Hogenboom 2016). In the canton of El Chaco, the millennium school of Santa Rosa del Chaco was inaugurated in 2014 with much pomp and ceremony.[2]

In this context, expectations among the local population mainly concentrated on economic growth and local development. Ten years after construction began, however, the results were not all positive. The small town of San Luis provides an example. As explained by one local leader, this settlement was started by a group of farmers about fifteen years ago and expanded with the arrival of workers when construction of the CCS began (2009–2010). San Luis is part of the project's area of direct impact and was also the location of the San Luis Ventana 2 campsite. Due to migration caused by labor demands, residents of San Luis came from other towns and Andean provinces and even from Colombia (Polanco 2013, 63). The influx of workers and the construction of the campsite created temporary demands for room and board. People in the town and surrounding area adapted houses and invested in restaurants and small businesses. Once the campsite was completed six months later, however, the workers moved to it and took with them the economic activity that had started to develop.

This is one example of how a project like the CCS can alter the social and economic dynamics of an area of impact without improving the well-being of its residents. It is important to emphasize that in its initial stages, the CCS offered employment to thousands of workers, both directly and indirectly. Between 5,000 and 6,000 people worked on the Project. Approximately 3,000 from El Chaco were hired by Sinohydro for construction, while another 3,000 were hired by third-party companies to do infrastructure work.[3] While agriculture is one of the most important activities in the area, once hiring began, people abandoned their fields, believing the company would provide a stable salary.

Another source of income derived from the project in the early stages was land sales. While these cash flows were tempting, these were dependent on the construction of the project. Job and service demands created an "economic enclave" (Cardoso and Faletto 1978) that encouraged people to shift from productive and subsistence activities to those dependent on the project, all while fostering migration. Once the project was complete in 2016, the need for labor dropped dramatically. At the present time, there are only about 150 workers in the CCS, working in shifts of fifty (CELEC 2020). As expected, this cutback impacted local people, particularly those who had sold or abandoned their land in order to work for the CCS, as well as those who had migrated to the area (Polanco 2013).

In interviews held in the municipality of El Chaco and the town of San Luis, it became clear that residents and authorities alike feel that "the project has left more promises than solutions."[4] Disenchantment is widespread among residents, who perceive the current state of things as far short of the promises originally made to them.

To overcome this situation, residents opt for investing in and improving agricultural and cattle activities and further developing the tourism industry. The region is already known for adventure tourism, including kayaking and rafting in the Quijos River, which came to a halt due to the CCS closing and/or limiting access to tourists and local residents (Polanco 2013, 97). Workers in the town of Borja reported that fewer tourists come to stay in the area because the routes for kayaking and rafting have been limited by the project. In an area where 87 percent of the territory is located in protected areas (Polanco 2013, 98), an incentive for tourism, there are restrictions as the CCS is considered to be an area of national security.

The chronology does not end well. After the CCS was inaugurated in 2016, a series of unfortunate events took place, and many of the pieces of the hydroelectric project started collapsing. As early as 2014, workers and technicians noticed cracks in the dam. Years later a government report showed that there were 7,648 fractures in the machinery due to the use of low-quality steel and the poor welding done by Sinohydro (Casey and Krauss 2018). The most dramatic events took place at the beginning of the COVID-19 pandemic in February 2020, when the San Rafael waterfall imploded (*El Comercio* 2020; Paz 2020b). As Vásconez explains in her chapter in this volume, the "hungry waters" ate away at the Quijos River's banks and a month later, the riverbed collapsed and provoked ruptures in adjacent oil pipelines, impacting the economy of Ecuador and causing long-term environmental damage (*Mongabay Latam* 2020; Pallares 2020).

The physical and environmental disasters and infrastructure damage demand further reflection on the local "economic development" scenario discussed above. Once the construction of the project was finished, promises of development, economic growth, investment, and jobs collapsed. Even the highly publicized millennium school looks deteriorated. Many students have gone back to community schools.

What is behind the technical problems, disastrous events, and unfulfilled expectations? In the following section, we will explore the "rise and fall" of the millennium schools in Ecuador, in order to analyze the shift in political agendas as well as the financial debacle of the Moreno administration.

MILLENNIUM SCHOOLS AS VANITY PROJECTS

Unidades Educativas del Milenio (UEM), roughly translated as "millennium schools," are, according to the Ministry of Education's website, "high-level experimental public educational institutions, based on innovative technical, pedagogical, and administrative concepts, a benchmark for new public education in the country." The Correa government's rhetoric around these schools focused on the promise of free public education through megaconstructions with state-of-the-art infrastructure and technology. Millennium schools were set against community schools: President Correa noted that his government would close community schools, which he called "precarious schools" and "poverty schools."[5]

Millennium schools have been analyzed by social scientists like Torres (2017) as "social frauds" and definitely not an educational model to follow. Torres talks about illusions driven by the promises of the millennium schools: the fantasy of standardized and innovative education understood as a path to modernity. As Drouet points out, millennium schools served only 2.4 percent of students in the public education system in 2017 (2019). Drouet illustrates how the construction of a "modern" educational infrastructure, by itself, does not improve student performance or the quality of education.

The framing of UEM schools as mega-infrastructure allowed for a discourse shaping them as part of a historical vindication of rights. In the case of the Amazon, the government emphasized that oil royalties financed the projects. An article by journalist Jaime Giménez talks about "schools for the forgotten" and looks at the Nuevo Rocafuerte and Yasuní UEM schools (Giménez 2016). Both suffered from lack of teachers, lack of infrastructure maintenance, and the cancellation of bilingual intercultural education programs. Despite this, a rhetoric of redistribution claimed, as a supposed victory, that 20 percent of the existing UEM in Ecuador were located in the Amazon[6] and that places such as El Pangui, strongly impacted by the Mirador Project, also had a UEM (*El Telégrafo* 2015a). There are no clear numbers on how many UEM are still operating.[7]

Due to the enormous costs of megaschools, the new government started building the so-called Unidades Educativas Siglo XXI (twenty-first-century schools) with prefabricated materials provided by China Railway Corporation. Another policy was the reopening of smaller community schools. This is the case of Santa Rosa del Chaco, whose director reported that about two hundred students left because the community intercultural schools, originally located in or close to communities, were allowed to reopen by current President Moreno. In January 2019, the government announced that it would reopen one hundred community schools each year until the end of its administration. Nevertheless, of the community schools it had promised to open in 2019, the Ministry of Education only opened sixty-one, with an investment of US$2.2 million dollars (Machado 2020).

THE POLITICS BEHIND COCA CODO SINCLAIR

The construction of large infrastructure and extractive projects such as the CCS, Mirador, and the millennium schools were part of the post-neoliberal nationalist agenda of Rafael Correa. Correa saw large-scale oil and mineral extraction as key to this new agenda of social welfare and redistribution (Hogenboom 2012; Arsel and Avila 2011). However, while extractivism was considered crucial to increase the production of wealth and achieve higher levels of development (Arsel, Hogenboom, and Pellegrini 2016), the long-term goal of Correa's administration was to change the country's productive matrix: to transition from an economy based on resource extraction and export to one that privileges diversified production, knowledge capacity, biodiversity, and eco-efficiency (Secretaría Nacional de Planificación y Desarrollo 2012). The goal was to change the productive matrix and solve the energy crisis through the construction of hydroelectric projects such as the CCS (Lopez 2009, 3). In this scenario, megaprojects located in thirteen provinces were considered strategic and, as such, the earnings and royalties produced by them should have benefited the local populations in those provinces (Fernández-Salvador 2018, 216).

Correa's program had important political and symbolic implications. By prioritizing social programs and investing in public infrastructure, the government portrayed large-scale mining as necessary and desirable to improve the conditions of local people and achieve *Buen Vivir*.[8] Oil extraction and projects such as the CCS were considered key in contributing to local development and generating wealth to be invested in programs and infrastructure work. The CCS and Mirador Project became emblematic, with China as the main lender. Infrastructure work at all levels saw capital investments and booming economic activity in the area, which increased expectations among local population.

More recently, President Moreno's handling of the COVID-19 pandemic pushed economic and social austerity as well as prioritizing control over epidemiological surveillance. According to the Social Observatory of Ecuador (2020), there have been US$1.336 billion cuts in social programs. Five hundred thousand people are newly unemployed and 200,000 have fallen into underemployment. Extractivism has not stopped during the pandemic.

In May 2020, President Moreno announced the elimination of the fuel price subsidy, cut salaries for public officials by 16.66 percent, and continued with the suppression and merger of state entities and public companies. Moreno's government faces a governance crisis at all levels, as exemplified by irregularities in the purchase of medical supplies (España 2020); documented cases of bodies of COVID-19 victims that got lost in hospitals of the public health system (CDH 2020); and massive protests against economic policies (*BBC Mundo* 2020). Economic, cultural, political, and social inequality in Ecuador has been aggravated not only by the pandemic but by the political decisions of the current government.

THE OIL SPILL AND 2020 SPREAD OF COVID-19 IN THE AMAZON

This chapter has emphasized the effects of government policies on local Amazonian populations as part of larger epistemological framings and discourses. The following are some concluding remarks regarding the marginality of these communities in the context of the CCS and the global pandemic.

The current state of affairs around the CCS has provoked reaction in the media and among environmentalists, nongovernmental organizations, and scientists. There has been concern about the technical details behind the catastrophic events beginning in February 2020 (Casey and Krauss 2018; Paz 2020b), as well as the political and economic implications (Pallares 2020) of the CCS. Our focus remains on the local and Indigenous communities. When the oil pipes collapsed on April 7 in the midst of the 2020 COVID-19 lockdown, news of the oil spill was obscured by the public health emergency. Furthermore, while the OCP (Oleoducto de Crudos Pesados—Heavy Oil Pipeline company) stopped on the evening of April 7, neither the company nor the government informed the people in the affected communities about the rupture. As discussed by Basantes (2020), the livelihoods of Amazonian Indigenous communities depend greatly on the rivers, which are also an essential aspect of Indigenous communities' cosmology.

In addition to the effects of the worst oil spill, Indigenous and mestizo communities face the threat of the COVID-19 virus: "The overlap of two crises in one of the world's most biodiverse hotspots has made a bad situation even worse" (Picq and Kohn 2020). In fact, the Amazon is among the most affected regions in the pandemic, facing severe outbreaks. While government efforts in Ecuador have been concentrated in urban areas where contagions are in the thousands, rural populations are in dire need of attention (Paz 2020a). Many Indigenous groups have decided to isolate themselves and return to their communities, but there is still the danger that mining and oil workers entering their territory might bring the virus (*Al Jazeera* 2020).

The series of events and disasters occurring around the CCS together with the ongoing public health emergency have only unveiled the deep structural and environmental racism of Ecuador. After fifty years of oil exploitation, Indigenous and marginalized mestizo people in the Amazon remain excluded. People's lives continue to be less of a priority than the resources extracted from their territory.

The latest news regarding the construction of a road in the middle of the Yasuni Park, very close to the territory of the Taromaneni and the Tagaeiri (both Indigenous groups in voluntary isolation) in the midst of the pandemic (Paz 2020b), is a sign of how little these human beings matter to the policies or practices of extractivism and developmentalism in postcolonial states such as Ecuador. As Bonilla showed in her chapter in this volume, this negligence is not only immoral and heartbreaking, it is also a violation of rights protected by Ecuadorian and international law.

NOTES

1. Ecuador has twenty-four provinces, divided into cantons. The mayor and the municipal council are the elected governing bodies in the cantons, which comprise urban and rural parishes.

2. https://educacion.gob.ec/unidades-educativas-del-milenior/.

3. Municipality of El Chaco Employees, Personal Communication, March 3, 2020.

4. Municipality of El Chaco, Personal Communication, March 3, 2020.

5. https://youtu.be/7X1zHEkHQDU.

6. https://www.presidencia.gob.ec/la-amazonia-cuenta-con-el-20-de-las-unidades-educativas-del-milenio-construidas/.

7. Torres (2017) establishes a chronology that begins in 2008, when the first UEM was inaugurated in Zumbahua, Cotopaxi.

8. *Buen Vivir* or *Sumak Kawsay,* a Kichwa concept that can be translated as "life in fullness," was adopted as part of the political discourse of Correa's government and incorporated in the Constitution of 2008. For more on Correa's project, see Arsel, Hogenboom, and Pellegrini 2016; van Teijlingen and Fernández-Salvador Forthcoming; Fernández-Salvador 2018.

REFERENCES

Al Jazeera. 2020. "Escaping Coronavirus in Ecuador's Amazon." *The Take (Podcast).* July 27, 2020. https://www.aljazeera.com/podcasts/2020/07/27/escaping-coronavirus-in-ecuadors-amazon.

Amar, Paul. 2013. *The Security Archipelago: Human-Security States, Sexuality Politics, and the End of Neoliberalism.* Durham, NC: Duke University Press.

Arsel, Murat. 2012. "Between 'Marx and Markets'? The State, The 'Left Turn' and Nature in Ecuador." *Tijdschrift voor Economische en Sociale Geografie* 103, no. 2: 50–163.

Arsel, Murat, and Natalia Avila Angel. 2011. "State, Society and Nature in Ecuador: The Case of the Yasuní-ITT initiative." *NEBE Working Paper* 2, ISS/Hivos/USFQ/LIDEMA.

Arsel, Murat, Barbara Hogenboom, and Lorenzo Pellegrini (eds). 2016. "The Extractive Imperative and the Boom in Environmental Conflicts at the End of the Progressive Cycle in Latin America." *Extractive Industries and Society* 3, no. 4: 877–79.

Basantes, Ana Cristina. 2020. "Una mancha de petróleo que jamás se borra." *GKCity,* June 14, 2020.

BBC Mundo. 2020. "Coronavirus en Ecuador: las multitudinarias protestas por las drásticas medidas económicas y recortes de Lenín Moreno." May 26, 2020. https://www.bbc.com/mundo/noticias-america-latina-52814371.

Bebbington, Anthony, and Denise Humphreys Bebbington. 2011. "An Andean Avatar: Post-Neoliberal and Neoliberal Strategies for Securing the Unobtainable." *New Political Economy* 16 (1): 131–45.

Cardoso, Fernando, and Enzo Faletto. 1978. *Dependencia y Desarrollo en América Latina*. México: Siglo veintiuno.

Casey, Nicholas, and Clifford Krauss. 2018. "El gobierno ecuatoriano apostó por China para una represa que ahora se resquebraja." *New York Times*, December 24, 2018. https://www.nytimes.com/es/2018/12/24/espanol/ecuador-china -prestamos-represa.html.

CDH (Comité Permanente por la Defensa de los Derechos Humanos). 2020. "Informe cuerpos extraviados." June 10, 2020. https://www.cdh.org.ec/ informes/461-informe-cuerpos-extraviados.html.

CELEC. 2020. "Directorio completo de la Institución." https://www.celec.gob.ec/ ley-de-transparencia.html-directorio.

Davidov, Veronica. 2013. "Mining versus Oil Extraction: Divergent and Differentiated Environmental Subjectivities in 'Post-Neoliberal' Ecuador." *Journal of Latin American and Caribbean Anthropology* 18, no. 3: 485–504.

Drouet, Marcelo. 2019. "Evaluación de Impacto sobre logro y matrícula del programa: Unidades Educativas del Milenio." Master's thesis, FLACSO Ecuador. https://repositorio.flacsoandes.edu.ec/handle/10469/15903.

Ecuador Estratégico. n.d. "USD 106 millones han sido invertidos en obras de desarrollo en Napo." https://www.ecuadorstrategicoep.gob.ec/usd -106-millones-han-sido-invertidos-en-obras-de-desarrollo-en-napo/.

Ecuadorian Comptroller's Office (Contraloría General del Estado). 2018. *Examen Especial a la ejecución, terminación, liquidación y recepción de los contratos de construcción y fiscalización del Proyecto Hidroeléctrico Coca Codo Sinclair.* https://www.contraloria.gob.ec/WFDescarga.aspx?id=57460&tipo=inf.

El Comercio. 2020. "El Coca-Codo puede esfumarse en el río." April 13, 2020.

El Telégrafo. 2015a. "La Amazonía tiene su novena Escuela del Milenio." *El Telégrafo*, October 5, 2015. https://www.eltelegrafo.com.ec/noticias/sociedad/6/ la-amazonia-tiene-su-novena-escuela-del-milenio.

El Telégrafo. 2015b. "Regalías que generó el Proyecto Mirador en Pangui permitió la inversión en Proyectos Educativos en el Cantón." October 10, 2015. https://www .eltelegrafo.com.ec/noticias/politica/2/regalias-que-genero-el-proyecto-mira dor-en-pangui-permitio-la-inversion-en-proyectos-educativos-del-canton.

ENTRIX. 2009. *Estudio de Impacto Ambiental del Proyecto Hidroeléctrico Coca Codo Sinclair. Construcción de la vía de acceso al embalse compensador.* Quito: ENTRIX.

España, Sara. 2020. "Una oleada de casos de corrupción golpea Ecuador en medio de la pandemia." *El País*. June 4https://elpais.com/sociedad/2020-06-05/una-oleada -de-casos-de-corrupcion-golpea-ecuador-en-medio-de-la-pandemia.html.

Garzón, Paulina. 2018. "Implicaciones de la relación entre China y América Latina. Una mirada al caso ecuatoriano." *Ecología Política* 56: 80–88.

Giménez, Jaime. 2016. "Colegios para los olvidados de Ecuador." *El País*. September 6, 2016. https://elpais.com/elpais/2016/09/05/planeta_futuro/1473095204_176169 .html.

González, Mario Alexis. 2020. "Coca Codo Sinclair, el principal sospechoso de la erosión en el río Coca." *Primicias*, April 27, 2020. https://www.primicias.ec/noticias/economia/erosion-rio-coca-coca-codo-sinclair.

Gudynas, Eduardo. 2009. "Diez tesis urgentes sobre el nuevo extractivismo." In *Extractivismo, Política y Sociedad*, edited by Centro Andino de Acción Popular (CAAP) and Centro Latinoamericano de Ecología Social (CLAES), 187–225. Quito: CAAP.

Fernández-Salvador, Elena del Consuelo. 2018. "The Shuar and Large-Scale Mining in Zamora Chinchipe. A Study of Ethno-politics and the Struggle over Natural Resources." PhD dissertation, ISS-Erasmus University Rotterdam.

Hogenboom, Barbara. 2012. "Depoliticized and Repoliticized Minerals in Latin America." *Journal of Developing Societies* 28, no. 2: 133–58.

López A., Víctor. 2009. "No solo '. . . una forma inteligente de sembrar el agua para cosechar energía.'" Implicaciones del Proyecto Coca Codo Sinclair para la Amazonía Ecuatoriana." *Memoria del 5to Encuentro Nacional del Foro de los Recursos Hídricos*: 209–20.

Machado, Jonathan. 2020. "La fe no alcanzó para inaugurar las escuelas prometidas en 2019." *Primicias*, January 8, 2020. https://www.primicias.ec/noticias/sociedad/escuelas-rurales-comunitarias-comunidades/.

Miranda, Boris. 2019. "Coca Codo Sinclair: los problemas de la multimillonaria represa que China construyó en Ecuador." *BBC Mundo*, February 25, 2019. https://www.bbc.com/mundo/noticias-america-latina-47144338.

Mongabay Latam. 2020. "La erosión de la Cascada San Rafael rompe oledouctos y contamina el Río Coca." May 2, 2020.

Pallares, Martín. 2020. "Coca Codo Sinclair: ¿pagará la China por el inminente desastre?" *4Pelagatos*, April 20. https://4pelagatos.com/2020/04/20/coca-codo-sinclair-pagara-la-china-por-el-inminente-desastre/.

Paz, Antonio. 2020a. "Covid-19 llega a los indígenas waorani mientras que otros pueblos enfrentan nuevos problemas." *GKcity*, May 21, 2020.

Paz, Antonio. 2020b. "Ecuador: gobierno reconoce que la erosión de la cascada San Rafael podría afectar la hidroeléctrica Coca Codo Sinclair." Mongabay *Latam*, July 14, 2020.

Picq, Manuela, and Eduardo Kohn. 2020. "An Oil Spill in the Time of Coronavirus." *Al Jazeera*, July 14, 2020. https://www.aljazeera.com/indepth/opinion/oil-spill-time-coronavirus-200710101154552.html.

Polanco, Daniela. 2013. "Hidroelectricidad y Turismo en la Amazonía: El caso del Proyecto Hidroeléctrico Coca Codo Sinclair en el cantón El Chaco, provincia de Napo." Masters thesis, FLACSO-Sede Ecuador.

Secretaría Nacional de Planificación y Desarrollo (SENPLADES). 2012. *Transformación de la Matriz Productiva. Revolución Productiva a través del conocimiento y el talento humano.* Quito: Ediecuatorial.

Social Observatory of Ecuador. 2020. *Autoritarismo ante una pandemia que no da tregua.* https://www.covid19ecuador.org/analisis.

Torres, Rosa María. 2017 "Elefantes blancos: la estafa social de las escuelas del milenio." *Plan V,* April 3, 2017. https://www.planv.com.ec/historias/sociedad/elefantes-blancos-la-estafa-social-escuelas-del-milenio.

van Teijlingen, Karolien, and Barbara Hogenboom. 2016. "Debating Alternative Development at the Mining Frontier: *Buen Vivir* and the Conflict around El Mirador Mine in Ecuador." *Journal of Developing Societies* 32 (4): 1–39.

van Teijlingen Karolien and Consuelo Fernández-Salvador. Forthcoming. "¿La minería para el 'Buen Vivir'? Large-Scale Mining, Citizenship and Development Practice in Ecuador's Correa." *Latin American Perspectives.*

Viteri, María Amelia, and Manuela Picq, eds. 2014. *Queering Narratives of Modernity.* New York: Peter Lang.

"Yes We Do Exist": Ferrogrão Railway, Indigenous Voices in the Trail of Trade Corridors, and Building the Axis of a "Brazilian Pragmatist Policy" toward China

Diana Aguiar

AT THE END OF HIS first year in office in October 2019, Brazilian president Jair Bolsonaro embarked for China. Upon arriving in Beijing, he said he was not embarrassed to be there as he was in "a capitalist country." This weird caveat made sense in the context of justifying the change of tone Bolsonaro had adopted regarding China. During his presidential campaign, he had doubled down on anticommunist rhetoric. In February 2018, on a visit to Taiwan, he also declared that China was "buying up Brazil."

Bolsonaro's rhetorical shift was pragmatic. As Rodríguez's and Saggioro Garcia and Curty Pereira's chapters point out in this volume, China is Brazil's largest trading partner. Rural businessmen were concerned that the malaise between the Brazilian government and the Chinese, detailed by Zhou's chapter in this volume, would contaminate their business prospects, which are considerable. According to Zhou:

> In 2009, China became Brazil's largest trading partner. And more recently, in 2018, China-Brazil bilateral trade exceeded US$100 billion, with Brazil becoming the first country in Latin America to cross that monetary threshold with China. Over the past decade, Brazil's trade surplus with China accounted for about 40 percent of Brazil's total foreign trade surplus. China simultaneously became a significant source of investment for Brazil. (75)

The sheer size of the Chinese presence in Brazil and the promise of future investments led to pressure against Bolsonaro to abandon his ideological discourses with regard to the Asian country. Less than a month after the president's visit to Beijing, there was no lack of mutual praise for Sino-Brazilian relations at the Eleventh BRICS Summit in Brasília. There was also an unusual retraction. In a private meeting with the leaders of the other four BRICS (Brazil, Russia, India, China and South Africa) countries, the Brazilian president said that his criticisms of China during his presidential campaign did not reflect the truth.

This pragmatic shift involves not only the commercial aspects of the Brazil-China relationship but also investments. At the 2019 summit, Bolsonaro criticized the demarcation of Indigenous lands by previous governments, which he claimed would no longer take place. At the end of the meeting, Chinese president Xi Jinping stated that Brazil and China would continue to discuss an alignment between the Belt and Road Initiative (BRI) and the Investment Partnership Program. This "alignment" and its contentious relationship with Brazil's Indigenous policy are key to understanding the geopolitics of infrastructure that unites Chinese interests and those of Brazilian soy exporters, with the Brazilian Amazon as one of its most crucial backdrops.

The Investment Partnership Program is presented by the Brazilian government as the largest program in the world for leasing assets to the private sector. At the time of the Eleventh BRICS Summit, Bolsonaro was determined to guarantee the Chinese presence in Brazilian auctions. As positional stability is not a strong point of the current government, Sino-Brazilian harmony was short lived. As Zhang reports in this volume, it lasted until the outbreak of the COVID-19 pandemic in early 2020. After that, the political deterioration fermented by the Bolsonaro government's ineptitude made Sinophobic attacks (associating COVID-19 with the Chinese, à la Trump) an easy way for the president and his closest advisors to shift public focus from their inability to deal with the pandemic.

This is not a tension that is immune to reactions from supporters of the president. Many soy producers are concerned about losing parts of their main market. Furthermore, they want to resolve one of the biggest obstacles to their expansion and profit: the logistics infrastructure for more efficient transportation of soy to China (see Molina and Munduruku's and Oliveira's

chapters in this volume). The soy barons know that without Chinese investments, these infrastructure projects are not likely to get off the ground. This
is particularly the case with the most expensive, controversial, and important of these projects: the EF-170 railroad, better known as the Ferrogrão.

A DESTINY SET BY SOY?

At first glance, a rural businessman from the Brazilian state of Mato
Grosso, a Chinese family, and a Munduruku Indigenous village on the
Tapajós River (a tributary of the Amazon River) do not have much in common. However, a series of multiscale transformations turned soy into a
fraught topic for all of these stakeholders: it is the basis for profits for the
first, a change in alimentary habits for the second, and a threat to territorial rights for the third. This improbable interweaving wasn't created
by the grain itself; it is the result of its transformation into a commodity through a complex chain that includes corporate technological packages, computerized machinery, and transnational financial and logistical
schemes.

It was not always thus. The process of "conservative modernization"
that led soy monocultures to dominate the landscapes of central Brazil—
the "conquest" of the Cerrado (the Brazilian savanna) by soybeans—had
something of an air of the old US "winning of the west." The Brazilian state,
especially during the civil-military regime (1964–1984), dedicated itself to
this "conquest" through a violent process of expanding the agricultural
frontier, opening roads, privatizing land, promoting research, extending
credits, subsidies, and territorial (re-)arrangements. Even following the
redemocratization of the country in the 1980s, several normative adaptations—particularly the easing of environmental protection measures—have
continued to be carried out by the state under successive left- and right-wing
governments in order to promote the advance of the soy frontier.

SOY EXPANSION THROUGHOUT CENTRAL BRAZIL

The expansion of soy monocultures devastated the Brazilian savannah
over the last four decades, transforming the country into the world's largest soy exporter, controlling 42 percent of the global total. The exponential
increase in the participation of China in Brazilian global soy exports over
this period is reflected in a mutually dependent commercial relationship.

At the same time, agrarian transformations derived from this process have served as fuel for the intensification of enclosure in Brazilian agricultural frontiers. The Cerrado (especially in Mato Grosso and, more recently, its transitional areas in the Amazon and the so-called Matopiba) has been the main stage for this process. As these frontiers are distant from the established exporting ports of the Brazilian center-south, this process became a "logistical issue" for Brazilian agribusiness, driving political pressure for the implementation of new export routes.

NEW SOY ROUTES

As China became the main destination of the soy produced in Brazil, the Pacific took over from the Atlantic as the priority location of the commodity's largest trade routes. This was coupled with increasing consumption of other commodities by the Chinese—and more broadly Asian—market. Consequently, there has been an accelerated and unprecedented process of rerouting trade, with the Pacific as its backbone. As Zhang describes in this volume and elsewhere (Zhang 2017), this process is increasingly unfolding through a strategy of territorial control and hyperconnectivity designed by the Chinese state. The BRI is the greatest expression of this strategy.

The spatial reorganization of the metabolism of capitalism around China implies the redesign or reconfiguration of veins that allow commodities to flow. This is a phenomenon of global proportions that can be read as the expression in our time of the cyclical hegemonic disputes over the commercial dominion of strategic commodities. This cycle is the first marked by rising Chinese hegemony. The phenomenon is also part of the hegemonic impulse, in the hyperfinancial phase of the cycle (Bunker 2005), to resolve cyclical crises of overaccumulation through spatio-temporal fixes. This is what we are seeing with China and its "New Silk Road" (Harvey 1985).

Ultimately, appropriating territories is a central imperative of the continuously turning wheel of capital accumulation, as capitalist strategies constantly seek to annihilate space by time. This implies a constant quest to subordinate regions that follow different logics. The Tapajós Basin is being transformed into a "new soy route" as an Amazonian mirror of what the "New Silk Road" is on a geopolitical scale. Agribusiness sees the potential of the Tapajós to fulfill its self-proclaimed "logistical imperative": namely, to transport soy more efficiently from the agricultural frontiers in Central Brazil to soy's new priority destination, China. Based on the constitution of "corridors" as new types of proliferating "global territories," efficient flow management techniques seek to make each link in the supply chain productive (Mezzadra and Neilson 2013).

The transmutation of soy from a simple grain into a commodity is dependent upon its ability to travel. Between the harvesters in Mato Grosso and its final use as animal feed in China, soy needs to travel an immense distance at a cost that makes its production chain profitable. This ultimately means reducing the time it travels through space. This is where Tapajós's transformation into a soy route comes in.

But this is not the only outflow route being promoted by Brazilian rural producers. There are several other logistical corridors radiating from central Brazil, creating a "War of the Routes" in which projects are competing. Each of these serves the interests of a different (and even divergent) set of regional oligarchies and capital factions that seek to shape public infrastructure programs in a highly speculative dynamic (Aguiar 2019).

The new soy route projects competing in recent years can be characterized, roughly speaking, as those seeking a Pacific exit, crossing other countries in South America (bioceanic routes), and those seeking ports in the Brazilian North Atlantic (the so-called Northern Arc). Although the Pacific projects have mobilized public debate and historical-political imagery of Brazil as a regional power and promoter of regional integration, it has been the North Atlantic projects that have been consolidated into public programs. From these northern ports, soy flows through the Panama Canal and then across the Pacific.

These are not routes designed by a single government: they are projects that have been shaped over years of disputes and multiscale political negotiations, launched during previous governments, which shows the continuity of the "logistical reason" that guides public debate on infrastructure. Many of these projects have not been completed. In other cases, they have not even broken ground. This is characteristic of infrastructure megaprojects due to their size and their long-term returns on investment. These aspects are aggravated, however, in (semi-)peripheral countries and frontier regions. In the case of Brazil, they've also been negatively impacted by the deep political crises of recent years. Project and investment announcements must thus be taken with a grain of salt, understood as part of the speculative dynamic that is intrinsic to the War of the Routes (Aguiar 2019). Many of the existing highways that the current government's program intends to expand and grant to the private sector have a central role in expanding the flow of soybeans. Among the projects for new routes, there is an emphasis on railroads focused on the export of soy. The China Communications Construction Company (CCCC) signaled its interest in the auction for the West-East Integration Railway (FIOL) and Ferrogrão (in the Tapajós corridor) licenses before the return of Brazil-China tensions in the wake of the COVID-19 pandemic. All these projects, if carried out, would promote the expansion of soy production in Brazil, leaving a trail of devastation and violated rights along their routes.

THE TAPAJÓS LOGISTICS CORRIDOR

There is no more frantic axis of expansion than the set of routes that make up the Tapajós logistics corridor. The oldest of these is BR-163, one of the roads opened by the civil-military regime half a century ago. Connecting the state of Mato Grosso to Santarém, the road was designed to export agricultural commodities produced in central Brazil, particularly soy. It is symbolic of "conservative modernization" in Brazil's backlands, a process that has been marked by private and violent appropriation of common land, as well as the genocide of Indigenous peoples.[1]

To become a soy export route, BR-163 needed to connect to other routes that would lead to Brazil's North Atlantic ports. With the expansion of soy production in the north of Mato Grosso and the increase in Chinese demand from the 2000s on, trading companies such as Bunge and Cargill began to design and operate port terminals in Itaituba, where BR-163 connects with the navigable portion of the Tapajós River. Camoça and Hendler's chapter in this volume offers an overview of what this has meant for local communities. There are no accurate estimates of the investments being made in and along the corridor, but it is estimated that more than twenty ports may be operating in the region in the next decade (Aguiar 2017).

The Middle Tapajós around Itaituba is the epicenter of the overlapping routes and projects putting pressure on forest peoples. Among these, none is as controversial or as much of a priority for agribusiness as Ferrogrão. This ambitious railway project aims to transport 25 million tons in its first year of operation and, by 2050, to haul 42.3 million tons per year, mainly of soy and corn. The Mato Grosso Institute of Agricultural Studies even projected a 70 percent expansion in the state's soybean and corn crops in ten years if the railroad is built. Mato Grosso is currently responsible for one-third of Brazil's soy production.

The trains are expected to cross almost a thousand kilometers, right through the middle of the Amazon on the edge of several Indigenous Lands and protected areas (many of which will be reduced to allow the passage of the railway). It will also heavily impact upon Indigenous territories not yet demarcated by the Brazilian state. It should thus not be surprising that, at the BRICS Summit, Bolsonaro made a point of emphasizing his government's opposition to the territorial rights of Brazil's Indigenous peoples, as provided for in the current federal constitution.

The dialogues announced by Xi Jinping at the end of the same summit regarding the "alignment" of the Chinese BRI programs and Brazil's PPI (Investment Partnerships Program) are an example of China's pragmatic approach toward its "New Silk Road." Several Latin American countries joined the initiative, but Brazil's refusal does not mean that country is less attractive to investors. Contradicting the fears of imperialist schemes that surround the BRI, China has not imposed on Brazil any projects designed by Beijing.[2] The projects that are attracting Chinese capital have been designed and negotiated by local and national forces. China has adopted a diplomatic approach that recognizes this correlation of forces, seeking to align them with its own interests. This is certainly a more favorable posture to enlist Brazilian support.

In the case of Ferrogrão, the CCCC signaled its interest in competing in the auction that will grant the right to construct and operate the railway for sixty-five years. Such a bid would probably imply financing by Chinese public institutions. This is not the only possibility, however. There is a lot of speculation about how feasible construction costs will be, and Ferrogrão has a unique mix of capital interests that are considering the project.

The Pirarara consortium[3] (formed by Amaggi, LDC, Cargill, Bunge, and ADM) was at the forefront of the Ferrogrão proposal from 2012 until the project's absorption into the infrastructure program of the Dilma Rousseff government. The consortium is considering investing in the megaproject, something unusual for commodity trading companies. This fact draws our attention to the activism of rural capitalists in Mato Grosso in defense of the railroad. In 2018, the Association of Soybean Producers of Mato Grosso decided to create a fund for investment in the project. This is possibly more an act of political pressure, given that the total amount foreseen for the construction and the time it would need to be completed (about a decade) is enough to scare any producer who operates with cash flows driven by a harvest cycle. But if this financing scheme were to get off the ground, it would be something unprecedented in the world for a logistics project of this size.

For agribusiness, the project to transform Tapajós promises a priority export corridor, which already has a head start in its disputes with other routes. For the geopolitics of Chinese infrastructure, the project is part of a strategy of ensuring stable supply routes for strategic commodities and a massive spatio-temporal fix that China's overaccumulated capital needs. The Brazilian state—more and more at the service of a neoliberal accumulation regime (Dardot and Laval 2014)—is responsible for managing the disputing interests, channeling them into infrastructure programs, as well as regulating, securitizing, and making possible the Tapajós Corridor and other projects. For Indigenous peoples and traditional communities whose territories are along these new routes, it makes little or no difference whether the project is Chinese or funded by other sources of capital. It is undeniable that the spectacular rise in Chinese demand for commodities has promoted the expansion of Brazil's soy frontier and, more broadly, a process of redesigning trade routes that subjects certain territories to conflicts with logistics-driven capital. At the same time, the fact that Chinese companies are signaling interest in investing funds in this sort of thing may make feasible infrastructure projects that would otherwise be difficult to carry out. In this sense, soy has promoted the unlikely interweaving of conflicting destinies and dynamics revolving around the design of new logistical corridors. But, like a prophecy never fully realized, inscribed in these projects and their materialization are the inevitable encounters of different intentions and rationalities. These, in turn, produce destabilizing frictions (Tsing 2004).

IN THE WAY OF SOY: INDIGENOUS AND TRADITIONAL PEOPLES' TERRITORIES

The first meeting between non-Indigenous travelers in Tapajós and the Munduruku seems to have taken place in 1768, leading to the region being labeled as Mundurukania (Torres 2014). The Munduruku's presence is ancient. Some of the painted ceramics found in archaeological excavations are the "oldest known specimens of ceramic in the Americas, dating to approximately 8,000 BP" (Rocha and Oliveira 2016, 398) and have graphic styles that the Munduruku still paint on their own skins today. Relegating this ancestry to an endangered past, French traveler Henri Coudreau, who toured the Tapajós in 1895, asked:

> Who knows if the last Mundurucús, who are gradually becoming extinct in these increasingly deserted areas, will not survive long enough to see the passage of the first locomotives of the 'Grande Central Ando-Paraense'? (Coudreau 1940, 15; original spelling)

Contrary to Coudreau's predicted extinction, and as Molina and Munduruku's chapter in this volume shows, today the Munduruku are the most forceful resistance group opposing the megaprojects that seek to establish themselves in the region.

In January 2020, the group published a letter denouncing the multiple development schemes that threaten their lands. "The government is interested in expelling us in order to build large enterprises such as the Ferrogrão, hydroelectric plants, waterways, and ports to transport large quantities of soybeans and corn to China and Europe" (Ipereg Ayu Munduruku 2020). In March of the same year, Munduruku leader Alessandra Korap spoke at a public hearing of the Human Rights Commission of the Federal Senate, claiming that the government wants to "build Ferrogrão as if we did not exist in the territory. But we will say 'Yes, we do exist'" (TV Senado 2020). Territorial tensions in the Middle Tapajós are the result of a collision of territorialities—of state, capitalist, Indigenous, and riverine peoples—that have distinct and contradictory logics of space-time. These tensions reveal the illusions, rooted in assumptions of fluidity through frictionless space, that are inscribed in projects of capitalist accumulation. For state and capitalist territorialities, dependent on control and predictability in managing the movement of commodities through space, the Amazonian frontiers represent spaces to be domesticated along with the peoples of the forest. Those regions that are links in a supply chain are areas in which attempts are being made to impose flow control techniques. However, at every point in any logistics corridor, this operation is susceptible to different threats. In frontier regions, we see the most radical opposition of worlds: on the one hand, the modernity of the just-in-time supply chain and, on the other, the temporalities of peoples who have lived in dialogue with the cycles of nature, their potential, and restrictions for thousands of years. The resistance of Indigenous peoples and traditional communities to the new soy routes are symbolic of this conflict. In addition to the Tapajós Corridor, other logistical projects in various regions of Brazil are encountering fierce resistance to their implementation. The BR-135 duplication project in Maranhão has direct impacts on *quilombola* territories in the state, such as Santa Rosa dos Pretos. For Josicléa Pires da Silva, one of the main *quilombola* leaders, this type of project is a sort of a "death in life": they are "the white modernity that de-envelops; that cuts off living bodies—trees, streams, animals, and family nuclei—to lay hundreds of kilometers of inert asphalt and iron" (Mundo Preto 2017).

There is not necessarily any interest in Chinese investment in the BR-135 duplication project, but the road makes up a logistical corridor to the port of São Luís do Maranhão for Matopiba soybeans whose main destination is China. One of the ports under construction for the expansion of the complex, Porto São Luís, has the CCCC as a partner and is the focus of intense conflicts with artisanal fishing communities in Cajueiro. Oliveira's article in this volume offers an on-the-ground view of what the new port has meant to the residents of the traditional communities whose lands it has taken.

Quilombola and traditional communities are among the most threatened by projects for new soy routes, precisely because their territories are the result of centuries-old resistance to slavery, "white modernity," and subordination to "development" processes. They are territories that have managed, to some extent, to constitute themselves as autonomous spaces. They thrive in the "in betweens" of the agricultural and mineral frontiers and are seen as a potential "stock" of wealth in processes of spatial expansion of accumulation. As a reaction, the *quilombola* communities of Bebedouro and Araçá-Volta, in Western Bahia, threatened by another soy route project (FIOL), have denounced the violation of their Right to Free, Prior, and Informed Consultation (FPIC), in accordance with Convention 169 of the International Labor Organization (ILO). Railway building in the region brought devastation and disruption to *quilombola* ways of life. Since the railroad project has been on the national agenda, demarcation of *quilombola* territory has stopped. The railroad was designed to export soybeans from the Cerrado of Bahia through the port of Ilhéus. It is currently under the control of the Brazilian state, which is conducting construction via the Valec company. The railroad is scheduled to be offered up for private management after it is constructed, and the CCCC has shown interest in acquiring it. In the Lower Tocantins, other *quilombola* communities—Abacatal, Laranjituba, and Africa—are resisting ventures involving a port complex and the so-called Ferrovia Paraense railway. The state government of Pará signed a term of intent with the CCCC for railroad feasibility studies, which would combine the export of soy from the Cerrado and the Cerrado-Amazon transition area, as well as ores mined in the Carajás region. The route of this railroad would cross *quilombola* and traditional territories across eastern Pará. In reaction, *quilombola* communities put together consultation protocols in which they interpret the Right to FPIC based on their own political culture. These resistance processes[4] are examples of how the illusions of smooth logistics can be disturbed by on-the-ground realities. Taking place across multiple regions and landscapes, with different histories of territorial occupation, the resistances these projects generate add disobedience and insurgency to a destiny traced by soy, its logistics, and capitalist and state agents.

CONCLUSION

In December 2017, a group of Munduruku warriors armed with bows, their bodies painted with ancient graphic designs, prevented the public hearing on Ferrogrão in the city of Itaituba. They carried with them a banner that read "The Munduruku people say 'No Ferrogrão!' China: the soy you buy has Indigenous blood in it. At Tapajós, it will not pass. Water is life."

The encounter that gave rise to this Munduruku reaction may be the most intense representation of global connections (Tsing 2004) on Brazil's frontiers. Miles away, the soybean fields in Mato Grosso are the promise of modern agribusiness and high technology inscribed in the simplest of grains transformed into a commodity. To be a commodity inserted in global chains, soy must have its production process—including its transportation to China—operate smoothly. There can be no discontinuities or friction. Everything must be under control—military, legal, digital, territorial, and cartographic control.

But in the way of the soybeans are the Munduruku and other Indigenous peoples, *quilombola*, and traditional communities. The friction they impose hinders the logistical, financial, and capital planning of extraction operations. The frontier (Martins 2014) cannot be ignored because it causes failures in the operating system. Friction "refuses the lie that global power operates like a well-oiled machine" (Tsing 2004, 6).

While the projects of the geographic expansion of capitalist accumulation presuppose a smooth, flat, and frictionless terrain, the frontier serves as a reminder that no capitalist project runs in territories as they are in the pages of designs. As it causes friction, each project must also find a grip on these territories, interspersed by the cracks created by preexisting tensions and those caused by the project itself. Insubordinate and insurgent territorialities disturb—sometimes fatally—the most Cartesian of plans.

NOTES

1. Recognized by the National Truth Commission in its final report (2014), which investigated human rights violations during the dictatorship.

2. The notable exception is the Ferrovia Bioceânica Railway connecting central Brazil to the Pacific, via Peru. The project was an expression of Chinese influence and was included in a federal infrastructure program during the government of Dilma Rousseff. For many reasons, it seems to have been taken off the agenda (Aguiar 2019).

3. Led by the Amaggi company, owned by Mato Grosso ruralist and the world's largest soy producer, Blairo Maggi.

4. As part of long-term research on logistical corridors and territorial conflicts in Brazil, between 2015 and 2019, I visited the various territories mentioned in this work and talked with social leaders, attending meetings where the projects mentioned here were under debate. I thank these Indigenous peoples and *quilombola* and traditional communities for the trust in sharing their perspectives.

REFERENCES

Aguiar, Diana. 2017. *A Geopolítica de infraestrutura da China na América do Sul: um estudo a partir do caso do Tapajós na Amazônia brasileira*. Rio de Janeiro: FASE and Action Aid.

Aguiar, Diana. 2019. "As veias abertas para a expansão do capital: tensões territoriais no projeto de transformação do Tapajós em corredor logístico." PhD dissertation, Universidade Federal do Rio de Janeiro.

Arrighi, Giovanni. 2010. *The Long Twentieth Century: Money, Power and the Origins of Our Times*. London: Verso.

Bunker, Stephen. G. 2005. "Preface: Finding the Global in the Local." In *Globalization and the Race for Resources*, edited by Stephen G. Bunker and Paul S. Ciccantell. Baltimore: Johns Hopkins University Press.

Conab—Companhia Nacional de Abastecimento. 2020. *Acompanhamento da Safra Brasileira de Grãos 7*, no. 9 (June). Brasília: Conab.

Coudreau, Henri. 1940. *Viagem ao Tapajós*. São Paulo: Companhia Editora Nacional.

Dardot, Pierre, and Christian Laval. 2014. *The New Way of the* World: *On Neoliberal Society*. London: Verso.

Harvey, David. 1985. "The Geopolitics of Capitalism." In *Social Relations and Spatial Structures*, edited by D. Gregory and J. Urry, 128–63. Basingstoke, UK: Macmillan Education.

Ipereg Ayu Munduruku. 2020. *Carta Munduruku no encontro indígena na aldeia Piraçu, TI Capoto Jarina*. São José do Xingu (MT).

Little, Paul Elliott. 2001. *Amazonia: Territorial Struggles on Perennial Frontiers*. Baltimore, MD: Johns Hopkins University Press.

Martins, José de Souza. 2014. *Fronteira: a degradação do Outro nos confins do humano*. São Paulo: Contexto.

Mezzadra, Sandro, and Brett Neilson. 2013. "Extraction, Logistics, Finance: Global Crisis and the Politics Of operations." *Radical Philosophy* 178: 8–18.

Mundo Preto. 2017. "Escoando o produto do saque." http://mundopreto.com.br/escoando-o-produto-do-saque/

Rocha, Bruna C., and Vinicius Honorato de Oliveira. 2016. "Floresta virgem? O longo passado humano da bacia do Tapajós." In *OCEKADI: Hidrelétricas, conflitos socioambientais e resistência na bacia do Tapajós*, edited by Daniela F. Alarcon, Brent Millikan, and Mauricio Torres, 395–416. Brasília: International Rivers.

Torres, Mauricio. 2014. "De seringais, gateiros e garimpos: o Alto Tapajós e a resistência de suas gentes." In *Tapajós: Hidrelétricas, infraestrutura e caos*, edited by Wilson Cabral de Sousa Junior, 37–61. São José dos Campos: ITA/CTA.

Tsing, Anna. 2004. *Friction: An Ethnography of Global Connection*. Princeton, NJ: Princeton University Press.

TV Senado. 2020. "CDH—Impactos socioambientais do corredor logístico da Amazônia oriental," March 10, 2020.

United States Department of Agriculture. 2018. *Production Supply and Distribution Online- Custom Query. United States Department of Agriculture: Foreign Agricultural Service -Production, Supply and distribution*.

Zhang, Xin. 2017. "Chinese Capitalism and the Maritime Silk Road: A World-Systems Perspective." *Geopolitics* 22, no. 2: 310–31.

Green Marketing Extractivism in the Amazon: Imaginaries of the Ministry versus Realities of the Land

Maria Elena Rodríguez

THE PRESENT CHAPTER ANALYZES foreign direct investment (FDI) of Chinese companies in Brazil, particularly in two "sensitive" regions: the Amazon and the Brazilian Cerrado. We look at what are the projects, priority sectors, and impacts of these investments. Today, China is the main investor in Brazil and, in fact, in Latin America as a whole. Below, we analyze a series of investments made during the past ten years, collected and organized in the database of the China Panel of the BRICS Policy Center of the Pontifical Catholic University of Rio de Janeiro.[1]

In recent decades, cooperation between China and Brazil has been characterized by breakthroughs that attracted the attention of the international community (see Zhou in this volume). Brazil became the first country to establish a strategic partnership with China in 1993—a partnership that was upgraded to the status of "comprehensive" in 2012.

By 2009 China had become Brazil's largest trading partner, with bilateral trade exceeding US$100 billion in 2018. Although Chinese investments have slowed in Brazil due to the multiple political, economic, and health crises in that country, they are still significant, and nothing suggests that they are likely to disappear. More importantly, Chinese money is moving into new sectors and new regions of Brazil that are ecologically and culturally sensitive (as the articles by Molina and Munduruku, Felipe and Raimunda Costa, Aguiar, and Thomaz et al. in this volume detail).

CHINESE INVESTMENT IN LATIN AMERICA

During his visit to China in October 2019, Brazilian president Jair Bolsonaro pragmatically promoted bilateral relations between the two countries and invited Chinese companies to participate in Brazilian oil and gas auctions. This was a significant policy change, and Bolsonaro's about-face is a side-effect of Brazilian dependence upon China.

Despite what Bolsonaro said, China is not buying Brazil: Brazil is selling itself to China. More specifically, Brazil is offering up the Amazon and the Cerrado to China. This not only involves the expansion of the agricultural frontier and an increase in soybeans destined for the Chinese market; Brazil is presented as a playground for all sorts of profitable enterprise, particularly involving energy generation and transmission (see as Thomaz et al. in this volume). This is a continuous project that is on-going despite tensions between Beijing and Brasília. It engages state and municipal governments that make "pilgrimages" to China to showcase the business opportunities of the Brazilian north. Authorities promise tax incentives and land while cutting through the red tape of environmental licensing, just so they can see a project completed. As the governor of Pará said regarding his 2019 visit to China, the idea is to attract investments to the state (Secretaria de Comunicação Pará 2019).

Analyzing the spatial distribution of FDI projects since 2003, one sees a large concentration in the State of São Paulo (the largest financial and industrial center in Brazil). The number of projects and the robustness of investments in the Amazon and in the Cerrado biome are impressive, however. The Amazon has been undergoing rapid territorialization by national and international agents whose investments revolve around megaprojects (Castro 2016). These are similar to those that took place during Brazil's military regime, when the prospect of connecting the Amazon to the rest of the national economy through fiscal incentives and the creation of infrastructure took place. Today, "intervention" in the Amazon is occurring under the competitive capitalist insertion of the region into global productive and financial circuits.

No foreign presence in the Amazon has been as strong and broad as the Chinese today. The Amazon is strategic: the "vital space of the twenty-first century" (Amin 2015). This is not only due to its huge stock of natural resources, but also the wide-open opportunities of the region. In this new international dynamic, the Amazon has become a center of attention in the search for the resources needed to keep the global economy growing. For Porto-Gonçalves (2005), the Amazon is presented "as if it were certain countries' backyard," a "periphery of peripheral countries." This results in the region being globally understood as a "superlative natural resource reserve, which can be squatted, appropriated."

The projects we mapped between 2010 and 2019, both in the Amazon and in the Cerrado, Brazil's tropical savanna, show a predominant Chinese interest in the energy sector. In fact, of the thirty projects identified, twenty are in energy generation, transmission, and distribution infrastructure, and even in some wind and solar projects, especially with the installation of plants in the Cerrado. Investments total more than US$24 billion. The capital invested in these projects comes mainly from Chinese state-owned enterprises (SOEs), which have been acquiring a stake in new sector projects or in existing infrastructure.

An interest in entering and dominating the market, as well as the search for profit and the dissemination of a Chinese technological standard, led China to a deeper and wider expansion strategy in Brazil. Two highly competitive Chinese SOEs with great technical capacity have dominated investments in the Brazilian electric sector: State Grid (working in the energy transmission sector) and China Three Gorges (CTG, focusing on energy generation). Together, these two megacompanies are responsible for eleven of the fourteen investments (78.5 percent) in electricity in the Amazon and the Cerrado.

The largest investments in hydroelectric plants in Brazil are dominated by the CTG and its subsidiary, CTG Brasil, which has been operating since 2013. CTG Brasil is the second largest private energy producer in Brazil, generating 8.28 gigawatts. China also owns 15,761 km of transmission lines in Brazilian territory. Pride of place here goes to State Grid Brazil Holdings, which belongs to the State Grid Corporation of China and which, through Xingu Rio Transmissora de Energia (XRTE), controls the transmission line of the Belo Monte Hydroelectric Power Plant, extending from Pará to Rio de Janeiro. This project is worth R$8.7 billion and holds 2,500 kilometers of transmission lines.

Brazil follows the global pattern of Chinese investors in several countries, which is to command and control a certain sector. Chinese investors now collectively own about 11 percent of total power generation assets in

Brazil. China reigns over this segment as the largest energy distributor in Brazil today. Energy is a vitally important field for the Chinese. Without energy, larger projects are not feasible. The kingpin of the entire Amazonian geo-economic system revolves around the generation and transmission of energy.

China has made demands about energy from the moment its companies moved into the Amazon. This is the case, for example, of two planned railroads in the states of Pará and Mato Grosso (Ferrovia Paraense SA and Ferrogrão), both of which are fundamentally important for the exportation of soy production. These two railroads would lower the price of Brazilian soy. According to Deng (2009), Chinese multinational companies tend to acquire strategic assets: resources and capacities that can reinforce competitive advantages of the companies and of China in international expansion and the global market.

REGIONAL CONTEXT

Latin America is positioned in the world market as a major supplier of raw materials. On the demand side, China is currently the third largest consumer of gas and the second largest consumer of petroleum, while concentrating more than 30 percent of the global demand for raw materials such as copper, soy, iron, and steel. China is an essential trading partner for Latin America. But the relationship between China and Latin America is not limited to raw materials. Project financing and direct investment by Chinese companies are also important in the region and becoming more so. Only twenty years ago, financial relations between China and Latin America were practically nonexistent; now they are enormous. China has greatly increased its presence in the world since the 2000s, by promoting a strategy it calls "Going Global." This involves capital outflows that take the form of infrastructure projects, financing, and FDI.

The first significant change came in 2008, when the Chinese government launched a "white paper" on Latin America and the Caribbean (Ministry of Foreign Affairs 2008). This document pointed to China's growing strategic interest in the region due to the immense natural resources and agriculture outputs found there, which mesh with the demands of Chinese interests. The "white paper" identified four objectives related to improving political harmony between China and Latin America: economic cooperation and mutual gain, cultural relations, personal exchanges, and the general advance of the principle of a single, unified China. This last objective sought to reduce in number Taiwan's Latin American allies.

The second "white paper," published in 2016 (Ministry of Foreign Affairs 2016), reaffirmed the guidelines of the first, while bringing into play other strategic sectors such as infrastructure for agriculture, energy resources, and sustainability (renewable energy). Logistics and telecommunications, information, and communication were also touched upon. The Chinese government emphasized incentives for Chinese companies to invest in the region, allowing Latin America to progress and increase its capacity for autonomous development. Eighty-six percent of China's FDI in Latin America during the 1990s-2010s focused on raw materials.

China's share of total global FDI grew from the 2000s on, but it was only in 2010 that the country became a significant investor. In 2012, it became the third largest provider of FDI in the world, with around sixteen thousand companies controlling some twenty-two thousand subsidiaries in 179 countries, with an accumulated capital of US$530 billion (Chen and Perez Ludeña 2014). In 2015, China became the second largest global investor behind the United States, with a total investment value of US$145.7 billion, representing 9.9 percent of the world total (Ministry of Commerce 2010).

The "Going Global" program has been the main instrument promoting the internationalization of Chinese companies. It allows massive financing and preferential conditions from official Chinese financial entities, particularly the EximBank of China, as well as tax reductions, logistical support, and the facilitation of administrative processes involving direct investments abroad (Acioly and Leão 2011). Companies that invest overseas have no foreign currency purchase restrictions. Since 2008, the China Banking Regulatory Commission has allowed commercial banks to finance all types of acquisitions and transactions abroad. Financial institutions such as China Investment Corporation have thus decided to invest part of their assets in foreign projects, to the tune of around US$200 billion (Sevares 2015).

As stated by Dussel-Peters (2012), the Chinese government can do this because the Chinese companies with a capacity to invest are mainly state owned. If they are not, they must exist in an environment in which the central or local government controls the incentive systems, taxes, credits, and permissions needed to function. As a result, between 2000 and 2015, approximately 87 percent of Chinese investments in Latin America and the Caribbean had been made by SOEs while only 13 percent had been made by private companies (Gallagher 2016).

Chinese companies have expanded into a wide range of countries and industries. According to data from the Ministry of Commerce of the People's Republic of China (Mofcom), Asia receives almost three-fourths of Chinese FDI, with Hong Kong being the first recipient and the platform that channels most of these investments outward. Latin America and the Caribbean are the second largest destination, with investments predominantly made in financial centers (the Virgin Islands and Cayman Islands) that operate as investment platforms. Less than 10 percent of Chinese investments are distributed between Brazil, Peru, Venezuela, and Argentina (Dussel-Peters 2012).

Bernal Meza and Xing (2020) conclude that China seeks oil and mineral resources in Latin America and the Caribbean. Other analysts say that Chinese companies seek a long-term development strategy for the region. Still others (who take Brazil as a reference) show that China's FDI is mainly driven by market or trade opportunities.[2]

With regard to Latin America, official sources point out that Chinese FDI has grown significantly since 2010, a year in which it jumped to almost US$30 billion, a value equal to everything that China had invested in the region up to that moment. Nevertheless, these sources differ significantly in terms of the values they report. For example, ECLAC estimates a value of $6.9 billion in 2015 while Mofcom reports that $12.6 billion has been invested. Reports regarding amounts invested per country also differ greatly. According to Mofcom, the Virgin Islands and Cayman Islands captured 86.35 percent of Chinese FDI between 2010–2015. Meanwhile, ECLAC claims that Brazil and Peru received about 75 percent. This is because the Chinese system registers investment flows by initial destination. Operations carried out through third-party markets are thus difficult to trace. Transnational companies are acquiring increasingly complex organizational structures and often do not invest directly from their headquarters, using subsidiaries located in territories with tax advantages (CEPAL 2018). Chen and Pérez Ludeña (2014) explain that several purchases (stock packages of large companies, for example) have been made through tax havens or other destinations outside the two countries involved in an FDI. They are difficult to track without recourse to journalistic articles or statements by businessmen.

In Brazil, the situation is no different. The bond between China and Brazil is based on a broad commercial and investment relationship. After 2005, Brazil also became a significant destination for Chinese FDI, first in the commodities sector, then in a wide range of infrastructure projects. Up to 2009, Chinese direct investment fluctuated considerably. After that year it accelerated, seeing rapid growth in terms of value. In 2010, China became Brazil's largest source of investment. To exemplify the size of Chinese FDI in Brazil, let us look at 2010, when Brazil became the main destination for Chinese investments, receiving US$15 billion, which amounted to 15 percent of Brazil's total FDI that year.[3] Brazil accounted for about a quarter of the acquisitions made by China abroad during that year (SEAIN 2018). There was not only an increase in the amount the Chinese invested, however: Chinese companies from new economic sectors also arrived in Brazil. According to ECLAC (CEPAL 2018), from 2005 to 2017, Brazil received 55 percent of all investments made by Chinese companies in Latin America, with around US$54 billion invested in some one hundred projects (see Pedlowski, this volume, for details on where and how some of these monies were invested).

Up to 2017, for every R$10.00 that entered Brazil to buy a company or an asset, R$3.00 came from China. Chinese inroads in Brazil during this period amounted to R$60 billion. China became the country's largest foreign investor in mergers and acquisitions, surpassing the United States and other investors. In fact, it is worth noting that, until the end of the last decade, the most significant investments in Brazil came from the US. Between 2003 and 2019, China surpassed the US with an FDI in Brazil of US$71 billion as compared to the US's US$58 billion (despite US investments being spread over a larger number of projects). China intensified purchases of Brazilian companies in 2017: 12 percent of the companies sold that year had Chinese buyers in deals totaling US$8.5 billion, according to a study by the British consultancy Dealogic (2018). This movement was more intense than in previous years. Between 2009 and 2016, the share of Chinese investments in Brazil never exceeded 4 percent of the volume invested in mergers and acquisitions in the country. In 2017, however, 35 percent of the amount spent by foreigners on acquisitions in Brazil came from China.

US direct investments in Brazil are concentrated in the industrial sector, which represents 32 percent of investments since 2003. Other important sectors are financial services (15 percent), telecommunications (12 percent), and electricity (10 percent). The US share of investments in other sectors is relatively marginal (SE-CAMEX Ministério da Economia 2019). Since the mid-2000s, investments by Latin American companies in the region have also been "a growing phenomenon" (CEPAL 2012).

According to researchers from the Fundação Dom Cabral, "in 2006, more than 50 percent of the acquisitions of companies in Latin America were by Latin American companies themselves" (Almeida and Cretoiu 2008, 9), a situation that has radically changed since 2011, when there was a 50 percent reduction in "trans-Latin" FDI flows (CEPAL 2005).

If in 2017 Chinese direct investments in Brazil reached US$11.3 billion, by 2018 they dropped to US$2.8 billion due to uncertainties caused by the presidential elections, the anti-China rhetoric of future president Jair Bolsonaro, and expectations of changes in regulatory frameworks. As the country accounted for 42 percent of all investments in Latin America, the drop in flows to Brazil explains much of the -5 percent decrease in the region. A few industries showed growth in FDI flows after 2018, mainly those in extractive sectors. In 2019, Chinese investments in Brazil grew slightly.

Chinese FDI had previously been concentrated in agriculture, mining, and oil. Recent years have seen increasing investments in the energy and electricity sector. When analyzing Chinese investments since 2003, a clear and growing preference for the energy sector has been observed (SEAIN 2018).

While agriculture, mining, and oil extraction represent 3 percent, 7 percent, and 25 percent respectively of the total Chinese investments since 2003, the electricity sector alone represents 45 percent of the total value of these investments. In 2011, 33 percent of the resources involved in Chinese operations went into this area. This number then fell, reaching 2 percent in 2013, but it resumed growth from 2015 on, when energy generation and transmission in Brazil received large investments from Chinese SOEs. Auctions in the electricity sector in Brazil in 2016, 2017, and 2018 contributed to this growth.

Based on data from the American Enterprise Institute and the Commission for National Development and Reform (Puty 2018), 96 percent of

Chinese investments in Brazil between 2003 and 2017 involved the direct participation of SOEs. These included at least 52 investing companies from 2003 to 2017, 46 of which were public and limited companies with majority state shareholder participation. According to general secretary of the Brazilian Association of Chinese Companies, there are more than 300 Chinese companies investing in Brazil, 31 of which are among the Fortune 500 (Zhang 2020, 54).

The flows described above follow the global trend of Chinese investment, whose defining characteristic is the "investing company." Chinese investment firms are almost exclusively dominated by SOEs. According to China's Ministry of Commerce (2010), SOEs represented some 70 percent of China's global FDI in 2009. Since SOEs dominate the natural resources sector in China, they also dominate investment in resource-rich countries such as Australia, Canada, and Brazil, as well as in sub-Saharan Africa. All major Chinese transactions in the minerals, energy, and oil and gas sectors in Australia between 2006 and 2012 involved an SOE (Ritchie n.d.).

Investment was weak in 2019. Nevertheless, all the Brazilian pilgrims to China came home with promises and memoranda of intent. Initially 2020 looked to be promising. Brazil would once again be on the Chinese agenda. But the arrival of the COVID-19 pandemic dashed those expectations, aggravating the economic crisis underway in Brazil. Attracting foreign investment, especially in infrastructure, has become seen as way of accelerating Brazil's economic recovery—or, at the very least, softening its fall.

The best option in this scenario would be to resort to Brazil's newest friend and investor, China. This means that the Chinese presence in Brazil may become even more accentuated in upcoming years. Reductions in the country's regulatory burdens have facilitated the arrival of companies willing to reduce Brazil's logistical bottlenecks. Nobody is more interested than China in setting up an extensive infrastructure network in the Cerrado and in the Amazon. New roads and rail networks, supported by expanded energy grids, will facilitate the shipping of commodities such as iron ore and soybeans. But in Brazil, more minerals and more soy mean more trees felled, more Native peoples displaced. A diplomat from the Chinese embassy in Brasília said in August 2019 that Brazil has very restrictive environmental laws and that the incineration of the Amazon was "manufactured" (Ministry of Commerce 2010). While the entire world understood the deforestation of the Amazon and the Cerrado as an international crisis, China remained silent.

The current moment is thus decisive. The new wave of investment may bring more devastation, or it may be an opportunity for China to show environmental responsibility and ensure sustainable development of global resources. It is time for China to consider a different route of operations abroad by implementing an environmental policy that effectively monitors and controls the environmental and social risks associated with Chinese credit and investment activities.

NOTES

1. All data regarding Amazônia and the Cerrado cited in this text can be found on BRICS Policy Center-Painel China site, http://www.bricspolicycenter.org/painel-china/

2. Personal communication with Wangfei, 2020.

3. Data from the Painel China database.

REFERENCES

Acioly, Luciana, and Rodrigo Pimentel Leão. 2011. "China." In *Internacionalização de empresas: experiências internacionais selecionadas*, edited by Luciana Acioly, Luis Afonso Fernando Lima, and Elton Ribeiro. Brasília: IPEA.

Almeida, André, and Cretoiu, Sherban. 2008. "Internacionalização de empresas: a experiência brasileira e o contexto latino-americano." *Revista Dom* 2, no. 5 (March/June).

Amin, Mario Miguel. 2015. "A Amazônia na geopolítica mundial dos recursos estratégicos do século XXI." *Revista Crítica de Ciências Sociais* 107: 17–38.

Bernal-Meza, Raúl, and Xing, Li (eds). 2020. *China-Latin America Relations in the 21st Century: The Dual Complexities of Opportunities and Challenges*. New York: Palgrave Macmillan.

Castro, Edna. 2016. "Formação socioeconômica do estado do Pará." In *Formação socioeconômica da Amazônia*, edited by Edna Castro and Indio Campos. Belém: NAEA/UFPA.

CEPAL. 2005. "Balance preliminar de las economias de América Latina y el Caribe." Santiago de Chile: Cepal.

CEPAL. 2012. "O investimento estrangeiro direto na América Latina e Caribe 2011." Santiago de Chile: Cepal.

CEPAL. 2018. "O investimento estrangeiro direto na América Latina e no Caribe 2018. Documento informativo." Santiago de Chile: Cepal.

Chen, Taotao, and Miguel Pérez Ludeña. 2014. "Chinese Foreign Direct Investment in Latin America and the Caribbean." *ECLAC Series* LC/L.3785. http://

www.cepal.org/en/publications/35908-chinese-foreign-direct-investment
-latin-america-and-caribbean.

Chinese Government. 2008. "China's Policy Paper on Latin America and the Caribbean." http://www.gov.cn/english/official/2008-11/05/content_1140347.htm.

Dealogic. 2018. "M&A Highlights: Full Year 2018." https://www.dealogic.com/insight/ma-highlights-full-year-2018/.

Deng, Ping. 2009. "Why Do Chinese Firms Tend to Acquire Strategic Assets in International Expansion?" *Journal of World Business* 44: 74–84.

Dussel-Peters, Enrique. 2012. "Chinese FDI in Latin America: Does Ownership Matter?" BU Working Group on Development and the Environment in the Americas. http://www.redalc-china.org/monitor/2016-01-10-23-02-57/docu mentos-de-investigacion/205-dussel-peters-enrique-2012-chinese-fdi-in-latin -america-does-ownership-matter.

Gallagher, Kevin P. 2016. *The China Triangle: Latin America's China Boom and the Fate of the Washington Consensus*. Oxford: Oxford University Press.

Ministry of Commerce, People's Republic of China (Mofcom). 2010. 2009 Statistical Bulletin of China's Outward Foreign Direct Investment. http://hzs.mofcom.gov .cn/accessory/201009/1284339524515.pdf.

Ministry of Foreign Affairs of the People's Republic of China. 2008. *China's Policy Paper on Latin America and the Caribbean*. https://www.fmprc.gov.cn/eng/zxxx/t521025.htm.

Ministry of Foreign Affairs of China. 2016. *China's Policy Paper on Latin America and the Caribbean*. https://www.fmprc.gov.cn/mfa_eng/zxxx_662805/t1418254 .shtml.

Ortiz Velásquez, Samuel. 2017. "Inversión extranjera directa de China en América Latina y el Caribe, aspectos metodológicos y tendencias durante 2001–2016." *Economía Informa* 406.

Oliveira, Eliane. 2019. "Brasil é um dos países mais rigorosos nessas questões ambientais, afirma diplomata chinês." *Jornal OGlobo*. September 23, 2019. https://oglobo.globo.com/economia/brasil-um-dos-paises-mais-rigorosos-nessas -questoes-ambientais-afirma-diplomata-chines-23899850.

Porto-Gonçalves, Carlos Walter. 2005. *Amazônia, Amazônias*. São Paulo: Contexto.

Puty, Claudio A. C. B. 2018. *Estratégia de internacionalização de estatais chinesas e o Brasil*. Brasilia: IPEA.

Ritchie, Duke. n/d. "Chinese Outward Foreign Direct Investment." *China Go Abroad*. http://www.chinagoabroad.com/en/commentary/chinese -outward-foreign-direct-investment.

SEAIN—Secretaria de Assuntos Internacionais—Ministério do Planejamento. 2018. "Boletim de Investimentos chineses no Brasil No. 7." https://www.gov.br/econo mia/pt-br/centrais-de-conteudo/publicacoes/boletins/boletim-de-investimen tos-estrangeiros/arquivos/boletins-de-investimentos-estrangeiros-2013-china/ boletim-de-investimentos-chineses-no-brasil-7deg-bimestre-setembro-dezem bro-2018.

SE-CAMEX Ministério da Economia. 2019. "Boletim de Investimentos Estrangeiros—Países Selecionados." http://www.economia.gov.br/central-de-conteudos/publicacoes/boletim-de- investimentos-estrangeiros.

Secretaria de Comunicação Pará, Secom Pará. 2019. "Governo do Pará vai a China atrair investimentos para o Estado." *Agência Pará*. May 23, 2019. https://agenciapara.com.br/noticia/12910/.

Sevares, Julio. 2015. *China. Un socio imperial para Argentina y América Latina*. Buenos Aires: Edhasa.

Zhang, Xin. 2020. "Dedicar-se a servir de impulsionador da Cooperação sino-Brasileira" *Revista Nordeste* 14 (163): 54–55. https://www.mfa.gov.cn/web/zwbd_673032/gzhd_673042/P020200818133886565061.pdf.

PART 6
RACE, CLASS, AND URBAN GEOGRAPHIES

Steel Industry's Legacies on the Outskirts of Rio de Janeiro and White Brazilian Capital-State Alliances: A Feminist Approach

Ana Luisa Queiroz, Marina Praça,
and Yasmin Bitencourt[1]

SO FAR IN THIS VOLUME, the chapters on Brazil have mostly focused on the impact of megaprojects financed by the Chinese in the northern region of Brazil (Molina and Munduruku, Camoça and Hendler, Felipe and Costa, Aguiar, Rodríguez). Because the north of Brazil contains diverse and fragile social and physical ecosystems and is emphasized by the global mediascapes and imagescapes regarding Brazil, it is easy to forget, as Rodríguez reminds us, that China has significant interests in the industrialized southeast of Brazil as well. In this chapter, we will thus follow the electrical transmission lines discussed by Thomaz et al. in this volume, south from the Xingu to Rio de Janeiro, where energy is being harnessed by a series of new steel plants and Chinese enterprises.

For fourteen years, lives have been affected by Ternium Brasil's operations. Formerly the ThyssenKrupp Companhia Siderúrgica do Atlântico (CSA), Ternium Brasil is located in the neighborhood of Santa Cruz in the West Zone of the city of Rio de Janeiro. The installation and operation of the largest steel complex in Latin America has been altering the ways of life of the populations that have historically inhabited the region: some 217,000 people live there.[2] Today, the residents of this territory are on the margins of a highly polluting megaenterprise.

When analyzing Ternium Brasil and its relations with the territory that surrounds its installations, we can see a set of damages that can be qualified as "a standard package" of megaproject impacts. Women, especially Black women, are one of the most vulnerable groups in this scenario, as they already face hostile conditions arising from the patriarchal organization of society. These conditions are reinforced by the operation of the megaprojects in the territories to such a degree that we can say that these projects cause a sort of "repatriarchalization" (Queiroz and Praça 2020).

The objective of this chapter is to reveal the set of specific impacts on women caused by megaprojects, in this case, Ternium Brasil in Santa Cruz. We begin with women's perceptions as the base point for our analysis. Our contribution is directed toward the debate regarding socioenvironmental conflicts and the repertoires of resistance to capitalist, racist, and patriarchal models of development, in this case represented by the actions of the steel company and its allies.

Ternium's relationship with China in this case is less in the sense of investments or export, because the acquisition of steel is currently not China's focus. Here, we are more concerned with recognizing China's relevance as an actor contributing to the international maintenance of a model that impacts heavily on the lives of women. We analyze material collected by the Alternative Policies Institute for the Southern Cone in the Santa Cruz neighborhood, interviews,[3] journalistic articles, reports, environmental impact studies, and a related bibliography.

CHINESE BEHAVIOR IN LATIN AMERICA AND THE CARIBBEAN

The relationship between China and Latin American countries has attracted the attention of since the 2000s due to significant increases in trade flows and political exchanges between the Asian giant and the region. In Brazil, China entered the country through foreign direct investment, loans, and trade. Trade relations have become the most important field in this relationship since China has become Brazil's largest trading partner (Agência Brasil 2019). However, many diverse Chinese investments in Brazil have taken place over the past few decades (Garcia 2018).

When we look at the Chinese presence in Latin America and the Caribbean, we see that the region has become relevant to the Asian country's interests. From 2007 to 2018, Chinese investment in the region totaled around US$115 billion (Conselho Empresarial Brasil-China 2019, 21), with Brazil being the main concentration of these resources, absorbing 49 percent of them. In second place comes Peru with 19 percent, then Argentina with 10 percent, and Chile with 8 percent. In Brazil, the main destination of Chinese capital has been the energy sector with 53 percent of all investments, followed by mining (30 percent), agriculture (5 percent), and transportation, finance, and chemicals, each with less than 5 percent (Conselho Empresarial Brasil-China 2019, 24).

China's arrival has reinforced existing situations, mainly in the sense of reaffirming and contributing to the maintenance of the international division of production. The current model of capitalist, racist, and patriarchal development, which destroys traditional forms of life and common goods in the territories it colonizes while homogenizing and alienating forms of production, also serves Chinese interests. We thus understand that the impacts experienced by women in this scenario are related to megaprojects receiving investments by and selling products to China. So far, China's activities in Latin America and the Caribbean have not guaranteed any transformation in the relations of power and autonomy in the region, or on the impacts on the territories to which China allocates resources.

CASE OF TKCSA/TERNIUM BRASIL

CSA was built in 2006 and opened in 2010. It was initially managed by the German group ThyssenKrupp, which held 73 percent of its shares. The remaining 27 percent belonged to the Brazilian company Vale S.A.[4] Violations have been occurring since the construction of the steel complex began, extending to the present. Up until September 2016, the company operated via a conduct adjustment agreement (CAA).[5] The operating license granted by the State Environmental Institute (INEA) was not in full compliance with the conditions of the CAA (O Globo 2016). The relationship of the company with the state government of Rio de Janeiro ensured that CSA's noncompliance did not stop its activities. To the contrary, the company has enjoyed substantial municipal, state, and federal tax exemptions and benefits.[6] According to an article in O Globo (2016), "at the end of July of this year, the Public Ministry of the State of Rio de Janeiro sued to try to prevent the granting of the operating license without further analysis of the environmental impacts."

In 2017, the complex was sold by ThyssenKrupp to Ternium S.A. for €1.4 billion, changing its name to Ternium Brasil (Cavalcanti 2017). The steel-maker is part of the Techint Group (TG), a business conglomerate founded in Italy in 1945 that currently operates on a global scale. The group began operations in Latin America and the Caribbean in the 1950s. Today it is in some eleven countries, including China with its Tenova and Tenari projects. TG has annual sales of more than US$20 billion and employs around 57,000 people. In Santa Cruz, it annually produces 5 million tons of steel and has 4,100 employees. TG is a member of the entities in Brazil that control the country's steel, energy, and mineral sectors and that have a deep capacity for connecting with and influencing various spheres of the state. Their corporate website says "Ternium is the largest steelmaker in Latin America. We produce special steels with a focus on the customer, safety, and respect for the environment. The company has already invested R$11 billion in Brazil and is the largest shareholder in Usiminas, the main producer of flat steel in the country" (Ternium n.d.).

Despite publicly presenting itself as a company managed and financed by the German multinational Thyssenkrupp, CSA has a strong connection with Chinese companies, mainly the state-owned CITIC Group. Most of CSA's infrastructure was constructed under the coordination of some six hundred Chinese engineers (Scofield Jr and Batista 2007). Despite the partnership being announced as a successful integration of Brazil into international production chains, the result was disastrous from an environmental point of view. CSA has been accused of massive damage to the region, such as contamination of fishing grounds and illegal deforestation. Particulate material derived from the steelmaking process was released in the air and reached surrounding cities, with profound impacts on the health of the inhabitants. Thyssenkrupp blamed the Chinese: the structures responsible for the containment, built by CITIC, were not adequate and did not follow "International standards" (*Deutsche Welle* 2017). The accusations are similar to those made against the Chinese in other contexts and presented in Brito's chapter in this volume, in a racialized logic where the Chinese are associated with cheap products. CITIC is not only present at CSA, however. In 2017 alone, the company invested more than US$3 billion in the Brazilian agricultural sector, mainly in traditional products exported to China (Freitas 2017), and it still works with mining and heavy machinery.

SANTA CRUZ: LIVED IMPACTS OF A SACRIFICE ZONE

Santa Cruz is one of the neighborhoods with the lowest human development index in the city of Rio de Janeiro (0.742), with a majority Black population (65 percent according to the 2010 Brazilian Institute of Geography and Statistics census). The region has historically been marked by family farming, artisanal fishing, and shellfish collection. From the 1970s onward, it became an industrial district. This is when Ternium Brasil became established. The neighborhood is directly connected to Sepetiba Bay, a factor of paramount importance for projects in Santa Cruz and Itaguaí. This is where the steel mill's port and docks are located, giving it strategic importance in terms of transportation of commodities and steel exports (Instituto Pacs 2015).

The steelmaker's huge revenues do not create improvements in the lives of residents. CSA's activities have been characterized by violations of rights and impacts that affect health and work in the region. Organized resistance to the company has been ongoing for more than a decade, led by a collective of residents from the outskirts of Reta João XXIII, fishermen, and young people. This coalition has the support of civil society organizations, elected officials, public defenders and district attorneys, and FIOCRUZ, among other actors.

We have already mentioned some of the impacts of CSA's activities. Others will be mentioned further on that are directly related to women. These include impacts on ways of life, employment, and income. In particular, the local fishing grounds and associated enterprises have been largely shut down, causing the loss of jobs and income for the population. Tailings contamination has increased the mortality of fish and other marine species.[7] Then there is water consumption: Ternium consumes 1.5 billion liters/day or 570 billion liters/year: the equivalent of a city of 6.1 million inhabitants. Other negative impacts have been seen in other Latin American countries. In Argentina, the Techint Group has been accused of collaborating with state terrorism during the dictatorship; in Mexico, Indigenous peoples accuse Las Ensinas (a Ternium subsidiary) of association with a drug cartel in order to ensure the safety of TG's activities and the persecution of local leaders; in Guatemala, Ternium was indicated as of the sixteen companies that most violate workers' rights in Latin America.

IMPACTS ON WOMEN BY THE LARGEST STEEL MILL IN LATIN AMERICA

Capitalist, racist, and patriarchal development deliberately ignores the existence of antispatial society (Santos 1979). It is impossible to disassociate the material and symbolic marks inscribed on territories from the operations conducted within them that alter the landscape and the lives of residents. In Santa Cruz, the impacts experienced by women can be described in three general categories: economic, health, and violence.

Megaprojects such as Ternium Brasil move into territories claiming to promote development. They have a model specifically based on the exploitation of natural and human resources and on alienation and avoidance of responsibility for their actions. In the case studied here, as in others, women were largely excluded from the production process, which attracted men from other regions (and even from other countries). In an interview, resident Maria Regina de Paulo talks about how her expectations of jobs and life improvements through work have been frustrated: "Few people here have worked with CSA. They had to get people from outside to work there. For many, it was a dream that became desperation afterward."[8]

Women are on the margins of the "development" process created by CSA. Paid reproductive work, such as cleaning and cooking services, is almost their only opportunity to be included in the local labor market. This is work that, when obtained, is devalued in relation to other positions in the production chain, subsequently increasing women's economic dependence on men in their family circle.

CSA is accused of being responsible for raising CO_2 emissions by in 76 percent in the city of Rio de Janeiro (*Jornal O Globo and Jornal Extra* 2009). The pollution caused by the steel company exceeds the average recommended by the World Health Organization according to monitoring conducted by the Popular Health Surveillance Project in 2017 (Instituto Pacs 2017), through measurements made by the Martha Trindade Collective.[9] The increase in dust, silver rain, and other pollutants has direct impacts upon the health of women. Furthermore, by being more concentrated in activities related to cleaning and sanitation, these women are more exposed to the toxins concentrated on sidewalks, houses, and in the air:

> It's soot, all the time. It's impossible to fish. When we sweep the balcony and the sidewalk dust, all that dust comes out. . . . Before, I didn't get

home so much and didn't even see it, but a couple of days ago I swept the sidewalk and sat in the sun, it looked like there was glitter all over my body.[10]

In addition to high exposure to toxins, women suffer from the effects of housework overload:

The issue of megaenterprises such as the steel industry affects, most of the time (and in many ways), the homemaker, who is always managing [the house]. [This] is the woman and she always is greatly worried that a child will get sick and she will not be able to afford treatment. Then there is the issue of cleaning the house, which affects the women a lot because of pollution. This is the job that the woman ends up having to do: all the housework and still work outside the home. Many times, she is on her own, too, and I believe that this has great effects when it comes to care. And she ends up not taking care of herself, because she is always taking care of the people around her. The women I have contact with here live with this reality of taking care of other people a lot and they end up not taking much care of themselves.[11]

Overwork and a constant state of anxiousness are elements revealed by the Martha Trindade Collective in the daily lives of women in the neighborhood, directly affecting their health. This takes place in a context where neither the state nor the company contributes to the existence or maintenance of local public health facilities. Residents report respiratory, cardiac, skin, allergic, infectious, and inflammatory diseases, in addition to anxiety and depression disorders.

There was a time when I stopped working [outside the home] because I had an itch and I didn't know what it was. My eyes were very red, my mother couldn't breathe. . . . When I stayed at home with her in 2007, I saw what was happening. There were people dying and health problems. The health post had no doctor to take care of people. My mother was suffocating at home and we didn't know what was going on. They said "It's progress; things will get better." And it really didn't get better. It just made our situation worse.[12]

People get sick. My daughter is allergic. This week she is covered in red spots, with little red balls. And my nephew also has respiratory and skin problems. Fifteen, twenty years from now, everyone will have cancer in Santa Cruz.[13]

One of the challenges of registering these damages and making companies responsible is the invisibility of these women's work. The exploitation of reproductive work is fundamental to capitalist development, naturalized as a manifestation of care and love (Federici 2017).

Among the anxieties and fears that impact on the mental health of women in Santa Cruz has been the effects of the arrival of men from outside the neighborhood. This is a recurrent theme in interviews. According to the Federal Council of Engineering and Agronomy (Santos 2010, 236), the CSA project planned on hiring thirty thousand workers for its implementation. Although only about 2 percent of this workforce was made up of Chinese (Instituto Pacs 2017),[14] there was no strategic plan for their social integration with residents of the neighborhood. The sudden presence of a bunch of foreigners in a peripheral neighborhood with no prior history of tourism or interaction with foreign cultures directly changed people's daily lives. Physically and culturally different and unable to speak Portuguese, these Chinese were maximally visible as outsiders in Santa Cruz.

> When [the Chinese] arrived, there was a time when people said there were folks dressed in orange walking up and down behind the river, there. They started to say that there were Chinese in the TKCSA Works and that's how I found out [about their presence]. Because the people who lived nearby saw them.[15]

Just as in other megaprojects that involve a large male labor force hired from outside, the women and young people from Santa Cruz felt the need to become more alert on the streets: "There were these stories of rape, of having to be careful on the street.... Even more so because we were young at the time. I didn't understand these things very well, but I had to learn to deal with them, to be more careful with these things. That's how I remember the start of the company," recalls one of the young women of the Martha Trindade Collective.

Through the investigation of the patterns of specific impacts on women caused by megaprojects, it has been observed that the presence of men from other Brazilian states in the territory constitutes a risk and can directly increase violence against women, or at least cause this impression on women. Among the consequences of this male concentration are an increase in the number of rapes and unplanned motherhood, single motherhood, or denials of paternity generated by encounters with outside men. All of this works as mechanisms for the impoverishment of women (Queiroz and Marina Praça 2020).

This pattern, observed in Brazil when megaprojects are installed and operated, strengthens a culture of fear and caution among women, which can be reproduced and aggravated when those identified as outsiders are not from other states but from other countries. In the case of TKCSA's installation, given the pervading sexist violence of Brazilian society itself, many women are taught to fear "strange men" from infancy on. The perceived "invasion" of a community by men who have no local ties to it is often understood by local women as one of the most direct and violent impacts they suffer in the context of megaprojects.

In Santa Cruz, the beginning of construction intensified fears that already existed in a neighborhood historically neglected by the government:

> Aside from the fear of being among many men we don't know, which is a problem that was pointed out by our mothers (in my case only my mother), there is the normalization of the fact that van drivers are going out with girls our age. . . . But we knew who the men were that bothered the girls here. When men showed up that we did not know and had no idea of where they came from, it was more complicated. I was very scared because many of my friends were showing off, because the men themselves manipulate women by saying that they are "very mature," even though they were clearly under age and often not even with fully developed bodies.[16]

The woman quoted above demonstrates how these fears manifest in concrete behaviors in the community. Local women feel they know who the local "risky" men are. This is an important survival skill in a context where violence against women is rarely punished. A great influx of unknown men increases local women's sense of danger, exemplified in the quote by accusations of pedophilia and other sex crimes. This reaction could have been anticipated by the project's organizers and dealt with through community outreach projects and by reinforcing local women's organizations.

This engendered impact is not even considered when megaprojects of this sort are planned and implemented. Without the mediation of companies or the state in interactions between "outsider" workers and the local community, the vulnerability of women and foreign workers is simultaneously aggravated: the former related to patriarchy and the latter to xenophobia. Without proper research about cultural interaction, the presence of foreign workers and the impacts of the companies' production modes in the different territories where they operate may place communities and especially women and foreign workers in situations of risk.

By analyzing the contexts in which steel megaprojects operate, we can establish that their impacts are difficult to repair. In response to these impacts, women in Santa Cruz have been mobilizing to demand shares in the company and places at the policy-making table in the state. In an interview, Regina Marins recalls one of the demonstrations at the door of TKCSA, highlighting neighborhood mothers:

> I went to protest myself. I woke up one day at 5 am and I went with three mothers to the door of Colégio Japão, which is 50 meters away from the company's gate. We stopped at the gate and blocked traffic up Avenida Brasil. And that's how we managed to get the Chinese workers' buses out of there, because the way they were being parked, we couldn't send our children to school.[17]

In addition to street demonstrations, women and other residents mobilized through the legal system by filing lawsuits claiming financial damages as compensatory measures for the impacts caused by the TKCSA. Although justice is slow and the returns on lawsuits are not always positive, this is one of the ways women and other residents have recorded their stories and made them visible:

> I have a suit I filed with my mother because of a flood caused by a 90° deviation [in a watercourse] that they did. This diversion prevented the water from draining. The water came in and didn't go out. I had huge losses. I went to the courts with my mother and explained everything we had lost. When the flood happened, I was with my mother in Minas Gerais. I was her caregiver, and I was unable to return. The people who were here [at that time] said that the water entered the house and destroyed

everything. The house was closed for a month and sewage water was in here for a week. Whoever was here when it happened was able to clean the house, and those who weren't had to clean up afterwards. When I arrived back in town with my mother, I wanted to go back, but there was no way we could. We had to stay. We slept in the living room. Everything was rotten: the bed, the refrigerator. . . . It was the flood that ended everything here. We suffered from material losses and health problems. My mother became very ill and died in 2016, on February 3.[18]

To date, there have been four types of lawsuits filed against the company. The first sort, seeking individual remedial actions, totals 238 cases combined in a class action that brings together three elements: air pollution caused by the operation, structural impacts on housing, and flooding that occurred due to the manipulation of water courses. The second type of suit is an administrative improbity action filed by the Public Prosecutor's Office regarding the improper granting of environmental authorization for the complex to begin its preoperational stage. The third suit is a public civil action filed by the Public Ministry/RJ against Ternium Brasil, the State of Rio de Janeiro, the INEA, and the Municipality of Rio de Janeiro. Its objective is to prevent INEA from issuing the final operating license for the steel complex without first completing technical studies demanded by the state environmental licensing process. Finally, an action for collective redress has been filed by local fishermen against Ternium Brasil, alleging environmental damage caused by the complex.

CONCLUSION

Chinese investments and activities in Brazil and Latin America are structurally inserted in a capitalist, racist, and patriarchal model. The relationship between the case of Ternium Brasil and China is in this structural field. Steel production takes place in the economic sector that receives the greatest Chinese investments in Brazil, and the company in question ships part of what it produces to Asia. Additionally, the Techint conglomerate maintains activities in China through the Tenova and Tenaris groups.

Despite the indirect character of Chinese capital in the steel complex (via CITIC), we believe we must denounce this model and present the main impacts this type of project has on women's lives. These include loss of ways of living, work, health, and traditional identities.

Resistance to development megaprojects has historically been carried out by traditional communities in which women have great power. Women have also suffered differential and disproportionate impacts due to these projects. Women's struggles against large corporations need to be supported. Changes in the practices of megaprojects will only be possible through the radical transformation of the structural and structuring model of capitalist relations.

Complaints to the company; the formation of local, national, and international alliances; resistance by affected territories and bodies; participatory environmental monitoring; critical research; lawsuits—these along with many other activities are the ways that women, residents, fishermen, and young people have challenged megaprojects' untrammeled operations in the territories in which they live. These groups seek to exist in the midst of the transgressions and losses they experience by being forced to share space with a megaproject that follows an international logic of production and ignores existing laws, lives, and historical practices in the territories it colonizes.

NOTES

1. Researchers and popular educators of the Alternative Policies for the Southern Cone Institute (Instituto Políticas Alternativas para o Cone Sul–PACS).

2. Available at: https://www.data.rio/app/bairros-cariocas.

3. The interviews in this chapter are quoted with the permission of the interviewees.

4. Vale S.A sold its interests to ThyssenKrupp for US$1.00.

5. The CAA is an agreement that establishes conduct considered inappropriate by public defenders and civil organizations involved in a legal case.

6. The company received federal subsidies through the Banco Nacional de Desenvolvimento Econômico e Social, as well as being declared exempt from many taxes while generating credits that could be applied to others. At the state level, it received resources from Fundes and the deferment of its ICMS taxes. At the municipal level, it saw the reduction of its ISS quotas. The total value of all the financial inducements and incentives received by the company was around R$2.5billion.

7. Mulheres atingidas: territórios atravessados por Megaprojetos. Instituto Pacs, 2021.

8. Interview with Maria Regina de Paulo, 2020.

9. The Martha Trindade Collective is composed of youth from the Santa Cruz neighborhood of Rio de Janeiro. Its goal is to link actions and information in and

about the region to debates regarding health, the city, and the environment. The group was organized in 2017 through the Vigilância Popular em Saúde project that measured the air quality in the region together with FIOCRUZ.

10. Interview with Regina Marins, 2020.

11. Interview with Martha Trindade Collective, 2020. https://pacsinstituto .medium.com/mulheresterrit%C3%B3riosdeluta-a-voz-da-juventude-do-cole tivo-martha-trindade-em-santa-cruz-74bd279fe583.

12. Interview with Maria Regina de Paulo, 2020.

13. Interview with Regina Marins, 2020.

14. In addition to the absence of any planning geared toward better integrating workers into the region, TKCSA was denounced by the Public Labor Ministry in August 2008, due to the presence of 120 Chinese who were working without a labor contract.

15. Interview with Maria Regina de Paulo, 2020.

16. Interview with Collective Martha Trindade, 2020.

17. Interview with Regina Marins, 2020.

18. Interview with Maria Regina de Paulo, 2020.

REFERENCES

Agência Brasil. 2019. "China é o principal parceiro comercial do Brasil." https:// agenciabrasil.ebc.com.br/internacional/noticia/2019-11/china-e-o-principal -parceiro-comercial-do-brasil.

Cavalcanti, Glauce. 2017. "Ternium conclui aquisição da CSA e siderúrgica muda de nome Desembolso com a operação fecha em € 1,4 bilhão." *O Globo*, September 7, 2017. https://oglobo.globo.com/economia/ternium-conclui-aquisi cao-da-csa-siderurgica-muda-de-nome-21797404.

CEPAL. 2018. *Explorando nuevos espacios de cooperación entre América Latina y el Caribe y China*. Segunda Reunião Ministerial do Fórum da Comunidade de Estados Latino Americanos e China. Santiago, Chile, Janeiro 2018.

Conselho Empresarial Brasil-China. 2017. *Investimentos Chineses no Brasil 2016*. Rio de Janeiro: CEBC.

Conselho Empresarial Brasil-China. 2019. *Investimentos chineses no Brasil 2018—O quadro brasileiro em perspectiva global*. Rio de Janeiro: CEBC.

Deutsche Welle. 2017. "Como a ThyssenKrupp fez no Brasil um dos piores negócios da indústria alemã." https://www.dw.com/pt-br/como-a-thyssenk rupp-fez-no-brasil-um-dos-piores-neg%C3%B3cios-da-ind%C3%BAstria -alem%C3%A3/a-37697527.

Federici, Silvia . 2017. *Calibã e a bruxa: mulheres, corpo e acumulação primitiva*. Tradução: coletivo Sycorax. São Paulo: Elefante.

Freitas, Tatiana. 2017. "Citic vê Brasil como motor de crescimento após acordo com Dow." *Uol Economia*. https://economia.uol.com.br/noticias/ bloomberg/2017/12/12/citic-ve-brasil-como-motor-de-crescimento-apos-acor do-com-dow.htm.

Garcia, Ana Saggioro. 2018. *Investimentos da China no Brasil, África do Sul e Índia: arranjos institucionais, atores e impactos.* Rio de Janeiro: Instituto PACS/ ActionAid Brasil.

Instituto Pacs. 2015. *Baía de Sepetiba: fronteira do desenvolvimentismo e os limites para a construção de alternativas.* Rio de Janeiro: Site do PACS. http://biblio teca.pacs.org.br/publicacao/baia-de-sepetiba-fronteira-do-desenvolvimenti smo-e-os-limites-para-a-construcao-de-alternativas/.

Instituto Pacs. 2017. *Vigilância popular em saúde e ambiente em áreas próximas de complexos siderúrgicos.* Rio de Janeiro: Instituto Pacs, JnT, and FIOCRUZ. http://biblioteca.pacs.org.br/wp-content/uploads/2018/11/Relat%C3%B3rio -Final-Final.pdf.

Jornal O Globo and Jornal Extra. 2009. "CSA aumentará em 76% o lançamento de dióxido de carbono na atmosfera." November 5, 2009. https://extra.globo.com/ noticias/rio/csa-aumentara-em-76-lancamento-de-dioxido-de-carbono-na -atmosfera-194138.html e http://oglobo.globo.com/rio/mat/200...dioxido-de -carbono-na-atmosfera-914629793.aspJustiça.

Global and Instituto Pacs. 2017. *Relatório de Violações de Direitos Humanos na Siderurgia: o caso da TKCSA.* Rio de Janeiro: Instituto PACS e Justiça Global. http://biblioteca.pacs.org.br/publicacao/relatorio-violacoes-de-direitos-hu manos-na-siderurgia-o-caso-tkcsa/.

O Globo. 2016. "Rio de Janeiro concede licença de operação à siderúrgica CSA." September 29, 2016. https://oglobo.globo.com/economia/negocios/ rio-de-janeiro-concede-licenca-de-operacaosiderurgica-csa-20199990.

Queiroz, Ana Luisa, and Marina Praça. 2020. *Dos impactos à defesa: mulheres, corpos-territórios e direitos humanos.* Periódico Massa Crítica, Edição 75, Instituto PACS. http://biblioteca.pacs.org.br/publicacao/dos-impactos-a-defesa-mul heres-corpos-territorios-e-direitos-humanos/.

Santos, Milton. 1979. *Espaço e Sociedade.* Rio de Janeiro: Vozes.

Santos, Rodrigo Salles Pereira. 2010. "A Forja de Vulcano: siderurgia e desenvolvimento na Amazônia Oriental e no Rio de Janeiro." PhD dissertation, Universidade Federal do Rio de Janeiro.

Scofield Jr., Gilberto, and Henrique Gomes Batista. 2007. "Chinatown à vista." *Jornal O Globo.* February 2, 2007. https://www2.senado.leg.br/bdsf/bitstream/han dle/id/405332/noticia.htm?sequence=1&isAllowed=y.

Ternium. n.d. "Conheça mais a Ternium." https://br.ternium.com/pt/nossa -empresa.

Rio de Janeiro's Unruly Carbon Periphery: Community Entrepreneurs, Chinese Investors, and the Reappropriation of the Ruins of the COMPERJ Oil Port-and-Pipeline Megaproject

Fernando Brancoli and Wander Guerra

CHINESE PRESENCE IN RIO DE JANEIRO: FROM CITY HALL TO LOCAL LEADERS

In February 2021, Eduardo Paes, the mayor of Rio de Janeiro, celebrated the Chinese New Year under the eye of Yang Wanming, Chinese ambassador to Brazil. Paes stated that Rio was ready to be part of the "New Silk Road" and that the city is "open to investments, cultural exchanges and new ties with our 'Oriental brother.'" In his reply, Yang promised Beijing's support in the fight against COVID-19 across the state of Rio de Janeiro (Diário do Povo 2021).

Despite the warmth of these official speeches, another celebration that took place in the same week demonstrated how Chinese presence in the state of Rio de Janeiro is more complex than classical institutional and diplomatic relations can account for. In the city of Itaboraí and the community of Itaoca, about 50 kilometers from the capital of Rio, a group of about fifty people celebrated the reopening of a dock to handle oil tankers. Although more modest, this celebration was attended by representatives of Brazilian and Chinese oil companies, as well as local leaders.

The event is important for understanding the Chinese presence in Rio de Janeiro, as it represents the intermingling of the consequences of Beijing's influence on issues involving public security, racism, and the fragmentation of the Brazilian actors interested in dealing directly with China. Itaoca concentrates not only the ruins of the Rio de Janeiro Petrochemical Complex (COMPERJ), now in the process of being reconstructed with Chinese capital; it also brings together a complex network of subnational actors who are interacting directly with Beijing.

Chinese policy in Brazil, as demonstrated by Saggioro Garcia and Curty Pererira's and Aguiar's chapters in this volume, was historically built through relationships with institutionalized actors in the federal government, principally the Ministries of Foreign Affairs and Agriculture. Other authors in this volume such as Vasques have pointed out that over the last decade Beijing has also approached city halls and governors. Itacoa/COMPERJ shows that China has scaled its actions to include even more local actors, such as community leaders and groups. To date, there has been little reflection regarding this movement and how, in the medium term, it may represent a new Chinese tool in Brazil.

The Itacoa community in Itaboraí is currently led by organized groups often accused of being armed militias. Though these accusations have been denied (*O Globo* 2017), experts point out that criminal militias often use legitimate residents' organization to mask their activities. These militias are different from the drug trafficking groups that have become symbols of the state abandonment in Rio. They were created in the 2000s by ex-police and firefighters with the aim of "organizing" these spaces supposedly abandoned by the state (Rodrigues, Brancoli, and Amar 2017; Brancoli 2020). They maintain themselves by levying illegal taxes on the local population and selling drugs and weapons in this "stateless vacuum." Within this logic, formal institutions are presented as emanating from a unified actor—the state—which is usually presented as a solution to crises of governance. To the extent that the security dilemmas are caused by the absence or the malfunctioning of the state, the resolution of this crisis needs to occur through the restructuring of the state. In this view, the reconstruction of the state in Rio is made possible through Chinese investment.

CHINESE INVESTMENT IN RIO DE JANEIRO

As Rodríguez has pointed out in their chapter, China has been expanding its presence in Latin America since the beginning of the 2000s. In 2015, within the establishment of the framework of the forum between China and the Community of Latin American and Caribbean States, Chinese president Xi Jinping indicated that the Asian country would invest around US$250 billion in the region over the next decade. Between 2007 and 2018, China invested around US$115 billion in Latin America and the Caribbean (LAC), according to data from the China Global Investment Tracker.

The flow of Chinese investments in Brazil can be split into four phases. Up to 2010, Chinese companies were mainly interested in the commodities sector. From 2010 to mid-2013, Chinese investments shifted towards the industrial sector. The third phase was characterized by investments in services, notably by Chinese banks. Finally, the last phase began in 2014 with large investments in electricity and infrastructure. In this last phase—on which most of the Brazil-focused chapters in the present volume have focused—investments were made in areas with great growth potential, such as petroleum and gas, agribusiness, and technology. Pedlowski's chapter in this volume documents the chronology of China's interest in the Porto do Açu megaproject in Rio de Janeiro state. Initially conceived as a multinodal shipping, processing, and manufacturing site, Porto do Açu only gained significant Chinese investments after it became focused on oil and mineral exportation.

In 2018, Chinese investments in Brazil amounted to approximately US$3 billion. If we include announced investments, the total amount of Chinese investments in Brazil in 2018 reached approximately US$4.5 billion. But despite Chinese rhetoric, its contributions to LAC fell sharply between 2017 and 2018, as Rodríguez's chapter in this volume details. Data compiled by Boston University's Global Development Policy Center (2020) indicate a 58 percent decrease between the two years, emphasizing the irregular intensity of investments in the region. But even with fewer Chinese investments, Brazil continues to be a center of gravity for the Asian country's contributions to the LAC. Practically half of Chinese investments in the region between 2007 and 2018 were directed to Brazil. This is a considerably higher percentage than seen in Peru, the second largest LAC destination for Chinese investments, which received 19 percent of the total. Similarly, data compiled by the Latin America and the Caribbean China Network (Red ALC-China) corroborate that Chinese investments in the region have Brazil and Peru as the largest recipients, with amounts totaling US$48.5 billion and $15.7 billion, respectively.

Even with the drop in investments, Brazil has continued to be central to China, a situation that has persisted since 2010. According to data presented by the Chinese Embassy, the States of São Paulo and Rio de Janeiro have concentrated most of China's investments. Rio, according to the same source, has received 10 percent of all Chinese investments as compared to the other twenty-six Brazilian states.

As Baptista (2016) points out, Chinese investments in Rio have always been large, increasing from 2010 on. Between 2001–2012, according to UNCTAD (2019), based on Ministry of Commerce (Mofcom) data, these flows increased, especially between 2003–2010, when they jumped from US$7 million to US$487 million. With regard to the ways Chinese investments enter the state of Rio de Janeiro, various projects have been identified in the automotive, steel, and energy sectors. Mergers and acquisitions were predominantly carried out by Chinese state-owned companies, both in terms of the volume of capital invested and the number of projects. This data supports our statements regarding Rio de Janeiro's new role as a base for supplying resources to China. When we consider the mode of entry (mergers and acquisitions), the sector entered (energy), the reason for the investments (a search for resources), and the large number of projects involved, we gain a picture of the inflow of Chinese capital in the state, mostly coordinated by Chinese central state-owned companies, that conforms to new territorialities active in the process of Rio's territorial restructuring.

Baptista (2016) argues that these projects allow us to understand the state of Rio de Janeiro in a context in which China seeks to ensure control of strategic resources. The author identifies the large Chinese state-owned companies involved in this process. The survey described in this chapter identifies investments by three other Chinese companies: CR Zongshen, Wuhan Iron Steel Group, and Northern China Railway.

Chinese investments in Rio must be understood as part of the city's long-term dynamics. Rio de Janeiro was the capital of the Empire and later of the Republic of Brazil, but its status waned from the 1960s on, with the transfer of the capital to Brasília. This period also saw Rio supplanted by São Paulo as Brazil's primary industrial center. The fall of the city's prestige has only increased along with its problems of violence and deindustrialization.

It is in this context that investments linked to oil and gas extraction began from the 2000s on. The discovery of large oil reserves along the coast of the state represented an increase in Rio's exploitable natural resources and an improvement in the city's (inter-)national image. This context must be understood because Chinese investments cannot be comprehended only in terms of the entry of new companies and capital into Rio. The Chinese presence is part of a greater rebirth of the city and state. Both the Chinese government and the leaders of Rio de Janeiro have expressed appreciation of this dimension. In advertising published in 2009 in Rio de Janeiro newspapers, the Chinese Consulate claimed that China was "investing in the best city and the best people in the world." Then mayor of Rio de Janeiro Eduardo Paes said in an interview that "the arrival of Chinese companies was a clear sign of prestige and the development of [the city's] image in the world" (Possa 2021).

Optimism also overflowed among the general population, mainly with regard to promises of new jobs and the development of hitherto poor regions. It is within this structure that COMPERJ developed.

COMPERJ: INVESTMENTS AND RUBBLE

COMPERJ bears the marks of the changes that have occurred in the first decades of the twenty-first century in Brazil and Rio de Janeiro. Here, we will address three of these.

During the 2007–2014 period, the company was an important symbol of the new developmentalism[1] being implemented by the Workers' Party (PT), which had taken power in 2002. As part of the Growth Acceleration Program (GAP),[2] the company incorporated important elements of the development project as it was then conceived of by the PT: public-private partnerships, state investments in strategic sectors, and the exploitation of commodities.

Thanks to a favorable situation in the international market (with increases in prices for commodities and partnerships with countries like China) the new developmentalism succeeded during the first decade of the century . . . at least partially.

When it began in 2007, the first phase of the PAC emphasized modernization of Brazil's petroleum sector. This period saw one of the largest investments in Petrobras's history. COMPERJ was envisioned as producing various petroleum products in an attempt to generate added value, despite intensifying the Brazilian economy's dependence on raw materials export.

Additionally, investments in COMPERJ and its associated ventures sought to attract private investments—both national and international—as an integral part of Brazil's economic growth (Marquezino and Araújo 2014; Vieira 2015; Rodrigues and Salvador 2011). Here we have the first meaning of COMPERJ: a symbol of the success of Brazilian developmentalism and the economy in the first decade of the twenty-first century.

A second component of COMPERJ's tangle of changing meanings was that the company also represented a widely discussed phenomenon called "the war of places," where regions, cities, and territories are subjected to the logic of market competitiveness and fight to attract investments (Barral Neto, Passos, and Silva Neto 2008).

It is important here to go back a bit and understand that between the 1960s and 1990s, the state of Rio de Janeiro saw its prestige erode both nationally and internationally. In this scenario, a need arose in the late 1990s and early 2000s to make Rio de Janeiro—and especially its metropolitan region—attractive to foreign and national capital. From 2002 on, a rare alignment occurred between the federal, state, and municipal governments. The federal government decide to bring public investments back to Rio de Janeiro, mainly in the form of infrastructure, to make the state and metropolitan region competitive once again. The territory of Rio de Janeiro thus became the stage for several large strategic projects (Vieira 2015; Cepemar Consultoria and Meio Ambiente 2007).

COMPERJ's location is permeated with contradictions, however. Itaboraí, a satellite city east of Rio, was the location chosen for the complex (Faustino and Furtado 2013). Allegations were made that the project was thus channeling opportunities toward the Metropolitan Region of Rio, despite the fragile environment that would surround the complex.[3]

CHINA AND COMPERJ: AN UNRULY CARBON PERIPHERY?

The abandonment of COMPERJ's construction and the entry of Chinese investors must be understood within the context of the return to systemic crisis in the state of Rio de Janeiro. This materialized in growing popular discontent, particularly due to the previous unrealized promises of development and employment. The fact that the city of Itaboraí was chosen for the installation of the petrochemical center generated even more commotion, as it was an area with historically high poverty rates.

Within this context, it is not surprising that the announcement that Chinese companies were interested in resuming the COMPERJ project generated a lot of attention. In July 2018, Petrobras announced a business agreement with China National Petroleum Corporation International (CN-PCI), a CNPC subsidiary, for the construction of a refinery at the site. As previously mentioned, China already had indirect investments in Rio de Janeiro's petroleum and gas systems. For example, it had been operating in the city of Campos since 2003. But COMPERJ was China's first explicit joint venture in the metropolitan region. The optimism lasted for just over a year. In September 2019, the two companies concluded that the completion of the refinery was not economically attractive.

This did not mean, however, that Beijing was leaving COMPERJ completely. CNPCI opened a direct line to community leaders from Itaboraí. According to the leaders heard by the authors, China had a "genuine" concern for the well-being of the local population. These people made direct comparisons with previous investors, who were understood as focusing on profits. It is still too early to affirm whether this perception will expand to other Chinese investments in Brazil, but it is peculiar how China has already created a narrative about its social concerns.

This is relevant when we note that the project's objective is mainly to guarantee the construction of a gas pipeline in lower Guanabara Bay, connected to the Duque de Caxias refinery. The Chinese goal at this point seems to be maintaining control of essential commodities through a new strategy. China now positions itself as a state concerned with local populations and community dynamics. We can thus see a change from the period in which Beijing negotiated with governments. Today, in the context of a serious economic crisis with political leaders reorienting Brazilian alliances, the Chinese government has not abandoned its objectives in the region. It has, however, expanded the range of actors with whom it will negotiate. This is not, therefore, an abandonment of institutional channels to guarantee investments, but an understanding of the diversity of agents involved in such projects and their differing expectations.

It is interesting to think about these movements through Mitchell's (2011) reflections on "carbon democracy." Mitchell's eponymous book is not a study of "democracy and oil," but of "democracy like oil." In it, Mitchell treats fossil fuels not as a commodity, but as an industrial complex interacting with social and technological components. This perspective guides Mitchell in his exploration of the impact of fossil fuels on political systems. Economics, "the central object of democratic politics in the West," emerges as an abstraction, escaping the limits of the material universe. Likewise, Mitchell argues that petroleum infrastructure should not be seen as mechanisms that guarantee oil supplies and prices, but also as a manifestation of power dynamics and politics.

The North-South dynamic itself is part of the power relations that materialize in the oil trade. Mitchell pointed out that over the nineteenth and twentieth centuries, Global North oil companies limited oil production and slowed the development of industry in developing countries, building an American-European monopoly. As a result, they also "impeded the ability . . . to build effective methods for advancing egalitarian political claims" (2011, 86) in colonies worldwide. Restrictions on oil production and development in these colonies resulted in populations unable to take advantage of their natural resources and unable to exercise political will, (re-)generating the claim that said populations were "in need of development." An example of this sort of discourse can be seen in Gustavo Oliveira's chapter on Amazonian entrepôts in this volume, where local resident's supposed lack of ability to generate political will justifies their abuse/tutelage by metropolitan companies. Behind this rhetoric was the "need for materials unavailable in industrial regions," as well as the need for safe oil transportation. The need to sustain the empire in these terms was heightened by World War I.

China's connections to local leaders are part of a dynamic in which Beijing acts more assertively in terms of its economic policy in Brazil. Previously, China has kept distant from debates in Brazil. Since 2020, however, this has changed. With the arrival of diplomats who are younger and aligned with the "wolf warrior" style of leadership, China's performance has become more mediatized and assertive. It is important to understand that this is not a question of replacing the strategic actors with whom Beijing is engaged, but of engaging with a wider range of actors who have the capacity to meet China's strategic objectives. Added to this is the maintenance of the Chinese discourse that, unlike those of the countries of the Global North, Chinese investment tools respect sovereignty and local development. The first wave of investments in Itaboraí represented a more traditional model of development, where the exploitation of commodities did not consider the impacts on local communities or the possibility of making technology and wealth spread horizontally. Today's grammar is one of investments focused on the communities that surround the spaces that are to be exploited. It is too early to say whether this discourse of horizontality and reconstruction will materialize into concrete projects, but China's recent diplomatic and media movements deserve to be recognized.

The economic and health crises currently raging in Brazil are changing the constellation of internal political forces and opening windows of opportunity for international actors to act more assertively in the largest country in South America. In the specific case of China, this has become visible in terms of media narratives and investment strategies. At the current moment, China is clearly signaling that it intends to act at different levels of government and with different levels of leadership in Brazil. Although these changes are still underway, it is already possible for us to assume that they will change the way Brazil and China interact.

NOTES

1. A model of economic development structurally based on neoextractivism, characteristic of the PT government in the first decade of the 2000s (Bresser-Pereira 2010; Lima 2011; Mattei 2011; Branco 2009; Sampaio 2012; Svampa 2011; Acosta 2011; Milanez and Santos 2013).

2. The set of investments by the federal government in logistics, urban, and energy infrastructure that sought to resume and execute major development projects throughout Brazil.

3. The area of influence (Area Directly Affected, Area of Direct Influence, and Area of Indirect Influence, according to RIMA) of the Rio de Janeiro Petrochemical Complex contains seventy-four Natural Conservation Units. In addition, the region's water scarcity, the fragility of the Guanabara Bay ecosystem, the arrival of new urban settlements, and possible sources of contamination were not considered (Soares 2012; Cepemar Consultoria and Meio Ambiente 2007; Moyses 2010; Andrade Filho et al. 2015).

REFERENCES

Acosta. A. 2011. "Extrativismo e neoextrativismo: duas faces da mesma maldição." In *Descolonizar o imaginário: debates sobre o pós-extrativismo e alternativas ao desenvolvimento*, edited by G. Dilger, M. Lang, and J. Pereira Filho, 46–85. São Paulo: Editora Elefante. Fundação Rosa Luxemburgo.

Andrade Filho, J. M., E. B. M. Barros, C. N. Francisco, A. C. Di Maio, and I. O. Pires. 2015. *Diagnóstico dos instrumentos legais de gestão territorial da área de influência do Complexo Petroquímico do Rio de Janeiro—COMPERJ*. September 2015.

http://marte.sid.inpe.br/col/dpi.inpe.br/sbsr@80/2008/11.17.23.28/doc/3447-3453
.pdf.

Baptista, T. J. 2016. "Os investimentos da República Popular da China no estado do
Rio de Janeiro: novas territorialidades no processo de reestruturação territorial fluminense no início do século XXI (2010–2013)." PhD dissertation, Universidade do Estado do Rio de Janeiro.

Barral Neto, J. F., W. S. Passos, and R. Silva Neto. 2008. "O petróleo como grande
financiador da 'Guerra de Lugares: o caso dos municípios da Bacia de Campos."
RJ. *Cadernos IPPUR* 22, no. 2 (August/December). http://www.ippur.ufrj.br/
download/pub/caderno_2008_2.pdf.

Branco, R.C. 2009. "O novo-desenvolvimentismo e a decadência ideológica do es-
truturalismo latino-americano." *Revista Oikos* 8, no. 1. http://www.revistaoikos
.org/seer/index.php/oikos/article/viewArticle/132.

Brancoli, Fernando. 2020. "Coronavirus Puts Criminal Governance at a Crossroads: Parastate Authority Creeps Further into Everyday Life in Rio de Janeiro's
Favelas as Militias Seize the Pandemic to Expand Their Control." *NACLA Report on the Americas* 52, no. 3 : 246–251.

Bresser-Pereira, L.C. 2010. "Do antigo ao novo desenvolvimentismo na América
Latina" http://www.bresserpereira.org.br/papers/2012/12.Do_antigo_ao_novo
_desenvolvimentismo.pdf.

Coelho, B. H. S, C. L. Loureiro, M. A. Irving, and D. G. Soares. 2015. "Conflitos entre o COMPERJ e a gestão de áreas protegidas: o Mosaico Central Fluminense
como possibilidade de enfrentamento a impactos socioambientais de grandes
empreendimentos industriais." *Revista Desenvolv. Meio Ambiente* 35: 259–73.
http://revistas.ufpr.br/made/article/view/42103. Accessed on: 01/14/2016.

Cepemar Consultoria and Meio Ambiente. 2007. *RIMA–Relatório de impacto ambiental. Implantação do Emissário Terrestre e Submarino do Complexo Petroquímico do Estado do Rio de Janeiro–COMPERJ.* Rio de Janeiro: Petrobras.
https://petrobras.com.br/lumis/portal/file/fileDownload.jsp?fileId=8A6E0796
4136B60A0141605BFDFE70FC.

Diário do Povo Online. 2021. "Embaixada Da China No Brasil Realiza Evento Online Do 'Ano Novo Chinês 2021.'" February 8. http://portuguese.people.com.cn/
n3/2021/0208/c309809-9817482.html.

Faustino, C., and F. Furtado. 2013 "Indústria do petróleo e conflitos ambientais na
Baía de Guanabara: o caso do Comperj." *Relatório da Missão de Investigação e
Incidência.* Plataforma Dhesca—Relatoria do Direito Humano ao Meio Ambi-
ente. Rio de Janeiro.

Global Development Policy Center. 2020. *China-Latin America Economic Bulletin
2021 Edition.* Boston: Boston University. https://www.bu.edu/gdp/2021/02/22/
china-latin-america-economic-bulletin-2021/.

Lima, S.C. 2011. "Da substituição de importações ao Brasil potência: Concepções
do desenvolvimento 1964–1979." *Revista Aurora* 5, no. 7 (January). http://www
.marilia.unesp.br/Home/RevistasEletronicas/Aurora/4castrolima34a44.pdf.

Marquezino, G. M. S., and J. Araújo. 2014. "Uma análise da inserção do programa de aceleração do crescimento (PAC) no distrito de Itambi/Itaboraí-RJ e suas implicações no contexto socioambiental." *Revista Movimentos Sociais e Dinâmicas Espaciais* 5, no. 3. http://www.revista.ufpe.br/revistamseu/index.php/revista/article/view/95.

Mattei, L. 2011. "Gênese e agenda do 'novo desenvolvimentismo brasileiro.'" In *IV Encontro Internacional da Associação Keynesiana Brasileira (AKB)*. Rio de Janeiro: *Anais eletrônicos*. http://www.ppge.ufrgs.br/akb/encontros/2011/10.pdf.

Milanez, B., and R. S. P. Santos. 2013. "Neodesenvolvimentismo e neoextrativismo: duas faces da mesma moeda?" http://www.ufjf.br/poemas/files/2014/07/Milanez-2013-Neodesenvolvimentismo-e-neoextrativismo-duas-faces-da-mesma-moeda.pdf.

Mitchell, T. 2011. *Carbon Democracy: Political Power in the Age of Oil*. London: Verso.

Moyses, Y. 2010. "COMPERJ e unidades de conservação: contradições no território." In *I Congresso brasileiro de organização do espaço e X Seminário De Pós-Graduação em Geografia*, 1: 5858–78. Rio Claro: UNESP.

O Globo. 2017. "Chineses Planejam Investir Pelo Menos R$ 32 Bi No Rio." https://oglobo.globo.com/economia/chineses-planejam-investir-pelo-menos-32-bi-no-rio-21598090.

Petrobras. 2007. *Relatório de Atividades*. http://www.investidorpetrobras.com.br/pt/relatorios-anuais/relatorio-de-administracao.

Petrobras. 2015. *Relatório da administração*. http://www.investidorpetrobras.com.br/pt/relatorios-anuais/relatorio-de-administracao.

Possa, Julia. 2021. "Iniciativa Chinesa, 'Maior Programa De Infraestrutura Do Mundo' Mira Brasil." Poder360, November 15. https://www.poder360.com.br/brasil/iniciativa-chinesa-maior-programa-de-infraestrutura-do-mundo-mira-brasil/.

Rodrigues, T. A., and E. Salvador. 2011. "As implicações do Programa de Aceleração do Crescimento (PAC) nas políticas sociais." *SER Social* 13, no. 28: 129–56. http://repositorio.unb.br/bitstream/10482/9689/1/ARTIGO_ImplicacoesProgramaCrescimento.pdf.

Rodrigues, Thiago, Fernando Brancoli, and Paul Amar. 2017. "Global Cities, Global (In) Securities: An Introduction." *Contexto Internacional* 39, no. 3: 467–476.

Sampaio, P. A. Jr. 2012. "Desenvolvimentismo e novo desenvolvimentismo: tragédia e farsa." *Serv. Soc. Soc.* 112: 672–88. http://www.scielo.br/scielo.php?script=sci_arttext&pid=S0101-66282012000400004.

Soares, D. G. 2012. "Conflito, ação coletiva e luta por direitos na Baía de Guanabara." PhD dissertation, UFRJ/IFCS.

Svampa, M. 2011. "Extrativismo neodesenvolvimentista e movimentos sociais: Um giro ecoterritorial rumo a novas alternativas?" In *Descolonizar o imaginário: debates sobre o pós-extrativismo e alternativas ao desenvolvimento*, edited by G. Dilger, M. Lang, and J. Pereira Filho, 140–71. São Paulo: Editora Elefante. Fundação Rosa Luxemburgo.

UNCTAD. 2019. *United Nations Conference on Trade and Development. World Investment Report 2019: Special Economic Zones.* New York: United Nations. https://unctad.org/system/files/official-document/wir2019_en.pdf.

Vieira, T. W. M. 2015. "Novo desenvolvimentismo e conflitos ambientais: o Complexo Petroquímico do Rio de Janeiro e os pescadores artesanais da Baía de Guanabara." Master's thesis, Universidade Federal do Rio de Janeiro.

From Cheap Credit to Rapid Frustration: China and Real Estate in Rio de Janeiro

Pedro Henrique Vasques

THE YEARS FOLLOWING the outbreak of the Brazilian economic crisis between 2013 and 2014 have been marked by a decrease in public and private investments, reducing the possibilities open to Chinese capital. One of the alternatives that has tried to guarantee the permanence of the Chinese presence in Brazil during this crisis was the channeling of financial resources toward real estate projects. This emerged in a scenario characterized by a drastic reduction in public investments and the weakening of large companies in the construction sector as a result of corruption convictions. In Rio de Janeiro, Chinese resources have become a means of maintaining the dynamism of the real estate sector. However, the deepening of the crisis and the complicated requirements for access to international credit have made these partnerships largely unfeasible, killing private-sector optimism.

This chapter looks at an area of Chinese investment that is otherwise not discussed in this volume: attempts by Chinese investors to enter the real estate sector in Rio de Janeiro via civil construction during the second decade of the twenty-first century. Sino-Brazilian partnerships in agricultural, infrastructure, and industrial projects with public and private actors during the 2000s are widely known, as the chapters by Rodríguez, Molina and Munduruku, Oliveira, Camoça and Hendler, Felipe and Costa, and

Thomaz et al. in this volume have documented, as are the denunciations of human rights violations that have been linked to these projects.

The analysis presented below is based on information obtained from Chinese investors in Brazil, as well as from document collections on the subject. The chapter has been divided into three sections in addition to introduction and conclusions. In the first part, we describe the Rio de Janeiro "bonanza" between the years 2003 and 2012, when there was a rise in civil construction stimulated by public investments. In the second section, we look at the events between 2013 and 2016, highlighting Brazil's political and economic crises as a window of opportunity for Chinese investments in the real-estate sector. In the third section, we analyze key episodes that took place between the 2016 and 2020, explaining the collapse of the optimism associated with the promises of state reforms and the deepening of the political and economic crises. We hypothesize that, even in the face of uncertainties caused by COVID-19, the Chinese will probably maintain their investment plans in Latin America and especially in Brazil, aiding possibilities for access to cheap credit for several sectors, especially civil construction, to reemerge.

2003–2012: GROWTH AND BONANZA

In 2003, there was a significant change in the Brazilian political scenario with the election of Luiz Inácio Lula da Silva of the Workers' Party (PT) as president of Brazil. In Rio de Janeiro, however, the first decades of the 2000s saw the decline of the Democratic Party and the limited electoral strength of the PT in the state (2003–2018) and municipal (2009–2018) elections. These were dominated by the Brazilian Democratic Movement Party (PMDB), one of the largest and most solid conservative blocks in the country. In 2006, however, the PT chose to form an alliance with the PMDB as a strategy of resisting the fragility imposed upon the PT by the political-legal developments associated with Penal Action 470.[1] At that time, Lula was running for his second term (which he won in 2008). There were numerous political implications associated with the PT-PMDB alliance, but for the purposes of the present analysis, we are interested in only one of these: the alignment that was formed beginning in 2006 between federal and state governments in Rio de Janeiro (and which, in 2009, also included the city government). This convergence is important because it caused state and municipal governments move away from their historic opposition to the federal administration and to begin to work with it. This shift facilitated large transfers of public resources, allowing all levels of the government to act to promote development and stimulate investments.

It must be remembered in this context that the PT governments (Lula's two terms and Dilma Rousseff's first) were characterized by the adoption of a neodevelopmental economic model. This period was marked by strong state stimulation of investments, especially in infrastructure. In the case of Rio de Janeiro, works aimed at hosting megaevents (e.g., the 2014 FIFA World Cup and 2016 Olympic Games) or related to the Growth Acceleration Program (PAC) and the Minha Casa Minha Vida (MCMV) housing program were key in this respect. It is also during this period that oil discoveries off the coast of Rio de Janeiro (2006) were announced and began to be exploited (2008). Unlike the 1970s, when the Campos Basin reserves were found and Brazil was in a negative economic situation, the beginning of the twenty-first century found the country experiencing a period of economic boom. In the 2000s, this discovery produced strong incentives for technological and industrial development aimed at offshore exploration, significantly expanding the scale of national oil production and situating Rio de Janeiro as a pole for supplying goods and services to the petroleum sector in the South Atlantic. The expansion of oil production caused an increase in tax revenues, contributing to balancing public accounts, favoring the growth of several sectors of Rio's economy, and giving autonomy to less privileged regions of the city and state (Melo and Oliveira 2015).

Even with the outbreak of the international financial crisis in 2008, the Brazilian federal government's investments in Rio were maintained. The relatively low impact of the crisis in the country was due to the rapid adoption of countercyclical measures by the Brazilian government, particularly those related to expansionary macroeconomic policies responsible for stimulating the domestic market (Lima and Deus 2013). This ended up benefiting Rio de Janeiro. As Silva explains (2017), the first years of the twenty-first century were very positive for Rio de Janeiro, especially the period between 2010 and 2012 when the state grew above the national average. During this period, there was much growth in the civil construction sector stimulated by the aforementioned countercyclical measures of the federal government, as well as by the promises of investments associated with megaevents. This movement generated jobs and income, but it also contributed to the expansion of social inequalities, reflected both in the interventions carried out by the state (particularly land expropriations) and in increasing real estate prices. Rio de Janeiro became one of the most expensive places to live in Brazil, and a significant part of this was due to housing rental or purchase costs. This dynamic is best explained by the number of expropriations and removals carried out in the period: sixty thousand people were displaced from their homes and territories to make way for a municipal project in which they were marginalized (Azevedo and Faulhaber 2015). The city and state's status as an international showcase and the commitments made by external actors to projects in Rio were used as justifications for ignoring fundamental rights and responding with violence to the constitutionally guaranteed resistance to these projects by residents and social movements.

2013–2016: FROM OPTIMISM TO DEEPENING CRISIS

The boom in both Brazil and Rio de Janeiro declined in 2013. It also saw a sequence of broad popular demonstrations. Countless developments can be associated with the events of June 2013, among them the rise of today's conservative and authoritarian movements, as well as the large increase in the use of police force against protesters. However, for the purposes of this chapter, this period and its associated political demonstrations mark the emergence of political and institutional instability that saw the beginning of the collapse of the PT-PMDB alliance. Federal financial flows toward the State and Municipality of Rio began to dry up. Even with the reelection of Dilma Rousseff (PT) and Governor Sérgio Cabral (PMDB) in 2014, the years that followed saw the deepening of a financial crisis that heavily affected Rio de Janeiro, especially when combined with the drop in petroleum prices. Associated with the economic decline that characterized this moment were the first fruits of the investigations conducted by the Federal Police and Public Prosecutor's Office under the popular rubric of Operation Lava Jato. These investigations produced effects on the private sector.

It is important to remember that "Operation Lava Jato" refers to a set of investigations into corruption conducted by the Federal Police. Although they implicated several political parties, the operation gained notoriety because of the investigations carried out against leftist leaders and social actors belonging to or linked to the PT. The operation contributed to the condemnation of ex-president Lula and to the stimulation of widespread antagonism to his party. This was decisive in the 2018 elections, which saw Jair Bolsonaro's election to the presidency. Bolsonaro then named Sérgio Moro—one of those responsible for the conviction of former president Lula—to the post of minister of justice, which Moro held until April 2020. More recent investigations by the press based on information made available by hackers have revealed that the public agencies linked to Operation Lava Jato had the support of US intelligence agencies and that their investigations were permeated by irregularities, reinforcing some of the defendants' denunciations of widespread arbitrariness in the investigations. The progressive rupture of the PT-PMDB alliance and the evolution of lawsuits to combat corruption produced significant changes within Rio's real estate sector. To understand this, one must remember that the government and party convergences referred to above created a large flow of financial resources into Rio in the previous years. Second, one must also remember that the investments resulting from these transfers were mostly directed toward the execution of major public works. These, in turn, were carried out by large business groups in the civil construction sector—such as Odebrecht, Andrade Gutierrez, and OAS. A large number of these companies ended up being convicted of corruption in the numerous investigations in and around Operation Lava Jato. The drastic reduction in the flow of federal funds to the State of Rio de Janeiro occurred almost simultaneously with the abovementioned imprisonments, asset blocking, and fines. One of the consequences of this process was the weakening of the civil construction conglomerates operating in Rio. Opportunities for access to credit were also impacted. This scenario allowed small and medium-sized companies in the construction and real estate sectors to begin competing for the spaces vacated by the corporate conglomerates condemned for corruption. At the same time, the scarcity of public resources made it easier for other actors to offer credit. This was the context that made it possible for Chinese investors to move into the construction sector in Rio de Janeiro.

The real estate sector was anchored in the expectation that, even in the face of the economic crisis and the political instability that culminated in the impeachment of Dilma Rousseff in 2016, civil construction would continue in view of the Olympic Games. This belief contributed to stimulate optimistic and protectionist behavior in the sector that avoided reducing prices while it could. It also kept real estate acquisition going and new public works moving along. One must remember, however, that the dynamics of real estate and construction follow a different flow in relation to other productive processes. This is a sector that is characterized by its slowness, both in times of economic recovery and in situations in which it is necessary to wind down activities. As a result, the stock of residential and commercial enterprises in Rio increased even while the market lost dynamism. The slow pace of action was accentuated by the high expectations created by megaevents. In other words, not only was a large flow of capital expected into Rio de Janeiro during these events, but it was also believed that the events themselves would provide a showcase that would soon increase international interest and investment.

In this context, Chinese behavior was unusual. Convinced by the optimism spread by the Rio de Janeiro real estate sector and despite the on-going political and financial crises, the Chinese floated proposals for financing and executing projects, supplying labor and/or inputs, and even undertaking joint projects. After all, the Chinese had had some success in conducting partnerships in the infrastructure and industry sectors with Brazilian companies and Brazilian governments. In the case of Rio de Janeiro, these included a partnership with ThyssenKrupp Companhia Siderúrgica do Atlântico (currently, Ternium Brasil). The Chinese seemed poised to expand their investments to include civil construction as well. This reorganization of investments would be in line with the Chinese political-economic strategy for Latin America, aimed at maintaining and increasing China's influence through participation in large projects and the provision of cheap credit. In the Brazilian case, with the decline of large public investments, the Chinese entry into the real estate sector appeared as an alternative, guaranteeing the permanence of the Chinese presence in Brazil.

We can see this playing out in the contrast between Chinese state investment strategies and the private interests of the Chinese in Brazilian territory. The article produced by the Chinese real estate platform Juwai stands out here. Entitled, "Why the Rio Olympics Isn't Drawing Chinese Buyers to Brazil" (Juwai 2016), it presents research that showed that Chinese interest in acquiring residential properties in Brazil had been declining substantially since 2015—this despite the fact that the Olympics, as a rule, represents a seal of approval for international investors. The article presents five reasons for this behavior: the devaluation of China's currency against the Brazilian Real, making the acquisition of real estate less attractive as compared to purchases in other countries; low public and individual security, an element the Chinese consider to be very important; environmental irregularities, related to water quality in particular; difficult international connections, characterized by the long duration of flights between China and Rio de Janeiro; and political instability, marked at that time by the impeachment of President Dilma Rousseff, the trial of former president Lula, and corruption scandals that involved the interim president, Michel Temer. In view of these elements, while Chinese interest in Brazil declined in 2015, Chinese interest in acquisition of real estate in Tokyo skyrocketed, looking toward the 2020 Olympic Games.

Individual Chinese investors could not be certain that the crisis that began in 2014 would not be deeper than that experienced in the 1980s and 1990s. As indicated by Mercês and Freira (2015), the situation in Rio de Janeiro was so critical that between 2015 and 2016, 420,000 jobs were lost, a number higher than during the earlier period. This scenario was accompanied by a sharp drop in taxes collected, which was even more intense than the reduction in economic activity would account for. This shrinking of revenues produced a large hole in Rio de Janeiro's public budget. Cuts in expenditures and other adjustments were not enough balance accounts, demonstrating Rio's economic dependence on national and international circumstances. Although Mercês and Freira defend the need for further cuts as a way out of the fiscal crisis, it is evident that such a project—which would wipe out an already very precarious state—would not be enough to solve the public deficit and stimulate the local economy (Sobral 2017). To make matters worse, petroleum prices have continued to decline since 2014 (Pedrosa and Corrêa 2016).

The crises that erupted from 2014 onward are indispensable for constructing an understanding of the Brazilian political-economic scenario during that period. However, the delay on the part of the construction sector in understanding the depth of the problems seems to have been motivated by unrealistic optimism and an unsustainable protectionism. This made the sectors' planning strategies obsolete during this downturn, placing the sector in a precarious position. This difficulty in understanding the scenario seems to have been the main factor that prevented Chinese investment proposals from going ahead. Representatives of Chinese investors in Brazil report that confidentiality agreements have been signed and draft contracts have been written. However, none of the real estate businesses the Chinese are involved in have prospered. It is interesting to note that, unlike the Chinese performance in large infrastructure projects in Brazil, which was often associated with human rights violations, in the real estate sector, the granting of Chinese credit has been characterized by a strict concern with following international standards. These requirements represented barriers to small and medium-sized business groups who wanted to access Chinese financial resources. The barriers became almost insurmountable with the deepening of the crisis and the indebtedness of the private actors involved. It should be noted that, in addition to lending money at low interest rates, Chinese investment funds were committed to further reducing the cost of financial resources if the project included both the loan and the execution of the work itself. This implied the use of Chinese technology, inputs, and labor. However, as reported by representatives of Chinese investors in Brazil and confirmed by the reports of the Brazil-China Business Council, no works in the real estate sector were identified in the period.

2016–2020: FROM EXPECTATIONS FOR RENEWED GROWTH TO FRUSTRATION

The impeachment of Dilma Rousseff (PT) propelled Vice President Michel Temer (PMDB) to the presidency from 2016 to 2018. The new administration signaled to the market that state reforms would be adopted, notably in the fields of labor, social security, tax, administration, and federal law. The Temer government's agenda also included privatizations and concessions in strategic sectors such as sanitation, electricity, and environmentally protected spaces. However, weakened by investigations regarding his involvement with corruption, Temer was unable to promote significant advances in this political agenda before the end of his term in 2018. At that point, Jair Bolsonaro was elected president in the midst of an election characterized by the spread of hate speech, fake news, and antagonism against former president Lula and the PT. In addition to the controversies and illegalities that marked this period of Brazilian democracy, the new government committed itself to the market to prioritize the state reform agenda, which was personified in the figure of the new minister of economy, Paulo Guedes. This commitment renewed the optimism of several sectors of the economy, and, for Chinese investors, it represented a positive indicator for the resumption of investments in Brazil. The new government's main targets remained focused on the infrastructure sector and, in particular, on basic sanitation, a policy that is essentially conducted by the public authorities in Brazil and that has been the subject of regulatory reform aimed at expanding private participation.

Despite his speeches, Bolsonaro's government showed itself incapable of leading the state reforms demanded by the market, paving the way for other actors to take the lead. This was mostly the legislative branch, which is responsible for discussing and approving social security reform. Driven by conflicts, the combative federalism promoted by the federal executive hinders or prevents linkages while stimulating clashes between the constituted powers. These conflicts go beyond the federative relationship, reaching into the press and the opposition and even including other nations such as China. The Brazilian government's rapprochement with the Trump presidency was accompanied by its decision to vilify China, producing a political-diplomatic departure that contradicted the Bolsonaro government's previous approximations to China. This shift highlights the Brazilian government's difficulty in maintaining alliances over the medium or long term. In any case—and in addition to the accumulated political wear and tear—up until the outbreak of the pandemic in 2020, we saw a resumption of private investment in Brazil, including Chinese investors. In the civil construction sector, the Chinese conglomerate Xuzhou Construction Machinery Group (XCMG) stands out. XCMG came into the country after the Chinese creation, in 2020, of a bank in Brazil that focused on infrastructure. There have also been investments in petroleum and the expressions of interest in the highway, rail, and port sectors (Scaramuzzo and Pereira 2020). These last two are considered strategic for the exportation of the agricultural commodities the Chinese desire.

The economic downturn of the recent years and the negative developments associated with Brazil's poor management of the public health crisis put Rio de Janeiro in an extremely difficult position from which to recover. In this context, it is possible that the real estate sector in Rio will remain very weak over the next few years. If the federal government maintains its antagonism toward the State of Rio de Janeiro, it will be necessary for the state to seek other forms of financing, whether for public or private works. In this context, the resumption of Chinese investments in the country may represent a feasible alternative for accessing credit in Rio, especially considering that the state will increasingly be able to rely on the revenues of the oil industry in order to finance public expenditures. It remains to be seen whether such resources will be accompanied by compliance with national and international human rights regulations or if, given the precarious political and financial condition of the state, everyone involved will ignore these rules, allowing further violations as a "necessary" counterpart for the recovery of the local economy.

CONCLUSION

In the midst of the first decade of the twenty-first century, Rio de Janeiro went through a period of economic boom made possible by a vigorous international scenario, high oil prices, the hosting of mega-sporting events, and an unprecedentedly high level of interfederative articulation. These factors gave Rio's economy a high degree of dynamism, particularly with regard to civil construction. However, the decline of this period has been characterized by a confluence of political and economic crises that have led to the collapse of public investment programs as well as the condemnation of politicians and large civil construction conglomerates, culminating in the impeachment of Dilma Rousseff in 2016. Among the numerous developments associated with these crises, the restructuring of the real estate sector stands out. In the case of Rio de Janeiro, the vacuum produced by the judicial removal of the large companies active in the state represented an opportunity for small and medium-sized groups that, as public credit dried up, began to seek out other sources of funds. At this moment, Chinese investors appeared as an alternative. In a scenario where partnerships with the Brazilian government were reduced, it became necessary to create other ways of guaranteeing that Chinese capital in Brazil.

From the perspective of the postpandemic world, it is estimated that the resumption of China's growth will become a priority for that nation's government. This is of fundamental importance for maintaining that government's internal political legitimacy and its authoritarian model. Although this move would reinforce the need for concentrating investments in China itself, the intensification of the country's dispute for international dominance with the United States has produced the need for the Chinese to remain in the territories where their influence is currently under a certain degree of tension. In the case of Brazil, this presence is reflected both in the Chinese importation of Brazilian commodities and in the participation in and promotion of investments. In this sense, the decline of the neodevelopmental model championed by the PT governments does not seem to represent an obstacle to those Chinese interested in injecting resources into Brazil. Accelerating privatizations and concessions opened by the Bolsonaro government present a new opportunity for China, and the arrival of XCMG in early 2020 expresses Chinese interest in this model. Even in the uncertain scenario created by the global health crisis, there is little doubt that should the Brazilian government be successful in opening state concessions to the private sector, the Chinese will be important players in this dynamic.

On the other hand, the rise of conservative authoritarianism amid the collapse of liberal Western democracies and the strengthening of the Chinese presence at this time of institutional fragility may contribute even more to this process. In the name of resuming national economic growth, collective and individual rights guarantees may be made even more precarious, giving rise to new human rights violations in projects in which the Chinese are involved.

NOTE

1. Popularly known as the "mensalão" (big monthly allowance), Penal Action #470 fought the executive branch's purchase of congressional support.

REFERENCES

Azevedo, Lena, and Lucas Faulhaber. 2015. *SMH 2016: Remoções no Rio de Janeiro Olímpico*. Rio de Janeiro: Mórula Editorial.

Juwai. 2016. "Why Rio Olympics Isn't Drawing Chinese Buyers to Brazil." August 18, 2016. https://list.juwai.com/news/2016/08/why-rio-olympics-is-not-drawing-chinese-buyers-to-brazil.

Lima, Thaís Damasceno, and Larissa Naves Deus. 2013. "A crise de 2008 e seus efeitos na economia brasileira." *Revista Cadernos de Economia* 17, no. 32 (January/June): 52–65.

Melo, Hildete Pereira de, and Adilson de Oliveira. 2015. "Café e petróleo: Um paralelo histórico." *Cadernos do Desenvolvimento Fluminense* 7 (January/June): 91–104.

Mercês, Guilherme, and Nayara Freira. 2017. "Crise fiscal dos Estados e o caso do Rio de Janeiro." *Geo UERJ* 31: 64–80.

Pedrosa, Oswaldo, and Antônio Corrêa. 2016. "A crise do petróleo e os desafios do pré-sal." *Caderno Opinião*. Rio de Janeiro: FGV Energia.

Scaramuzzo. Mônica, and Renée Pereira. 2020. "Brasil volta à rota de investimento dos chineses." UOL Estadão, December 1, 2020. https://economia.uol.com.br/noticias/estadao-conteudo/2020/01/12/brasil-volta-a-rota-de-investimento-dos-chineses.htm.

Silva, Eduardo Fernandez. 2017. *Evolução da economia do Estado do Rio de Janeiro na segunda década do século XXI*. Estudo Técnico. Consultoria Legislativa. Brasília: Câmara dos Deputados.

Sobral, Bruno Leonardo Barth. 2017. "A crise no Estado do Rio de Janeiro entendida não apenas como uma questão financeira." *Geo UERJ* 31: 34–63.

The China-Ecuador Economic Relationship's Impact on Unemployment during the Administration of President Moreno

David F. Delgado del Hierro

OVER THE LAST DECADE, China has expanded its international relations with around one hundred countries. Latin America and the Caribbean have been important strategic targets for Chinese investment, as reflected in the Asian giant's current New Silk Road[1] project (Sieren 2019). As many authors in this volume have discussed, especially the chapters by Reyes Herrera and Mosquera Narváez, China's search for partners and resources came at time when many in Latin America were turning away from Washington and Wall Street. Van Teijlingen and Hidalgo Bastidas's chapter reminds us that Ecuador went one step further:

> When the charismatic, self-proclaimed post-neoliberal Rafael Correa was elected president of Ecuador in 2007, one thing was clear: the World Bank and the International Monetary Fund—institutions that influenced the country's economic policy in the 1980s and 1990s—would no longer have it their way. Employing popular anti-imperialism, Correa defaulted on foreign debts, expelled the World Bank's country manager, and unilaterally renegotiated terms of payment. This move cut off Ecuador's access to finance, but Correa didn't care. He had found a new and very powerful ally across the Pacific [China]. (234)

With this project of meeting Latin America's new demands for finance in mind, and with the intention of stimulating the economy and freeing up Asian markets through channeling of investments to other parts of the world, in 2014 Chinese president Xi Jinping promoted the creation of the Asian Infrastructure Investment Bank (AIIB n.d.). Because gaining access to international financing is a challenge for smaller countries, often due to demanding conditions imposed by lenders, contracting debt with a creditor like China, which does not impose domestic policy conditions or specific limits as to the amount to be lent, can be attractive. In this context, especially because Chinese investments "come without questions about human rights or the nature of the government in power," the People's Republic of China has become Ecuador's main creditor (Vidal Liy 2018).

As of 2020, Ecuador has enjoyed forty years of bilateral relations with China (Araujo 2020). During this period, China "has become a key market for Ecuador's exports," reaching eighth place among other importing countries in terms of direct foreign investment (Astudillo and Vinueza 2020). Starting in 2007, the Ecuador-China relationship began to intensify, to the point that during the 2009–2018 period Ecuador signed 74 contracts with Chinese companies worth approximately US$8 billion (La Hora 2019), with 64 contracts awarded to 18 Chinese companies during the 2015–2017 period alone (*Plan V* 2019). China became Ecuador's largest supplier in terms of the total amount contracted (Fundación Ciudadanía y Desarrollo 2018). Finally, more than 70 percent of Ecuador's bilateral debt is currently with China, and almost all financing obligations are payable in future shipments of presold oil, "which has led Ecuador to a financial dependence that is without precedent when compared to other countries" (de la Paz Vela Z. 2019).

This chapter discusses Ecuador's unemployment—currently aggravated by the COVID-19 pandemic—in the context of economic measures taken by the current government as it confronts institutionalized corruption, overpriced contracts, and excessive debt, and in light of the Ecuador-China economic relationship from 2016 to the present. Unlike Mosquera Narváez in this volume, who adopts a "win-win" framework for understanding this relationship, this chapter highlights many of the predatory terms of that relationship and the consequences for Ecuadorian workers.

OVERPRICING IN CONTRACTS WITH CHINESE COMPANIES

During the administration of former president Rafael Correa (2007–2017), contracts were awarded to various Chinese companies, notably China CAMC Engineering, China Gezhouba Group, and Sinohydro, for the construction of large-scale infrastructure projects (*El Universo* 2017).

Sinohydro was in charge of building the Coca Codo Sinclair hydroelectric project, the "largest construction in national history" (Pallares 2020). However, it was later found that during the construction, "it used nonconforming materials . . . [and] did not carry out adequate quality control or technical procedures" (Contraloría General del Estado 2018). After construction was completed, the presence of 7,648 cracks in the plant's infrastructure resulted in an interruption of operations in 2019 (Ministerio de Energía y Recursos Naturales No Renovables del Ecuador, n.d.), which caused the state to incur a loss of approximately US$93.88 million (Miranda 2019).

China National Electronics Import and Export was contracted to install and supply an electronic ankle bracelet system for Ecuador's law enforcement and corrections agencies. The company billed US$1,058 for each device, equivalent to an 800 percent markup according to investigations conducted by *Focus Ecuador, Plan V, Mil Hojas,* and *La Hora*.[2] Similar overpricing issues have been reported with China Gezhouba Group (a contractor involved in the development of Universidad Yachay,[3] China International Water and Electric, and China CAMC Engineering).[4] Overpricing was also found in multimillion-dollar contracts with companies from other countries, such as the Brazilian conglomerate Odebrecht (*El Comercio* 2017) and South Korea's SK Engineering and Construction (*Plan V* 2018).

The inflation in most of these contracts arose through selection processes conducted "as though there were only one bid under consideration, and no real competition." Of 48 contracts totaling US$7.3 billion and financed with Chinese loans, only 8 arose from bid selection processes and 40 were awarded without a formal bid—a practice that disregarded laws and the economic common sense that "intense competition in bidding can significantly reduce prices" (*El Universo* 2017).

The bid selections involving Chinese companies were conducted in secret. This led to the harsh criticism that Ecuador's "opacity problem" was "a constant and concerted manner in which the Correa administration entered into investment contracts with Chinese companies" (*La Hora* 2019).

THE MORENO ADMINISTRATION INHERITS AN ECONOMIC CRISIS

During the Correa administration, when the price of raw materials reached a historical high-water mark, 40 percent of the state's contribution to the Ecuadorian Social Security Institute (ESSI) was eliminated, a measure the Constitutional Court declared unconstitutional in 2019. The former president "doubled Ecuador's debt" and "left the country with a negative economic growth" of -1.2 percent, "with a high public deficit" and "the highest unemployment since the international recession of 2008" (Blasco 2019). While the administration initially lowered the country's public debt to 16.8 percent of GDP in 2011, the debt rebounded to 45.4 percent of GDP by the end of Correa's term. To pay for the Chinese portion of this debt, the administration agreed to ship presold petroleum to the Asian giant, "committing . . . 90% of [Ecuador's] exportable crude . . . until 2024" (Kraul 2018).

The debt with China became onerous with the global drop in the price of oil, Ecuador's main source of export income. Therefore, in December 2018, President Lenín Moreno visited China to join Ecuador to its "New Silk Road" initiative (*La República* 2018), with the objective of securing more flexible terms for the repayment of its Chinese debt.[5]

At the end of Correa's term, his administration reported US$27.871 billion in public debt. However, just days after assuming office, the current president revealed the figure was actually US$41.893 billion (España 2018). Foreign debt accounted for 72.4 percent of this revised amount, confirming the "growing trend of indebtedness from 2011 to 2017" (*Gestión Digital* 2020). Because this new figure exceeded 40 percent of the GDP, and as there were express regulations that prohibited such a level, the Moreno administration chose to repeal said laws. In a similar transparency effort, in April 2019 the Ministry of Economics and Finance (MEF) changed its method of calculating Ecuador's public debt, including items that were not previously reflected (MEF 2020b, 4).

In December 2019, using its new method, the MEF calculated Ecuador's foreign debt at US$41.493 billion, and as of April 2020 total public debt is estimated at US$57.182 billion or 52.14 percent of GDP—a figure that is expected to increase with the 2020 COVID-19 pandemic (MEF 2020a, 13).

ECONOMIC MEASURES DURING A SOCIAL AND HEALTH CRISIS

In the face of this financial crisis, President Moreno ordered budget cuts and requested loans from multilateral development banks. In February 2019, his administration announced US$10.2 billion in "rescue" loans from the International Monetary Fund, the World Bank, and the Inter-American Development Bank, although this financing came with structural adjustment conditions. Thus, on October 1 of the same year, the administration issued Decree 883, a package of austerity measures designed to save the government approximately US$2.27 billion per year (Orozco 2020).

On October 3 in response to the decree's termination of gasoline subsidies, the public transportation sector canceled its services and drivers blocked roads in protest. The next day, the Confederation of Indigenous Nationalities of Ecuador announced an indefinite strike and massive march on the capital. In response, the government declared a state of emergency (En los Valles 2019). This national strike, which resulted in US$821.68 million in losses and damages (Banco Central del Ecuador 2020), ended on October 14 when the government agreed to repeal the austerity package (*El Comercio* 2019). For a more intimate narrative of the protests, see Correa et al. in this volume.

In February 2020, just four months after this failed reform attempt, Ecuador confirmed its first case of COVID-19. Weeks later, in the midst of a global pandemic, the Moreno administration announced a new package of economic measures (*El Comercio* 2020). The MEF confirmed the reduction of more than US$98 million in allocations to public universities, an action criticized by the Inter-American Commission on Human Rights (Trujillo 2020) and eventually suspended by Ecuador's Constitutional Court (García 2020). The latter finally decided that the measure had no effect on an education, and the reduction was thus maintained (Corte Constitucional 2020).

As the government struggles to address the pandemic, it also faces questions of widespread corruption—especially in its public health system. In April 2020, it was reported that the Teodoro Maldonado Carbo Hospital had been purchasing surgical masks at three times the market price (Basantes 2020). Shortly thereafter the Ecuadorian media reported overpricing of more than 1,000 percent for body bags sold to the Los Ceibos Hospital in Guayaquil (*El Universo* 2020a).

IMPACT ON UNEMPLOYMENT

Between Ecuador's excessive Chinese debt and the overpricing and mismanagement that has plagued the public budget, fulfillment within the foreseeable future of the constitution's declaration of a right to employment[6] does not appear likely. In the National Survey of Employment, Unemployment, and Underemployment, the numbers show that in December 2016, at the end of the Correa administration, national unemployment reached 5.2 percent (INEC 2016, 10–14). By September 2019, the figure dropped slightly to 4.9 percent (INEC 2019, 9–13), a trend that corresponds to a slight decrease in Ecuador's Chinese debt.

To sustain its economy in the crisis environment inherited from the Correa administration, in March 2019 Ecuador acquired a US$4.2 billion International Monetary Fund loan, which was conditioned on Ecuador implementing fiscal reforms, flexible hiring, a reduction in the size of the state apparatus, and the withdrawal of fuel subsidies. The economic measures Ecuador has implemented in the service of these conditions had both direct and indirect effects on unemployment.

Among measures that directly affect employment are the temporary decrease in the working day for government employees and a corresponding decrease in the minimum monthly wage from US$400 to $300 (Orozco 2019); the decision not to renew temporary employment contracts for civil servants in administrative positions, which has affected 2,279 employees in the Ministry of Public Health alone (*Nodal* 2020b); and the liquidation, selling-off, or merger of ten state-owned entities, including TAME EP Linea Aérea del Ecuador, Ferrocarriles del Ecuador EP, INMOBILIAR, Empresa Pública Siembra EP, and Medios Públicos de Comunicación del Ecuador EP. In response to these closures, protesting workers have raised questions about rampant mismanagement. One of their attorneys, Juan Pablo Albán, stated in reference to TAME that "what's responsible for the company's debts isn't the 932 workers, but rather [the company's] poor administration" (*El Universo* 2020b). Similar criticisms have been directed against Medios Públicos (*Nodal* 2020b) and Correos del Ecuador EP (*Primicias* 2020a).

The Law of Humanitarian Support to Combat the COVID-19 Health Crisis, approved by Ecuador's National Assembly in May 2020, allows employers and workers facing situations of force majeure to negotiate up to a 50 percent reduction in the length of the working day and reductions in salary (and corresponding Social Security contributions) of up to 45 percent. Under the slogan "Employment yes, slavery no," the Unitary Workers Front and the General Workers Union have protested this measure and requested a presidential veto (*El Universo* 2020c; *Primicias* 2020b).

As for measures that affect unemployment indirectly, the timing of a recent payment of US$341 million toward the reorganization of Ecuador's foreign debt has been questioned. Made during a global health crisis, several experts have observed this money could have been useful to "face the health emergency the country is going through" (*Nodal* 2020b).

Other deleterious effects on unemployment are not expected to be immediately noticeable. For example, the International Labour Organization has estimated that the exhaustion of the ESSI's pension fund will be accelerated by the economic effects of the COVID-19 pandemic and that it could be completely depleted within seventeen to twenty years, if the government continues its 40 percent contribution, or otherwise in as few as seven years (Alvarado 2020). These projections are based on an estimated GDP contraction of 6 percent due to the pandemic and a fiscal deficit "projected at no less than 8.7% of GDP . . . [and that] the labor market reflects an increase in the unemployment rate and levels of informal employment." The number of ESSI-affiliated workers could suffer an overall wage decrease of 7 percent and that "total national wages could drop by 17%" (International Labour Organization 2020).

In this context of a contracted economy, liquidations and mergers of public companies, the liberalization of fuel prices, and the continued payment of foreign debt (despite the urgency of the COVID-19 health crisis), there will be a significant increase in national unemployment, as well as a general decrease in wages and reduced quality of public services, and therefore a proliferation of informal and precarious work. For marginalized populations, like the Shuar and other Indigenous communities, this is only the latest crisis compounding the generations of crises they have struggled to survive, as Pullaguari, Bonilla, and others in this volume have illustrated.

The arrival of the COVID-19 pandemic, aside from aggravating these circumstances, has also given visibility to structural problems that have been dragging Ecuador's economy down for over ten years.

NOTES

1. China's 2013 Belt and Road Initiative is often referred to as the "New Silk Road" project, or "*la Nueva Ruta de Seda*" in Spanish.

2. *Focus News Ecuador* (a.k.a. Focus Ecuador), *Plan V*, and *Fundación Mil Hojas* are Ecuadorian online investigative news publications. *La Hora* is a tabloid newspaper published in Quito, Ecuador (La Fuente 2017).

3. The Universidad de Investigación de Tecnología Experimental Yachay. *Yachay* is Kichwa for "knowledge."

4. Universidad Yachay purchased eight Mettler Toledo pH-meters at US$8,391.50 per unit, when the domestic market price for the same instrument was US$1,990.00. (Aguilar 2016).

5. Since 2017, Ecuador has reduced its Chinese debt. In 2019, balances payable reflected a decrease of approximately US$6 billion, however China continues to be the country's largest creditor, accounting for 64 percent of its total foreign debt.

6. Article 33 of the Ecuadorian constitution provides that, "as a source of personal realization and economic foundation, employment is a social right and duty as well as an economic right."

REFERENCES

AIIB. n.d. "About AIIB." https://www.aiib.org/en/index.html.

Aguilar, Roberto. 2016. "Yachay, la universidad que produce . . . sobreprecios." *Conexiones 4P/ EL Enfoque/ Info.* August 8, 2016. https://4pelagatos .com/2016/08/08/yachay-la-universidad-que-produce-sobreprecios/.

Alvarado, Priscila. 2020. "El fondo de pensiones del IESS durará 10 años menos debido a la pandemia, según la OIT." *El Comercio*, May 21, 2020. https://www .elcomercio.com/actualidad/fondo-pensiones-iess-pandemia-oit.html.

Araujo, Alberto. 2020. "China celebró los 40 años de relaciones diplomáticas con Ecuador." *El Comercio*, January 16, 2020. https://www.elcomercio.com/actual idad/ecuador-china-celebro-relaciones-diplomaticas.html.

Astudillo, Ericka, and Dayana Vinueza. 2020. "China es el tercer destino de productos del Ecuador." *El Telégrafo*, January 2, 2020. https://www.eltelegrafo.com .ec/noticias/economia/4/china-tercer-destino-productos-ecuador.

Banco Central del Ecuador. 2020. "Paralización de octubre de 2019 dejó daños y pérdidas por US$821,68 millones." January 17, 2020. https://www.bce.fin.ec/ index.php/boletines-de-prensa-archivo/item/1347-paralizaci%C3%B3n-de-oc tubre-de-2019-dej%C3%B3-da%C3%B1os-y-p%C3%A9rdidas-por-usd-82168 -millones.

Basantes, Ana Cristina. 2020. "La metástasis de la corrupción." *GK*, May 10, 2020. https://gk.city/2020/05/10/corrupcion-hospitales-ecuador/.

Blasco, Emilio J. 2019. "La crisis económica que dejó Correa en Ecuador." *ABC Internacional*, October 15. https://www.abc.es/internacional/abci-crisis-economi ca-dejo-correa-ecuador-201910150209_noticia.html.

Constitución del Ecuador, Registro Oficial 449. October 2008. Artículos 3.1, 33 y 34.

Contraloría General del Estado. 2018. "Contraloría identifica 7648 fisuras en Coca Codo Sinclair." *El Comercio*, November 15, 2018. https://www.contraloria.gob .ec/CentralMedios/CGENoticias/20544.

Corte Constitucional. 2020. Sentencia No. 34-20-IS y acumulados, Quito D.M. August 31, 2020. https://drive.google.com/file/d/1_e7fXA-sljB6qLTsot8y5vzL77Ws wIGo/view).

de la Paz Vela Z., María. 2019. "¿A cuánto finalmente asciende la deuda? Todas las deudas del Estado." *Revista Gestión* No. 266: 12–19. https://revistagestion.ec/sites/default/files/import/legacy_pdfs/266_002.pdf.

El Comercio. 2017. "Procesado admite que facturaba con sobreprecio en obras de Odebretch." September 20, 2017. https://www.elcomercio.com/actualidad/procesado-factura-sobreprecio-odebrecht-fiscalia.html.

El Comercio. 2019. "Lenin Moreno deroga el Decreto 883 que eliminada el subsidio a los combustibles." October 14, 2019. https://www.elcomercio.com/actualidad/lenin-moreno-deroga-decreto-883.html.

El Comercio. 2020. "Por coronavirus, toque de queda en Ecuador de 14:00 a 05:00." March 24, 2020. https://www.elcomercio.com/actualidad/toque-queda-ecuador-coronavirus-covid19.html.

El Universo. 2017. "Seis firmas acaparan las obras costeadas con créditos chinos." October 15, 2017. https://www.eluniverso.com/noticias/2017/10/15/nota/6430801/seis-firmas-acaparan-obras-costeadas-creditos-chinos.

El Universo. 2020a "Cuatro detenidos y 12 retenidos tras allanamientos para investigar compra del IESS de bolsas de cadáveres." May 4, 2020. https://www.eluniverso.com/noticias/2020/05/04/nota/7831137/fiscalia-realiza-allanamientos-investigar-compra-iess-bolsas.

El Universo. 2020b. "Empleados de TAME piden que Gobierno reconsidere decisión de liquidar línea." May 23, 2020. https://www.eluniverso.com/noticias/2020/05/23/nota/7849611/empleados-tame-piden-que-gobierno-reconsidere-decision-liquidar.

El Universo. 2020c. "La posibilidad de cambiar los contratos de los trabajadores activa protesta de sindicatos." May 18, 2020. https://www.eluniverso.com/noticias/2020/05/17/nota/7844199/reformas-laborales-contratos-emergencia-protesta-ley-humanitaria.

En los Valles. 2019. "Cronología del Paro Nacional en Ecuador." October 23, 2019. https://enlosvalles.wordpress.com/2019/10/23/cronologia-del-paro-nacional-en-ecuador/.

España, Sara. 2018. "Ecuador destapa deudas ocultas de la gestión de Correa." *El País*, July 14, 2018. "https://elpais.com/internacional/2017/07/14/america/1499989552_044307.html" https://elpais.FCD.

Fundación Ciudadanía y Desarrollo. 2018. "Un análisis de las compras públicas realizadas por el gobierno entre 2015 y 2017." *Observatorio de Gasto Público* (March): 1–18.

García, Andrés. 2020. "Sectores sociales esperan pronunciamiento de la Corte Constitucional por recorte a la educación superior." *El Comercio*, May 11, 2020. https://www.elcomercio.com/actualidad/corte-constitucional-recorte-educacion-superior.html.

Gestión Digital. 2020. "Bonos, multilaterales y China acaparan la deuda del Ecuador." February 26, 2020. https://www.revistagestion.ec/economia-y-finanzas-analisis/bonos-multilaterales-y-china-acaparan-la-deuda-del-ecuador.

INEC. 2016. "Encuesta Nacional de Empleo, Desempleo y Subempleo." *Instituto Nacional de Estadística y Censos* (December): 1–53.

INEC. 2019. "Encuesta Nacional de Empleo, Desempleo y Subempleo." *Instituto Nacional de Estadística y Censos* (September): 1–52.

International Labour Organization. 2020. "OIT evalúa efectos de la COVID-19 en la sostenibilidad de las pensiones de invalidez, vejez y muerte en Ecuador." May 20, 2020. https://www.ilo.org/lima/sala-de-prensa/WCMS_745272/lang--es/index.htm.

Kraul, Chris. 2018. "Por los créditos negociados con China, Ecuador se enfrenta a un enorme déficit presupuestario." *L.A. Times en Español*, December 10, 2018. https://www.latimes.com/espanol/internacional/la-es-por-los-creditos-nego ciados-con-china-ecuador-se-enfrenta-a-un-enorme-deficit-presupuestari o-20181210-story.html.

La Fuente. 2017. "Sobreprecio en grilletes chinos adquiridos con deuda externa pagada con petróleo." *Periodismo de Investigación*, November 20, 2017. https:// periodismodeinvestigacion.com/2017/11/20/sobreprecio-en-grilletes-chinos-ad quiridos-con-deuda-externa-pagada-con-petroleo/.

La Hora. 2019. "Contratos con empresas chinas blindados por la Ley de su país." June 06, 2019. https://lahora.com.ec/noticia/1102248665/contratos-con-empre sas-chinas-blindados-por-la-ley-de-su-pais.

La República. 2018. "Ecuador se suma a la iniciativa china de la Nueva Ruta de la Seda." December 12, 2018. https://www.larepublica.ec/blog/politica/2018/12/12/ ecuador-se-suma-a-la-iniciativa-china-de-la-nueva-ruta-de-la-seda/.

Lucero, Karen. 2020. "Bonos, multilaterales y China acaparan la deuda del Ecuador." *Revista Gestión*, February 26, 2020. https://www.revistagestion.ec/econo mia-y-finanzas-analisis/bonos-multilaterales-y-china-acaparan-la-deuda-del -ecuador.

MEF—Ministry of Economics and Finance of Ecuador. 2020a. "Boletín de Deuda Pública Interna y Externa." https://www.finanzas.gob.ec/wp-content/uploads/ downloads/2020/05/Presentacio%CC%81n-Boleti%CC%81n-de-Deuda-Pu%CC %81blica-Abril-2020_2605.pdf.

MEF—Ministry of Economics and Finance of Ecuador. 2020b. "Circular No. MEF-VGF-2020–0003-C." April 16, 2020. https://esigef.finanzas.gob.ec/esigef/Ayuda/ MEF-VGF-2020-0003-C.pdf.

Ministerio de Energía y Recursos Naturales No Renovables del Ecuador. n.d. "Central Hidroeléctrica Coca Codo Sinclair." https://www.recursosyenergia.gob.ec/ central-hidroelectrica-coca-codo-sinclair/.

Miranda, Boris. 2019. "Coca Codo Sinclair: los problemas de la multimillonaria represa que China construyó en Ecuador." *BBC News Mundo*, February 25, 2019. https://www.bbc.com/mundo/noticias-america-latina-47144338.

Montaño, Doménica. 2020. "Recortes en el presupuesto de universidades públicas genera rechazo." *GK*, May 6. https://gk.city/2020/05/14/medidas-cautelares-sus penden-educacion-superior/.

Nodal. 2020a. "Ecuador, asambleístas criticaron al gobierno por el pago de la deuda externa y plantearon juicio político por el manejo de la emergencia sanitaria."

April 16, 2020. https://www.nodal.am/2020/04/ecuador-asambleistas-critica ron-al-gobierno-por-el-pago-de-la-deuda-externa-y-plantearon-juicio-politi co-por-el-manejo-de-la-emergencia-sanitaria/.

Nodal. 2020b. "Gobierno de Ecuador despide a más de dos tercios de los trabaja-dores de los medios públicos." May 27, 2020. https://www.nodal.am/2020/05/ gobierno-de-ecuador-despide-a-mas-de-dos-tercios-de-los-trabajadores-de -los-medios-publicos/.

Orozco, Mónica. 2019. "Alza del salario básico será de US$6 en el 2020; el SBU pasa a US$400." El Comercio, December 27, 2019. https://www.elcomercio.com/actu alidad/incremento-salario-basico-2020-400.html.

Orozco, Mónica. 2020. "Recorte de gasto pública y deuda plantea Gobierno para afrontar escenario económico." El Comercio, March 10, 2020. https://www.el comercio.com/actualidad/recorte-gasto-publico-deuda-plantea.html.

Pallares, Martín. 2020. "Coca Codo Sinclair: ¿pagaría la China por el inmi-nente desastre?" Conexiones 4p/El enfoque, April 20, 2020. https://4pelaga tos.com/2020/04/20/coca-codo-sinclair-pagara-la-china-por-el-inminente -desastre/.

Plan V. 2018. "Así se armó el negocio de la Refinería del Pacífico." January 2, 2018. https://www.planv.com.ec/investigacion/investigacion/correa-testigo -honor-la-delincuencia-organizada-la-refineria-del.

Plan V. 2019. "Las grandes obras públicas del Correato fueron financiadas y con-struidas por China." April 9, 2018. https://www.planv.com.ec/historias/politica/ grandes-obras-publicas-del-correato-fueron-financiadas-y-construidas-china.

Primicias. 2020a. "Histórico: precios del petróleo caen a menos de cero por barril." April 20, 2020. https://www.primicias.ec/noticias/economia/ historico-precios-petroleo-caen-menos-cero/.

Primicias. 2020b. "Trabajadores, maestros y estudiantes protestan contra el Gobierno." May 22, 2020. https://www.primicias.ec/noticias/sociedad/ trabajadores-tame-maestros-estudiantes-protestan-gobierno/.

Sieren, Frank. 2019. "La nueva ruta de la seda china: ¿Oportunidad o amenaza?" El Mundo, September 21, 2019. https://p.dw.com/p/3QoOt.

Sosa, César Augusto. 2019. "El atraco de la década." El Comercio, December 23, 2019. https://www.elcomercio.com/opinion/atraco-decada-iess-rafael-correa.html.

Trujillo, Yadira. 2020. "CIDH se pronuncia por recorte a universidades del Ec-uador." El Comercio, May 11, 2020. https://www.elcomercio.com/actualidad/ recorte-presupuesto-universidades-cidh-emergencia.html.

Vidal Liy, Macarena. 2018. "La nueva ruta de la sea, el gran plan estratégico de China." El País, December 3, 2018. https://elpais.com/economia/2018/11/30/ac-tualidad/1543600537_893651.html.

Villavicencio, Fernando, and Cristina Solórzano. 2018. "Así se armó el negocio de la Refinería del Pacífico." Plan V, January 2, 2018. https://www.planv.com.ec/in-vestigacion/investigacion/correa-testigo-honor-la-delincuencia-organizada-la -refineria-del.

PART 7
HYBRIDITY OF TRANSNATIONAL LABOR

Savage Factories of the Manaus Free Trade Zone: Chinese Investments in the Amazon and Social Impacts on Workers

Cleiton Ferreira Maciel Brito

AMAZONIA'S SAVAGE FACTORIES

It is a misconception that the Amazon is a vast, wild rainforest, broken only by slash-and-burn agriculturalists, agribusiness plantations, and the sorts of megaprojects described by Rodríguez, Molina and Munduruku, Oliveira, Camoça and Hendler, Felipe and Costa, and Thomaz et al. in this volume. Since the nineteenth century, capitalist economic globalization has targeted the Amazon and, in the twentieth century, industrial capitalism began to really take off in the region. An excellent example of this is that in the main Amazonian city of Manaus, a productive space emerged as a direct result of one of the main creations of capitalism in Brazil: the Manaus Free Trade Zone (MFTZ). How the factories and workers of this zone have resisted or been forced to change due to the recent influx of Chinese investment are the focus of the present chapter.

Created on February 28, 1967 by the Brazilian military government, the MFTZ was one of the world's first free zones. Its main "competitive advantage" is that it operates under a different tax policy from the rest of the country, offering tax and nonfiscal incentives for companies. The zone was partially a response to the interests of global capital, which sought to circumvent labor costs and also the taxes levied by nation-states. For local elites, this was justified because "the cost of doing business in the Amazon" would be greatly reduced.

According to its creators, the MFTZ would result in the development of a commercial, agricultural, and industrial hub. Only the commercial/industrial parts of this project ever got off the ground, however, with the Manaus Industrial Hub (MIH) taking pride of place (Seráfico 2011).

Since the 1970s, the MIH has attracted a profusion of factories from all over the Earth. In the 1970s and 1980s, US, European, and Japanese capital investment dominated the MIH. During this period, jobs in the hub were strongly Taylorist. This was a period in which unions emerged, presenting strong challenges to capital.

In the 1990s, the "Asian tigers" arrived, particularly South Korean companies. The Japanese management model became standardized in the hub. It is also at this point that a certain "standard" was established for national and local workers: under union pressure, they gained labor benefits and profit-sharing agreements. Worker involvement in workplace management became common, and workers were awarded recognition and productivity bonuses to remove them from the influence of unions and increase productivity (Valle 2007).

Since the 2000s, China has emerged as an investor in Manaus. More than twenty Chinese state, semistate, and private factories have come into the hub. In 2014 these accounted for almost 10 percent of the MIH's total employees.

In the context of the arrival of these factories, polls (Fraga and Rolli 2011) showed that 42 percent of the workers of Chinese companies in Brazil quit their job in the first year of their employment, representing a 68 percent higher turnover rate when compared to European or American companies.

This went against the Japanese model that had been implemented in Brazil. On the other hand, it seemed to confirm the findings made by international research, which had been pointing out precarious work conditions in Chinese factories, both at home and overseas (Lee 2009; Gao 2004; Pun and Chan 2012; Meunier 2012; Burgoon and Raess 2014; Andrijasevic and Sacchetto 2016). It has thus become necessary to know what the managerial model of Chinese factories in Brazil is and to show, sociologically, its impacts on work.

Between the 2013 and 2017, I carried out ethnographic research[1] in four Chinese factories in the MIH. These were a privately owned chipboard factory; a privately owned television, notebook, and tablet factory;

a motorcycle factory (set up with state capital); and an air-conditioning plant, partially operating with state capital (semistate capital). I also formed relations with the Chinese in these factories and outside of them. This proved to be important in understanding the daily lives of expatriate workers. My investigation's main discovery was the establishment of a Chinese model of production in Brazil whose elements had significant impacts on local workers and, in the face of the perceptions and reactions of local social agents, has both suffered adaptations and hardened controls (Maciel Brito 2017).

CHINESE SAVAGERY OR CHINESE ADAPTATION: IMPACTS ON UNIONS

The arrival of Chinese factories in the Amazon—to use a classic expression by Karl Marx—was something of a "ghost" haunting the region. Representatives of the Metallurgists Union of the State of Amazonas expressed varied views on the Chinese factories in the MFTZ. The union president presented his vision to me in these terms:

> The worst Asian businessmen are the Chinese. They think, for example, that when a manager goes to the production line to teach, he must yell at everyone. Usually, they do not have their own building: everything is rented, due to the imposition [of rules] by their country. In reality, these companies are state-owned. It is not like in Brazil. They come here, but it's all the state. They have no power here. Anything they do here, they must report there.

The union president also spoke of the difficulties that union leaders met in making Chinese companies comply with labor standards and agreements forged by class entities: "You have to confront them directly, because when the justice system fines them, they don't care. We are going to close those companies."

Finally, the union leader pointed out that the Chinese do not give any autonomy to Brazilian workers. They strictly control the production process through managers. "Production managers are everything. They do not have a national management group. And that is a form of control. . . . And this is precisely so they don't have to pay out social benefits. . . . We in the union prefer that they leave Brazil."

Meanwhile, in the opinion of another union leader, the arrival of Chinese companies is a new issue, and the union was still studying how they would behave in terms of labor legislation. According to this leader, nothing had yet happened to justify an occupation of a factory, in contrast to the union president's opinion.

According to yet a third leader, as soon as the Chinese companies arrived in Manaus, they began to break labor agreements. Many of them preferred to pay a fine rather than comply with a court order. However, according to this third leader, this relationship was slowly changing, and the Chinese had adapted.

The data I collected in the field displayed more "Chinese adaptation" than "Chinese savagery." This because, despite the union president having reported physical aggressions against workers, nonpayment of wages, and noncompliance with Brazilian laws, no data from the period studied showed this. In addition, the information collected in the Labor Court did not show a greater number of lawsuits against Chinese companies as compared to other the companies of other countries operating in the MIH.

In fact, the "disorganization of work" promoted by the Chinese went beyond what the unions reported, having diffuse impacts in Manaus. At the same time, however, it was very specific and unique, as shown by the shop floor data shown in the following sections.

MANAGEMENT VIA EXPATRIATION: IMPACTS ON CONTROL OF FACTORY SUPERVISION

With regard to factory control and supervision, research data shows heavy pressure from the Chinese and little autonomy granted to workers in terms of decision making. In the case of workers in the administrative sector of one factory where I conducted research, every purchase above US$2,000 had to be approved by headquarters in China.

Allied to this was a strong presence of supervisors on the factory floor: something that went against the 1990s trend of the Japanese model of production, which promoted the end of direct factory supervision. "When the Chinese guy sees something dirty, he complains to the supervisor and the supervisor complains to us. The Chinese are very demanding, they have many supervisors. I never saw that in any other company."[2]

Workers also reported that supervisors always passed along the production line to see if the employees were working correctly. When they saw something that disagreed with what they thought was correct, they did not teach the workers: "They take us off the job and call in other employees to take over." According to this interviewee, this happened because "the Chinese do not like mistakes, and they want us to do everything right the first time. For example, a boy was soldering wrong. The Chinese guy saw it, pulled the solder iron out of the kid's hand, and started doing it himself. They do, but they don't teach."[3]

Directly linked to the issue of factory control is the fact that the Chinese do not share information with Brazilians. According to my interviewees, Chinese management controls information about everything that happens in the factory: defects in the components, what must be done to fix them, actions to be developed throughout the year, annual production goals, ideas on how to develop new products, how to operate a particular machine that arrives from the headquarters in China, and so on. Finally, I observed macrocontrol emanating from China, exercised through information technology. This was structured in something called the Global System, through which the headquarters in China could see the Manaus factory floor and direct production there from China through direct contact with Chinese expatriates.

THE NO-FEELINGS POLICY: IMPACTS ON PARTICIPATION AND AWARDS

Another element of this "shock" is the lack of Chinese companies' appreciation of workers' creative capacity. According to my interviewees, the Chinese are not open to dialogue in the factory. They do not accept new ideas and they weave a vertical web of relationships where the ideas of managers are the correct ideas: "The Chinese way is terrible. They are hard-headed. We must do as they teach. If you say your way is better, they don't accept it."

For workers, this process has resulted in little motivation to work in Chinese companies since they do not feel valued by management. According to the workers, in the other MFTZ companies—mainly Japanese (Honda, Yamaha, Showa, Konica, Sony) and European (Siemens, Bic, Nokia,[4] Philips[5])—their ideas were accepted by managers, and many of them were rewarded. They could also count on gaining more in profit-sharing plans for their ideas. This did not happen in Chinese companies; to the contrary. According to workers, the Chinese leadership reconfigured what was "normal" in the management practice of the MIH:

They are cold in dealing with employees. They don't even say "Good morning." The Dutch did. The Dutch let us have ideas. The Chinese don't. They did not like us to have ideas or opinions about how to change our position or improve something.

These references to the management style of other MFTZ companies were constant in the interviews I carried out, showing that the Japanese model of production was the workers' reference for management. The workers always drew on comparisons with their old jobs, indicating that they felt they were more valued, respected, and part of a "team" that could "collaborate in the management of the company" in the old companies.

The lack of valorization of workers was reflected not only in the absence of a policy for participatory management, but also in the absence of tools for workers to evaluate the factories. There was little incentive for improving and training the workforce.

Many interviewees remarked that Chinese management did not invest in training courses or in the education of workers, demanding that workers pay for technical courses or college themselves. For the workers, this was a step backward. In many non-Chinese MFTZ factories, 50 percent of the cost of a university course was paid for by the company, or they periodically referred workers to technical courses with a view toward obtaining better training for their work force.

For the interviewees, this lack of training was worsened by the lack of opportunities for growth in the company. Senior positions were largely occupied by Chinese, who ended up promoting other Chinese. Furthermore, according to the workers I interviewed, a higher hierarchical level means a higher salary, and this did not interest management, given that a Chinese employee receives a lower salary than a Brazilian in the same job: "It's very difficult to grow in the company. At Konica,[6] I got a promotion after two years. I've been here for five years now and I still haven't got a promotion."

LAW IS THE LIMIT: IMPACTS ON LABOR RIGHTS AND SALARIES

Linked to this was the issue of wages. A line worker told me, for example, that in his previous job his salary was R$1,042, but that in a Chinese company the same job paid only R$908. Another worker reported a similar fact: "A worker doing my job at a Dutch company earns R$1,900, but here with the Chinese it's only R$1,500. Supervisors at the Dutch company earned R$4,000: here, it's R$2,800."

The workers also pointed out that that many of the benefits they received at other companies were less in Chinese companies. These include basic rations packages, which in Japanese companies was R$200 and in Chinese companies only R$70. They also indicated benefits to which they were entitled in other companies but which Chinese management had excluded or which could only be accessed through additional payments. This was the case, for example, with dental plans. European companies covered all members of the worker's family, but workers in Chinese companies had to pay R$12 out of their salary.

This "Chinese aggressiveness" toward labor benefits was confirmed by a human resources manager at a Chinese factory that had previously belonged to the Dutch:

> One aspect of Chinese culture is, of course, being more aggressive regarding spending than the Dutch were. In fact, the Dutch were not at all aggressive about spending. They had, in my view, a culture of accumulating many benefits for their employees. But the Chinese do not. They are very careful with the organization's expenses. They do not give out benefits or contributions other than those that are required by law. Those that are required by law, sure. They give those. But those that are not required by law? Those they question and then they start getting rid of them. Those that are not essential, they eliminate.

This same process was also pointed out by the workers I interviewed. According to them, this particular Chinese factory laid off a large part of the personnel who used to work under Dutch management. This was done, according to a foreman, with a view to "not incite other workers to want to earn a higher salary, because that company was a mother." Later, wanting to take advantage of the employees' manufacturing experience with the type of equipment produced at the factory, the company rehired the employees, but with lower wages and benefits than they previously earned under the Dutch.

The information I compiled allows us to compare between companies of various national origins in the MIH, and it backs up my interviewees, showing that the Chinese do not break labor laws in terms of wages, nor fail to grant legally required benefits.

Levels of wages and benefits are above legal minimums and the minimums agreed upon with workers. But when compared to other MIH companies, the Chinese spend much less than the Japanese, European, and South Korean companies. In the motorcycle sector (which is more structured, with greater professional qualifications and deeper local roots) Japanese factories pay much higher wages and benefits than Chinese factories.

Nevertheless, the data also shows that one cannot say that the Chinese are "enslaving" the local labor force or failing to comply with labor legislation in terms of wages or morals, as global and local narratives about Chinese factories tend to claim. What becomes clear is a model that is very focused on technical management, directly impacting on relationships with the local worker and workers' perception of Chinese factories. Minimum legal wages and benefits, little management participation by workers or unions, and heavy surveillance of workers all exemplify this model.

CONCLUSION: THE SOCIAL IMPACTS OF A NEW GLOBAL PRODUCTION MODEL

The presence of Chinese factories in the Amazon is recent, particularly in terms of their productive logic, and there is a lack of studies evaluating the consequences of the Chinese way of organizing work in the region. And yet, looking at the Chinese presence in the Amazon can contribute to assembling the puzzle that is the study of globalized China. It was in this sense that I carried out field research at the MIH.

This article has empirically evaluated how the Chinese model was affecting work relations on the factory floor, particularly with regard to the workers in Manaus. The data I collected has pushed me theoretically to understand how these elements are related to the history of transformations of work in the MIH and how the Chinese model has established itself as a way of managing and producing.

In this sense, then, I want to highlight two points:

- In general, Chinese factories have deepened the production pattern and technological regime arising from the economic globalization of the 1990s, accentuating the importation of low-cost inputs and with little local industrialization.

- On the factory floor, the Chinese have promoted a (dis-)organization of work that contrasts with the managerial style of the so-called Japanese model.

I believe that both the deepening of the technological pattern resulting from globalization and the "(dis-)organization of work" promoted in the factories I investigated are part of the China's effect on global and local production.

In the case of Manaus, strong socioproductive ties between parent and subsidiary companies generate fragile local socioproductive ties. External regulation has been stronger than internal regulation, since there is a state/capitalist legal regime at work regulating international Chinese companies. This is more organized and controlled than the global capitalism of the late twentieth century, involving state regulation of productive processes on the one hand and regulation by the nascent domestic capitalist class on foreign investments on the other.

These forces, in turn, take shape in the lives of the Chinese expatriates who are used to dense state, corporate, and subjective surveillance. In this situation, institutional and social forms intertwine to create a controlled expatriation: contract lengths, living for work, family needs, distance, factory dormitory policies, national pride, and personal responsibility are much emphasized in this model. Chinese expatriates are thus part of a process that shifts property (the sale of labor) and managerial/political control in the course of Chinese internationalization. Unlike other types of expatriation, the Chinese live in constant quarantine and have their lives organized by the company, with little relationship to the social environment of the region in which they are working.

This is the *Chinese model of production*, which has as its backdrop a productive system produced in Manaus under a "Western" market ethos and managed under a state/collective ethos organized in China. The questions that unfold are why this model is different from the Japanese management model in the MIH and why it has not resulted in a type of management with more "participatory" opportunities.

I tackle these questions by building a typology: *participatory management via subjective control vs. technical management via direct control*. The Japanese model—still dominant in the MIH—is an example of the first management style, in which the collective has folded in favor of the individual.

This occurred because it had to face another collective—the unions—and because in the face of greater control by national institutions over imports and local production chains, the Japanese had to make greater concessions to local social agents, including workers. Hence, a management style with greater social interaction was born in the Amazon.

Going in the opposite direction, Chinese factories (and their community spirit) seek to collectively discipline importation, external interests/demands, and management, the fundamental components that make up the Chinese model. An initial stage of this model is a system of exchange values based on the dissemination of manufactured products and the importation of cheaper inputs, machines, and equipment in high quantities under a Brazilian system that is fiscally weak and with relatively few applicable taxes.

The corollary is a structure that depends on no mediations without Chinese actors, either in production or importation. This structure takes advantage of the institutional fragilities revealed by globalization and the gravitational effect of the Chinese economy on production capacity, product costs, and global resources. We can thus say that, to all effects, the Chinese Model deepens the dependency of underdeveloped countries upon the centers of global production. But that is not all it does.

In its second stage, the model establishes *political control of management* on a global level, with controlled expatriates who are integral parts of a strategic agenda involving Chinese importation of technology and raw materials. This leads Chinese factories in Brazil to create tight, symbiotic connections with their home companies. The consequence of this model is a combination of the market and state in these factories, which are thus able to control importation and labor costs, as well as manage the bodies and life trajectories of the Chinese expatriates who work for the companies.

In this context, a necessary input for Chinese production would, in theory, be a dependency or vulnerability that generates a bargain in the MIH. However, the Chinese production model works in such a way that it supplies a dependency without the need for any intermediaries or agents from outside the model. What is more, the use values of the resources (raw materials) employed in production are also locally transformed into exchange values (merchandise), since the Chinese factories also sell inputs to other companies.

This generates a set of manufacturing sites that are weakly rooted, without the need for negotiation with local laws, and that, indeed, are almost independent of the city which they are situated. They have no political agenda for investment nor needs that engender local ties. The result is greater managerial rigidity and an economic agenda self-supplied by China. This is a labor model that is more Made in China than Produced in Manaus, and it results in relatively little gain for the work it consumes.

NOTES

1. Doctoral research undertaken at the Federal University of São Carlos, São Paulo. The resulting thesis was awarded Honorable Mention in the Sociology category from the Ministry of Education of Brazil in 2018.
2. Line worker. Interview with the author, 2015.
3. Accountant. Interview with the author, 2017.
4. Bought by Microsoft in 2013.
5. Bought by the Chinese.
6. A company in the MIH.

REFERENCES

Andrijasevic, Rutvica, and Devi Sacchetto. 2016. "Foxxconn Beyond China: Capital-Labour Relations as Co-determinants of Internationalization." In *China at Work: A Labour Perspective on the Transformation of Work and Employment in China*, edited by Mingwei Liu and Chris Smith. London: Palgrave Macmillan Education.

Burgoon, B., and D. Raess. 2014. "Chinese Investment and European Labor: Should and Do Workers Fear Chinese FDI?" *Asia Europe Journal* 12, no.1–2: 179–97.

Fraga, Érica, and Claudia Rolli. 2011. "42% deixam empresas chinesas no país em 1 ano." *Folha de São Paulo*, São Paulo, May 8, 2011. https://www1.folha.uol.com.br/fsp/mercado/me0805201104.htm.

Gao, Y. 2004. *Chinese Migrants and Forced Labour in Europe*. Working Paper 32. Geneva: International Labour Office.

Lee, Ching Kwan. 2009. "Raw Encounters: Chinese Managers, African Workers and the Politics of Casualization in Africa's Chinese Enclaves." *China Quarterly* 199: 647–66.

Maciel Brito, Cleiton. 2017. "Made in China / Produzido no Polo Industrial da Zona Franca de Manaus: o trabalho nas fábricas chinesas." PhD dissertation, Universidade Federal de São Carlos.

Meunier, Sophie. 2012. *Political Impact of Chinese Foreign Direct Investment in the European Union on Transatlantic Relations*. European Parliament Briefing Paper. Brussels: European Parliament.

Pun, N., and J. Chan. 2012. "Global Capital, the State and Chinese Workers: The Foxconn Experience." *Modern China* 38, no. 4: 383–410.

Seráfico, Marcelo. 2011. *Globalização e empresariado: estudo sobre a Zona Franca de Manaus.* São Paulo: Annablume.

Valle, Izabel. 2007. *Globalização e reestruturação produtiva: um estudo sobre a produção offshore em Manaus.* Manaus: Editora da Universidade Federal do Amazonas.

National Development Priorities and Transnational Workplace Inequalities: Challenges for China's State-Sponsored Construction Projects in Ecuador

Rui Jie Peng

IN THE AGE OF GLOBALIZATION, China's state-owned enterprises (SOEs) and capital are spearheading foreign direct investments and development projects in the Global South. Chinese state-driven foreign investments in Latin America represent the fastest growing and one of the most important global investment flows (Chen and Ludeña 2013). This has led to a proliferation of infrastructure projects often run by Chinese state-owned construction firms that employ both Chinese and local workers. Under threat of looming global recession and China's slowing economic growth, the Chinese government has strong incentives to stimulate growth and employment through "Stepping Out" and internationalization. As a result, Chinese SOEs and investments are steadily expanding in countries like Ecuador and Brazil and are expected to grow, creating more transnational workplaces in Latin America.

In many Chinese companies, Chinese and Ecuadorian personnel work together. Because Chinese SOEs account for most of these workplaces, Chinese workers have increasingly been cast as foot soldiers in development projects. Between 2013 and 2014, as Chinese investments in infrastructure and energy projects in Ecuador were exploding, I conducted ethnographic field research at the Coca Codo Sinclair hydroelectric project (CCS) that a Chinese state-owned construction company, Sinohydro, was building in eastern Ecuador.

As a Chinese person and graduate student at the time, I gained permission from the company to stay at the main project camp in to conduct ethnographic research. This opportunity allowed me to gain firsthand exposure to the company's organizational dynamics and Chinese and Ecuadorian workers' lived experiences of geopolitical change. My ability to speak Chinese and Spanish and my position as an independent researcher helped me build rapport with both Chinese and Ecuadorian workers. I observed how the company's operations and local regulations are reshaping labor relations and social dynamics. I studied how workers from different racial and national backgrounds interpreted two different sets of labor laws and how they managed workplace inequalities. My goal was understanding how transnational workplace inequality and national-racial boundaries interrelate. I found that workers' class, race, gender, nationality, citizenship, and legal status stratify their labor tasks and statuses. By examining microlevel interactions between Chinese and Ecuadorian workers, I argue that global capital, national hierarchies, and development priorities shape the structure of labor control and workers' lived experiences of workplace inequalities (Peng 2017).

I begin by examining China and Ecuador's national discourses about development, investment, aid, and debt. I focus on how South-South flows of capital and national development priorities act as macrostructures undergirding workers' lived experiences with inequalities and their agency in a transnational workplace. I further discuss what these workplace inequalities and intergroup dynamics might mean for labor relations, foreign policy, and global capital accumulation strategies, especially as we confront challenges from the COVID-19 pandemic, a looming economic recession, and China's intention to play a more visible role in the Global South.

CHINA'S "STEPPING-OUT" AND TRANSNATIONAL LABOR CONTROL

Since the 1980s, the Chinese government has encouraged SOEs to "step out" through various foreign direct investment (FDI) schemes. To counter Western domination in the international development arena, the Chinese government has tried to frame its FDI and development projects as "South-South cooperation" (Ferchen 2011), emphasizing its role in promoting equal and sustainable development in the Global South. After Chinese

SOEs first established joint ventures in Africa and Latin America, they prioritized creating mutual benefits and boosting political ties with host countries (Lee 2017). As the Chinese economy began to experience overcapacity in the late 2000s, Stepping Out to the Global South meant seeking a larger market share. In its attempt to gain power and reshape a new world order in international relations and development, the Chinese government initiated the Belt and Road Initiative (BRI) in 2013 to leverage geopolitical power and weave Eurasia, Southeast Asia, and Eastern Africa into "a tight network of economic, cultural, political, and strategic relations" (Callahan 2016). Latin America was included as part of China's Twenty-First-Century Maritime Silk Road in 2017 and its recent New Health Silk Road agenda for the pandemic. Ecuador ranks fifth for Chinese FDI in Latin America (Gonzàlez 2018) and has contracted Chinese SOEs to develop its oil, mining, and hydropower sectors.

Such national development priorities are so ambitious that they shape Chinese employees' everyday experience with the organization of work and labor control in transnational workplaces. Specifically, the Stepping Out and South-South cooperation discourses imply a new international development order, motivating Chinese SOEs to structure highly disciplinary labor regimes for their Chinese workers. One way they do so is to structure job hierarchy, provide services for employees, and internally regulate grievances based on *danwei* (the socialist work unit). Before China's 1978 market reform, *danwei* was a physical workplace and organizing principle that organized employees' work and personal lives and aided in implementing socioeconomic imperatives such as delivering state welfare services. As a workplace, *danwei* encompassed institutions such as lifetime employment, inheritable jobs, and affiliated schools and hospitals (Gu 2001). As an organizing principle, *danwei* facilitated the planned economy by enforcing labor and social control (Frazier 2002). Since large SOEs began to operate overseas in the 1980s, *danwei* as a physical workplace that accommodated planned economy, welfare provision, and job guarantees is no longer viable. However, many Chinese SOEs overseas continue to draw from the *danwei* ethos to implement labor control in transnational workplaces.

Starting with the recruitment process for the CCS, Sinohydro hired Chinese workers through its state-owned branch under Chinese labor regulations, and Ecuadorian workers through its international subsidiary under local labor regulations. Under this organizational structure, Ecuadorian workers experienced much state oversight when they navigated the transnational workplace, but minimal state intervention in how they conducted their personal lives. In one sense, Chinese workers working abroad may seem to be working in a stateless situation because they have neither recourse to Chinese labor laws nor practical access to Ecuadorian protections. Viewed from another perspective, they were intensely governed by the state institutions and political imperatives—more so than their Ecuadorian counterparts. At the CCS, all Chinese workers lived in enclosed base camps offering housing, dining, and clinics. Apart from managers, the Chinese workers stayed in cramped dormitories and spent most of their time at work. Sinohydro not only strictly forbade the Chinese workers from going outside the camp without company approval but also withheld workers' passports and deposited their salaries in China. Such tight labor and social controls draw from the *danwei* principle, but specific labor management practices constitute new organizational strategies in the transnational workplace.

Chinese workers drew heavily on the "tough hydro-worker" identity to come to terms with family separation, long hours, and inferior work conditions. Following the principles of *danwei*, including obedience to authority, loyally, and integrity, the Chinese workers in Ecuador increasingly identified with and internalized beliefs in "self-sacrifice" and "technical excellence" to cope with the intense control of their work and lives. I found that most Chinese SOEs were concerned about the political stability and safety in their host countries. Chinese employees considered strict surveillance in their personal lives necessary for ensuring their safety and work performance. These workers were also motivated by the "tough hydro-worker" ethic to work overtime without pay and remain compliant so that they could secure permanent employment and future higher-paying work-abroad opportunities. Although safety measures were necessary, Chinese employees subjected to strict control eventually became submissive to the company, which undermined their ability to demand improved conditions. Facing the absence of state protection in their workplace and the omnipresence of state intrusions in their personal lives, many Chinese employees rejected protest. This further facilitated the development of stereotypes regarding their Ecuadorian counterparts.

In turn, when Ecuadorian workers observed Chinese workers, they stereotyped their Chinese counterparts as "workaholic" and "model workers," portraying them as submissive and unconcerned about better work conditions. Such stereotyped interpretations, however, ignored the underlying constraints Chinese workers experienced. As we can see in Brito's chapter on laborers in the Manaus Free Trade Zone in this volume, such readings of Chinese workers are not exclusive to Ecuador.

ECUADOR'S DEVELOPMENT MODEL AND THE OPENING OF OPPORTUNITIES FOR WORKERS

Ecuador has historically relied on exporting primary resources and commodities: cacao (1895–1920), bananas (1948–1970), and oil from 1972 to the present (Riofrancos 2017; Purcell and Martinez 2018). In the early 1970s, influenced by criticisms of the center-periphery world system and dependent relations with the US, Ecuador's military governments pushed state control over national resources. They used oil revenues to finance social spending and infrastructure development (Rosales 2017). Under this "resource nationalism" model, military governments used future oil production to secure international credits, resulting in a twenty-fold surge in foreign debts from 1971 to 1981 (Acosta 2013). However, after oil prices plummeted in the 1980s, forceful state control over natural resources and development plans gave way to growing pressures to commit to neoliberalism. This move marked the beginning of a series of structural reforms that created favorable conditions for foreign investment, particularly in the oil industry (Rosales 2017). Ecuador's neoliberal era arguably ended—and state control returned—with the election of leftist president Rafael Correa in 2006, and the 2008 Constitution that endorsed a just, sustainable, and environmentally friendly developmental model under the Indigenous concept *Sumak Kawsay* (Caria and Domínguez 2016). Correa took aggressive measures to reassert state power and break away from neoliberal orthodoxies and traditional Western financial institutions. As van Teijlingen and Hidalgo Bastidas's chapter in this volume relates, under Correa's leadership, Ecuador defaulted on US$3.2 billion of foreign debts, increased the government's share of petroleum profits, and implemented a series of redistributive policies aimed at improving people's lives (Silva 2016).

A central contradiction undermined these national development objectives, government legitimacy, and relations with social movement activists and critical leftist intellectuals: the government expanded resource
extraction by claiming that this would fuel short-term industrial and social
development, changing the country's commodity exportation model (Caria
and Domínguez 2016; Purcell and Martinez 2018). When such development
lacked capital, the Ecuadorian government deepened economic and political ties with China. Increasing volumes of Chinese state capital in the
natural resource sectors prompted further criticisms that the government
was reproducing the neoliberal extractivist model (Silva 2016; Riofrancos
2017). Correa's government then prioritized an even more aggressive development plan to expand hydropower and change the productive structure
of the economy. This politicized the hydroelectric projects being built with
Chinese loans and construction companies. It could be argued that the CCS,
the largest project, became an intensely politicized domain in which the
Ecuadorian state could assert power to boost its legitimacy. In interviews
with Ecuadorian workers in the project, I heard many call it "the presidents'
project." They recalled presidential visits to project sites. Some remembered
shaking hands with President Correa and Vice President Glas in person.

Faced with contested national discourses for economic and social development, the post-neoliberal Ecuadorian government increased oversight to guarantee Ecuadorian employees' rights as a means of justifying
its legitimacy. They institutionalized protections for workers and refrained
from severe repression of collective labor organization (Hawkins 2011). This
commitment to labor rights created political openings for Ecuadorian workers to push for labor protections through various protests at Chinese state-
sponsored projects. At the CCS, I observed that Ecuadorian workers could
leverage governmental oversight and appeal to labor laws to make demands
on management. As a result, they maintained eight-hour work schedules
and upheld higher security standards compared to their Chinese counterparts. One of the key arrangements that contributed to workers' organizing capacity was that the Ecuadorian state established a presence through
its Ministry of Labor (MOL), which supervised the hiring of Ecuadorian
workers by Sinohydro. The MOL implemented an Internet-based system
at the company, La RED Socio Empleo, which followed and recorded employment history, current status, work hours and overtime, as well as other

administrative data for every Ecuadorian employee. Under this system, the human resources staff would complete an online application to centrally administer Ecuadoran employees' procedures, wages, and other benefits. The Ecuadorian human resource manager at the CCS project explained that government intervention ensured that Ecuadorian employees receive proper compensation for hours worked. Those who decided to quit their jobs could easily collect their pending payments. The MOL also assisted in implementing the new Labor Codes, providing workers with adequate information on and access to state laws and protections for labor rights.

Such guaranteed state support created advantages for Ecuadorian employees in defending their labor rights and improving working conditions. Ecuadorian worker representatives actively negotiated with Sinohydro for better conditions through the sanctioned company platform. Chinese workers did not have such institutionalized protections and channels for demanding improved treatment. They stereotyped their Ecuadorian counterparts as "lazy" and "demanding" because they considered the Ecuadorian workers unwilling to work overtime without compensation. These perspectives obscured how Ecuadorian workers' histories of resistance and the political moment aided struggles for rights and protections.

In summary, the convergence of two sets of national development objectives and discourses in one transnational workplace reveals how the histories and politics around the global flows of capital and resources shape the social organization of work and protection for workers. At the CCS, pervasive stereotypes emerged in the Chinese-sponsored transnational workplace as the Chinese and Ecuadorian workers rationalized inequalities in labor relations and rights. On a broader level, these national-racial boundaries developed and intensified as China stepped out to pursue investment and development and as the Ecuadorian government leveraged Chinese financing for alternative development paths. Casting labor rights and work cultures as inherently national-racial qualities, however, masks such structural forces as national discourses and international hierarchies that shape how distinct groups perceive themselves and each other, reinforcing transnational workplace inequalities. These antagonisms not only disrupt possibilities for transnational solidarity; stereotypes and mutual mistrust can potentially undermine the promises of knowledge and skill transfer that many Chinese investments and projects set out to deliver to Ecuador.

THE CRISIS AND RESPONSES FROM THE CHINESE
GOVERNMENT

Since its initial entry into Ecuador, Chinese state-sponsored projects have seen incidents of workers' physical abuses and fatal injuries, reports of violations of workplace safety regulations, and protests and resistance from workers and impacted communities (Ellis 2018). For example, as Pullaguari documents in this volume, in the Mirador Copper Mine in Ecuador's southern Amazonian region, the Indigenous Shuar people have mobilized race and class discourses to resist the abuse and the hegemonic practices of modernization. Local communities near the CCS base camps also had high expectations for long-term investments to improve health and education infrastructures but only experienced short-term business opportunities. In addition to tense labor and community relations, quality and budget control issues have haunted Chinese-sponsored projects in Ecuador. In April 2020, as Fernández-Salvador and Viteri write in this volume, the dam caused massive erosion to the riverbed, resulting in pipeline ruptures and a disastrous oil spill in the nearby communities. More recently, after the current Ecuadorian president Moreno took office, several former officials were either charged or sentenced for receiving bribes from Odebrecht, a Brazilian construction company that is the main competitor of the Chinese. Ecuador's former president Correa was convicted by the top court for corruption charges (Cabrera 2020). More investigations are underway. Since March 2019, President Moreno has been surrounded by corruption probes for accepting bribes from the Chinese to facilitate the agreements of the CCS project.

These controversies are destabilizing Chinese investments and projects in Ecuador. They are compounded by Ecuador's shifting political preferences for sources of development funding. The Moreno administration has adopted more pro-Western attitudes in designing Ecuador's development programs and has started rapprochement with institutions like the International Monetary Fund and the World Bank (Ellis 2018). Delgado in this volume also notes how overpriced contracts with Chinese companies and excessive foreign debt accrued during the Correa administration have played a crucial role in the current social and economic crises in Ecuador, which have worsened amid the COVID-19 pandemic. Challenges arising from the economic crisis, the COVID-19 pandemic, and the neoliberal reforms could chart new courses for government intervention and labor regulation in future Chinese state-sponsored transnational workplaces.

The other possible source of change is the Chinese government. Faced with instability in its foreign investments and projects, as well as economic and political challenges posed by the COVID-19 pandemic, the Chinese government has begun to increase support for its BRI project. In March 2020, the Chinese Ministry of Commerce issued an announcement outlining the procedures the China Development Bank (CDB) should follow to identify and provide financial support to overseas Chinese projects (Ministry of Commerce of the People's Republic of China 2020). There are five central measures aimed at making loans more readily available. First, the CDB will leverage its designated BRI loan and increase support for enterprises and projects impacted by the pandemic. Second, the CDB will designate US$5 billion to support central government-owned enterprises and subsidiaries to resume production. Third, the CDB will reassess the financial risk and permit low-risk enterprises to renegotiate loan terms to help these projects resume work. Fourth, the CDB will simplify loan application processes for qualified enterprises. Finally, the CDB will increase multilateral collaborations with overseas financial institutions to diversify sources of loans for these projects.

By closely reading news reports in China that explain the official rhetoric, I find that the government initiated such measures to ensure the viability of Chinese FDIs and international development projects in the pandemic: 2020 marks the first year without a government target for annual GDP growth since China's 1978 market reform (Feng and Cheng 2020). Chinese state-sponsored enterprises and projects overseas have now become even more important in stimulating China's overall economy and employment. The government seeks to leverage the global health crisis to deepen bilateral financial exchanges and collaboration and reshape the international value and commodity chain. The combination of motivations to stimulate the economy and promote the BRI has translated into more visible measures to support and encourage Chinese state-sponsored projects overseas. The Chinese government has leveraged the "New Health Silk Road" rhetoric and agenda to channel medical-humanitarian assistance to Latin American countries (Koop 2020) while boosting China's image. These initiatives will likely translate into future collaborations and increase the number of transnational workplaces, thus exerting a profound influence on the development and well-being of the Global South.

Civil society groups in the Global South have begun to initiate dialogues with the Chinese government. In response to new stimulus measures by the Chinese Ministry of Commerce, a group of nongovernmental organizations (NGOs), consisting of 260 organizations working in the Global South, sent a letter (Zhong 2020) outlining suggestions for how Chinese projects should move forward. This group of NGOs seeks to strategically use the Chinese government's language and rhetoric in an appeal for more environmental and social responsibility. Building on this logic, this group further appeals to the Chinese government to only fund projects that have met certain standards: having obtained community consent through consultation, observing local standards for environmental protection, and ensuring the health and sustainability of their workers. The group expands the definition of "risk" (*feng xian*) used in the Chinese government's announcement, which originally referred to "controllable financial risk." The NGOs demand that the CDB honor commitments to "controllable risk," not only in the financial sense but also in terms of the health of workers and communities and the overall environment by highlighting the COVID-19 pandemic as a health crisis for human beings and the planet. In all these instances of strategically using Chinese government rhetoric, the group of NGOs has centered broad social and environmental issues and pressured the CDB to observe high standards in selecting targets of supportive loans. In doing so, they have implicitly portrayed many of the Chinese-sponsored projects as having failed to meet these socioenvironmental goals.

This group of NGOs has recommended a list of projects and urged the Chinese Ministry of Commerce not to fund them during the new round of increased financial support. Three Chinese-sponsored projects in Ecuador (the Mirador Copper Mine, Rio Blanco Copper Mine, and San Carlos Panantza Copper Project) appeared on the list. The NGOs' appeals closely reflect how such projects have fared in Ecuador. Not only have Chinese-sponsored mining projects witnessed worker protests and injuries, but these projects have had considerable influence on the health and livelihoods of workers, local and Indigenous communities, and the planet (Erazo 2012). This event is a telling instance of how, according to Vásconez in this volume, civil society and public discourses about such Chinese investments as the CCS became reinvigorated in the wake of a series of environmental disasters and the ongoing COVID-19 pandemic. Despite the international pressure, however, there is yet to be a formal response from the Chinese Ministry of Commerce.

As my examination of the Chinese-sponsored CCS project in Ecuador reveals, China–Latin America relationships and engagements are in a historic process of rapid change and transformation. My ethnographic research in Ecuador captures a short period in the life of the CCS project. While it documents how national development objectives and historical labor institutions and struggles underpin the lack of labor protection among Chinese workers and the guarantee of labor rights and negotiation among the Ecuador workers, these relationships can rapidly shift. As we see in the COVID-19 pandemic, differences in development objectives and labor regulations, as well as misunderstanding and stereotypes among workers on Chinese-sponsored projects, might exacerbate existing inequalities and lead to negative health impacts. Neoliberal labor reforms and inadequate social investments will likely increase health risks and precarious labor conditions among workers in Ecuador. In light of these changes, we can analyze how the Chinese government's increased support for these overseas projects might have a broader influence on its foreign investments and strategies, and how such adjustments interact with changing policy and development priorities in countries like Ecuador during the COVID-19 pandemic. I suspect that to push Chinese government agencies to act "responsibly" in investments and projects, it is not enough to organize and pressure the CDB. More synergistic measures to identify political allies in the destination countries and leverage domestic laws and regulations can aid in the effort of achieving equity and protection for workers, communities, and the overall environment.

REFERENCES

Acosta, Alberto. 2013. "Extractivism and Neoextractivism: Two Sides of the Same Curse." In *Beyond Development: Alternative Visions from Latin America*, edited by M. Lang and D. Mokrani. Quito: Rosa Luxemburg Foundation.

Cabrera, León. 2020. "Ecuador's Former President Convicted on Corruption Charges." *New York Times*, April 7, 2020.

Callahan, William A. 2016. "China's 'Asia Dream': The Belt Road Initiative and the New Regional Order." *Asian Journal of Comparative Politics* 1, no. 3: 226–43.

Caria, Sara, and Rafael Domínguez. 2016. "Ecuador's Buen Vivir: A New Ideology for Development." *Latin American Perspectives* 43, no. 1: 18–33.

Carrion, Carmen. 2019. "El 'dosier Lenin' que incrimina al presidente de Ecuador por un piso en Villajoyosa." *El Confidencial*, March 7, 2019.

Chen, Taotao, and Miguel Pérez Ludeña. 2013. "Chinese Foreign Direct Investment in Latin America and the Caribbean." ECLAC (Economic Commission for Latin America and the Caribbean).

Ellis, Evan. 2018. "Ecuador's Leveraging of China to Pursue an Alternative Political and Development Path." *Journal of Indo-Pacific Affairs*, Fall: 79–104.

Erazo, Paúl Mena. 2012. "La mayor organización indígena de Ecuador se moviliza contra Correa." *El País*, March 8, 2012. https://elpais.com/internacio nal/2012/03/08/actualidad/1331190707_452752.html.

Feng, Emily, and Amy Cheng. 2020. "China Abandons Economic Growth Targets Amid Pandemic." *NPR*, May 22, 2020. https://www.npr.org/2020/05/22/860667352/ china-abandons-growth-targets-for-1st-time-in-40-years.

Ferchen, Matt. 2011. "China–Latin America Relations: Long-Term Boon or Short-Term Boom?" *Chinese Journal of International Politics* 4, no. 1: 55–86.

Frazier, Mark W. 2002. *The Making of the Chinese Industrial Workplace: State, Revolution, and Labor Management.* Cambridge: Cambridge University Press.

González, Anabel. 2018. "Latin America—China Trade and Investment Amid Global Tensions." Atlantic Council. https://atlanticcouncil.org/wp-content/ uploads/2018/12/Latin-America-China-Trade-and-Investment-Amid-Global -Tensions.pdf.

Gu, Edward. 2001. "Beyond the Property Rights Approach: Welfare Policy and the Reform of State-Owned Enterprises in China." *Development and Change* 32, no. 1: 129–50.

Hawkins, Daniel. 2011. "The Influence of Organized Labour in the Rise to Power of Lula in Brazil and Correa in Ecuador." *Labour, Capital and Society / Travail, Capital et Société* 44, no. 2: 26–55.

Koop, Fermin. 2020. "Coronavirus Reshapes China's BRI in Latin America." *Dialogo Chino*, July 30, 2020. https://dialogochino.net/en/infrastructure/36699-co ronavirus-reshapes-belt-and-road-in-latin-america/.

Lee, Ching Kwan. 2017. *The Specter of Global China: Politics, Labor, and Foreign Investment in Africa.* Chicago: University of Chicago Press.

Ministry of Commerce of the People's Republic of China. 2020. "Announcement for Using China Development Bank's Financial Services to Support Building High-Quality Belt and Road Initiative during the Covid-19 Pandemic." March 2, 2020. http://www.gov.cn/zhengce/zhengceku/2020-04/08/5500262/files/3312eef 0d5064f88b031b35be098d6a5.pdf.

Peng, Rui Jie. 2017. "One Transnational Project, Two Labor Regimes: The Workers' Experience with Labor Process and Racialization on a Chinese Hydroelectric Project in Ecuador." Paper presented at the Society for the Study of Social Problems Annual Meeting. Montreal, Canada.

Purcell, Thomas F., and Estefania Martinez. 2018. "Post-Neoliberal Energy Modernity and the Political Economy of the Landlord State in Ecuador." *Energy Research & Social Science* 41: 12–21.

Riofrancos, Thea. 2017. "Extractivismo Unearthed: A Genealogy of a Radical Discourse." *Cultural Studies* 31, no. 2–3: 277–306.

Rosales, Antulio. 2017. "Contentious Nationalization and the Embrace of the Developmental Ideals: Resource Nationalism in the 1970s in Ecuador." *Extractive Industries and Society* 4, no. 1: 102–10.

Silva, Verónica. 2016. "The Return of the State, New Social Actors, and Post-Neoliberalism in Ecuador." *Latin American Perspectives* 43, no. 1: 4–17.

Van Teijlingen, Karolien, Esben Leifsen, Consuelo Fernández Salvador, and Luis Sánchez-Vázquez. 2017. *La Amazonía minada: minería a gran escala y conflictos en el sur de Ecuador.* Quito: USFQ Press.

Zhong Shan, Ministro. 2020. "Re: Apoyo a la construcción de "alta calidad" en el Cinturón y la Ruta de la Seda—cómo las entidades chinas pueden proteger a las personas y el medio ambiente en un mundo de Covid-19." Letter correspondence. April 19, 2020.

Rio's Phantom Dubai? Porto do Açu, Chinese Investments, and the Geopolitical Specter of Brazilian Mineral Booms

Marcos A. Pedlowski

EVEN THOUGH IT HAS BEEN a private enterprise since its foundation, the Açu Industrial Port and Logistics Complex (hereafter, Porto do Açu) is a very complete application of the neodevelopmentalist model (Bresser-Pereira 2006). This is especially true with regard to the strategies adopted during the governments of Luís Inácio Lula da Silva and Dilma Rousseff to leverage the process of economic growth in Brazil based on so-called public-private partnerships. Porto do Açu, like several other ports that were enlarged or built after Lula's rise to the presidency, began construction in 2007 in the municipality of São João da Barra along the northern coast of Rio de Janeiro. Initially conceived during the tenure of Governor Rosinha Garotinho (2003–2006) to be a medium-sized port exporting the oil produced in the Campos Basin, the project was radically expanded in 2007 by Garotinho's successor, Governor Sérgio Cabral (Pessanha 2017). Eike Batista also joined the project at that time. Batista was the founder and chief executive officer of the EBX Group. He presented the new governor of Rio de Janeiro with an ambitious plan to build a port, industrial, and logistical complex that, in practice, would be a modified form of the neodevelopmentalist model conventionally known as a Maritime and Industrial Development Area (Wang, Chen, and Ma 2018).

The alliance between Cabral and Batista resulted in the replacement of the minimalist version of Porto do Açu with another project that planned for the construction of a port and industrial megacomplex. This would house two steel foundries, two thermoelectric plants, a cement plant, and a shipyard, in addition to the port terminal. The complex would also be coupled with a pipeline beginning 552 km away in Conceição do Mato Dentro, a mining town where iron ore deposits (at that point belonging to MMX, one of the companies that made up the EBX Group) are located (Pedlowski 2013). This model saw Port of Açu as not only a raw mineral commodity shipping point but also a complex where minerals would be processed into products in the enterprise's various industrial units. The objective would be to add value to these goods while meeting the demands of global markets, especially those of China. Batista claimed that the Porto Açu megaproject would take up 90 km², an area equivalent to the island of Manhattan. Batista's main promise—widely echoed by the media—was that Porto do Açu represented economic redemption, not only for the municipality of São João da Barra where the project would be installed, but for the entire North Fluminense region.

This redemption would take the form of a significant increase in jobs and tax receipts. As a counterpart to the cycle of growth and development that was supposed to start with the construction of Porto do Açu, steps would have to be taken at the local level for the venture to become a reality. The first step was to remove around 1,500 families of small farmers and artisanal fishermen from their homes within the 7,500-ha area that had been chosen to house the complex. The second step was to adopt a fragmented environmental licensing process, so that the different parts of the Porto do Açu project would be evaluated individually and separately. This was supposedly done to achieve greater speed in the licensing process (Latini 2016).

Due to the large size of Batista's project, it immediately became apparent that the construction of the complex could not take place without direct participation by different levels of government (from federal to municipal). EBX Group did not have the ability to solve the different aspects required to implement Porto do Açu (Moraes 2017). In the list of things understood as preconditions for the undertaking were financial grants to carry out construction. As important, however, were the removal or modification of several different laws that hindered the implementation of the complex in the area where Batista wanted to build. Porto do Açu was an enterprise that was supposed to be constructed solely with private capital. It was thus not part of the federal government's Growth Acceleration Program launched in 2007. Batista lobbied incessantly, however, for access to government-subsidized credit lines. Several campaigns were successfully carried out so that Porto do Açu could be awarded credit with interest subsidized by the National Bank for Economic and Social Development and other government sources, such as the Maritime Fund. Legal and administrative measures were also adopted at the state and municipal levels to enable the rapid implementation of the complex, even if this meant the use of EBX Group's private police and security forces to forcibly remove the legitimate landowners without the financial compensation provided for in the federal constitution.

The present chapter details China's wavering involvement in a project that, to a certain degree, exemplifies the issues discussed in the other Brazilian chapters in this volume. Built on confiscated land with little to no input from affected communities, financed by multiple investors through tortuous multilateral structures, originally created to industrialize a backwoods area of the southeast but subsequently transformed into a much reduced, resource-export oriented operation, the Porto do Açu megaproject well illustrates Brazilian dreams, Chinese practicalities, and the results the "strategic partnership" and "inevitable marriage" between the two countries have on local and traditional communities and their surrounding environments. The chapters in this volume by Vasques, Rodríguez, and Queiroz, Praça, and Bitencourt remind us that Brazil is a geographical and economic giant—however debilitated by its crises—and that Chinese investments and interests in the country extend to many economic sectors and regions.

INCONCLUSIVE ATTEMPTS TO TRANSFORM PORTO DO AÇU INTO A HIGHWAY TO CHINA

Eike Batista always saw Porto do Açu as a superhighway linking Brazil to the prosperous Chinese market. To move from plan to action, Batista put together a delegation to visit China in July 2009. Among those in the Brazilian delegation were the governor of Rio de Janeiro, Sérgio Cabral Filho; the state secretary for economic development, Júlio Bueno; and the mayor of São João da Barra, Carla Machado. After making visits to several Chinese cities (including Beijing, Shanghai, and Wuhan), Batista met with the president of the Wuhan Iron and Steel group (Wisco). He managed to gain a promise that one of the biggest steel groups in China would invest US$5 billion to build one of the steelworks that were in the original

Porto do Açu model. In December 2009, Batista returned to China and came back to Brazil with the good news that he had started negotiating a partnership to set up a scooter and moped factory in the Porto do Açu industrial area. At the same time, Batista announced Wisco's acquisition of 21.5 percent of the shares of MMX, the EBX Group's mining company, which would ensure a sustained supply of iron ore for the future steel-works in Porto do Açu.

In addition to news about these economic partnerships, Batista also circulated rumors that then Chinese president Hu Jintao would visit Porto do Açu in 2010 during his visit to Brazil at the invitation of President Lula. Although the Chinese president did not come, a large delegation of Chinese businessmen visited the site in April 2010 under the leadership of Deputy Foreign Minister Jiang Yaoping. This congregation included the president of the China Chamber of Commerce, Zhang Yujing. The visit was spun by Batista and representatives of the Rio de Janeiro government as an un-equivocal demonstration that Rio (and by extension Porto do Açu) had guaranteed Chinese investment in Brazil.

Despite all the rumors and expectations, the Chinese group backed out of the project in November 2012 amid conflicting news in the Brazilian press about the fate of the proposed steel works in São João da Barra. The lack of a railroad that could connect Porto do Açu to MMX's iron ore terminal in Porto Sudeste, 300 km away from São João da Barra, figured prominently in these stories.

Batista's initial reaction was to wave away the loss of the Wisco part-nership. At the time, he claimed that Porto do Açu's profile was changing to become a niche for companies focused on supplying the deep-water oil fields off the coast. Coincidentally or not, however, in October 2013 (less than a year after Wisco left the Porto do Açu project), the conglomerate of companies created by Eike Batista began to implode. A major cause of this disaster was the unfounded expectations regarding the potential of the oil fields acquired by OGX, the EBX Group's oil company (Gaspar 2014). The catastrophe forced Batista to hand over controlling interest of the main jewel in his crown, Porto do Açu, to a private equity fund specializing in energy production: EIG Global Partners, headquartered in Washington, DC.

This transfer did not mean the abandonment of the project of trans-forming Porto do Açu into an important logistics node for the global trade in mineral commodities. The search for Chinese partners also continued, as well as efforts to attract Chinese political and commercial leaders to the venture. An example of this was the visit by Li Jinzhang, the Chinese ambassador to Brazil, who came to Porto do Açu in July 2017 with a delegation of Chinese businessmen. The ambassador, however, did not go beyond politely recognizing the potential for partnerships with Chinese companies.

In May 2019, in a clear effort to move beyond diplomacy to the creation of partnerships, the Brazilian subsidiary of EIG Global Partners, Prumo Logística Global, signed an agreement with the Chinese state-owned Guangzhou Port Group, the manager one of the China's principal ports. As reported by the press, this agreement aimed at sharing practices and knowledge about port operation and management, in addition to strengthening cooperation in investments and business development. The obvious (but unstated) objective was to finally attract Chinese investments to finance the energy projects underway in Porto do Açu, particularly the construction of two thermoelectric plants. It should be noted that Prumo Logística Global had already signed a similar agreement with the Port of Antwerp in 2017, agreeing to invest US$20 million in Porto do Açu.

The agreement with the Port of Antwerp associated a respectable brand with the Porto do Açu, but another of its practical consequences was the hiring of professionals from the Belgian port to occupy key positions in the Porto do Açu's international relations division. The first of these was Tessa Major, who was previously responsible for port projects at the Port of Antwerp International. Major occupied Porto do Açu's post of director of international business and innovation. Prumo Logística also hired Maartje Driessens, another professional with previous connections to the Port of Antwerp. Driessens became the general manager of strategic partnerships, not only with China but also with India, in an apparent effort to associate Porto do Açu with other BRICS (Brazil, Russia, India, China, South Africa) countries. In both cases, what seems to be the goal is the creation of international partnerships.

INTERNATIONALIZATION OF PORTO DO AÇU AND ITS REINFORCEMENT AS A GEOGRAPHICAL ENCLAVE

One of the consequences of the search for international strategic partnerships in Porto do Açu has been the strengthening of its condition as a multinational geographic enclave in São João da Barra. As a result, the population that inhabits the territory tends to see Porto do Açu more as an inexhaustible source of social and environmental problems than as the promised instrument of regional economic redemption.

The fact that most of the small farmers expropriated by the Rio de Janeiro government have not yet been compensated for the loss of their properties is the main element contributing to tensions between the local population and the port. But environmental problems caused by the project are also aggravating tensions. The best example of these can be seen in the salinization of the waters and soils in the area, caused by technical failures in the construction of the project's retaining pools. This damage has prevented farming and artisanal fishing in and around the lagoon system and has thus interrupted the social processes of (re-)production that existed in the area before the Porto do Açu project landed atop of it.

Prumo Logística's position has been to transfer responsibility for the socioenvironmental problems to different levels of the Brazilian state. This fact has also aggravated local opposition to the project. Understandably, the people affected by the Porto do Açu compare the increasing fortunes of the enterprise's foreign partners with the losses that residents have incurred. A revealing discourse that many traditional residents of the area employ to describe Porto do Açu is that "outsiders arrived to take without asking or paying for that which already had owners."

CONCLUSION

Porto do Açu is a perfect case study of the socioenvironmental effects of the projects developed to boost Brazilian port infrastructure during the governments of presidents Lula and Rousseff. As a product of this neodevelopmentalist period, Porto do Açu synthesizes in a unique way the tensions between demands for economic growth and the rights of the groups that traditionally inhabit the areas chosen as platforms for the export of mineral commodities. The vagaries of the project, which has undergone multiple changes and adjustments since its implementation in 2007 and the beginning of its operations in 2014, make Porto do Açu a unique case in efforts to expand the channels for the exportation of the commodities produced in Brazil. Therefore, it deserves continuous attention. Finally, it is necessary to keep an eye on Porto do Açu to see if the effort to transform it into a kind of superhighway from Brazil to China will bear fruit or if everything will remain limited to the scope of protocols of intention, signed in formal events and then tabled for future reference.

REFERENCES

Bresser-Pereira, L. C. 2006. "O novo desenvolvimentismo e a ortodoxia convencional." *São Paulo em Perspectiva* 20, no. 3: 5–24.

Gaspar, M. 2014. *Tudo ou Nada*. Eike Batista e a verdadeira história do Grupo X. Rio de Janeiro: Editora Record.

Latini, J. R. 2016. "A avaliação de impacto ambiental (AIA) enquanto instrumento participativo e preventivo no contexto do neodesenvolvimentismo: o caso do Complexo Logístico Industrial do Porto do Açu (CLIPA)." Master's thesis, Centro de Biociências e Biotecnologia, Universidade Estadual do Norte Fluminense.

Morães, Roberto. 2017. "ISS das atividades portuárias: o caso de Santos e do Porto do Açu em SJB." http://www.robertomoraes.com.br/2017/12/iss-das-atividades-portuarias-o-caso-de.html.

Pedlowski. M. A. 2013. "When the State Becomes the Land Grabber: Violence and Dispossession in the Name of 'Development' in Brazil." *Journal of Latin American Geography* 12, no. 3: 91–111.

Pessanha, R. M. 2017. "A relação transescalar e multidimensional "Petróleo-Porto" como produtora de novas territorialidades." PhD dissertation, Faculdade de Educação, Universidade do Estado do Rio de Janeiro.

Wang, H., T. Chen, and H. Ma. 2018. "Different Institutions, Distinctive Trajectories? Revisiting Maritime Industrial Development Areas with Cases on China's Liaoning Coast," *Growth and Change* 49, no. 1: 165–88.

Index